Handbook of Property Management

OTHER McGRAW-HILL BOOKS BY ROBERT IRWIN

Computerizing Your Real Estate Office

The McGraw-Hill Real Estate Handbook

Mingles: A Home Buying Guide for Unmarried Couples (paperback)

Timeshare Properties: What Every Buyer *Must* Know!

The New Mortgage Game

Protect Yourself in Real Estate: The Complete Beginner's Guide (paperback)

The Real Estate Agent's and Investor's Tax Book (with Richard Brickman)

How to Buy a Home at a Reasonable Price (paperback)

How to Buy and Sell Real Estate for Financial Security (paperback)

Handbook of PROPERTY MANAGEMENT

Robert Irwin
Editor in Chief

McGraw-Hill Book Company

New York St. Louis San Francisco Auckland Bogotá Hamburg
Johannesburg London Madrid Mexico Montreal New Delhi
Panama Paris São Paulo Singapore Sydney Tokyo Toronto

SPECIAL NOTE TO READER

This publication is composed of chapters contributed by different authors who express their opinions on the subjects covered. Neither the publisher, the editor, nor any of the authors, however, is engaged in rendering legal, accounting, tax, or investment services. Some of the material covered by this book may be affected by changes in the law or changes in the interpretation of the law since the book was written. In addition, laws may vary between states. For legal, tax, accounting, investment, or any other expert advice, the reader should secure the services of a competent practitioner in the field. The editor, authors, and publisher hereby specifically disclaim personal liability for any loss incurred as a result of material presented in this book.

Library of Congress Cataloging in Publication Data

Main entry under title:

Handbook of property management.

Includes index.
1. Real estate management. 2. Real estate investment. I. Irwin, Robert, date.
HD1394.H318 1986 333.5'068 85-14979
ISBN 0-07-032114-0

234567890 DOC/DOC 8987

ISBN 0-07-032114-0

The editors for this book were Martha Jewett and Norma Frankel, the designer was M. R. P. Design, and the production supervisor was Teresa F. Leaden. It was set in Baskerville by Achorn Graphics.

Printed and bound by R. R. Donnelley & Sons Company.

CONTENTS

PREFACE

Whether you are a landlord with a single house or an asset manager with a portfolio of thousands of units, if you are reading this book, chances are you have property management problems and concerns.

As a property manager in today's world your role is increasingly complex and challenging. You are frequently sandwiched between the demands of owners and the needs of tenants. You must deal with lenders, government agencies, and maintenance and repair workers and get involved in a host of other areas in which you may have limited expertise.

Your job may seem impossible. On the one hand you must be careful not to discriminate; on the other you must see that property delivers the maximum on its rent potential. You may be called upon to settle domestic squabbles for tenants and the next day serve an eviction notice to the same tenants. You may have to get out there with a pipe wrench to fix a broken hot-water heater or manipulate tenant mixes for maximum profit in a multimillion-dollar shopping center. You may even be called upon to decide what computer system to purchase when you have no idea of how computers work!

It isn't easy being a property manager. And one of the trickiest problems is getting the right information. You may need to know:

How to improve your profits through better management

How to deal with difficult tenants

How to hire the right on-site manager

What kind of lease is best for you

How to handle an eviction

What to do about maintenance, insurance, and taxes

The best way to deal with a government agency

How to avoid a discrimination charge

What to do about rent control

Whether it is time for a computer, and if so, which software to get

These are some of the problems of property management.

MAKING THIS BOOK

A considerable amount of thought went into the best way of presenting useful answers to the above questions in this book. Several concerns had to be addressed. For example, how can an answer be made understandable and relevant for both a single-unit owner/landlord and an asset manager with a portfolio of thousands of units?

There were two solutions. The first was to design most chapters so that the reader could build on knowledge gained in them. The authors start off simply and then go on to more complex ideas and concerns. In this fashion even the complete novice will be able to follow; at the same time the already sophisticated asset manager will also gain vital information.

The second solution to serving both the "ma and pa" landlord and the asset manager was to divide the book into sections. By checking the section and chapter titles, regardless of your questions or your present degree of expertise, you should be able to turn quickly to the areas relevant to you and your concerns.

Another desire in making this book was to keep the writing easy to read and consistent. Fortunately, the authors selected are all quite good writers. The readability may vary from chapter to chapter, but no chapter should be either incomprehensibly difficult or below the reader's level.

Finally, there was the matter of getting up-to-date, accurate information. For this the editor relied on the credentials, experience, and knowledge of the individual contributors. Contributors to the *Handbook of Property Management* include attorneys, professors, and brokers. Most important, however, all of them are intimately involved with property management. Many are property managers themselves. Others teach seminars on various aspects of property management. Still others are involved in legal or insurance aspects. All are knowledgeable and bring to their chapters the most up-to-date information as of the time of writing.

THE GOAL

The goal was to come up with a highly practical book that a property manager could use on the spot. Yes, it had to include theories. But more important, it had to have concise, concrete answers that could be put to immediate use.

As editor in chief, I feel that this goal was realized. Regardless of the area in which your need may fall, regardless of how many units you may be managing, you should be able to find a quick, clear answer to your property management questions somewhere in this book.

ROBERT IRWIN

CONTRIBUTORS

Bowen Ballard has 21 years of experience in residential and commercial property management and related real estate fields. He is a partner, property manager, and appraiser for Ballard Realty Companies and is president of Ballard Mortgage Company.

Mr. Ballard received a B.S. in commerce and business administration from the University of Alabama. He has been on the board of directors of the Colonial Bank, Montgomery Area Chamber of Commerce, National Association of Home Builders, Alabama Association of Home Builders, Alabama Association of Realtors, and Montgomery Board of Realtors.

Mr. Ballard is a certified property manager (CPM) and past president of the Central Alabama Institute of Real Estate Management Chapter.

Joseph W. DeCarlo is managing partner of J. D. Property Management Company in Costa Mesa, California. He holds a certified property manager (CPM) designation from the Institute of Real Estate Management; a California real estate brokers license; a California general contractor license, and an N.A.S.D. license.

Mr. DeCarlo received his B.A. and M.B.A. from Syracuse University. He has been an instructor in property management and real estate for the past eight years at Santa Ana College and Coastline College and is a frequent speaker at seminars on property management.

Mr. DeCarlo is vice chairman of Coast Colleges Community District Real Estate Advisory Board. He is a planning commissioner for the city of Costa Mesa and has published articles on property management in apartment magazines.

THOMAS W. DOOLEY is proprietor and president of TWD & Associates, a real estate and general management consulting organization specializing in franchising, training, marketing, futurism, and company evaluation. He previously was a special representative for Homes for Living Network, St. Louis, Missouri; chief executive officer for Gallery of Homes, Inc., Elmhurst, Illinois; and executive vice president of the Realtor's National Marketing Institute.

Mr. Dooley is the author of two books: *Real Estate Brokerage in the '80s—Survival among the Giants* (Real Estate Education, 1980) and *How to Afford Your Dream Home in Bad Times as Well as Good Times* (Real Estate Education, in press).

Mr. Dooley is currently director of graduate studies at the College of Business and Teachers of Lewis University. He previously was with the Department of Management, College of Business, Northern Illinois University. He holds an M.B.A. in business administration–management from Xavier University, Cincinnati; an M.A. from the University of Toronto in philosophy; and an A.B. from Thomas More College in Lakeside Park, Kentucky.

RUTH I. FRISHMAN, J.D., a California attorney and real estate broker, is a well-known real estate management consultant, popular seminar leader, and nationally published author.

Ms. Frishman has managed more than 4000 units of housing, including FHA/HUD, condominium associations, and mobile home parks. She currently teaches property management at the University of California and a graduate course in housing development and management at the University of San Francisco.

She has an A.B. in communications and public policy from the University of California at Berkeley and a J.D. from Golden Gate University Law School in San Francisco.

Ms. Frishman has served on the board of directors of numerous local, state, and national housing groups, including the National Commissioners Committee of the National Association of Housing and Redevelopment Officials (NAHRO), the Education and Research Advisory Committee of the California Department of Real Estate, the Alameda County Housing Authority Commission, the Northern California Association for Non-Profit Housing, the Mid-Peninsula Coalition Housing Fund, the Emeryville Community Development Advisory Commission, and the Marin Income Property Association.

In her spare time Ms. Frishman manages her own investment property.

DAVID L. GANZ, ESQ., is an attorney admitted to practice law in New York and Washington, D.C. He is the managing partner of Ganz, Hollinger and Towe, New York City, and a prolific writer and accomplished practitioner in a variety of fields. Admitted to practice before the U.S. Tax Court, state and federal courts, and the Supreme Court of the United States, he has represented landlords and tenants in litigation as part of an overall general civil practice. He is himself a landlord in New York City.

E. WILLIAM HAHN, Ph.D., who received his doctorate from Purdue University in the field of system optimization techniques, currently is an associate professor in the Management Science Department of the School of Government and Business Administration at George Washington University. He teaches courses and seminars in quantitative methods and computer information systems to students working toward the M.B.A. His research interest is the application of the microcomputer to the business environment.

Dr. Hahn is also president of Hahn Computer Systems, Inc. (HCS), a microcomputer software development firm located in McLean, Virginia. HCS concentrates exclusively on the development of software packages for the professional real estate broker and manager.

Dr. Hahn has directed research and development efforts on totally integrated management systems, including residential property management, condominium/association management, real estate office accounting, real estate office management, and apartment management. He has published articles in *Real Estate Today* and *Real Estate Business* on software selection techniques for real estate professionals.

MARLENE M. HAHN, ESQ., who received a law degree from The National Law Center of George Washington University, has more than twelve years of experience in the real estate business. She founded a Virginia real estate firm specializing in residential sales and property management and operated it for 10 years.

Ms. Hahn has given real estate courses at both Northern Virginia Community College and the University of Virginia. Active in the Northern Virginia Board of Realtors, she currently chairs the Computer User's Group and is a member of the Information Systems Committee. As director of operations of Hahn Computer Systems, Inc., she frequently works directly with real estate professionals in helping determine their needs with respect to an automated system. She has published articles in *Real Estate Today* and *Real Estate Business* on software selection techniques for real estate professionals.

LOUIS B. HANSOTTE is a practicing attorney and the senior partner of the San Diego law firm of Hansotte, Nostrand and Lange. He teaches "Legal Aspects of Real Estate" at the Grossmont Community College and has coordinated the college's real estate program.

Mr. Hansotte has taught real estate licensing courses and has been part owner of two license training schools in addition to authoring four segments of the California Department of Real Estate's multimedia presentation on legal aspects of real estate. He has lectured extensively and presented continuing education seminars on many aspects of real estate. He is the author of *Legal Aspects of California Real Estate* (Wiley, 1982).

Mr. Hansotte received his B.S. in engineering from the U.S. Military Academy at West Point, New York. He has a C.L.U. designation from the American College of Life Underwriters, Bryn Mawr, Pennsylvania, and an L.L.B. from La Salle Extension University, Chicago, Illinois. He is a real estate broker and a member of the California Bar Association.

K. REED HARRISON is an attorney-at-law in Westlake Village, California. He is also chairman of the board of directors of the Village Bank, N.A.

Mr. Harrison is admitted to practice before all courts in the state of California; U.S. District Court, Central District; Ninth Circuit Court of Appeals; and the U.S. Supreme Court. His law practice emphasizes real estate and commercial law, and he has represented numerous clients in both residential and commercial landlord–tenant disputes.

He is also a licensed real estate agent and personally owns and manages income properties.

GERALD E. KIMMER is president of Realty Management Services, Inc., in Minneapolis, Minnesota. He studied electrical engineering and graduated from the University of Minnesota with a degree in business management.

Mr. Kimmer worked for 20 years in retail management prior to becoming a partner in Realty Management Services, a property management and development company. He has been active in numerous business organizations and has taught real estate licensing courses.

JAMES H. KOCH publishes the monthly newsletter *Country Property*. He conducts popular seminars on country property investing and is an experienced investor in the field.

Mr. Koch has published six books: *Pitfalls in Issuing Municipal Bonds*

(Moody's Investors Service, 1975), *A Selected Annotated Bank Marketing Bibliography* (American Bankers Association, 1971), *How Banks Can Use Direct Mail as an Effective Marketing Tool* (American Bankers Association, 1972), *Profits from Country Property* (McGraw-Hill, 1981), *How to Get the Most Profit from Your Collectibles* (ARCO, 1982), and *Profits from Small Town Property* (Van Nostrand, 1983). In addition he has written numerous articles, including a long series for the magazine *Country Living*.

Mr. Koch received his B.A. from Carleton College, Minnesota, and did graduate work as a Woodrow Wilson fellow at Princeton. For many years he was with Dun & Bradstreet, Inc., as a reporter and middle-management executive. He then became a senior partner and, since 1972, president of Aquarian Advertising Associates, Inc., of New York City.

ROGER E. LIPMAN is president of R. E. Lipman Insurance Brokers, Inc. He holds degrees in electronic engineering and business finance as well as an M.B.A. His experience includes senior management positions with multinational electronics firms and extensive experience with commercial property insurance for real estate management firms. He is a chartered property casualty underwriter (CPCU) and holds an associate in risk management.

Mr. Lipman is a qualified instructor at the University of California extension in Berkeley, California. He has served on the city council and as mayor pro tem for the city of Benicia, California. He lectures on insurance topics before groups in the western United States.

THOMAS D. PEARSON, Ph.D., is program director and associate professor of real estate and urban development, Department of Finance, Insurance, Real Estate, and Law, North Texas State University, Denton, Texas, and vice president of production services at Lomas & Nettleton Mortgage Banking.

Dr. Pearson received his Ph.D. in economics from Georgia State University in 1974 and his M.A. in economics from Louisiana State University in 1966. He is a member of the American Real Estate and Urban Economics Association, Southwestern Society of Economists, and of the American Institute of Real Estate Appraisers and an affiliate member of the Denton Board of Realtors.

DAVID W. "DUSTY" RHOADES, CCIM, CPM, earned his B.S. at the University of Arizona and his M.S. in business administration, with a major in marketing, from Northwestern University. Mr. Rhoades has owned and managed apartment complexes in a number of sunbelt states.

Mr. Rhoades is a vice president of finance and development with the

Johnstown American Companies, Atlanta, Georgia, and is one of the very few ever to have attained both the certified property manager (CPM) designation awarded by the Institute of Real Estate Management and the certified commercial investment member (CCIM) designation awarded by the Realtors National Marketing Institute.

Mr. Rhoades has served as an executive in the areas of sales, marketing, and general management for such consumer-product companies as General Electric, Pillsbury, Schlitz, and Colgate. Prior to entering the real estate business he was president of an international food company.

DENNIS S. TOSH is holder of the J. Ed Turner Chair of Real Estate at the University of Mississippi. A licensed real estate broker, Dr. Tosh received a Ph.D. in real estate from Georgia State University. He is the author or coauthor of six books, including *Real Estate Principles for License Preparation* (Reston, 1984), *Real Estate Math Made Easy* (Reston, 1982), and *Guide to Examinations and Careers in Real Estate* (Reston, 1979).

Dr. Tosh was previously chairman of the Department of Economics and Finance at the University of Baltimore. He is currently a consultant on real estate licensing examinations for the Educational Testing Service (ETS) and the American College of Testing (ACT).

Dr. Tosh is a member of the Real Estate Educators Association, the Real Estate Centers Directors and Chairholders Association, the American Real Estate and Urban Economics Association, and the National Association of Corporate Real Estate Executives.

MARI TUSTIN has been in property management for fifteen years and is a licensed California real estate broker, a certified property manager, and a graduate of Dominican College of San Rafael with degrees in sociology and social science.

She is vice president and director of family housing for the John Stewart Company, Sausalito, California.

In a consulting capacity, Ms. Tustin has participated in feasibility studies and syndication of more than $400 million in residential, cooperative, and office properties and teaches management seminars throughout the country. Her particular expertise is in the rehabilitation and renewal of financially, physically, and socially troubled properties, which requires the cohesion of many resources beyond the purchase dollars.

She also serves small and independently owned businesses in an advisory management capacity.

WILLIAM J. WALLISCH, Ed.D., is a nationally known speaker and writer on communication, mass media, and the impact of technology on education. He is a tenured associate professor of English and communication at the U.S. Air Force Academy in Colorado Springs and a lieutenant colonel in the Air Force.

In 1982 Dr. Wallisch was named an American Council on Education fellow; subsequently he took his fellowship at the University of Pittsburgh. He is an honor graduate of the Defense Information School. Dr. Wallisch received his B.A. in English from Allegheny College and his M.A. in mass media from the University of Oklahoma, and has an Ed.D. in higher education governance from the University of Southern California. He joined the faculty at the Air Force Academy in 1976.

William C. Weaver, Ph.D., is the Gordon J. Barnett professor of real estate, College of Business Administration, University of Central Florida, Orlando, Florida. He received an M.B.A. from Loyola University in computer science and management and is a 1980 graduate of the School of Mortgage Banking. He is a Ph.D. in real estate and urban affairs.

Mr. Weaver has published in various real estate–oriented journals, including *The Real Estate Appraiser & Analyst, The Mortgage Banker, The Real Estate Securities Journal, The Appraisal Journal, Real Estate Today, Real Estate Issues,* and *Real Estate Review.*

Mr. Weaver's consulting firm, Real Property Consultants, specializes in complex real estate problems.

Handbook of Property Management

PART 1

Introduction to property management

CHAPTER 1

Dealing with tenants

Mari Tustin
The John Stewart Company
Sausalito, California

All you need is one tenant. Voilà! You are a landlord. Whether you own one rental house, thousands of rental units, or office space; whether you are self-employed or part of a property management team; your communication with your tenants will have certain common elements.

MANAGEMENT RESPONSIBILITY

It is estimated that 40 percent of all dwelling units in the United States are non-owner-occupied and that fully two-thirds of the wealth of this country is measured by its land, the natural resources on and within the land, and the physical improvements made on the land. If these two statements are taken as fact, the management of these dwellings and their occupants assumes gargantuan levels of importance. Real property, its owners, and its lessees constitute a major force in the economy of this country and exert a powerful influence on our lives. Through the industry of property management, people are employed, taxes are paid, and wealth is multiplied.

LANDLORDS VERSUS TENANTS

Those who own, control, or manage property have been dubbed *landlords,* while those who occupy property they don't own have been called *tenants*—both medieval terms. Progressive managers refer to present-day tenants as *occupants, residents,* or *lessees.*

Tenants are the income side of the balance sheet, the reason property managers are employed, and the manager's job security. Although they also are usually the source of a property manager's woes, tenants can help managers to become more professional.

Participants in the real estate industry apparently believe that most tenants pay their rent, since income projections provide for an average of only 5 percent per year in loss of income through vacancies and delinquencies. It is the job of the property manager to justify this belief. Property management is a relatively new profession, still struggling to find theories that explain what happens and provide techniques, tools, and guidance to improve the outcome. Managers need a workable framework within which to conduct their relationships with tenants and landlords.

ROLES IN TENANT-LANDLORD RELATIONSHIPS

Ordinary people change their behavior drastically when assigned roles and titles. Two equally educated, well-dressed, and successfully employed people often take adversary positions when one is given the role of tenant and the other that of landlord. Tenants frequently see themselves as powerless, unable to control the environment in which they live or work; landlords may see themselves as victims of tenants' whims. The issues that divide them are money and property but sometimes involve style and mannerisms. And the nature of the scenario that is played out between them often is dictated by their preconceived ideas of each others' roles. Tenants tend to see managers as having control, while landlords tend to see tenants as trying to undermine their control. Their approaches to one another can generate manipulation, power struggles, "lose-lose" situations, loss of time and money, and lengthy legal battles.

By looking more closely at the roles frequently played, managers can gain perspective and tools for creating a "win-win" situation. The following headings are not categories of people, but characterizations of how one group of individuals may approach another in a given situation. The participants act out their roles, but there is always a real person behind the role.

The Angry Tenant

Every property manager who has been around awhile has run into the angry tenant. It makes no difference that the landlord is not the actual irritant in the tenant's life. What matters is that at certain points in these tenants' lives they make contact with the landlord. If the tenant sees herself or himself in an adversary position to begin with, the connection with the landlord (or maintenance person, property manager, or owner) can be negative.

The angry tenant usually lets small issues go by, waiting for the right moment to sandbag the manager. If the tenant has a leaky faucet in the bathroom, he waits until the landlord sends a notice to "pay or quit," then barrages the manager with a tongue-lashing about how awful the entire building is, reminding him or her he won't pay until the issue is resolved.

This is the tenant who has had a bad day with his own client or has hurt himself on the job because he didn't get proper safety equipment from his employer. The tenant may have been angry all his life and felt he had to fight for every gain he ever made.

Often the angry tenant feels she has to look out constantly for Number One, since everyone else is out to do her in. Her children may be out of control; she may feel their dreams are gone and life has passed them by. The angry tenant may be the one who did not receive the social security check in the mail, the small businessperson who has mounting accounts receivable, or the construction worker who was laid off.

The anger is displaced, its true meaning usually deeply buried. Anger for this tenant has become an approach to all problems, but rarely has it been an effective solution. The anger alienates those around him, which makes him even angrier. This person sees himself as a "regular guy" and can't understand why the rest of the world doesn't see him in the same way. He may have been told not to be outwardly angry or "people won't like you," and that parental voice in his ears makes him even angrier. The steam builds, the cat gets kicked, the muscles get tighter, the jaws are clenched, and the eyes are on fire. These responses invite even more anger to be directed toward the tenant and even more alienation from those with whom he must deal.

She doesn't pay the rent on time (when money is not the issue), plays the music too loudly, takes two parking spaces for her new car, or refuses to pick up the debris in front of her pizza parlor in your commercial building.

Finally there is the confrontation—the tenant meets the landlord. The angry tenant is looking for a fight and waits for the landlord to sound the slightest bit abusive about the late rent, the trash, or the noise.

Even if the landlord is successful in putting the message across, the task is only seven-eighths completed by the tenant: the rent check arrives, but has the wrong amount; she switches to loud classical music instead of loud rock music; she picks up only part of the debris in front of the restaurant.

The angry tenant is making a statement: Anger is the tool that has been chosen to order the tenant's life. Having survived to this point, the lessee believes that anger is an effective tool. Not seeing the fallacy of this cause-effect relationship, the tenant continues to believe that only the tough win, and that overt anger is strength, which therefore gives power. The discomfort in the tenant's life is blamed on all those around him; he believes that if only all the *others* would change their ways, his life would work. The ultimate payoff is increased isolation, which the angry tenant sees as the only safe place. The fact that there are other choices is not available information.

Dealing with the angry tenant. The manager must decide on a response to this angry tenant. The manager, too, has choices: return the anger, be manipulated or intimidated by the anger, or defuse the anger as it comes. It is hardly a secret that people in managerial positions are called on to play many roles: lawyer, confidant, counselor, financial planner, organizer, consoler, parent, even magician.

In this situation, the manager must call on his or her resources as defuser or at least show an ability to resist becoming entangled in the web of the angry tenant. The manager does not have to become involved in the angry tenant's perception of himself or of the world. The manager can choose to remain outside that tangled mess and just be there. A manager must always have time in these situations: time to talk, time to listen, time to invite the tenant in to discuss the situation, time to acknowledge the tenant's anger, time to take another look at the situation, time to look behind the statement and behavior, time to gather wits, and time to remain kindly firm. But the property manager *must* take the time. To brush off the angry tenant is to escalate the confrontation to a war.

Turf. Resolution may depend on where the confrontation takes place. If it is the tenant in the manager's office, the manager might say, "Why don't you sit down and let's see what we can do." The manager can close the door and give the angry tenant the courtesy of respectful treatment. The manager shouldn't expect that his or her courteous actions will be reciprocated by the tenant; he employs courtesy because it is the most *effective* tool he can use, not because he expects to be rewarded for good behavior.

Some managers revel in the thought of a public fight and the opportunity to prove their superiority. Clearly this choice will never resolve an issue, for the tenant will, appropriately, wait for the next chance to get even.

A manager can defuse the situation with tone of voice, eye contact, and the offer of a cup of coffee or even a glass of ice water on a hot day. She should sit across from the tenant in another chair rather than behind the desk. Even if the issue is not legitimate, the manager need not put on a display of power or authority—the power already exists. The attempt to *prove* power reveals a question on the part of the manager as to whether or not it exists and who has it. The manager should keep her power—it can't be taken from her, but she can give it away.

Resolving the problem. The manager will not, cannot, and is not expected to resolve permanently the angry tenant's position in life. In fact, to attempt to do so is to tread on dangerous territory, which the manager is probably not qualified to do. If the manager feels a need to resolve the angry tenant's problem, he probably enjoys confrontations so that he can become caretaker or parent, and therefore be needed.

With all due respect for the complexity of human behavior, the manager's task at this moment is to resolve the issue, which may mean letting the angry tenant digress for a few minutes. The manager may learn that the angry tenant had a particularly bad day yesterday and can acknowledge that fact with sympathetic phrases such as "Sounds like that client really tried to do you in," or "That's quite a problem; have you decided how you are going to handle it?" Such defusing statements—acknowledgments of the tenant's situation—are frequently sufficient to allow the two to proceed with the issue at hand—the unpaid rent, the leaky faucet, the debris in the parking lot. True power and authority need not be displayed—they exist by virtue of position; the effective manager, as well as the angry tenant, are both aware of that fact. This is not the time to display plumage, but to get results. The tenant will probably continue to be angry, but the manager may no longer be the recipient of that anger. The results are achieved, the participants get on with their lives, and both sides feel that they have won.

If the manager does not assess the situation clearly, the war is on. The tenant will demand to speak to the supervisor, and the manager must take the supervisor's time to explain what is happening. The supervisor undoubtedly will be upset because she doesn't have the time to deal with these matters. What is worse, the supervisor may be even less capable of handling the angry tenant than the manager was. If the supervisor merely wants the angry tenant out of the office, she may make concessions to the tenant that will ultimately make life unbearable for the manager.

If the manager does not want to have her authority undermined, she must not give her power away by failing to resolve the issue in the first place. Stated another way, if you don't want your power taken away, don't give it away. Eventually, the supervisor will get tired of having to solve these problems, and the manager's job will be in jeopardy, and rightfully so.

Another possibility is that the supervisor will also be unable to defuse the situation or may be as adamant and headstrong as the angry tenant, in which case the tenant must seek higher authority—it is now a matter of saving face.

A manager is defined by the dictionary as one who guides or directs something, or one who is directly at the head of any undertaking. A true manager takes the responsibility for resolution and direction of any problem with which he or she is presented. It is a powerful position to be able to direct the actions of others toward a predefined goal. A confrontation by an angry tenant is definitely an opportunity for a manager to assess her abilities to define a problem, create a solution, and move toward goals. Firefighters don't fight fire with fire, and we don't throw a bucket of water to a drowning person. If the angry tenant hooks the manager's anger, they enter a war in which the outcome is unpredictable—a situation that benefits no manager. Good managers prefer to know the outcome beforehand, or at least the probability of achieving a successful one, which requires that they be detached from the other person, remain single-minded in purpose, and listen to the multitude of clues offered.

Most angry tenants will, in one way or another, let the manager know the real reason for the anger. Managers must discover it, acknowledge it, finish with it, and politely resolve their own needs: arrange for a specific time to pick up the rent check, complete the work for the leaky faucet, help find a high school student who wants to earn a few dollars by picking up the garbage in the parking lot of the pizza parlor during lunch hour.

Avoiding taking it personally. People scream at policies and rules, not at managers. Put succinctly by one administrator of a very large residential property, "A lot of them want to reduce the relationship to a personal one, because then they feel they have more power. If you allow them to offend you *personally,* you have reduced the encounter to a personal one." Taking things personally leads to frustration, more anger, guilt, and, ultimately, another form of power play. The manager should stick to policies and deal fairly, quietly, accurately, and with an openness to whether or not the policy is appropriate and fairly applied.

Tenants who are angry and hostile need to know that, despite their tantrums, the world keeps on turning just as before. To permit this behavior to result in concessions that would not have occurred otherwise merely reinforces the behavior. If the tenant is placated, he or she will keep using that behavior and keep expecting to be placated. Why change a behavior that works? To permit such behavior to escalate into a play for position, authority, and power is to shelve permanently the possibility for resolution.

The art of negotiation, particularly with a tenant who is behaving unreasonably, is to make concessions, but not ones that matter. This tactic is not to be used with the tenant who has a legitimate complaint such as clogged plumbing. I refer to the tenant whose demands and behavior seem to be unreasonable in terms of the problem presented. You must simply see that her refrigerator is working properly. You do not have to acquiesce to a new refrigerator because the tenant down the hall got one, nor do you have to justify or explain your behavior if in doing so no new light will be shed on the issue. When confronted with an angry tenant you might ask yourself questions such as these: "How much of this does the person really mean? What is the 'meat' of the story? Is the real issue the one being presented?"

The Lonely Tenant

The lonely tenant is usually found in residential properties but can also be observed in small commercial, retail, and office spaces. Such tenants are living a paradox: they want to be near and with others but manage to set up their lives to be alone—a safe place.

The situationally lonely tenant is a temporary characterization, for the tenant may not be totally responsible for creating the condition: A spouse dies, the only child moves far away, and a support system has not been created or is not available. It is a heartbreaking experience to see lonely tenants walking alone, eating alone, living in their apartments alone. They may be lost in yesterday and have not yet had the time or courage to create a new world. It is the divorced person, living alone without the big house and noisy kids; it is that very raw period between letting go of the past and adapting to the future. It is a time when every encounter with the environment brings grief and more withdrawal.

The lonely tenant tries the manager's patience by setting up issues just to get feedback; any kind of feedback from anyone will do: "forgetting" to pay the rent; sneaking a pet into the apartment; leaving the windows open when the sprinklers are on so the drapes get stained; forgetting to move the car on Tuesday mornings so the street sweeper can get through; complaining about a neighbor's noise that can never be detected by anyone else; calling the landlord and reminding him it's time to prune the trees outside the window. When there is a line at the office window on the first of the month, lonely tenants are on hand to air their problems.

The personal touch. No matter how we feel about these issues personally, we sooner or later face the fact that as professionals we must move on to other matters. First, however, there are certain human solutions that may help. For those persons who permit you to do so, a touch, a handshake, or a hug is in order, for most likely that is the sort of confirmation the tenant was seeking in the first place. The worst thing a manager can do when faced with the lonely tenant is to avoid the person or the issue.

Hiding, figuratively or literally, only makes the tenant work harder for confirmation of his existence. The tenant will become louder in the voicing of complaints and will make his stories longer and longer—until the goal of confirmation is reached. Rather than using the hide-and-seek tactic, the manager should greet this matter head-on—once again, by taking time.

You can recognize the loneliness and acknowledge it: Knock on the door while passing, bring a flower, ask about the tree in front of the unit or how the tenant's small business is doing.

A manager is not a manager if she or he does not take the time. It doesn't even have to be the manager who takes on the task—duties can be delegated, assigned, and shared. But if the issue is ignored, the problem will grow until the tenant moves or dies, and in the interim, people will groan when they see the lonely tenant coming. Better to handle the problem in *your* time at *your* convenience than be forced to handle it at someone else's demand.

Typical lonely tenants. We tend to have a notion that senior citizens are lonely, and some are. Some have spent a lifetime alienating friends and relatives and now wonder why no one comes to call. While it is not the manager's responsibility to change that history, one can be professionally effective without being patronizing. For managers of exclusively senior citizen buildings, a major part of the job centers around creating activities in which opportunity for friendship may arise. There will be those who do not choose to participate, and after a few friendly invitations they should not be continually needled to join in the activities.

In the building that is not occupied exclusively by senior citizens, the lonely tenant may be a little more difficult to single out. Still, the question is whether or not that tenant chooses to respond to invitations, which are the responsibility of management to extend. Not all the seeds that are scattered will take root and yield fruit.

The saddest lonely tenant may be the young teenager or adult, who may be lonely for very good reasons. Usually young persons congregate among their peers for confirmation and affirmation. However, if the peer group is basically a negative one, that is, one that thrives on socially unacceptable behavior, the young adult or teenager who does not want to participate and has no alternative group is indeed very lonely. Youth is a difficult age at best, even with full support of family, friends, school, and society. When the social context has no sanctions for positive or "different" behavior, the lonely tenant is really an outcast—a person without a passport.

If you spot this lonely tenant, seize the opportunity to help. Try to find some way to support the antisocial behavior he or she is exhibiting toward the basically antisocial group. As you scan the newspapers at night, check for appropriate job openings for this person. If you know of a softball league, get an application. One of the many hidden rewards of being a manager is the opportunity to change the direction of someone's life. Don't miss the opportunity, or shirk the responsibility, to help this tenant.

The lonely tenant may be found in other settings. A small commercial, retail, or office property may provide space for the professionally lonely: the small businessperson who operates with only a part-time office assistant; the retail outlet in which the proprietor works both the front desk and the repair shop in the back. While an abusive tenant can initially appear to be an angry tenant, the real story could be that of the lonely tenant.

Loneliness can be self-inflicted as a protective device against what the lonely tenant perceives to be a hostile and unfriendly world. This attitude can result in aggravation to the manager: rent payments that are forgotten, maintenance problems that go unreported and become extensive and expensive, lease renewals that remain unsigned or cannot be located beneath the pile of debris on the front desk. In their isolation, such tenants do not learn about the world they live in; therefore, they develop few coping measures and retreat even more into their isolation, and the cycle continues.

Once again, the manager's task is to find the time. If it is the manager's responsibility to protect the physical premises, the lonely tenant, who prefers that you stay out of his environment, must be addressed. Create a niche for yourself first—send a potted plant on the anniversary date of the lease (an effective management technique for all tenants, whether the property is 1000 or 100,000 square feet). If you come across an article about the business the lonely tenant is in, copy it and send it with a short note. If lonely tenants know you are aware of their existence and see you are not a threat to their sheltered world, your tasks as manager may become easier.

On the other hand, the manager must not interpret all lack of communication from a tenant as manifestations of loneliness. Some tenants are genuinely satisfied with their environment, believe the rent to be fair and equitable, pay it on time, and are very busy businesspeople, who do not care for management tactics they see as meddling.

The Criminal Tenant

Make no mistake—the "criminal tenant" may be better at his or her job than you are at yours. If the behavior displayed at your property is truly criminal and the tenant is not behind bars, he clearly knows something you don't. There is a fine line between criminal and obnoxious or unacceptable behavior, which our police officers know only too clearly. Don't act on authority you don't have or on information that may not be true. Weigh the quality and quantity of what you believe you see, note down any unusual behavior, and, if warranted, report the matter to the authorities.

This is sometimes a risky situation. If the criminal tenant has reason to believe you know something you shouldn't, and if the manager puts pressure on in other areas to try to "set up" the tenant for eviction, unless it is done with a great deal of caution and care, it can backfire.

You could find yourself with not only a criminal tenant, but a violent one. In one building, a loud party was actually an occasion for a dope pass; and the manager, in his zeal to set things right, was thrown over the balcony of the second floor after he was stabbed seven times (he survived).

Managers' lives have been threatened, and taken, for interfering with the criminal tenant. Remember, the criminal tenant has a great deal to lose by being uncovered, and some of these persons will not hesitate to protect their lifestyle. If in your research, unobtrusively and quietly conducted, you determine you are truly right, pursue the matter, if you choose to, through appropriate channels only.

The manager is not at liberty to risk property damage or personal injury to himself or others by taking on a role of law enforcement. There is also a fine line between situations you should report to the authorities and those with which you should not get involved. Only your personal conscience, and the law, can dictate where you draw the line, but your professionalism dictates what you do about it once you have made a decision.

What one person sees as criminal behavior may actually be a reflection of what we perceive to be "wrong." There are many different kinds of people, and, unfortunately, most of us make judgments about others. It would be extremely unprofessional and unethical to look for criminal behavior in any tenant who does not measure up to our own standards. We have freely chosen our standards, and tenants freely choose theirs.

Criminality versus morality. Confusing criminality with morality can be costly. One large apartment building, located in a neighborhood of very tidy middle-class apartments, seemed to be somewhat less cared for than its neighbors. New management was hired after the purchase by a new owner. The agent discovered through talking to some of the tenants that a few of the occupants were probably involved in prostitution, although there appeared to be no soliciting going on at the project. But through the comings and goings and conversations of those tenants, others had determined the area of their professional expertise.

The new property manager, offended by these persons on "his property" and eager to perform an outstanding service to the owner, promptly proceeded to look for ways to remove these clients from the premises. He succeeded—and lost some of his best-paying tenants.

At another residential property—an economically and socially troubled property—there lived an unusual tenant. He drove a very large and beautiful convertible and appeared to be an artist by trade. The top of his car was usually down while parked in the lot, although he never seemed to be missing any of his expensive camera equipment.

The housing project was indeed a tough one. Break-ins had been a common nighttime occurrence. An occasional murder or rape added to security problems. It wasn't apparent why this gentleman chose to become a resident of our project.

Within several months after his arrival, the rash of break-ins, burglaries, robberies, and even rapes had been reduced, and all appeared to be quiet. I had my suspicions as to his real source of income, but there was never any untoward behavior displayed at the project. In fact, since this gentleman and I had a mutual hobby—photography—we frequently discussed the latest techniques or equipment on the market.

About 2 years later, the gentleman was arrested, convicted, and sent to prison for selling narcotics. Within 2 months of his departure, the project was once again filled with police sirens every night.

We learned the reason for the change. During the gentleman's residency with us, he had made it quite clear to the thugs and hoodlums that there was to be no cause for the police to be on the property—that he intended to allow all his neighbors to lead quiet and peaceful lives. This well-spoken, very congenial, and well-educated gentleman clearly had his own ways of getting his point across. Once he was no longer on the premises, old rivalries and dissensions surfaced at the property.

I am not condoning drug dealings. I abhor them and am sick that so many of our nation's young people are lost to artificial and temporary "highs." I will continue to fight for stronger legislation and law enforcement as a private citizen. But as a property manager, in this case I had neither cause nor justification for interfering.

If he displayed unusual behavior, I didn't notice it. Others in a position to investigate and pursue the matter clearly did. And in some ways, the innocent people of that project benefited by his presence. For 2 years they could safely walk to the trash bins at night or do their laundry in the twilight hours without fear of loss of life or limb.

The "Retired Attorney" Tenant

Some of my best friends are attorneys; this characterization has nothing to do with the previous professional status of the occupant. It is a syndrome that reveals itself by the manner in which the tenants perceive themselves (although a retired attorney on the board of directors of a condominium or in the tenant association of an apartment building may find herself in this category!). It is not the information such a tenant has or doesn't have that characterizes the syndrome, but the manner in which the information or knowledge is used.

This occupant may quote law by code and section or cite state health regulations with fascinating accuracy. She knows the covenants, conditions, and restrictions (CC&Rs) thoroughly. And to what purpose? It depends. This tenant can be extremely helpful in management meetings. She provides the necessary information immediately so that the meeting need not be postponed until another day while research is done.

Make these tenants allies or they will definitely be adversaries. If the retired attorney's purpose is to inform others, keep herself informed, and assist with solutions, management has not only an ally, but an informed lessee.

On the other hand, if the use of known or imagined information is based on the need to find some form of security, this tenant simply becomes a "loose screw." She consumes meetings with lengthy oratories and raises the pitch of meetings from functional to angry. She can be out to be heard and to make sure everyone is listening. She is not unlike the retired contractor who continually tells you how your building is falling apart, the retired doctor who advises you of the numerous health hazards in the dining room, or even the retired manager who constantly presents you with better ways of doing your job.

Efficient managers recognize that they cannot control which situations come to them, but they can control their reactions to those situations. They recognize that there is no perfect building, no perfect tenant, nor any system without problems. They recognize that they have been hired precisely because these problems exist, and it is their task to work within the framework of people and events that are not perfect and will never be made so.

As an astute manager, determine the validity and accuracy of retired attorneys' information and use it. Assign them tasks that genuinely need to be done, such as research. Ask the retired attorney to bring you at least three solutions for every problem uncovered, to provide documentation, and finally, to recommend one of the tentative solutions with reasons for that choice. If you decide that the research and conclusions are valid, your valuable retired attorney can save you much time and money. If you conclude the work submitted is more puff than cream, thank the tenant for the work and get on your way.

If the retired attorney chooses anger as a response to rejection, the problem and its solution move to another category. Many times the misuse of previous professional expertise comes from anger. The world no longer "needs" this person, who has now been retired to pasture. Those years of training, productivity, and social contribution are over. In days gone by, the retired attorney's phone may have rung with people needing help to solve problems. Now he gets only an occasional call for golf or the movies. He sees his productive life as over—retirement has been forced on him by the circumstance of time. He fights for continued recognition based on previously satisfactory standards.

The manager accepts but does not patronize. Younger managers of senior citizen retirement communities frequently make the mistakes of patronizing, talking slower or louder, or using less sophisticated language to the residents. These tactics are not only demeaning, but a total denial of the lives they have led, an acquiescence to and support of the misconception that there is something negative about getting older.

When the retired attorney believes she has been belittled, if she has any power and clout left—particularly if the expertise is valid and useful—she will not accept lightly the attack on her character. She has won many battles, is a survivor, and will willingly take on another fight. She can put a tenant body in arms, bring in state and local authorities, and generally wreak havoc with management organization, not to speak of the budget.

It's best for managers to acknowledge the possible power; do homework for themselves; and research, correct, or address issues that are genuine trouble spots. It's a tough battle, but most assuredly one that builds character!

We'll return to tenant roles, but now let's consider other aspects of dealing with tenants.

TENANT ORGANIZATIONS

Tenant organizations are born of one of three situations: written regulation (condominium and cooperative residential and office buildings), request from management for assistance, and reaction, usually negative, to management. A tenant organization that perceives its roles as adversarial or reactionary to management will cause much pain to a manager or administrator. It creates a "demand" situation, frequently established with "win or lose" criteria. The tenant organization so composed perceives itself as having been victimized by management and having no possibility for communication other than through organized power and a show of strength. It doesn't matter at this point exactly what the real issue is. The point is that the organization perceives the issue in a certain way, and that is what is real for the members. To attempt to use logical or statistical analysis (logical as perceived by management) or legal threats will only serve to escalate the crisis. If that's how the tenants feel, then that's how they feel.

The question becomes, do you as management *know* how they feel? Did you ever acknowledge how they feel? Can you or did you acknowledge that you can see how some action on your part could have invited the group to feel the way it does? Or did you retreat into landlord-tenant roles, quote the house rule, or circle in red the pertinent section of the lease and send it to all tenants? Two parties determined to have a fight will achieve exactly that.

Avoiding Hostility

In the rent-up of one large apartment building, owners had provided a model of the building and a schematic indicating the future installation of cable television. Nowhere in the written document was the promise of cable TV made, but the implication was there in the drawing. Due to a slow rent-up, ownership decided to forgo the installation of the cable TV. A few tenants demanded the amenity. Management snubbed their feelings about having been deluded and pointed out that no one had actually promised them cable TV. The contest escalated, and a class action suit was filed, led by a tenant who knew the law, had the resources to pursue the matter, and was angry that he had been ignored and his intelligence insulted. The tenants won, the owner had to install cable TV, and the management firm was fired.

Was there an easier and less costly solution? Certainly. When the ownership first made the decision not to go ahead with cable television, a letter to or a meeting of existing tenants to explain the problem would have been in order. A reduction of the monthly rent for the existing tenants of as little as $2.00 per month might have solved the problem. A few tenants might have moved but probably not many; few tenants were even aware of the problem until several angry tenants brought the matter up to the entire tenant body. At the time of the letter, the schematic of the units showing cable access should have been removed for the benefit of future applicants. The total cost would have been minimal compared with the legal costs involved in continuation of the argument. Instead, management defied the tenants, attempted to prove a point using power, and lost the case—and the contract. Management threw down the gauntlet without having predetermined the outcome.

In another case, collaboration between tenants and management allowed resolution of a potentially explosive situation with a high degree of professionalism. Management was told by ownership to increase rents to an exorbitant level for the purpose of increasing the value of the property for resale. Management recognized the lack of care permitted by the restrictive budget allotted and advised the owner that the rents could probably not be justified in terms of the services rendered and that the income level of the tenants probably could not tolerate the drastic increase. It continued to advise the owner that because of a shortage of comparable rental units in the area, the community could not absorb those who would have to move, creating the potential for a rent strike in this consumer-oriented community. Management presented to ownership the maximum rents it believed could be obtained—and these only if some expenditures for repairs were made.

The amounts proposed by management were less than those desired by the owner but to settle for these levels would be far less costly than an enraged tenant body. Management called a meeting of all tenants, at which the proposed annual budget was broken down for each tenant in terms of the monthly rent they paid: so much for mortgage interest, gas, electricity, trash removal, grounds maintenance, repairs, services, and so on. Most of the tenants were surprised at the quality and degree of documentation they were provided in support of the proposed rent increase. No one raised any objections to the amount included as a fair return to the owner. Various tenants agreed to head committees to look into existing expenses and to determine what repairs would be the most necessary or yield the greatest benefit in terms of their needs and those of the owners.

One committee found that the rate charged for electricity was erroneous, and significant refunds were made to the building. Another group was appalled at the cost of repairs due to tenant abuse and helped management formulate a set of house rules and lease clauses that might reduce the economic burden on all tenants. Management made the necessary repairs after taking into consideration the tenants' requirements and its own requests. The entire process took less than a month, and no loss of rents was incurred. Some managers or administrators might have called this process "inviting the fox into the chicken coop," but this author calls it effective management.

THE WRITTEN WORD

Much of our interaction with tenants must be based on written documentation. Management frequently relies on the written word to solve all problems: the lease, addenda, and attached rules. While usually (but not always) effective in a court of law, strict adherence to the quotation of chapter and verse of the lease and house rules will not always solve problems. We live in an age in which people want to know what is happening to them and want to understand, if not be involved in, the decisions that affect their lives.

We have all seen leases and house rules that would exceed *War and Peace* in length and are treated by virtue of weight and volume as the final authority. There are also leases, known as rental agreements, that hardly fill up one side of a piece of paper, which management deems allows it the freedom to make up rules as it goes along. Neither extreme, nor anything in between, will create flawless management unless and until the written word, and the behavior that enforces it, has as its *intent* the resolution of problems, the protection of the premises, and the quiet enjoyment of the tenants, along with mechanisms for enforcement. Documents that stem from an attitude of punishment absolutely and clearly invite the behavior they purport to eliminate.

Twenty pages of house rules that list one hundred "don'ts" are not conducive to smooth management and positive tenant relations. Some of us set ourselves up for battle because we believe we have to fight to win. Extensive and negative house rules draw the battle lines. A tenant who is disposed to using anger or manipulation will be invited by these negative rules to display behavior antagonistic to management, and management frequently takes the bait.

What is it about some management firms that makes their job seem so easy? Why do some buildings live for years in peace while others are constantly in a state of turmoil? From one perspective, the issue is rules versus style. The most effective management teams establish written documents and regulations designed to promote positively the smooth flow of income and expenses. The rules are stated in a positive fashion, they are brief, and they are nonrepetitive. (House and building rules should not include complete rephrasings of the lease.) And the style of these managers permits time—time to talk to tenants, time to explain consequential behavior, time to provide assistance, time to suggest alternatives, time to make a phone call to ease a weary mind.

The written word is a tool for management to use, the authority on which some decisions are based. The written word is not intended to substitute for personal connections. In the hierarchy of property management, subordinates are frequently relegated to creating status reports, and it is forgotten that an economically profitable piece of income-producing property is based on communication—lots of it and most of it positive. If we don't walk our properties, talk to the tenants, chat with the groundskeepers, and thereby put our "ear to the ground," we will be ill prepared to resolve problems and respond to emergencies. No manager manual or other form of the written word—and there are some mighty thick manuals—can ever account for all problems.

Written words for use in property management—whether leases, rules, addenda, or manuals—should be succinct enough to provide direction but brief enough to be immediately understood and enforced. If the rule is basically unenforceable, leave it out. If the rule is a plea for certain types of behavior, it can never be more than just that—a plea—and it should be stated as such. Try a printout or brochure that says, "Can you help us: have your guests park in unassigned spaces; latch trash enclosure gates on exiting." Trying to evict someone for not behaving as requested may be impossible. A statement threatening that eviction will follow if the behavior is *not* exhibited lowers credibility regarding the enforceability of the entire contents of the document.

THE TENANT WHO IS RIGHT

In a very subjective business such as property management, "right" is frequently a matter of perspective. Over the years I have found tenants as a group to be mostly cooperative and agreeable, sometimes surprisingly so even when their complaints are improperly addressed or not addressed at all. In some cases, tenants are clearly not aware of their rights and available legal remedies, and management steps in to take advantage of this ignorance.

Management has also been known to display favoritism or respond to tenants judgmentally. The favorite tenant who plants lots of flowers may be given first priority when his or her freezer will no longer freeze ice cream, while the troublesome tenant must wait days in 100° weather for the air conditioner to be repaired. Judgmental management bears its own seeds of destruction to a management firm or owner who practices it. Businesspersons and world leaders know that effective leadership does not depend on whether or not we like our clients or constituents, but whether or not the duties as prescribed can be performed fairly and equitably with the proper goals and results in mind.

This is not to say that we are not entitled to our prejudices—we all have them, cultivated and nurtured for years. But to conduct our behavior from the perspective of these prejudices is poor business practice, consumes much energy and time, and may lead to legal conflict and economic disaster.

Whatever the nature of the property being leased, tenants have a right to expect certain items to work, in conjunction with the terms of the lease or according to local, state, and federal laws. While unreasonable demands by a tenant may stem from other issues, when tenants are clearly within their rights to make demands, management can take one of the following positions.

"Right" versus "Wrong"

If management or ownership, at any level, demands that it be "right" before an issue is resolved or even addressed, the contest is on. The vast majority of tenant-oriented laws on the books today in all 50 states stem from very poor *management* decisions. Management fails to make a proper decision in the first place, personalities become involved, and management compounds the error with additional mistakes. The rivalry escalates to court. Most "bad" (from management's perspective) legal decisions have come from bad cases, and most cases are brought to court by management. The precedents these cases establish wreak havoc on the industry and frequently induce investment money to seek rewards from sources other than income property, particularly residential income property. There is absolutely no harm in granting an apology to a tenant and *immediately* resolving an issue; the manager should continue to contact the tenant in the interim if resolution will take more than a day.

Managers who have not been embarrassed by their own decisions or reddened when confronted by an incensed tenant organization have not had the unforgettable experience of ultimate humility and learned the lesson it sears indelibly on the brain. The "right versus wrong" attitude stems in part from our social belief that mistakes are a sign of weakness and that important and successful people never make mistakes. A mistake—an erroneous decision—is evidence of someone having made a decision, having tried, having taken decisive action as best he or she knew how at the moment. To be able to recognize and correct a mistake is a gift. Never to admit to a mistake or, worse yet, to err by making no decision at all is very costly in the real estate business—or any business.

The Subservient Approach

In an effort to please anyone and everyone, some of us take the opposite approach, that of becoming totally subservient to the tenant. Tenants' every wish is granted, and we cannot humble ourselves enough. Managers with this problem are so engrossed in pleasing the tenant, the boss, and the owner that there is no longer a rhythm to management. A smooth operation is replaced by chaotic and random movements of staff.

This approach is a gross disservice to tenants and owners. Such a manager is frequently found on a project just purchased by new ownership after years of neglect to both people and property. The new manager, eager to display enthusiasm and an ability to "turn the project around," attacks every request from the tenant as his personal task in life. Instead of being presented with a hope for better living through planned operations and an orderly conduct of affairs, the tenants see that no matter how small their request, management drops everything to respond. The requests begin to build up, the good manager gets "burned out," none of the major issues are resolved, and the property deteriorates. Without a plan, there can be no planned action, nor can there be follow-through, quality control, assessment of goals, or purposeful decision making.

Subservient managers also reveal another aspect of their personality: the preference to make no decision at all and allow others to make the decisions by acquiescing to their every demand. One cannot formulate a goal and work toward that goal while at the mercy of every request made of us; this manager reacts to problems, always appears to be running, is always perspiring. Everyone, of course, can see how hard the manager tries, but soon everyone can also see how little the manager accomplishes. Subservience can be a cover for incompetence, an inability to create and/or follow a plan. Despite efforts to please everyone, no one is pleased, because the manager didn't bring competence to the job in the first place. Subservience is also a tool for deflecting the anger of tenants—the angry demand finds no resistance, but neither does it find resolution.

The Organizer

If any industry needs organizers, it is the property management business. The organizer takes every problem, every request, every issue, and puts them in a category: the "fix-it-now" category, the "list-for-the-maintenance-person" category, the "need-refrigerator-parts" category. These managers have a complete warehouse of information in their heads, with rows and rows of shelves full of places into which every request fits. Mention refrigerator, and these people pull the box labeled "refrigerators" from their mental shelf and can tell instantly which seven units need to have refrigerator doors resealed. When purchasing supplies, they know they need seven refrigerator door sealers and three for inventory. They send the maintenance person out with a checklist organized in accordance with the physical layout of the property. The work orders are sorted by priority, and next week's meeting with the owner is organized by subject. They have folders and keep notes on lined yellow paper neatly hole-punched and entered into folders.

Their staff talks smoothly and quietly, following their example. Procedures are written, rewritten, and constantly subject to change as they grow with the property. The tenants always know they are taking every action possible to deal with their problems because they know organized persons cannot have problems without solutions. And the solution may be the process of organization itself, from the point of view of both the flow of work and the attitude of the tenant who requires the assistance of the organizer. The tenant who is right need ask the organizer only once for assistance, and he can consider the job as good as done. Although there are other attributes required in an effective manager, it is the "organizer" characteristic that lends itself to solutions.

PROBLEM TENANTS

The Immoral Tenant

If you feel the need to act personally when you perceive "immorality," it must be done outside the context of your professional or ownership capacity. Being the owner or property manager does not give us the right to force, either directly or by threats or insinuation, our own standards on any tenant. We can't mix morality with economics. If, as property manager, you decide to take on the issue of morality, do not do so without previous discussion with and approval of the owner. It is mandatory that the owner be advised of your plan and reasons and of the financial or other consequences that may be incurred if your plan is executed. A good income property can become a financial disaster as a result of the actions of a manager with honorable intentions. If the owner's goals are physical renovation and increased income with a view to future sale, "cleaning up the property" can create expenses that are not affordable.

A Judgmental Issue

The place to deal with the immoral tenant, like the criminal tenant, is outside the office, on your own time and at your own expense, unless you are the owner and choose to accept the financial consequences. What is "immoral" is a matter of judgment, and as an owner or property manager, your basic question is one of goals. If, as owner, you bought the property to "clean it up," you need only recognize the economic consequences; if these weigh favorably in terms of your expected social consequences, then proceed. As a property manager, this is the time to compartmentalize—divide the behavior into categories. Behaviors that must be addressed from a professional management and economic standpoint should be considered regarding enforceability of sanctions and discussed with legal counsel. If any steps you want to take personally, on your own time and at your own expense, will eventually be detrimental to your professionalism or opposed to the owner's wishes or management policy, you must either find another job or refrain from acting.

The Manipulator

Manipulators feel that to get what they want they need only move people like pawns on a chessboard. They have decided that asking directly for what they want does not work. If the hot water heater is at too hot a setting, he or she sends in a small child with a bandaged hand to pay the rent. When the manager asks what happened, the child dutifully reveals the burn from the hot water. In an office building I once managed, the janitorial crew was negligent in refilling the paper accessories in the lavatories one weekend. The matter was brought to my attention effectively by a quiet, nondescript tenant. He waited until several clients were in the room outside my office and politely dropped on the secretary's desk the empty tissue roll and empty box of seat covers. A polite phone call would have been better from my point of view, but from the manipulator's perspective, directly addressing the issue is far less spectacular and powerful a method.

Manipulators display the behavioral traits of angry persons. They feel that a forthright statement of their needs will be met with denial, ridicule, or rejection. A direct statement of needs also displays a degree of vulnerability, and manipulators do not want the world to know that they, too, have unmet needs. Manipulators are actually very sensitive and astute persons, able to find quickly another person's sensitive buttons, soft spots, and vulnerable positions. They quickly put the manager in a defensive position, sometimes bringing in a third party to present their case. If the project happens to have a property manager who is equally adept at manipulation, the two of them can spar indefinitely, each outwitting the other. But the problem is never solved, and valuable management time is wasted.

Point out to the tenant, without denigrating the behavior, that you don't quite understand the nature of the request; guess at it if you have to, but do not "buy into" the behavior. Ask to be shown the problem directly, and then deal with it directly without taking side trips concerning the manipulative behavior. An attempt to outmanipulate the manipulator will waste valuable management time. Keep defining and redefining the problem until you and the manipulator agree on exactly what the problem is—then work on that.

The Con Artist

The con artist is a cousin of the manipulator. He or she is convinced that nothing in life can be straightforward, everything must be cloaked in subterfuge, and the route to completion and satisfaction must be circuitous and devious. Usually this is a conscious game for the tenant, to see if she can outwit you, but in some cases the behavior was learned as the only means to get her needs satisfied or even to survive. The con artist is a fast talker—a real smoothie—who dazzles you with a speech establishing her needs with total clarity and logic and then requests an immediate confirmation of the proposal, hoping to catch you off guard before you have had time to think about it. If you respond immediately, you are probably in trouble already.

The only way to deal effectively with this tenant is to indicate that you have heard the proposal and promise to think it over or discuss it with staff. Get back to the tenant soon, but at your convenience. Do not provide an immediate answer unless you are quite clear about what the real message was and what the real consequences of your decision are.

The Born Loser

The born loser is another type of manipulator. Born losers have sad eyes, walk with stooped shoulders, and predetermine that all their efforts will result in failure, then set out to prove how right they are. Alternatively, their outward stance may be one of bravado, showing the world they don't care that they never succeed, didn't want to anyway. As a tenant, the born loser is the nice person who tries your patience and breaks every rule, quietly and unobtrusively, until you have no choice but to issue a notice to terminate the lease. Born losers apologize each time they overstep the boundaries, but sooner or later repeat the behavior. As a property manager, you've spoken to them nicely, explained what you will have to do if they continue, and even apologized for having to do your job. They nod, give a very impressive and sad story, and promise never to do it again. A month later, you shake your head in dismay as they appear once more on the delinquent list. Born losers set themselves up to lose.

The Delinquent Tenant

When properties have rental delinquencies, you have probably noticed that the same names appear each month. Late charges do not bother these tenants—punitive charges seldom do. My firm encountered this problem more than our patience would bear, and a new policy was instituted at all properties (commercial, office, and residential):

1. We abandoned late charges—they never covered our administrative costs anyway.

2. Lease addendums were issued (in a manner pursuant to state and local laws) which stated that all rents are due and payable on or before the first day of the month in accordance with a specific paragraph of the lease. A notice to "pay or quit" is issued on the third day thereafter (details in accordance with whatever laws and regulations the property is subject to). If a tenant is served two such notices within one calendar year, the tenant is issued a notice to vacate the premises. A warning letter is issued with the first notice to "pay or quit."

The reaction was interesting. The first month the perpetually delinquent tenants were still delinquent. With the first "pay or quit" notice, the formal and standardized warning letter was attached, reminding tenants of the aforementioned lease addendum. The second month, more than 75 percent of the habitual delinquents paid their rent by the third day of the month. Those who didn't received a notice to "pay or quit" and subsequently received a notice to vacate the premises for lease violation.

Our entire stance was that the project was not designed to be a lending institution or public assistance service; those functions were performed by other organizations established and equipped to meet specific needs. Our project, whether residential or business, was established to provide a service of physical accommodation, and as long as management and ownership met their obligations, we expected tenants to meet theirs, particularly payment of rent. We could not very well go to the mortgagees of our property and give them all the sob stories that had been given to us concerning why the rents were not being paid on time.

We took two eviction cases to court the first go-around, and won both. This policy has now been in effect for over 5 years, the paragraph is a standard clause in our leases, and we are extremely successful in collecting rents on time. Every now and again we are tested, but we've done our homework and issued the proper warnings and notices. Often among the casualties is the born loser—the nice person who never pays the rent on time because there was vacation, or the car's transmission broke down, or the bank messed up the checking account. In many ways, the born loser is a manipulator, who uses tactics that generate sympathy to avoid commitments.

The Violent Tenant

The tenant who chooses violence when provoked is definitely in authority. Property management is full of the unexpected, and the mild-mannered tenant who physically abuses or injures the manager may come as a complete surprise. However, the situation is sometimes forseeable, and management should take all precautions not to invite the use of power. A manager shouldn't be a peacemaker when a police officer should be called in, and mustn't take on the roles of prosecuting attorney, judge, and jury if the matter is best solved in court.

Managers inherit situations and tenants when they take on rented property. An astute management agent or owner weeds out managerial applicants who seem to like to win fights. It is true that some properties require a very "strong" manager, but the strength should lie in the ability to make decisions, not in the ability to take on violent tenants.

It is important that managers don't attempt to "be one of them." The tenant who *chooses* violence is prepared to carry through until completion, while the manager who thinks about violence is probably not fully prepared to go "all the way." Furthermore, under no circumstances is it advisable for the manager to try to be "one of the gang." Trying to dress like, talk like, and look like the tougher tenants does not make the manager safe, not does it protect the property or other tenants.

I frequently manage very "rough" properties and have developed a style that works. (For one thing, I am here to tell the story while others aren't.) First of all, I always walk my properties, no matter how dangerous they appear. If I can't walk the property, I do not accept the management contract. Second, I do not try to "fit in." I wear whatever I wear and *always* dress professionally. When I walk the property, I do not tempt fate by carrying anything other than pad and pen. I want it to be perfectly clear to everyone that I carry nothing worth stealing and no weapons. When I need to take pictures, I carry a large camera in full view and request permission of any person whose picture I take. I make it obvious that I am taking pictures of the *property*. On many project, unit, or space inspections I have encountered the solicitation, purchase, or use of drugs. I say my "good morning" and keep right on going. It is not the time or place to confront the situation, and I have no intentions of being a hero. I have personally known a manager who was shot by a deranged tenant, another who was stabbed seven times and thrown over a second floor balcony, and several more at whom shots were fired. Others have been "pushed around" by violent tenants. Sometimes the best decision a manager can make is to decide to make another decision!

The New Immigrant

Unlike the preceding sections, this one does not present a characterization but a set of genuine problems for management and tenant concerning acculturation, or the process of acquiring the habits, traits, and style of a new social culture. We are a nation of immigrants. Most of us have parents or grandparents who came from other shores. The process of acculturation is difficult for everyone, and those of us who are already here do not always understand the behavior of the immigrant; some of us even fear or ridicule that behavior. The newcomer may find little sanction or approval for his or her traditional way of life. Related problems surface in the business of property management since most new immigrants rent homes, apartments, or places of business. These problems are particularly evident at or near points of entry into the United States: California, Florida, Texas, and New York.

Many new immigrants come to this country from a desperate situation—usually abject poverty or war. They may be misperceived as ignorant, stupid, or uneducated because their new environment is very different from what they have known. In the late 1970s we managed a large residential property that was very troubled, financially and socially. Vacancies exceeded 50 percent even with federal assistance for low-income families. We were approached by the authorities from a nearby military base who had housed the last of the boat people escaping Vietnam.

For months these people had been housed in large, temporary tent facilities at the base. These new immigrants were military officers and enlisted men, civil servants, and farmers. Those for whom sponsors could be found were soon transferred to those sponsors to begin a new life with help, guidance, and support. For others, the search for a sponsor seemed impossible; no one wanted the farmers and their families. The new immigrants spent months in the heat of the desert. The families were large, sometimes including six or eight children and maybe a grandparent. They had no wealth, or power, and no talents that seemed salable to the American public.

We had thirty-five vacant units at our project, and the housing officer of the base sought us out. Could we, would we, take these families if someone would guarantee the rent and security deposit? It was not an easy decision. The local newspaper had been on the track of the military base trying to learn where these families were to be sent, but publicity was the last thing these people, or our project, needed. After several late-night discussions, which included the federal agency that provided assistance to the project, we decided we would house the new immigrants. We had many problems to solve even before their arrival: many of the units were in a state of destruction, fit for no living person, and racial problems existed at the project. We knew some of the existing tenants would not want this new racial group, particularly when they found out that rent and food would be provided by yet another agency, even though it was private. "Why," these tenants would ask, "are the boat people being given so much attention when our own American poor need a helping hand?"

Under cover of night, for security and publicity reasons, we brought two busloads of these families into our project. Our many meetings and conversations with existing residents left us uneasy regarding what their responses would be when the buses arrived. I requested volunteers from our firm to accompany me to the site for the arrival and transition of the families; my staff had to agree to wear jeans and white T-shirts so that everyone would know who we were and that we were unarmed. Our identification was additionally revealed by the company logo emblazoned in red on the front and back of each T-shirt.

A tense situation. As the buses arrived at 2 a.m., the existing tenants were outside milling about. They knew by my presence that the new families were on their way. When the buses arrived, they were surrounded, and the bus drivers locked the doors and windows in fear. The temperature was over 80° that night. For several hours the impasse continued: I refused to call in the police. We simply kept talking and talking. Finally the tenants agreed to let us take the families to their units. One family at a time was led from the steaming bus to an apartment. We had only one man who spoke both English and Vietnamese.

The new immigrants were terrified; they were being separated from each other and could see that the "welcoming committee" was not particularly grateful for their arrival. Each family had to be shown the fundamentals of the unit: light switches, bathrooms, gas stove, refrigerator, air conditioner, and how to open and close the drapes and windows. Children were crying and adults were wanting to.

By 6 in the morning, the food truck still had not appeared; somehow it had been separated from the convoy. None of the immigrant families had food. Only one solution was immedately available: after all families were securely locked in their units, I took all our staff and their cars and we found an open grocery store. We bought chickens, vegetables, fruit, bread, milk, diapers, toilet paper, and whatever else we presumed the families needed on an emergency basis, and I wrote a check for far more than I had in my account. We set up a commissary in one of the vacant units, and one member of each new family was allowed to come and choose some basic foods. We forgot to buy pots and pans and utensils, but at least the children could drink milk and eat the bread and peanut butter.

Resolution at dawn. By the time the sun rose a new scene prevailed. Existing tenants were offering cooking utensils and supplies. Some offered last night's spaghetti or pot roast. One tenant was making Kool-Aid by the gallon. The lawns of the project were soon literally covered with tenants, old and new, eating a varied collection of food for breakfast. Children who were too small to speak any language were playing together. Babies were transferred back and forth for inspection. Teenagers shared their rock music, and adults were learning "thank you" in each other's language. Later that day the sponsoring agency arrived with more food and basic necessities, and our initial task was completed. We went home tired but fulfilled. We were not so naive as to believe that our problems were over, but at least we had begun.

We had taken on the responsibility of housing these new immigrants, and not totally from the goodness of our hearts: they appeared to be an opportunity to obtain rents and avoid the imminent foreclosure of the property. However, we were clear that we had at the same time chosen a new set of problems. Although the racial antagonism we feared had not materialized, localized incidents did occur. Our biggest problem was to provide security for all the residents and protection of the property. For the second goal we had to teach the new immigrants about the care of the units, and in a language we did not speak!

At times I grew frustrated at the new immigrants: Why didn't they understand the concept of a garbage disposal? Didn't *everyone* know about garbage disposals? Even my sociology background with extensive training in acculturation did not prepare me for this job. In the privacy of my own mind, I found myself thinking these people were not very bright. I was angry at the condition of the units, the lack of cleanliness according to my standards. I was nauseated by the multitude of cooking odors that greeted me when I went into an apartment and perplexed by the tenants' apparent liking for those odors. I was disgusted by what I perceived to be a total lack of manners at what they called an evening meal. My own prejudices and racism confronted me daily.

I wish I could say I was a patient teacher, or perhaps an eager student, but even when I became aware of my negative attitude, I was too embarrassed to deal with those thoughts and attitudes. Over the months I spent there, however, and that included most days and evenings, it was the new immigrants who provided the gifts, the teaching, and the training. They had brought courage; it wasn't I who had drifted out to sea on a boat never to see my homeland again. They sent their children out to play and off to school, displaying hope and trust that the schools and community would treat their children at least fairly, if not kindly. They learned *my* language and called me by name. Adults went to evening school to learn skills to seek employment and struggled with new words, new tools, new equipment. Their teenagers learned to wobble around like ours on the high-heeled shoes that were in vogue. They watched soap operas, "sit-coms," and Sesame Street on television. They began a whole new life and eventually dispersed into the wider society: some went to Minnesota, another family to South Dakota, another to Washington.

Most new immigrants will not arrive at your property so dramatically, but occasionally they will arrive. Many will be denied occupancy because of "lack of previous credit or landlord history" or because they are unable to complete the application properly or because their permission to be in this country in the first place is questioned. Those you do house, you thereby agree to teach how to live in your environment. Imagine a family that never had a vacuum cleaner or carpets to clean, or does not know how to clean drapes because they never had them before. Or a family that always cooked on an open fire and therefore doesn't know how to use a gas stove. Some new immigrants have had these amenities, and language and customs are the only barriers to cross. At any rate, you have taken on the responsibility of protecting the owner's physical investment. You must do what you need to do in terms of preparing yourself, but you mustn't fail to address the problems, and then reap the intrinsic rewards.

The new immigrant doesn't appear only in residential property. New immigrants lease commercial space, frequently for restaurants. When the new immigrant arrives, he or she is immediately concerned with making a living, and the details of how that is done may be confusing. The United States sees itself as a land of laws—rules by agreement—which are usually written; most tenants in all types of properties expect a written lease and acknowledge its rightful contents.

For example, on a triple net lease (tenant rents the space and pays for all taxes, insurance, and upkeep) for restaurant space in a commercial building, the tenant is clearly responsible for maintaining the plumbing. In one property, a new immigrant lessee did not understand about cold grease and clogged pipes, so when he sent all his cooking grease down the drain, the other lessees in the building experienced plumbing backups. The restauranteur would call us and request that we do something about the plumbing. Had the matter been a problem only for that tenant, I would have told him to call a plumber, at his own expense. However, the other tenants had every right to call me and complain and even to send me a bill for *their* plumber. In order to reach a solution and get on with my life, I enlisted the help of an interpreter and a plumber, and we installed a grease sump, at my expense, complete with many explanations regarding how to use it and what would happen if he didn't. Well, sometimes the pump works and sometimes it doesn't. My dilemma is whether or not to renew the lease next year. I could use this opportunity to be rid of the problem, or I could continue to go there and solve the problem, while the delightful new immigrant owner of the restaurant gratefully provides me with a delicious dinner—free.

THE "STRICTLY BUSINESS" SECTOR

Whether their property is in an office, retail/commercial, or industrial building, nonresidential tenants have a very different perception of the environment in which they are labeled "tenant." These tenants do not see the leased environment as a personal refuge—a cave safe from the hungry lions of the world; those rewards are sought elsewhere. The environment is the place the tenant goes to daily to accomplish something, to fulfill a task, to reach another goal for another purpose. The environment is simply *expected* to work. The plumbing is expected to be in order, doors securable, parking available, air conditioner issuing cool air, elevator speedy, roof keeping out the elements, and janitorial service ridding the premises of yesterday's news. While the lessees may display some of the characteristics of "tenants," they are basically tenants for only a portion of the day, unlike the residential tenant who is a tenant 24 hours a day, whether home or not. To the nonresidential tenant, the environment is purely service. The office or space is a commodity, not an end in itself.

Business Tenant Expectations

As occupants of a house, whether we are tenants or owners, we expect a certain number of items not to work from time to time. If one burner on the stove goes out, we use one of the other three until it gets fixed. If one light socket doesn't work, we find another until someone gets juice to the socket. We live for a surprising length of time with nonfunctioning or damaged parts in our physical environment (witness the condition in which some tenants leave their units and the repairs that must be made for new occupancy).

To the businessperson, on the other hand, a disruption in the physical environment can mean a disruption to the mechanism for producing income. The nonfunctioning item then becomes bigger than life in what is already a hectic business world. The leak in the corner of the warehouse is a small roof leak, and the inventory may be moved slightly while the first call to the maintenance or management company is made. Several days later the leak is larger and the inventory more cumbersome to move. As the owner of the business constantly walks around the puddle on the floor, she begins to seethe. And if the day has not been a particularly good one, the tenant calls the owner with a fury beyond that which even a good roof leak can generate. For the moment she can blame all her bad business decisions, or the recession, or the reduction in business due to rising interest rates on the leaky roof. At this point, she may well be beyond polite conversation, and the very last words she wants to hear are excuses.

While this is not the place to discuss the legal issues of implied habitability or the technicalities of lease agreements, it is the place to discuss the responsibility and rewards of providing leased space that functions so smoothly as to be virtually unnoticed by the tenant. At social gatherings, the conversation frequently turns to "our rental property," with much noise and ado about unreasonable tenants, while the speakers themselves are probably lessees in their own business enterprise and would not tolerate inattentive management.

Proper Maintenance

Nonresidential tenants, by virtue of their lease agreements, the owners' responsibilities, and the nature of business itself, present the fewest problems to property management. In return, management can ensure that the physical premises are maintained in a manner that totally conforms to the owner's obligations in the written agreements. If properly maintained, nonresidential tenants' spaces are the least likely to cause a phone call in the middle of the night for plugged plumbing. Renovations on turnover are less costly and turnover less frequent. Leases are for longer periods of time and rents easier to collect. If management pays attention to the maintenance required, the reward is a much higher margin of profit to both owner and management than obtained in residential properties. Businesspersons are doing exactly what you are doing—running a business. They do not need, and will not tolerate, neglect on management's part that causes them to function less efficiently in their business of making a living.

LANDLORD ROLES

Landlords too are ordinary people who may take on a preconceived role when given the title. The landlord perceives that the tenant will cause him or her turmoil, and then proceeds to create ways to cope with those problems even before they exist. Such solutions may be inappropriate.

One such landlord is the U.S. government (USG). Often property managers or owners representing the USG put themselves in the position of being all-powerful. Their responses sound like they come from manuals, and decisions always involve red tape, rules, regulations, and a series of approvals. All decisions must be "run up the ladder." The tenant is never sure exactly what the manager has said except that the solution will not be forthcoming soon. Thus the USG manager does not have to make decisions or take the responsibility for having made them.

The Righteously Indignant Manager

The righteously indignant manager wants the property and its tenants to be a reflection of what "ought to be" as opposed to the way things really are. This manager sometimes is totally ineffectual because the real source of a problem cannot be addressed—the manager spends time working on solutions to symptoms instead of problems. However, the righteously indignant manager can also be extremely successful if the desire for solutions is genuine, for she or he can act fast based on the need to "set things right."

My firm assumed management of one large residential property in a very hot, arid climate. The project had been sorely neglected by both the owners and the previous management company. Our project seemed to be the gathering place for the bulk of the city's illegal activities, and the owner faced losing his investment and tax shelter. Together we devised a plan for renovation: new managers, new landscaping, an exterior paint job, new appliances, and more security.

The property manager hired to oversee the task was a mature woman who had decided to come out of retirement when her spouse of many years died. Her accent was decidedly European and aristocratic, and she carried her very tall frame in a stately manner. She was outspoken, well-informed, and completely unafraid of power structures. She requested and obtained a meeting with the chief of police, the fire chief, and the city manager, explaining to them that she represented the new management firm and that the owner had agreed to make every attempt to restore this property to its original state. She then asked for their assistance, particularly night patrols by the police force and assistance from the arson investigation unit.

Their response was that our project had become the "bowels" of the city and that it was not their responsibility to clean up the mess. This righteously indignant woman, fully armed with facts and figures, stood up to her full stature and politely proclaimed that this property contributed over $34,000 per year in property taxes, employed more than ten persons directly, and paid hundreds of thousands of dollars for supplies and services to local merchants. For these contributions, and with the owner's written commitment to the management firm, she hesitated not a moment in politely demanding what was rightfully hers as a citizen, requesting a decision from these authorities regarding whether they intended to cooperate with her in revitalizing the property or force her to seek higher authority. Needless to say, their choice at the moment could only be cooperation, which she intended to pursue. As she left the meeting, she turned to the authorities and said, "Bowels, indeed!"

The Nice Guy Manager

The nice guy manager or owner is really more of a tenant than a manager. These managers put themselves on "their side." It is important to them that everyone likes them, sometimes at the expense of effective property management. They forgive transgressions of the terms of the lease, and owners find their receivables growing larger each month.

Each infraction of the rules has a credible excuse to the nice guy. He or she is also known as a "friend" to all the tenants, frequently joining their social gatherings and parties. How, then, on the third day of the month, can he issue notices to "pay or quit" and enforce them? Sooner, rather than later, he must be replaced.

The Absentee Owner/Manager

Absentee owner/managers receive in return exactly what they contribute to the property—neglect. Whether absent in body or spirit, this owner/manager extends to the tenants an invitation to just pay the rent and remain silent. This they will do until the unit or space is in complete shambles and the conditions no longer tolerable even to them, and then move. This style is useful for those who need to write off substantial sums of negative cash flow.

Owners and managers can also be angry, lonely, manipulators, con artists, and born losers. If they are anything other than professional managers, at any level, they will be at best temporary, lucky winners. If they are tyrants, they may win occasionally, but they will more frequently be nonproductive and inefficient. There is only one way to manage property professionally and effectively: be alert, be of a single purpose, and leave your games at home.

THE RIGHT STUFF

Like any profession, property management has its own requirements for success. That success is not measured by the quantity of property managed, but by the quality of the management process, with the final test of a fair and equitable financial return for the owner or investor. To achieve that return, certain qualities of personality are more useful than others, and certain behavior patterns produce better results with less effort than others. It is important to remember that there is a commonality of interest between landlord and tenant: Both want what they pay for; both want to have their stated and legal rights protected, and both want to achieve satisfaction. Economically and environmentally the needs and goals of the landlord and tenant are interlaced.

Collaborate

Consider collaboration instead of compromise. Compromise implies that each party has to give up something to achieve desired goals, whereas collaboration implies that both parties win. To achieve collaborative results, dialogue is required, and that takes time and the ability to listen. It is also necessary to take the responsibility of meeting contractual arrangements, written and oral.

Retain Your Authority

To direct behavior to a desired end, one must never give up one's authority. If you constantly refer to the "home office" as having the final decision-making power, you leave no power to yourself. Make the decisions, all the decisions you can, at your own level. It's alright to be afraid sometimes while making these weighty decisions, but you can make the decision anyway. If you want your authority to be with you in a pinch, don't let go of it on the daily matters. Keep what you have, for it will be needed.

Do Your Own Thing

Stick to your own game. Take a good hard look at your professional role, decide what decisions need to be made, and act on your own standards of behavior instead of responding to or imitating the other person's behavior. If you see yourself displaying any of the negative characteristics previously described, consider whether you want to continue that behavior based on how successful it is for you in achieving the desired results. Allow yourself the experience of changing your thought patterns and behavior.

I attended a conference once led by a leader of social change: Marilyn Ferguson, the author of *The Aquarian Conspiracy*. She told us:

> If you continue to think the way you have always thought, you will continue to get the same results. If you continue to act the way you have always acted, you will think the way you have always thought and continue to get the same results. If you continue to decide the things you've always decided, you will continue to act the way you have always acted and think the way you have always thought and continue to get the same results.

The choice is yours. If you can change your attitudes, thoughts, and actions and thereby achieve your own desired goals, you may also have a significant influence on how others live their lives.

Be patient if you do not always see your desired results for they are not always ours to see in our tenure. As a property manager, you are in a position to alter history, since every decision you make affects someone. If you have decided to provide the very best property that can be provided under the circumstances in which you operate, then do just that and don't compromise. There is no compromising on quality—poor tenants, small commercial tenants, or unsophisticated tenants deserve the same treatment as rich or sophisticated tenants. You may never know how you have changed lives by providing a family with a decent living arrangement or a small businessperson just starting out with a space that totally works. The result may not be yours to see, but you can be sure you have had an effect. It is not a question of whether or not your decisions will make a difference but of whether the effect you have will be intentional or unintentional.

Invite Solutions

You have the choice of inviting problems, conflicts, or solutions. Your very stance, manner, as well as words tell the other person what results you desire to achieve. If your message asks for negative results, you will be guaranteed to achieve just that goal. If your style invites and asks for positive results, consider them yours. Every problem carries within itself its own solution, and every solution harbors the potential for problems. In the process, you are always either part of the solution or part of the problem. When persons come to you with problems, ask them to present several possible solutions. You do not have a monopoly on solutions—they exist in every corner of the universe, and you need to be open to every one of them, regardless of the style in which they are presented. I once overheard my teenagers discussing with friends methods of behavior reinforcement used by their parents. My daughter said, "My mother uses the worst punishment of all. She makes me tell her exactly what the problem is as I see it and then asks me what consequences I would recommend. So I always know that whatever I do, I'm going to have to figure out my own payment."

Give Honest Assessments

Honestly assess the real rewards of this business, for it is easy to discount the many terrific relationships that are established, the positive results we achieve, or the good feelings we have when we know we've done a job well. Don't discount that nice birthday card from the tenant when you can't even figure out how she knew it was your birthday. What about the tenant who brings you a crate of peaches or the tenant who owns a print shop and at no cost prints the flyers for the annual barbeque? What about the senior tenant who is so very happy with her environment that she takes every opportunity to tell you so and her daughter brings you a bag of bulbs for the same reason? Don't forget the little kid hardly tall enough to reach the counter who brings in a dime he found on the laundry room floor, or the other little kid who is only 3 feet tall but has been sent out to empty the trash into a 5-foot-high container and figures out a way to do it instead of dumping the trash on the ground. The rewards are all around us, and in our haste and bustle to solve problems, we frequently forget to acknowledge all the gifts we have.

Listen to the messages that come to you without preconceived ideas about what the person is going to say or judgmental values that leave you deaf to the real message. If you're in a hurry to get in your response, you will have missed yet one more opportunity to make a resolution.

Do Your Homework

Above all, always do your homework. Leave the "shooting from the hips" to the spaghetti westerns. Know your property, know your tenants, know your alternatives, and do your research. You will still make mistakes, but they will be the best decisions you could have made at the time. They can be undone and redone much more easily than decisions made in haste. Be present and available to receive all the information coming at you; be a sponge that soaks up information and not the sieve that lets it all pass through. Once through with your decision, let go of it and get on to something else.

Be People Oriented

If you are not people oriented, you really need to find another way to make a living. Property management *is* people—you work for them and with them; you solve problems, and when more problems surface, you go right on solving them. There is not much demand for property managers for vacant buildings. And when you feel you have had just about enough of people, take time for yourself.

For too many years I have listened to stories about "burned out" managers and property supervisors. They complain about spending 12 hours a day on the job and getting phone calls all hours of the night. Just do what you can do and need to do in your regular day, and then get on with living the rest of your life. If necessary, make yourself find the time and energy to play. If you are an avid learner and take college or other courses at night, don't make them all real-estate courses. The best property managers are the ones who come to work refreshed each morning because their life is filled with other things besides property. They work hard and play hard and nothing short of disaster keeps them from the Wednesday night softball game or their morning run. Give yourself the same respect and courtesy you are required to give all your clients. You don't need to be a clock watcher—the effective manager eagerly fills the day with thoughtful decisions, and then just happens to be through when the day is over.

There is no separation between the individual tenant and the industry as a whole. Each tenant is a representation of the entire real-estate industry, and dealing with the tenant is really being a real-estate manager.

CHAPTER 2

Improving profit through more effective marketing

D. W. Rhoades
Johnstown American Companies
Atlanta, Georgia
W. J. Wallisch

Perhaps the best way to characterize *marketing* is to say it is a frame of mind, or an attitude. It's an approach you must take in order to realize fully the potential of the property you manage. The end result of effective marketing is an economically profitable and usually totally occupied apartment building, office complex, or bustling shopping center.

START WITH THE CONSUMER

The key to effective marketing is in your approach to the consumer and the way you fill his or her need for space to live in or work in. The process always begins with the consumer. The needs and wants of the consumer should be well represented in that ever-present little voice in your head called your conscience, which guides you to success. There's a jingle that goes like this:

> If you want to sell what John Smith buys,
> You'd better look at it through John Smith's eyes.

In short, you must understand what consumers want and give it to them. How you figure that out and present it is what we mean by marketing. In marketing we are constantly figuring out needs and filling them.

MASTER BASIC MARKETING PRINCIPLES

Volumes have been written on the subject of marketing. You can major in marketing in college and even get a Ph.D. in the subject. Moreover, the great American companies employ thousands of marketing and advertising professionals who spend each of their working days measuring the consumer needs of Mr. and Ms. "Public," not to mention their children and even their pets!

Don't let all that overwhelm or discourage you. Let it convince you that you must become familiar with the principles of marketing and develop a professional marketing attitude. Whether you do or not, your competitor probably will.

In essence marketing is the art of studying the habits, desires, wants, motivations, and purchasing decisions likely to be made by your clients. It's the study of human nature as it exists now and as it will affect the potential of your property to remain totally rented by satisfied clients. Your observations must be as thorough as possible and made consistently and carefully. Your analysis must encompass the entire spectrum of your market.

To get an idea of how vital marketing is in American business, consider the fact that more than $45 billion was spent on advertising and promotion last year. This substantial figure is almost 3 percent of the gross national product. Experts say that about one-half of every dollar a consumer spends today pays for the cost of marketing the product just bought. Everywhere in the business chain, marketing takes a big chunk of the total marketing budget. But few are willing to cut back on this expense, for they know it keeps them competitive. Without marketing, a business venture is blind and undirected. The firm of Dun & Bradstreet has attributed many business failures to a mistake in the marketing process. Not only must marketing be done, it must be done properly.

AVOID MARKETING MYOPIA

Good marketing mandates that you view your property from afar, in terms of the total market, and always through the eyes of those to whom you wish to market. You must be totally objective. Rationalization won't help you to evaluate your product properly, and *product* is a good term to use when you approach your responsibility to market properly.

Although it is said that we never again see a thing as we first see it, try to look at your property as if seeing it for the first time. Look for the blemishes as well as the strengths. Those who are looking at it from the standpoint of renting will see the blemishes—of that there is no doubt. Ask yourself what kind of persons would want to rent your property. Do they seek a comfortable living space? Are they looking for the ideal setting in which to spend their working day? Is yours the shopping center that offers the most in terms of attracting enough customers to their store, shop, boutique, or small eating place? Think of your residential properties as "living spaces" or "home environments" rather than simply "apartments."

ANALYZE THE NATURE OF YOUR BUSINESS

Ask yourself what business you are in. You really are in the business of helping people find homes. If you think of yourself as renting out mere apartments, you might find yourself with a lot of empty ones on your hands. Similarly, the nature of the working place is exceedingly important to those who will spend so many hours a day there. You must market a high-quality working environment, not mere "office space." Consumers are selective and shrewd; your marketing strategy must be in tune with those characteristics if you are going to keep pace with the times.

We are reminded of the phenomenon that took place when the railroads failed to understand that they were not so much in the railroad business as they were in the "transportation business." Many failed because they could not see the difference. You must see the difference and keep pace with sophisticated needs and tastes. Think about the impact of the terms *living space* and *home* in a colorful ad, and compare this to that black and white ad that starkly offers an "apartment" or "rooms to rent." The latter has the sound of the Great Depression about it, or a kind of turn-of-the-century bleakness. Consider that people create and do great things in their working environments, but they slave away in dingy offices. You must market your property so that customers know you have the places they want to live and work and shop in.

MODERN SHOPPING CENTERS

Modern shopping centers are superbly designed complexes wherein people are provided with an array of retail outlets. They are bright, attractive, and elegantly designed, and seduce potential customers with their physical attractiveness. They stress variety. Spaces in modern centers are marketed successfully if these features are highlighted. Marketing strategy and physical design can join forces to attract customers. Strategy should be compatible with design and should always aim at the tastes, desires, and wants of modern consumers. Marketing highlights strong features just as a carefully designed color scheme does. Gone forever are the days of dingy gray spaces.

The planned, or controlled, shopping center, usually located in a lucrative suburban shopping area, is the child of expert marketing. Each of the 10 to 100 stores in a center is carefully selected and balanced to appeal to the tastes and desires of those who live in the area. The key is "drawing power," which comes of careful marketing analysis. Who are the people? What do they want? Stroll through such a center and you see the answers: Restaurants, theatres, banks, and even brokerage houses and veterinary clinics blend in with the shops and stores that cater to the wants of today's suburban consumer. Nothing is left to chance; few stores survive long if they miss the market target aim.

Design Space Carefully

Space is well designed and used in such shopping centers. Not only are the stores efficiently laid out, but the broad walkways are retail avenues that can be rented out for selling or display for limited periods. New cars, storm doors, and a hundred other items can be displayed, which, with advertising, draw even more customers into the complex. Often there is a theme to the special displays on the walkways, such as "Home Show," "Outdoor Show," or "Better Living." The wise manager takes full advantage of their ongoing potential. The movielike marquee outside the center always advertises such special events.

We suggest you not only take advantage of such special events, but also use your open space for community service. Boy scouts, local community colleges, service organizations, and "get out the vote" campaigns can help you make a civic gesture and bring in crowds as well. Good marketing means exposure as much as anything. Advertising need not be confined to a "hard" ad about fall fashions. It can be as soft as a notice saying that the area boy scout council will be demonstrating programs in the mall this Friday, Saturday, and Sunday.

UNDERSTAND THE CONSUMER

Demographics

Be as thorough as the U.S. Bureau of the Census in learning about the makeup of your client area. What is the average income of the people living in your target market, of the people who require your services? How many children do they have? What is their education level? What do the figures tell you about their potential to require your services? Do they seem to be the group you have planned for? You can get this information from a number of sources including the latest census. We urge you to start out with this information as a bare minimum and progress to more sophisticated data.

Population studies are vital to the property business. For example, government studies on age distribution may reveal much in terms of a special interest area. The decreasing birthrate in the United States has resulted in a population that has a higher average age. For those of us who plan for living space, this means a market with an older average age and fewer families with young children. It means a focus on middle age. There's nothing especially complicated about this population analysis, but its value is immense. Professional market analysts carefully watch the population in terms of employment, marital status, and income. They know that the health of the market is tied to the behavior and makeup of the population.

Econographics

The economy has an immense effect on the behavior of the population. Industrial failures and successes affect consumer trends in any area. A business boom creates a surge of building activity and the demand for living space. A huge failure can create a ghost town overnight. Where the jobs are and who is being hired are directly proportional to the amount and kind of apartment space being rented. Businesspersons needing office space will also flock to a new boom area. The "high tech" phenomenon, for example, has changed the face of several areas. Large plants were constructed, which stimulated the need for living areas, more office space, and more places to shop. Interestingly enough, the "high techers" were not middle-aged; they were the unmarried "singles" who needed smaller units with lots and lots of recreational opportunity.

Psychographics

Age and income figures can tell you a lot about people, but attitude is a far better predictor. You must measure attitude to target a group—to anticipate and fill the members' needs. Although marketing experts can put data on raw income, age, education, and other demographic factors to good use, what they really strive for is an indication of how a target group reacts, buys, and makes choices. Only with such information can we take aim and meet needs.

The field of *psychographics* seeks to understand attitudes, with the aim of uncovering interests, motivations, and desires. It's clear that we must understand these human motivators to properly anticipate and provide for living, working, and shopping space. People will rush to obtain the right setting and reject outright the wrong one. If you research the attitudes of your target clients, they will beat a path to your doorstep.

Trendographics

We introduced the term *trendographics* based on the recent interest in trends in our society. We believe it is wise to monitor trends, especially in the property market. For example, the day is gone when the average person could afford to buy a condominium. The trend now is to go for an apartment. Knowing that, the wise marketing expert can meet the trend with the kind of apartment home the consumer is looking for. To keep up with trends you must become a student of human nature as it is affected by the pressures of society. Americans are very "trendy." The smart property manager knows that fact, measures the trends, and keeps constant tabs on how they affect the market.

Heavy Users

Marketing research experts who target beer drinkers will tell you that 55 percent of the beer sold in the United States is purchased by only 2 percent of the population. Smart people who sell products know exactly who buys them. Production is not left to chance. Ask yourself who the heavy users of your complex or center are. A thorough, intense study on your part will yield a composite of your heavy user group. Your marketing strategy must take that group into account; you must cater to that group and be sure you are making as many in that group as possible aware of your facility. They are out there, somewhere, looking for you. Let them know where you are. And target your marketing efforts in their direction.

Target Market

By putting all the previously presented information together, you should be able to come up with a clear picture of your target market. You will know who your potential clients are, where they live, how much money they make, how many children they have, and what motivates them. Your target market consists of the people most likely to pick up your brochures, spot your ad, or slam on the brakes when they catch sight of your facility. They are your life's blood and you must make it your business to keep your finger on the pulse of their moods. Above all, you must do a great deal of planning on behalf of their needs, which requires research and hard work.

MARKETING RESEARCH

There is much more to the science of marketing research than poring over census figures. A great deal of information may be found, for example, within the pages of your local newspaper. Here you find reflections of the trends and attitudes you need to know about to measure the market. Here also you can study your competition and how it advertises its wares. Where are the complexes like yours? What is the competition offering? Go beyond the newspaper and gather up all the brochures, free flyers, and printed material you can get your hands on. Try to identify the other fellow's strategy. Let him or her do some of your research for you.

SIZE UP THE SITUATION

By talking to your present clients you can learn about new attitudes and trends. You cater to a human consumer who is subject to change and capable of sudden impulse. By keeping up on attitudes, likes, dislikes, and trends in taste, you can keep your marketing picture up-to-date. Those who did not sense the trend from condominiums to apartments failed to keep abreast of the marketplace.

Go out and shop the competition yourself, as a way of measuring trends. Get in your car and see the other complexes that compete in your market. What are they offering that you are not? How do they fill or not fill the needs of your target group as you measured them? Were you on target? Were they? Did somebody think of something you didn't? You never will know unless you go out, shop the competition, and see what is happening in the market. If you are still not convinced, consider this one sobering thought: The customer shops the market. Your target group is out there in the marketplace, comparing facilities. Whatever best fills their needs will be successful. You must find out what is out there too!

DEVELOP A STRATEGY

Based on what you read, hear, and see, you can develop a final marketing strategy aimed at the right target. The better the research, the better the aim. The more time you put into market research, the more confident you will be about your ability to attract the kind of client you are looking for. The idea is to find each other, for you are both looking for each other. Your research will be put to the test every time the target group compares your facility with everything else in the market. The final reward will be a signed contract and a steady stream of serious lookers.

EXAMPLE OF GOOD MARKETING

Recently in the Denver, Colorado, area an apartment complex advertised a very exciting list of options available in their "home" units. The list was so extensive, the ad took up a full half page in a supermarket property flyer. We were so impressed with the marketing analysis that clearly went into that list that we think it's worth including in this section. Notice how all the consumer elements can be found in the wide range of options, how trends and human motivations are skillfully built into the offerings. Members of the target group could be intensely motivated to hop in the car and go see this truly modern living facility.

First described was the "Most Comprehensive Standard Kitchen Appliance Package in the Area!" This included a GE Space-Saver Microwave, GE Range, GE Dishwasher, GE Refrigerator, GE Full-Size Washer and Dryer, and a Disposal. Then came the range of standard features, designed for "gracious western living," presented like this:

> Fenced Private Patios; Sturbridge Exterior Siding; Italian Tile Entry Ways; Hand-Stained Wooden Handrails; Washable Interior Paint; Vaulted Ceilings; Custom Cabinetry (European Style); Pantry in Kitchen; Insulated Metal Entry Doors With Deadbolts; Fireplaces With Glass Doors; Italian Tile Hearths; Circulating Paddle Fans; Custom Made Mantels; One Car Detached Garages; Photo-Celled Garage Lighting; Designer Counter Tops (Many Different Styles); Ceramic Bath Tile; Casa Blanca, 3-Speed Fans; Choice of Up-Graded Carpeting; No-Wax Flooring in Bath and Kitchen Areas; Sliding Glass Patio Doors with Built-In Safety Locks; Custom Up-Graded Lighting Fixtures With Dimmer Switch; Built-In Bookcase; Double-Paned Wood Windows; Tongue and Grooved Flooring; Smoke Detectors; Pre-wired for Telephones; Colored Kitchen Sink; Colored Bath Fixtures; Kohler Plumbing Bath Fixtures; Extensive Exterior Landscaping; Across from 75-Acre Park; and a Great School District.

Lists Signal Luxury

Although simply a list, the preceding advertisement conveyed features that say "home," "warm," "exclusive," "plush," and "comfort" without using the words. Read between the lines and you come up with a pretty good description of the demographics of the target client, plus some ideas about the psychographics, trendographics, and heavy-use profile of the target market. The list is really bait, beautifully packaged, thrown right into the center of the target market pool. Not a long paragraph of prose, but a shopping list of comforts aimed at people with specific tastes, needs, and desires. It's a motivator, the kind of marketing package that causes action. And that's the key: Will your marketing plan cause action on the part of potential clients? This one did.

Develop a Consumer Profile

Look over the list again before you leave this section. Try your hand at writing out a consumer profile, based on the items contained in the list. Then, write up a list of your own, describing the kinds of options you are presently offering at your own facility. Pay attention to the way you describe those options; the writer of our list was very subtle and seductive in his approach. What does your facility have in common with the Colorado property? Where do you fall short? If a client were to shop your facility and compare it with the Colorado property, how would you stack up in his or her mind? How would you honestly compare the two?

Ask yourself what trends you see reflected in the Colorado list. Ask yourself if you are aiming at the same market. Look at the location of your property, and ask yourself if your area would support this kind of complex. What about your school district? Do you know how good it is? Marketing research dictates that you draw in as much power as you can from your geographic location and let that be a feature of your offering. The park in the Colorado list, for example, is a big plus for certain heavy-use groups but may be a negative feature for others.

THE LANGUAGE OF MARKETING

Marketing strategy has a great deal to do with language, with the skill of communicating properly with your target group. Great marketing communicates feelings and causes responses. There has been a good deal written about "body language" lately; properties communicate in the same way. Marketing a property requires a combination of words and physical structures, a mix of messages, both physical and nonphysical.

Think of the emotions the word *home* elicits in the comsumer. Everyone has a special image connected to that word, a personal ideal that suggests the warmth and comfort offered by the perfect living space. You must properly identify that image and then market it to the target.

TEST MARKETING

Earlier in the chapter we mentioned the fact that a number of railroads went out of business because of the failure to understand the nature of the business: transportation. Perhaps a vivid example of people who knew they were in the transportation business might be the Wright brothers. They were able to make the leap from bicycle to airplane, and they got there by testing and retesting the prototype of what would soon be mass produced and change the pace of world travel. Like the Wrights, you must keep up with the times and test out your hunches about what will be the new demands for the new age.

You keep up by shopping the competition and matching that with your own innovations. However, just because the complex down the street has installed paddle fans in each unit doesn't mean you must rush right in and do the same, no matter how promising the idea might be. The best thing to do is go into the test mode.

Large corporations do this all the time, spending as much as $50 million on an idea. Their marketing people will tell you that even with a price tag like that, only one product in four succeeds. But that doesn't discourage them from initiating more test cases. They know they must continue to test and experiment if they are to remain abreast with the competition and with consumer demands, changing tastes, and appetites for new and better products.

Create a Small Pilot Test

You have the luxury of keeping your testing on a small scale compared with the giants of industry. But like them, you must constantly test or find yourself behind the times, outdated, old-fashioned, and beaten out by the competition. Keep trying out new ideas in your building, but only in one or two units. We call this the "pilot plant" method, using just one apartment, office, or store as the guinea pig. Install the paddle fan. Put in the accent walls, fireplaces, carpet, grill, parquet entryway, wallpaper, flowers, signs, or special computer hookup in a single unit. Then watch what happens. Let the consumer tell you by way of acceptance. You soon may find yourself installing an innovation throughout the property, simply because the consumer said "yes" and demanded that it be the standard for the entire complex. Even though you meet with success on an item, you don't rest on your laurels. Nor does failure mean you quit testing. You should be testing something, somewhere in your unit, at all times.

Devise Imaginative Test Methods

If you can't install or build your innovation, you might want to have a sketch, model, or sample of what you could offer your clients. Keep carpet and tile samples on hand. Show them to clients and watch for responses. Be enthusiastic about test items; a client may move in based on the selection of a new item. You are absolutely on target if the consumer is making the choice, selecting the item.

Clients may tell you something is not a good idea. Fair enough. Don't be afraid to fail at the test level. It's a small but necessary investment. It shows you are looking ahead. It demonstrates your willingness to improve, to keep up with trends and changing tastes.

Feedback is an important element in the test and innovation process. When a client selects a test product, the word will soon spread. You hope for a domino effect that has your other clients knocking at the manager's door, asking for what they've seen in no. 12.

DEVELOP A MARKET PLAN

In the marketing process, as in any other facet of sound property management, you must commit yourself to a well-thought-out plan of action. We know how all-important it is for us to "know the numbers." If you develop a budget for your plan of action, you will be able to attack the target market with a steady aim.

Promotion

Your budget will determine your vehicle. You can, of course, choose from a wide range of "channels" over which you can send your marketing "message" to your target "receiver." You are the "sender," the marketing analyst with a product to sell. Radio, television, newspapers, and a wide variety of other media are available to you. In the property business, however, print seems to be the most cost-effective channel for the message.

Deciding when to send the message is an integral part of the process. The seasons can be key controlling agents in terms of your heavy-user target. Again, the person you are aiming for determines the timing. Is summer a factor? The start of the school year? Clearly your demographic research means a great deal here; it will give you your answers.

Remember that your target group is more likely to be out looking for you at certain periods. These potential clients will be traveling the roads and streets, shopping the complexes. They will be searching the newspapers and looking for printed material. You must be sure your message is there, ready to sell your product to the heavy user it's been designed for.

One of the most astonishing facts about the heavy-user market is that you very rarely have to make a determination about a client's qualifications for your product. The market is a self-selecting one; that is, people know what they want and where they belong. Clients self-select and self-qualify. The receiver you wrote your message for will find it, if you have put it on the right rack.

The "Shopper's Guide"

You need not spend megabucks advertising on all three TV stations, with spot plugs on the radio every half hour. You would go broke with an advertising budget allowing that. We think you should budget for something like the local shopper's guide, and we predict that about 40 percent of your clients will find you through such a guide. The other 60 percent will drive up and park right in front of your office, simply because they are out looking for you. They probably will have nothing more than a city map with them. But they know where they will work and where they want to live. Remember, they are self-selecting.

Price Range

Just from the looks of your facility, the heavy user will pretty well know what he is going to pay to rent space in your facility. But that "ballpark" price has a high and a low end. Never price all your units the same, for the price of any single unit is relative to its position within the complex as a whole. This is a commonsense matter, one your clients will readily understand. An office overlooking a bay, park, or other scenic area, for example, should be priced higher than one looking out over nothing. Each floor, view, and location has a different price tag. Good views and better access demand more money. Your marketing plan includes the ability to capitalize on choice views and features. It's fair and it's expected. It's good marketing to use everything to its fullest advantage. Within your heavy-user group, there's a subset of heavy window-overlooking-the-park users. Market that feature to its fullest extent.

By the Numbers

When you put your marketing plan into effect, "divide and decide." That is, give each person on your staff a piece of the marketing pie responsibility. A Program Evaluation Review Technique (PERT) chart, or something like it, can be useful here. It can help systematize who does what and when. The entire team should know at any given moment exactly what is happening and who is responsible for its execution. Lay out a schedule, and stick to it.

THE FUTURE

Marketing leads the way into the future. Once upon a time air conditioning was a unique feature in an office or apartment. Today you would be totally out of the market without it. Can you imagine a modern business office or apartment without it? Well, once it was part of someone's "test unit," and feedback and demand made it a standard feature.

Innovative Cycles

There is an identifiable cycle that accompanies any innovation. Something like air conditioning starts out as new, exciting, and modern. But soon it becomes so standard that it is noticeable only by its absence. All features pass through four stages on their way to ultimate obsolescence: introduction, growth, maturity, and decline.

Telephones, air conditioners, central heat, sliding doors, patios, elevators, escalators, neon lights, gas grills, indoor plumbing, ice makers, wall-to-wall carpeting, and gas lights were all once new and exciting innovations. The telephones are now pushbutton style and you can dial anywhere in the world on them. There are no longer operators in elevators. And gas lights went out with the turn of the century. If you examine this list, you can analyze how some items continually improved over the years, while others went out.

Restaging and Recycling

Some of the products on our list survived and became more exciting because innovators continually improved them. They, like their marketing analysts, stayed ahead of the times. Rather than let an item become so mature that it falls out of the market, marketing experts look for ways to "recycle" it and give it new life. The best of what we call marketing strategy is intensely alive when that takes place.

An outstanding example of restaging and recycling is occurring in cities all over the United States right now in what are known as "restored areas." An old, dumpy office building, built before the turn of the century, has gone to seed. It was everything you wouldn't want for business use: poor location, old-fashioned rooms, and clearly aged. But recycled it becomes very posh and "in." The old hardwood floors and other woodwork are refinished and recycled. The building takes on new life, new glamour. The entire block is recycled. Rent prices soar. Marketing, the handmaiden of such products, takes over. The old has become the new. The "out" has become the "in." It's not for everyone, but heavy users flock in. There is a waiting list. The same thing happens to the apartments that have been recycled nearby. An entire neighborhood blooms once more. Clever marketing—restaging and recycling—has been the key to the venture. Take a look at your property, inside and out. What can you reintroduce? What can be fixed up, recycled?

NEW PRODUCT DEVELOPMENT

The Greeks called it *inventio.* It's the process of making something where there was nothing before. Its more than following a trend; it involves the actual creation of products that consumers will flock to. Big business invests heavily in new products; they are the heart of the capitalist system, the grist of the trade mill.

Key In on the Modern Consumer

In the property business, new product development centers around the needs of the modern consumer. We tag along with what is new in society. For example, energy is a new concern that has produced a host of alternative systems. Innovative property managers are installing new products, such as wood stoves and solar panels, as the times demand.

Leisure and health are also major concerns. Thus hot tubs, spas, and clubhouses are found in more and more apartment complexes. Even office complexes have clubs and athletic facilities built right into the complex. Today's executives want to go downstairs for a game of racquet ball or tennis, or to take a run. And afterward, a sauna, Jacuzzi, or rubdown is just the thing to prepare them to tackle the work waiting in their in-basket upstairs.

Along with the concern for leisure and health comes flextime, a new concept in officework in which hours are arranged by the employee. Complexes should cater to those hours and the needs they create. The fitness center often becomes the first or last stop in the flextime schedule. Marketing strategy dictates keeping up with such new products and building them into properties.

Keep on asking yourself what is different. Once you find out, go out and test it. Strange, new products—products that match the times—will soon abound within your property, keeping you competitive and on the leading edge of what is happening.

Identify Trends

You must become a world watcher, a student of the society you live in. It takes practice to keep your finger on the pulse constantly. Read, listen, and watch. Talk with other managers. And talk with the people who sell products. Integrate the best into your marketing plan and into your property. And keep testing.

Talk to the Competition

We always ask ourselves, "What do the really smart people think of the market?" That is, what are the really successful people doing, selling, renting, or pushing right now? How do you find out? You ask them, and they will tell you. They are glad to tell you. People are flattered to be asked about their successes and will give you their insights and secrets in a minute. Ask fellow property managers, owners, builders, suppliers, and renters. They will give you a clear picture of the latest trends, what works and what doesn't work. Just keep asking and talking.

DEVELOP A MARKETING ATTITUDE

Once you start asking your questions, you will continue to do so because it will yield results. It's all part of the "think marketing" attitude you must develop. You are aiming for a "No Vacancy" sign that stays that way.

Even professional marketing experts survey each other to see what is going on across the entire spectrum of American marketing. As a matter of fact, the American Marketing Association surveyed over 500 recognized leaders in the marketing area, asking them about their hunches and thoughts in terms of reaching the American consumer of the 1980s. The association was interested in finding out about perceived trends in consumer behavior and how its members were engaging in new product development, strategy, and planning in terms of those trends. This survey, carried out by the professionals, is a model for what you should be doing within your own market. And it proves that one never becomes so successful that he or she can do without such a survey. The response to the survey was enormous. You, too, will get the answers to your questions, if you only ask. It's all part of sound and tested marketing analysis and of a well-honed marketing attitude.

A PROPERTY MANAGER'S APPROACH

There are, of course, other techniques besides the marketing analysis approach, which is based on the needs of the consumer. There is the strictly product-oriented approach, which says if you provide the best kind of facility it will sell itself. In some cases that works. There is also the hard-sell approach, which uses pressure tactics and zeal to grab clients off the street. We certainly would not argue with enthusiasm, and we urge you to be good salespersons. There is a lot to be borrowed from these narrow marketing approaches.

PRICE, PRODUCT, PROMOTION, AND PLACE

For years the standard marketing curriculum in our colleges of business has been oriented toward price, product, promotion, and place, the four

P's. No matter what textbook or article on marketing you pick up, you are almost sure to find a section on or mention of the four P's.

Price
Price is what you have decided you must charge for your property—the rent of the apartment, office space, or selling space. It is the payment the client must make to enjoy your unit. Price is an extremely flexible variable, and will vary even within your property. In another section of this chapter we mention the fact that units in a building vary in price depending on their location in the unit. Beyond that, the location and makeup of your property affect price. Price changes with trends; it should move upward because of your improvements and innovations. The economic picture affects price: Demand is a dynamic variable, subject to whim and dependent on sound marketing. Price assessment should be an ongoing part of your management style.

Product
Product is what you offer for exchange. In the case of property management, it is the unit you are offering a client to work in, live in, or sell in.

Promotion
Another word for promotion is advertising, although promotion involves more than an advertisement in a newspaper or renter's guide. *Promotion* is the entire gesture you make toward your client market, the words, ideas, and messages of all kinds that you direct toward potential clients. It's everything you do to cause them to rent your space. It is personal contact, advertising, publicity, public relations, and every subtle message your property sends out to the street in front of it. Promotion is the communication process between managers and their potential clients.

Place
The *place* is simply the point of contact. In the traditional sense of consumer product marketing, place involves how you deliver your product to the customer. For example, you might sell your product from an end-aisle display at the K-Mart store or in a door-to-door fashion. In property management, however, we like to think of place as your location. It isn't usually easy to change. The key issue is how to get your customers to come to you. How do they get your space "delivered" to them?

DEVELOP MARKETING FOCUS

Take a tip from Winston Churchill. Soon after he assumed his responsibilities as prime minister, he asked for a report on the status of the

British Navy. They brought him three volumes, each about 1½ inches thick. He said, "Pray tell, please bring me the status of the British Navy on only one sheet." Put your four P's on one sheet of paper. Like Winston Churchill, focus on what's important.

We have incorporated each of the four P's into sections of this chapter, just as you might incorporate these variables into your way of professionally managing your property. The four P's are another tool to use to structure your leadership and environment so you can "think marketing." Although marketing is far from an exact science, there are techniques and ways of observing client behavior that no sound decision maker can do without.

What we advocate is a total approach to marketing that incorporates consumer research, market analysis, market definition, product testing, innovation, planning, budgeting, pricing, and sound promotion. This approach is client oriented and keeps pace with trends. We think it yields long-term client satisfaction, the kind that keeps you way ahead of the competition. You might say our approach is environment oriented, because it taps in on the state of the society as it deals with the problems of finding the right place to live, the best place to work in, and the perfect spaces in which to shop. Above all, our approach is people oriented, rather than tied to bricks, concrete, steel beams, and dry wall.

AVOID THE "HARD SELL"

We don't think you need take the hard-sell approach. We see too much of that on television these days, where products are rammed down the throat of the consumer. When you have done the foolproof total market analysis, your property should sell itself. If you make it your business to analyze needs and preferences, you eliminate the need to "manipulate." Too often managers think they have to change attitudes on the part of consumers. Research and experience over the long haul have proved that it's most difficult to change attitudes. Rather than change attitudes, the true marketing professional measures them and capitalizes on the information. You do not change needs; you respond to them and anticipate them.

If you understand that you can't swim upstream against the needs, preferences, desires, and motivations of today's consumer, you are ready to hold up the image of your property alongside others on the market. You must be able to position your property in the market or you will not be the slightest bit competitive; positioning means *catering to the needs you have identified.*

TAILOR PRICE AND IMAGE

After you have done your marketing homework, you must allocate the funds and resources necessary to make your product fit the image the client is looking for. The image and the price must both be right for your market aim. When you know you look right, you tell the consumers so and tell them how to find you. Chances are they will do that by themselves.

When you read this description of a property in the Denver area, ask yourself how many sound marketing points you see in it.

> Apartment living should be easy. After all, it's home to more than half of the people in America. At Canterbury Square we believe that your comfort, cleanliness, courteousness, and a quiet environment are not extras. It is part of everything you can expect at a place you will choose to call home. Canterbury Square Apartment Homes in a quiet, established neighborhood. Come by for a visit and you can call us home.

This chapter should only be a beginning for you. It is designed to launch you into a deeper study of marketing. We encourage you to find marketing texts and study them. Above all, you should be marketing-minded. Remember that $45 billion figure we cited earlier. The real professionals in all aspects of American business depend heavily on marketing for their success. You too should be committed to marketing as a professional tool for better property management.

PART 2

The property manager

CHAPTER 3

Selecting a property manager

Thomas W. Dooley
TWD and Associates
Arlington Heights, Illinois

The management of real property is a complex enterprise. Functionally, the tasks involved can be divided into five major areas:

1. Leasing and renting of the property
2. Collecting rental payments
3. Administration of insurance
4. Maintenance of the property
5. Budgeting and record keeping

TYPES OF PROPERTY MANAGERS

Managers of property are a varied lot. First of all, there is the owner/manager. In a narrow sense, every home owner is a property manager. While he or she may not be involved in rental activities, certainly there are insurance, maintenance, and record-keeping functions to be performed.

Owners of multiunit residential properties often live in one apartment, rent or lease the remainder, and function as a landlord/manager for the entire project.

There are, of course, limitations to the "do it yourself" approach to property management. A single facility may have too many units or may be too complex in its tenant base to be capably managed by an owner/occupant or absentee owner. Ownership of multiple facilities adds significantly to the complexity of property management.

Professional Managers

When the scope of management responsibilities exceeds the capabilities, interest, or time commitment of an owner, he or she looks in the direction of "professional" property managers to take over the job. Precisely when that occasion might arise will vary among individual owners and under differing circumstances. If there is to be a standard rule of thumb, it might be stated that when owners find themselves beyond their scope of expertise, time availability, or viable economic return, they need to hire professional management.

Such a decison, however, is but the first of many. Determining that a professional property manager is needed is only the start, for property managers are a varied and sundry lot. Some are residential specialists, whereas others handle only commercial, mercantile, or industrial properties. There are those who prefer smaller units and those interested only in large projects. Neighborhood and area specialists abound.

Just as fields of interest vary, so does the level of skill and expertise of property managers. Their backgrounds differ widely too. Some have received specific training in the field of property management, while others wandered into the field from other real-estate pursuits, often as an adjunct to a brokerage business. Many have expanded into a "one stop" real-estate service facility and need property management as an essential ingredient.

Specialists

Even within a specific field, there are property management specialists for particular types of properties and for projects or buildings of different sizes. One the other hand, there are also generic property managers. They tend to be either small (often, one-person) firms or quite large enterprises handling all phases of management, with individual specialists concentrating on specific areas.

With such a wide variety of practitioners from which to choose, a property owner need explore all possibilities closely before selecting a management agent. That selection process of course presupposes another decision, that is, that an owner is going to engage a manager rather than attempt to do the job alone. That presupposition is not always valid, for there are many owners who serve as their own property managers, even when their holdings are fairly vast and varied.

CRITERIA FOR DETERMINING MANAGEMENT TYPE

While they are not always evenly applied by all landlords, the following key criteria should determine whether a "do-it-yourself" approach to management will work as well as hiring a professional manager:

How knowledgeable about real estate, including physical repairs, the owner is

How many units the owner has

Whether the owner lives on the premises

The age and general condition of the property

The economic value of the owner's time

Combining all these elements, one might reason correctly that owners' attempts to manage their property have a chance of success under specific conditions. The success pattern, however, is directly related to owners having or being able to acquire the skills and talents that a professional property manager ordinarily possesses. In most instances, owners with more than a casual real-estate investment fall short of the skill, talent, or time necessary to be their own managers and retain professional property managers.

The moment of decision is likely to occur early if the nature of the property is nonresidential. It also will be accelerated by the number of rental units, whether they are residential or nonresidential.

Most analysts suggest that a residential property with more than four rental units surely merits consideration for professional property management if the owner or a direct representative does not live on the premises. Even with on-site residency, observers suggest exploration of paid management if the total units are in excess of 20. Should a residential investment portfolio consist of single-family or two-family homes in multiple locations, the figures quoted as criteria for hiring management dwindle considerably, and the need for property management arises much sooner.

With nonresidential property, just about any facility beyond the size of a ministrip center or a single-unit industrial or warehouse building mandates management. Often holdings quoted as suitable for owner management are more economically efficient if managed professionally.

Once a basic decision to retain a property manager has been reached, an additional determination must be made as to whom.

MANAGER SELECTION

An owner requires the services of a professional manager who will produce the best overall results. Thus not only is the ability to show a high net income important, but so is maintaining the property in good condition. Some of the manager's capabilities lie in the realm of market familiarity. An agent must know what market conditions affect rental levels and other terms of occupancy. In large projects, it may be necessary for the property manager to have a group of assistants to handle various functions connected with the managed property. In such cases an owner needs to know and have confidence in the second level of employees in the management group. All these factors should be given attention when an owner selects a property manager.

Owners tend to focus attention on firms that are known from personal experience or general reputation to be highly competent. An owner who does not have access to such information probably will do well to confine a search for property management talent to practitioners in firms belonging to the Institute of Real Estate Management, a professional group affiliated with the National Association of Realtors. Should even more assurance of recognized competency be required, the owner may wish to insist on a manager who bears the designation certified property manager (CPM). To merit the title of CPM, awarded by the Institute of Real Estate Management, a manager must demonstrate both practical competency and theoretical mastery.

A WORKING RELATIONSHIP WITH THE MANAGER

In establishing an employment or service relationship with a property manager, an owner should insist on a clear understanding of duties and responsibilities. The most effective way to establish such an understanding is to execute a contractual management agreement. The agreement should cover whatever points the owner and/or manager think pertinent but most assuredly should address itself to such general items as an accurate identification of the property covered by the contract; a full identification of any and all persons having an ownership interest in the property along with corporate or partnership ownership, if any; the length of time the contract is deemed to cover; how money is to be collected, disbursed, and accounted for; various features connected with the manager's responsibilities for leasing, collecting rents, ending tenancies, evicting tenants, and so on; the amount of power the owner wishes to delegate to the manager; the responsibilities of the owner, including specific identification of any functions or tasks that the owner wishes to reserve from assignment to the manager; the basis, amount, method, and frequency of payment of management fees; and an arbitration clause for use in disputes between the parties.

Manager's Agreement

To refine the broad outline presented, it is wise for the owner and property manager to have an agreement regarding who is to perform a variety of specific functions. A checklist, added as an appendix to a property management contract, offers a good method of establishing clear-cut assignments. (See Figure 4-2, page 77.)

To ensure an optimal relationship, there should be regularly scheduled, face-to-face report and review meetings between owner and manager. If the property is managed by a large firm and involves work on the project by a number of different employees, the meetings should be conducted regularly and include both on-site management supervisors and executives of the management firm.

Finance

Another area in which very clear understanding between owner and manager must exist is that of finance. There must be a precise understanding in the following areas: amount and type of expenditures the manager may incur without specific permission from the owner; timing and format of financial reports to be rendered by the manager to the owner; method of handling, depositing, and remitting rental funds received by the manager; time and method of owner's remittance of fees to the manager; determination of whether the manager is authorized to make rental concessions, and if so, under what conditions and to what extent.

If part of the management function is to rent vacant units, the owner needs to reach agreement with the manager (and so stipulate in the contract) on a form of management by objectives (MBO), which commits the manager to certain performance levels within defined time limits. This requirement is especially pertinent when the manager is charged with renting up a new (or newly acquired) facility.

Consider this example: A new 40-unit apartment building is to be ready for occupancy on June 1. The manager and owner need to agree on mutual occupancy goals. Let us assume that the MBO goal is 70 percent occupancy (28 units) prerented by May 15 and 95 percent (38 units) rented by July 15. A PERT-type progress chart needs to be developed with agreed-on rental goals to be achieved at identifiable times, say, April 1, April 15, and May 1. On each target date, the owner and manager should confer to compare actual results with target plans. Adjustments in marketing approaches can be made if necessary.

RENTING UP

When faced with the need for a major renting effort, whether in a new building, renovation, or project with a high vacancy ratio, an owner should seriously consider paying rental bonuses to the management firm. If a bonus arrangement is established, the owner must realize that this compensation has no relationship to normal management functions (and fees) but rather is a reward for extraordinary marketing efforts. In some larger facilities, owners clearly recognize the distinction between renting functions and other property management tasks and engage a separate team of specialists for each. Thus it is not uncommon (especially in large, new buildings) to have a rental/leasing contract with one real estate firm and a management contract with another.

The concentration on specialization reflects the owner's recognition that a real-estate firm may excel in one function connected with property management but have less expertise in other operations.

SELECTING A MANAGEMENT FIRM

The process of selecting a management firm often hinges on the perceived reputation of the firm to handle a specific type and character of property in a certain geographic area. Skilled large-scale corporate owners recognize the importance of proper selection. As a result, they place the responsibility for selecting, controlling, and otherwise dealing with property management firms in the hands of a key executive.

Unfortunately, not every large-scale corporate owner is thoroughly skilled. As a result, it is not uncommon for the responsibility for physical facilities to be placed in the hands of an officer or other employee who knows or cares little about the function and its importance. A case in point is that of a Manhattan enterprise which recently acquired a seven-story headquarters building with total square footage in excess of 150,000. The company placed the responsibility for all property management, including extensive renovations and modifications, in the hands of its internal advertising director, whose position within the company is two notches beneath top management. The man is trying his best but his first love and area of past accomplishment is advertising and promotion. Building management takes a distant second place, and his lack of success has led the man to question his overall worth to the company.

This company fails to place proper emphasis on its very considerable real-estate asset, which in the long run probably will contribute far more to the success or failure of the company than its current advertising and promotion campaign.

A corporation more properly attuned to care and attention of all of its assets will place the internal responsibility for its real-estate holdings in the hands of an accomplished professional in the real estate field. While this person need not necessarily be a property management specialist, he or she should be sufficiently familiar with the field to know who the accomplished practitioners are and to execute a management agreement under which a responsible job can be achieved. That corporate official also must be able to monitor and control the effectiveness of the property management firm.

As we stated at the beginning of this chapter, property management is a complicated area of activity. Its complexity—and the need to master it professionally and profitably—is the same in large corporate real-estate holdings as it is in start-up four-flat investments.

CHAPTER 4

Hiring the on-site manager

Ruth I. Frishman, J.D., M.B.A.
Attorney at Law and Property Management Consultant
Emeryville, California

Good resident managers are the single most important link in your entire management chain. A good resident manager can often cover for a mediocre management company, but a good management company can never cover for a poor resident manager. Although good managers are not impossible to find, it is often a challenge to find the right manager for the right development. Good selection techniques are vital in reducing poor choices and the unnecessary aggravation and expense that follow. Once selected and hired, many managers are given little training or support, resulting in poor project management and resident relations as well as employee burnout and discontent. Therefore, training, supervision, and morale building are essential elements of a good personnel program.

Finally, resident managers tend to be an anomaly within the area of labor law because they live where they work and often work irregular hours. Close attention must be paid to the minimum wage and hour laws and proper payroll reporting procedures to avoid costly labor complaints and lawsuits.

HOW TO FIND A GOOD RESIDENT MANAGER

1. *Newspaper ads.* A blind ad in the classified section works best because it allows you to prescreen the applicant without tying up your office phone with unnecessary calls. You can evaluate how applicants present themselves in writing, and you can determine whether their initial qualifications meet your basic requirements before you set up the first interview. Sometimes you may even discover that your own employees are scouting new employment opportunities.
2. *Unemployment office.* Most state unemployment offices have job placement desks at which job openings can be listed at no cost to the employer. The people who apply through the unemployment office listings often tend to be highly motivated; they have gone out looking for a position rather than just hoping a good job would present itself in the want ads.
3. *Employment agencies.* In some larger urban areas there are placement agencies which specialize in placing on-site employees such as resident managers, and maintenance and janitorial workers.
4. *Management schools.* Often trade schools and community colleges which offer property management courses have placement offices. Instructors, who are usually active professionals in the field, can also help place students with associates in the field.
5. *Apartment associations.* Some of the larger local apartment associations have job-exchange services for their members, often at no additional cost.
6. *Other buildings.* Although some may feel that this is unethical, seeing what a manager currently manages is an effective way to evaluate his or her ability. Furthermore, you cannot "steal" a manager who is satisfied with her job, her salary, and the rapport she has with her current supervisor. Nor can you blame someone who chooses to move on to a better job.

SELECTING A MANAGER

Couples versus Individuals

Many property managers believe that resident managers come in twos, like the animals of Noah's Ark. Blindly hiring couples without examining whether such a policy best serves your management operation may result in some unfortunate choices. Often one strong spouse interviews and performs the job well. When you find out later that the other spouse cannot perform well or has a personality or drinking problem, you usually have to terminate both of them together. If you do plan to hire a couple, it is recommended that you interview both persons individually. If you would not hire each of them as individuals, you shouldn't hire them as a couple. Some people believe that when hiring a couple you get more work for less money. The other side of the coin, however, is that "you get what you pay for." An additional argument in favor of hiring individuals is that when a couple takes a vacation, quits, or is terminated, the building is left without any coverage. If you hire two individuals for the positions of resident manager and maintenance/assistant manager, the building will always be covered by one in the other's absence and you will have continuity when replacing one or the other.

Experienced versus Inexperienced

Although it is generally easier and quicker to train someone with experience, you occasionally find that some persons are so entrenched in their old ways of doing things that you cannot teach them anything new. In this situation, it is not so much a question of their experience, but rather their attitudes toward supervision and authority, and more important, their attitudes toward residents and their legal rights. The way we manage property today is substantially different from the way we managed it 15 or 25 years ago. Managers with outdated attitudes can create expensive lawsuits for their employers.

Inexperienced applicants can make good resident managers if they have two basic qualities: old-fashioned common sense and an ability to get along with people. If a person has these two qualities, the technical aspects of the job can be taught fairly easily.

Older versus Younger

Older resident managers tend to have more practical experience and better "people" skills. If they are semiretired, they are looking for a steady position that gives them job security and satisfaction. Although you don't want to select or reject employees based on age, which is discriminatory, it is important to be aware that younger people tend to be less stable as resident managers, change jobs more frequently, and are absent from the property more often than older people. In interviewing younger people for on-site positions, therefore, you may want to interview them in more depth regarding their short- and long-term goals, aspirations, and lifestyle. It is important for the applicant to understand that being a resident manager provides little privacy and requires an ability to get along with people under a variety of what often seem like impossible circumstances.

One circumstance in which hiring younger managers seems to work well is the hiring of graduate students in college towns. Graduate students often do not have much money, study long hours, and stay in one place for at least 2 years. They usually appreciate having a job that includes a place to live, which is often hard to find in college towns.

Resident Compatibility

A resident manager should be similar in socioeconomic status to the residents. A person from a blue-collar background will generally not be successful in a luxury high rise any more than a sweet grandmotherly type will be in a tough, low-rent urban development.

Disabled Persons

As long as the person has physical access to the units, you may find that a disabled person is one of the most hardworking, creative, and loyal people you have ever hired. You should not automatically exclude good workers because of invalid stereotypes.

In fact, you shouldn't automatically exclude any applicant from consideration just because she does not fit within your guidelines. The best managers this author ever hired were a couple, 26 years old, with no previous management experience, four children under the age of 6, and one Doberman pinscher!

HIRING PROCEDURES

Application for Employment

Make sure the application is completely filled out. Review the application in depth to ascertain the extent of the applicant's management, office, and maintenance abilities so that you can match the needs of the building with the skills of the manager (see Figure 4-1).

Interview

Do not make the common mistake that many interviewers make of monopolizing the interview or asking questions that can easily be answered with "yes" or "no." Ask open-ended questions such as the following that get applicants to start talking about themselves:

1. What are your specific skills and capabilities?
2. Why are you changing jobs?
3. What did you like best about your past jobs? What gave you the most satisfaction?
4. In what way did you contribute to positive changes in your last job? If you could have, what other areas would you have changed or improved?

5. Describe the best person you ever worked for.
6. What kind of people annoy you the most?
7. Describe how you handled an emergency.
8. How do you handle service requests, complaints from residents, late night lockouts, and so on?

You are looking for answers that reveal the applicant's character, loyalty, sense of responsibility, sensitivity to residents' needs, and common sense.

Remember that no business decisions, including the hiring and firing of employees, should be made in a discriminatory way (e.g., based on race, color, creed, sex). What you are interested in are the qualifications of the applicant to perform the job. Therefore, be careful of asking questions which can be interpreted as discriminatory (e.g., age, marital status, religious affiliation, nationality).

Explain to the applicant that you will be checking references, and ask if there are any situations or circumstances that she would like to explain before the calls are made.

References

Check all references thoroughly. Make sure your applicant is competent and trustworthy. You are entrusting the safety of the residents and the responsibility of a sizable investment and cash flow to the person you hire. You as the employer could be held liable to both the residents and the owner for injuries or damages suffered if you failed to screen your employees properly. If the applicant is currently managing a property within reasonable driving distance, take the time to check it out in person.

Credit Check

You are turning over the keys to a substantial amount of cash, equipment, and inventory, so you want to hire someone who is not over his head in so much debt that the temptation to "borrow" from the project's funds is more than he can resist. Ask the applicant's permission to run a credit check: to run one otherwise is breaching his right to privacy and, therefore, breaking the law.

Fidelity Bond Application

All employees should be covered by a blanket fidelity bond. The bonding companies are able to investigate the background of an employee more thoroughly than the average employer can. Although your regular policy will not cover ex-felons, you can get a special policy to cover such persons in some states.

RESIDENT MANAGER APPLICATION

1. Applicant's Name ______________________ S.S. # ____________

   Spouse's Name ______________________ S.S. # ____________

2. Present Address ____
   Street Address City State Zip

   How long ____________ Phone (Home) ____________ (Work) ____________

   Previous Address ____
   Street Address City State Zip

   How long ____

3. Employment History (Most recent first; include spouse's employment.)

Date From/To	Employer Name/Address/Phone	Building Name/Address/# Units	Title	Salary	Reason for Leaving

4. Abilities & Experience: Indicate "A" for you, "S" for spouse.

_____ Appliance Repair	_____ Formal Mgmt. Training	_____ Plumbing
_____ Boilers	_____ Gardening	_____ Recreation
_____ Bookkeeping	_____ Housing for Elderly	_____ Rent Collection
_____ Carpet Cleaning	_____ HUD Training	_____ Sales, Marketing
_____ Carpet Laying	_____ HVAC	_____ Swim Pool
_____ Carpentry	_____ Janitorial	_____ Tenant Unions
_____ Electrical	_____ Linoleum Laying	_____ Typing
_____ Elevators	_____ Painting	_____ ____________

5. Job Preference No. of Units Location Compensation Desired

   1st Choice ____

   2nd Choice ____

   3rd Choice ____

REPRINTED FROM: PROPERTY MANAGEMENT CAMERA READY FORMS, BY RUTH I. FRISHMAN, J.D., M.B.A

Figure 4-1 Resident manager application for employment.

6. Education

Applicant

High School ______________________________

College ______________________________

Other ______________________________

Spouse

High School ______________________________

College ______________________________

Other ______________________________

7. Credit References

Name ______________ Address ______________ Acct. # ______________

Name ______________ Address ______________ Acct. # ______________

Bank ______________ Branch ______________ Acct. # ______________

Bank ______________ Branch ______________ Acct. # ______________

8. Personal References

Name ______________ Address ______________ Phone (   ) ______________

Name ______________ Address ______________ Phone (   ) ______________

Name ______________ Address ______________ Phone (   ) ______________

9. General Information

How many people will be living with you? ______________________________

Is your health good, fair or poor? Spouse's health good, fair or poor?

Have you ever applied for Worker's Compensation? ______________ If so, explain ______________

____

Are you bondable? ________ Have you ever been bonded? ______________________________

Have you ever been convicted of a felony? If so, explain ______________________________

____

Do you have your own tools? ______________ Do you have a car? ______________

Do you have a truck? ______________ Do you have auto insurance? ______________

Applicant's drivers license ______________ Spouse's ______________

10. Person to notify in case of emergency: ______________________________

Address ______________________________

Relationship ______________ Phone (   ) ______________

It is understood that the above information is confidential and that all of the above is true and correct. Applicant and spouse authorize verification of any information herein including the running of a credit check.

______________________________ ______________________________

Applicant's Signature Date Spouse's Signature Date

Figure 4-1 *(Continued)*

W-4 Forms

All on-site resident managers are employees, never independent contractors. Therefore, they should be covered by workers' compensation, and the appropriate payroll deductions should be withheld from their earnings.

EMPLOYMENT CONTRACTS

All on-site employees should have written employment contracts to clarify their job duties, areas of responsibility, hours to work, days off, and compensation (see Figure 4-2).

The termination notice in the contract should be specifically spelled out. One to two weeks provides reasonable notice. Longer notice is not very practical because it is unlikely that an employee will give you more than 2 weeks notice of her intent to change jobs, and you may wind up paying additional wages in lieu of notice if you are the one terminating the employment. On the other hand, less than 1 week's notice is not fair to the employee who not only has to find a new job, but also a new place to live.

The contract should specify that the employee has 72 hours to vacate the premises when employment has been terminated. In other words, a 3-day notice period is written into the contract before the employee even moves into the unit.* The contract should state very clearly that occupancy of the manager's unit is premised exclusively on the condition of continued employment and that as soon as the employment terminates, so does the right to occupy the unit. You should emphasize that this is strictly an employment relationship, not a landlord-tenant relationship.

The job description must reasonably relate the hours worked to the hours for which the employee is paid. Otherwise, the resident manager may argue that he or she is working 24 hours a day and may possibly win a labor complaint against you for back wages for overtime. If you have a well-written contract with reasonable terms, most courts will honor it.

COMPENSATION

Resident managers can be paid by salary, by the hour, by apartment value in lieu of cash, or by any combination of these three methods. Managers paid on a salary are still subject to minimum wage and hour

*Check local state law.

laws unless they are exempt employees, which most resident managers are not.

Managers that are given an apartment in lieu of cash or a deduction off their rent are still employees and subject to minimum wage and hour laws. Remember, there is no such thing as a free apartment. It is an operating expense to owners, because it reduces the income they can collect, and it is compensation to employees. If the employee lives on the premises as a condition of employment and for the employer's convenience, however, the rental value of the apartment is exempt from FICA (Federal Insurance Contribution Act), FUTA (Federal Unemployment Tax Act), and federal income tax.

All employees, regardless of how they are compensated, must be covered by workers' compensation. Workers' compensation is not an area to cut corners on; it sets the limit on your liability for employees who are injured on the job. Without such coverage, your injured employee may wind up owning the building!

NEW EMPLOYEES

Once the employee is hired, give him or her an opportunity to read the company's personnel policy and ask questions. Review the entire employment contract and job description with him and reach a mutual agreement regarding the number of hours per week it will take to perform the assigned duties. Review the contract again in 90 days to confirm that the terms of the agreement are in fact workable. Do not minimize the time required in this area, because every minute spent in clarifying and defining company policies and procedures will save you hours of frustration and litigation down the road. If hiring a couple, negotiate separate job descriptions and compensation with each person.

The following points should be strongly emphasized since they are prime areas of litigation and liability:

1. Resident managers' right to occupy the apartment unit is exclusively conditioned on their continued employment.
2. Employees do not discriminate against applicants, residents, or other employees. To do so is grounds for immediate termination with no severance pay.
3. Other grounds for immediate termination include use of drugs, alcohol, or physical violence on the job or premises; theft or destruction of property; insubordination; and other blatant misconduct.
4. Time sheets are to be submitted each pay period unless the employee

Resident Apartment
Manager-Employer Agreement

This agreement, between ______________________________, hereinafter referred to as "manager" and ______________________________, hereinafter referred to as "employer" for the resident management of the property known as ______________________, located at ______________________________, California, shall be subject to the following conditions:

1. **Compensation:** Either (strike out the subsection which does not apply):
   a. Full compensation shall be $________ per month, payable semi-monthly by the ________ day and ________ day of each month,

   OR

   b. Full compensation shall be $________ per hour, plus overtime as required by law, for time spent carrying out assigned duties. If hours required to carry out assigned duties should exceed ________ hours in any workday or ________ hours in any workweek, manager shall notify employer prior to performing such services and obtain consent therefore except in an emergency, when manager shall notify employer of additional hours worked within 48 hours.

2. **Duties:** Duties assigned to the manager are those shown on Exhibit A, Assignment of Duties, which forms a part of this agreement, and which shall be subject to review within 90 days of signing of this agreement and annually thereafter.

3. **Apartment:** Since the apartment is provided as a condition of employment and at a reduced rate (see current General Information sheet for limitations) the manager will vacate the apartment immediately upon termination of employment. The rent on the apartment shall be $________ per month payable either (strike out one):
   a. By a credit against the agreed compensation

   OR

   b. By the ________ day of each month in cash.

   NOTE: Employers subject to Federal laws may use only alternative (b) for exempt employees.

4. **Days Off:** Shall be one day in seven.

5. **Excess Hours:** Manager shall record excess hours worked carrying out assigned duties on Exhibit B, Report of Hours Worked, and shall so arrange his time as to carry out assigned duties and to provide the opportunity for not less than six hours uninterrupted sleep each 24 hours except for emergencies affecting health or safety.

6. **Termination:** This contract may be terminated by either party (insert termination conditions):

   ____

   ____

Dated at ______________________________, California this ________ day of ____________, 19____

Signed ______________________________
Manager

____
Employer

CAA APPROVED FORM
CALIFORNIA APARTMENT ASSOCIATION
1.2 Revised 7/78

Figure 4-2 Resident apartment manager-employer agreement.

Exhibit A — Assignment of Duties

Place a ✓ in the box under the title of the one individual who is *primarily* responsible for each duty.

Duty	Manager	Co-Manager	Owner or Agent	Outside Contractor
1. Renting Activities				
Advertising preparation	☐	☐	☐	☐
Inserting ads in newspapers	☐	☐	☐	☐
Sign ordering and placement	☐	☐	☐	☐
Showing vacancies	☐	☐	☐	☐
Completing resident application, rental agreements, and accepting deposits	☐	☐	☐	☐
Keeping vacant units cleaned	☐	☐	☐	☐
Phone answering	☐	☐	☐	☐
2. Rent Collections				
Distributing rental collection cards	☐	☐	☐	☐
Collecting rents when due	☐	☐	☐	☐
Executing receipts for money collected	☐	☐	☐	☐
Serving late rent notices	☐	☐	☐	☐
Collecting late rents and late charges	☐	☐	☐	☐
Serving 3-day notices to move or pay	☐	☐	☐	☐
3. Administration				
Depositing collections in bank	☐	☐	☐	☐
Writing checks for accounts payable	☐	☐	☐	☐
Reconciling bank accounts	☐	☐	☐	☐
Preparing federal and state payroll forms	☐	☐	☐	☐
Preparing employee's bond applications	☐	☐	☐	☐
Keeping reports on rents in competitive units	☐	☐	☐	☐
Compiling rent change notices	☐	☐	☐	☐
Maintaining rent collection records	☐	☐	☐	☐
Preparing late charge or delinquent notices	☐	☐	☐	☐
Preparing 3-day notices to move or pay	☐	☐	☐	☐
Preparing and filing unlawful detainer actions	☐	☐	☐	☐
Enforcement of apartment rules	☐	☐	☐	☐
Filing small claims court actions	☐	☐	☐	☐
4. Record Keeping				
Income receipts	☐	☐	☐	☐
Expenses	☐	☐	☐	☐
Resident name register	☐	☐	☐	☐
Manager's weekly time report	☐	☐	☐	☐
Unit maintenance card	☐	☐	☐	☐
Monthly income statement	☐	☐	☐	☐
Monthly expense statement	☐	☐	☐	☐
Manager's weekly apartment report	☐	☐	☐	☐
Record of location by unit of all furniture and equipment owned by apartment	☐	☐	☐	☐
5. Cleaning Apartments				
Vacuuming carpets	☐	☐	☐	☐
Shampooing carpets	☐	☐	☐	☐
Refrigerator cleaning	☐	☐	☐	☐
Plumbing fixture cleaning	☐	☐	☐	☐
Drape cleaning	☐	☐	☐	☐
Window washing	☐	☐	☐	☐
Screen cleaning	☐	☐	☐	☐
Stove and oven cleaning	☐	☐	☐	☐
Wall washing	☐	☐	☐	☐
Cabinet and closet cleaning	☐	☐	☐	☐
Heater cleaning	☐	☐	☐	☐

Duty	Manager	Co-Manager	Owner or Agent	Outside Contractor
Cleaning Apartments (continued)				
Sink, shower, and lavatory cleaning	☐	☐	☐	☐
Floor washing and/or polishing	☐	☐	☐	☐
Ceramic tile grout cleaning	☐	☐	☐	☐
Light fixtures	☐	☐	☐	☐
Tops of doorway and window trim	☐	☐	☐	☐
6. Property Policing				
Facade cleaning	☐	☐	☐	☐
Entry cleaning	☐	☐	☐	☐
Garage oils on floors and pavements	☐	☐	☐	☐
Nite light setting (time clock)	☐	☐	☐	☐
Sign cleaning	☐	☐	☐	☐
Driveway cleaning	☐	☐	☐	☐
Walkway and lawn policing	☐	☐	☐	☐
Garbage area cleanup	☐	☐	☐	☐
7. Maintenance				
Carpet cleaning	☐	☐	☐	☐
Air conditioner cleaning	☐	☐	☐	☐
Recreation, sauna, and bathroom cleaning	☐	☐	☐	☐
Fishpond or fountain cleaning	☐	☐	☐	☐
Laundry room cleaning	☐	☐	☐	☐
Hallway cleaning	☐	☐	☐	☐
Lightbulb replacement	☐	☐	☐	☐
Carport cleaning	☐	☐	☐	☐
Hallway vacuuming	☐	☐	☐	☐
Warm air heat filter cleaning	☐	☐	☐	☐
Warm air heat filter replacement	☐	☐	☐	☐
Water heater draining	☐	☐	☐	☐
Stair and deck cleaning	☐	☐	☐	☐
Stair and deck sealing or painting	☐	☐	☐	☐
Plumbing stoppage	☐	☐	☐	☐
8. Repairs				
Door or window screen repair	☐	☐	☐	☐
Door or window screen replacement	☐	☐	☐	☐
Window pane replacement	☐	☐	☐	☐
Window crank repair	☐	☐	☐	☐
Window crank replacement	☐	☐	☐	☐
Air conditioner repair	☐	☐	☐	☐
Stove burners	☐	☐	☐	☐
Stove and oven handles or knobs	☐	☐	☐	☐
Refrigerators	☐	☐	☐	☐
Dishwasher repair	☐	☐	☐	☐
Door knobs and cabinet catch replacement	☐	☐	☐	☐
Door and cabinet hinge replacement	☐	☐	☐	☐
Carpet repairs	☐	☐	☐	☐
Painting	☐	☐	☐	☐
Plumbing faucet washer replacement	☐	☐	☐	☐
Plumbing replacements	☐	☐	☐	☐
Electric switch replacement	☐	☐	☐	☐
Electric fixture replacement	☐	☐	☐	☐
Stucco patching	☐	☐	☐	☐
Stucco painting	☐	☐	☐	☐
Front door painting	☐	☐	☐	☐
Fence repairs	☐	☐	☐	☐

CAA APPROVED FORM
CALIFORNIA APARTMENT ASSOCIATION
1.4 Revised 7/78

(continued)

Figure 4-2 *(Continued)*

Repairs (continued)

	Manager	Co-Manager	Owner or Agent	Outside Contractor
Fence painting	☐	☐	☐	☐
Disposal stoppage	☐	☐	☐	☐
Disposal repair	☐	☐	☐	☐
Disposal replacement	☐	☐	☐	☐
Toilet seat replacement	☐	☐	☐	☐
Toilet seal replacement	☐	☐	☐	☐
Toilet tank repairs	☐	☐	☐	☐
Removal of door locks	☐	☐	☐	☐
Replacement of keys	☐	☐	☐	☐
Water faucet replacement	☐	☐	☐	☐
Wall painting	☐	☐	☐	☐
Woodwork painting	☐	☐	☐	☐
Mahogany door cleaning	☐	☐	☐	☐
Mahogany door varnishing	☐	☐	☐	☐
Warm air heater thermostat repair	☐	☐	☐	☐
Warm air heater thermostat replacement	☐	☐	☐	☐
Warm air heater repair	☐	☐	☐	☐
Warm air heater replacement	☐	☐	☐	☐

9. **Landscape Care**

	Manager	Co-Manager	Owner or Agent	Outside Contractor
Watering lawns, shrubs, and trees	☐	☐	☐	☐
Watering planters and flower boxes	☐	☐	☐	☐
Mowing grass	☐	☐	☐	☐
Trimming grass	☐	☐	☐	☐
Trimming shrubs	☐	☐	☐	☐
Spraying shrubs	☐	☐	☐	☐
Fertilizing grass and shrubs	☐	☐	☐	☐
Repairing sprinklers	☐	☐	☐	☐
Replacing shrubs	☐	☐	☐	☐
Weeding lawns and planting areas	☐	☐	☐	☐

10. **Swimming Pools**

	Manager	Co-Manager	Owner or Agent	Outside Contractor
Cleaning and sweeping	☐	☐	☐	☐
Chemical replacement	☐	☐	☐	☐
Repair of equipment	☐	☐	☐	☐
Replacement of equipment	☐	☐	☐	☐
Testing and logging pH readings	☐	☐	☐	☐
Servicing filter	☐	☐	☐	☐
Water temperature regulation	☐	☐	☐	☐

11. **Miscellaneous**

	Manager	Co-Manager	Owner or Agent	Outside Contractor
Elevator cleaning	☐	☐	☐	☐
Roofing repairs	☐	☐	☐	☐
Master TV antenna and transformer	☐	☐	☐	☐
Snow removal and slippery walk protection	☐	☐	☐	☐
Personal property inventory	☐	☐	☐	☐
Furniture cleaning	☐	☐	☐	☐
Furniture repair	☐	☐	☐	☐
Furniture replacement	☐	☐	☐	☐
Vending machine repair	☐	☐	☐	☐
Vending machine collection	☐	☐	☐	☐
Vending machine stock	☐	☐	☐	☐

12. **Employee Relations**

	Manager	Co-Manager	Owner or Agent	Outside Contractor
Pre-employment and termination interviews	☐	☐	☐	☐
Hiring and discharging employees	☐	☐	☐	☐
Performance evaluation and counseling	☐	☐	☐	☐

13. **Other**

	Manager	Co-Manager	Owner or Agent	Outside Contractor
________	☐	☐	☐	☐
________	☐	☐	☐	☐
________	☐	☐	☐	☐

________________ Manager ________ Date ________________ Owner or Agent ________ Date

________________ Co-Manager ________ Date

Reviewed: Date ________________

Manager ________________ Co-Manager ________________ Owner or Agent ________________

Remarks ____

____

____

Reviewed: Date ________________

Manager ________________ Co-Manager ________________ Owner or Agent ________________

Remarks ____

____

____

CAA APPROVED FORM
CALIFORNIA APARTMENT ASSOCIATION

Figure 4-2 *(Continued)*

Exhibit B — Report of Hours Worked
(Not required of exempt employees)

Name ______________________ Position ______________________

Your workweek for payroll purposes begins at ______________ on ______________

and ends at ______________ on ______________

Days of Month		Worked Assigned Hours		Hours Worked (if other than assigned)		**Reason for absence or failure to work assigned hours.** If none worked due to illness or absence enter 0 in Total for Day column. Were excess hours authorized? Result of emergency? Explain in detail.
Day	**Date**	**Yes**	**No**	**Extra Hours (If any)**	**Total For Day**	

Payroll period from ____________ to ____________

______________________ Signature of Employee

______________________ Approved

CAA APPROVED FORM
CALIFORNIA APARTMENT ASSOCIATION
1.5 Revised 7/78 COPYRIGHT 1980

Figure 4-2 *(Continued)*

is exempt under state or federal law. The hours on the time sheet are to reflect those agreed on in the employment contract.

5. Employees are not to work overtime unless prior authorization is received or in the event of an emergency.

Introduce your new employee to the residents via a newsletter, announcement, or open house. This will avoid the problem of a new employee, completely unknown to the residents, attempting to collect the current month's rent, which the old manager has already absconded with.

AUTOMOBILE INSURANCE

All employees who own or drive automobiles should, regardless of their duties, be required to carry their own automobile insurance, with recommended limits of not less than $100,000 per person, bodily injury; $300,000 per accident, bodily injury; and $50,000 property damage. Evidence of such coverage in the form of a copy of the policy, a cover page of the policy, or a certificate of insurance should be provided at the time of hiring and on each anniversary of employment.

Requesting a certificate of insurance or being named as additional insured under the employee's policy, however, will alert the insurance company that the insured is using his car for business purposes, thereby raising his rates—a result most employees will resist.

TRAINING AND SUPERVISION

Policy Manuals

A good standard operations policy manual will have instructions, forms, procedures, and personnel policies clearly spelled out for the new employee. Requiring the new employee to read the operations manual the first week of hire will save you many hours and much effort in training and orientation.

Training Sessions

It is important to keep your employees updated as changes in the law and management policies occur. Training sessions are also good for morale. On-site employees are rather isolated and do not have a peer group with whom to interact. Such meetings give managers a chance to get together and exchange ideas and share problems.

On-Site Inspections
It is important to inspect the property at least once a month, not only to fulfill your legal responsibilities to your client, the owner of the property, but also for the morale of your on-site employees. They need to know that you are concerned about their job performance and appreciate their efforts when the job is well done.

Newsletters and Bulletins
Regular written communications from the head office keep the on-site staff informed about changes in the law, management policies, and maintenance techniques. It is also a way of giving recognition to your employees for ideas contributed and exceptional performance.

Seminars
There is no such thing as too much education. In fact, the basis of education is repetition. Many people need to be exposed to the same ideas several times before they grasp them. By supporting and encouraging continuing education for your employees, you are contributing to their professional growth and to the overall success of your operations.

Morale
In addition to the morale-building suggestions made above, consult with your staff when making major changes in policies or procedures or when preparing the annual budget. That is not to suggest a democratic process in which everyone gets one vote. You, as the supervisor, still get to "pull rank." Decisions are ultimately yours. But by including everyone in the process of making changes, you will get a much higher degree of cooperation and support from your staff when it comes to implementing the changes. Hearing their perspective will also help you to make better decisions. As a supervisor, you see the problem from a broad, long-range perspective, whereas resident managers tend to see the problem in short-range, finite detail. Both aspects must be considered to develop a satisfactory and comprehensive solution.

Support your staff's decisions with their residents and subordinates, and adhere to the chain of command. Don't allow others to go around the manager to you to get what they want. As soon as a manager has lost credibility, he or she has lost control of the project and must be replaced.

PERFORMANCE EVALUATION

Performance appraisal is equal to management development for both the supervisor and the employee. It is the supervisor's responsibility to be a role model, to show employees how to do the job, and to motivate them to do a better job.

Successful management regarding performance evaluation is based on the following assumptions:

1. People are an organization's most important resource.
2. People are capable of growth toward more effective behavior.
3. Supervisors can promote or impede the professional growth of employees.

A performance evaluation requires advance preparation. Review the performance file to determine if last year's goals and objectives were met, exceeded, or not met.

Hold a preliminary meeting with the resident manager and tell her what you want her to prepare for the next meeting. Have the employee take her share of the responsibility for the meeting by preparing her short- and long-range goals, assessing her strengths and weaknesses, and formulating a plan to implement her goals.

It is then the supervisor's responsibility to tie the employee's goals into the overall goals of the company. The goals should be mutually agreed on, but the supervisor can veto goals that are inappropriate, stick to those that are nonnegotiable, and negotiate the rest. Employees and supervisors should keep in mind that most employees want to please their supervisors.

Most employees underestimate their own potential and the value of the contribution they make to the company. Therefore, the supervisor's motive and attitude are more important in conducting a successful performance evaluation than any specific technique or skill. The ultimate objective is to encourage and motivate employees, not to punish or penalize them.

The evaluation should be based on the supervisor's personal experience and not on hearsay. There should be no surprises at the meeting; instead there should be regular communication throughout the year and a high level of trust and mutual respect, which allows disagreements to be aired easily. Nor should the performance evaluation be done at the same time as the salary review, which reduces the effectiveness of the performance evaluation and puts the supervisor in the incompatible roles of coach and judge at the same time.

DISCIPLINARY ACTION

A system of progressive discipline gives the employee adequate warning of poor performance and the company documentation in case the employee sues. As your company grows larger, it becomes more and more important to have written personnel polices and disciplinary procedures that are strictly adhered to in order to avoid claims of discriminatory, arbitrary, or unfair labor practices.

Documentation is crucial. Often there is plenty of verbal justification, but no written documentation in the file. Or what is worse—the only written items in the file are satisfactory appraisals and pay increases.

Do not lose sight of the other goal of discipline, which is to correct the employee's behavior. Discipline should be used as a positive management tool to modify employees' behavior and enable them to be more productive.

Discipline should progress as follows:

1. *Informal discipline.* Silence is tacit approval that current behavior is acceptable. If there is a problem, invite the employee in for a conversation. Keep the discussion open-ended, and listen for his or her explanation. Document in the file what occurred, when, where, what rule was broken, what changes will be made in the future, and that the employee was warned that continued breaches will result in termination.
2. *Formal discipline.* Be prepared with the facts, and come directly to the point with the employee. Allow the employee to respond. Ask in what way you can help the employee to change or improve his or her behavior, and set a review date. Document the details as if everything were going to be challenged in court because it just might be. Be clear, authoritative, and unequivocal in your warning. The employee must understand that his job is in jeopardy—this is part of "due process." Have the employee sign or acknowledge receipt of a written warning.
3. *Termination* (see section following).

TERMINATION

Employees have no inherent right to lifetime employment. However, the employer's right to "at will" termination is being greatly eroded today. It is well established that employers have an implied covenant of good faith and fair dealing with their employees. In several states, an employer can be sued simply for not being "fair" or "reasonable" in firing.

Furthermore, in most states, an employee is protected from arbitrary and capricious termination by his employer:

1. Due to discrimination (e.g., age, race, sex)
2. For refusal to work under unsafe conditions

3. For asserting civil rights (e.g., voting, jury duty, political beliefs)
4. If wages are garnisheed
5. For invoking protection under the minimum wage and hour laws
6. For engaging in union activities

Be careful of implied agreements in which employees may reasonably infer from verbal statements, length of employment, personnel policies, or other factors that they may be terminated for good cause only. For instance, courts have established various theories of "implied promises" of job security, ranging from what job recruiters say to positive job evaluations and promotions.

There comes a time, however, when an employee must be terminated either immediately for good cause (as spelled out in your personnel policy), because his or her behavior did not improve after performance evaluations or disciplinary action, or because the position has been eliminated and he is being laid off.

The termination should be handled by the highest level supervisor the employee deals with on a regular basis; this responsibility should not be delegated. Follow personnel policies and be consistent in applying them.

The termination should be done in person, not by phone or letter. Do not "drag out" the purpose of the meeting, but get straight to the point. Tell the truth, tactfully but straightforwardly. If you make up frivolous excuses, they may come back to haunt you in court. Use the documentation you have obtained.

Have the employee's severance check ready to hand to him at the time of termination. Include all accrued benefits to which he is entitled (e.g., severance pay in lieu of notice or vacation). If you are terminating the employee on site, ask for the project keys, petty cash, undeposited rent monies and other belongings to be turned over at this time. (However, you cannot "ransom" the termination paycheck for the return of these items.)

If you are terminating the employee for good cause, do so immediately at the time of the incident. Do not wait for a convenient time such as payday or until you have another person hired for the position or until you just can't take it another day.

Evaluate what went wrong to avoid having the same problem occur in the future. If an employee must be fired, it is usually less the fault of the employee than of management, who failed to screen, train, or supervise the person properly.

As a practical matter, progressive discipline and warnings often result in the employee quitting before being terminated. The advantages are that this reduces claims on the employer's unemployment fund, gets the employee out of the apartment unit sooner if he or she has another job lined up, and reduces bad feelings on the part of everyone.

WORKERS' COMPENSATION

Workers' compensation is required for all but specifically defined exempt employees. It covers all compensable injuries arising out of or in the course of employment. The injury must have occurred while the employee was performing the work for which he or she was engaged. For resident managers and other employees who are required to live on site, it often involves 24-hour coverage.

The insurance premium is based on the employee's full cash compensation and the fair market value of the apartment. The premium is paid by the employer at a rate established according to job classification.

There are criminal and monetary penalties for failing to cover employees with workers' compensation. Also liability insurance does not cover employers who fail to insure employees with workers' compensation.

INDEPENDENT CONTRACTORS

One area that creates a great deal of confusion, especially for small property management companies and property owners, is the distinction between an employee and an independent contractor. Often owners or management agents hire resident managers, cleaning people, or maintenance workers as "independent contractors" to eliminate the employer's expense of payroll taxes and workers' compensation insurance, only to find out afterward that the independent contractor was really an employee.

Do not confuse an independent contractor with a state-licensed contractor. An independent contractor has a legal status distinctly different from that of an employee. An independent contractor may or may not be required by the state to be licensed in a particular trade (e.g., electrician, roofer).

When hiring independent contractors, insist on proof that they have their own insurance coverage by requiring a certificate of insurance, which any professional insurance broker will provide on request, and execute a contract which states you will be submitting a 1099 form to the Internal Revenue Service (IRS) at the end of the year.

However, signing agreements with individuals stating that they are independent contractors does not necessarily make them so. The courts look at the substance of the arrangement, not the form of the agreement. If you find out after the fact that what you really have are employees, you may be responsible for both their share as well as your share of the payroll deductions that were not withheld, plus penalties and interest. If employees are injured without workers' compensation coverage, you may be liable for their injuries as well as criminal and monetary penalties.

The IRS Code and Regulations has categorized and described guidelines distinguishing between employees and independent contractors.

Factors indicating employee status include the following:

1. The employer furnishes the supplies, tools, and materials for the employee's use.
2. The employer gives instructions as to how, where, and when the job is to be performed.
3. The employer provides the training.
4. The employer requires that the services be rendered personally by the employee.
5. The employer has the right to discharge or terminate the employee at will.
6. The employer fixes the hours of work.
7. The employee is paid by the hour, week, or month.
8. The employee's business and/or travel expenses are paid by the employer.
9. The employer requires oral or written reports.

Factors indicating independent contractor status are as follows:

1. The independent contractor has a substantial investment in her own tools, supplies, materials, equipment, or facilities.
2. The independent contractor has freedom in his style of work, such as choosing his own methods.
3. The employer does not train the independent contractor.
4. The services can be rendered personally or by a substitute (e.g., a partner, subcontractor, or employee of the independent contractor).
5. The independent contractor realizes a profit (or loss) from his enterprise.
6. The independent contractor does not receive fringe benefits from the employer (e.g., vacation, sick leave, disability and health insurance).
7. The independent contractor usually works for more than one person.

The preceding guidelines can be summarized by noting one key characteristic: The more control the employer has over the situation, the more it looks like an employer-employee relationship rather than an independent contractor arrangement.

"CONSTRUCTIVE" EMPLOYEES

If you hire only one spouse as a resident manager, but you know that the other spouse, who has a regular full-time job somewhere else, occasionally helps out around the property on evenings and weekends, you have a "constructive" employee who is not on your payroll and therefore cannot be covered by workers' compensation.

The solution to the problem is either to inform the manager, in writing, that this situation will not be tolerated and jeopardizes continued employment, or to place the helpful spouse on the payroll for some minimal compensation.

LABOR LAW REQUIREMENTS

It is important to determine whether your property management operations are regulated under state and/or federal wage-hour laws. The most important federal law which applies to the apartment management business is the Fair Labor Standards Act (FLSA), which establishes standards of minimum wages, maximum hours, overtime pay, equal pay, and record keeping.

An individual employee is covered if he or she is engaged in either interstate commerce or the production of goods for such commerce. An employee is considered to be engaged in interstate commerce if she regularly uses any of the instruments of interstate communication, such as the mails or telephone, purchases or orders goods from other states, handles goods received from other states, or regularly travels across state lines in the performance of her duties.

The management company itself is covered by the FLSA if at least two of the company's employees meet the interstate commerce requirement and if the company's total gross dollar volume of sales is equal to or greater than $250,000, thereby extending the federal wage-hour coverage to all the employees of the firm.

The "white collar" exemption which exists for executive, administrative, or professional employees focuses on their duties and salary. For instance, an executive employee is one whose duties are primarily (at least 80 percent) intellectual, managerial, or creative. The duties also include the supervision of at least two other full-time employees and the ability to hire and fire. The employee must be paid a cash salary of at least $155.00 per week ($671.67 per month) exclusive of any apartment value. Many resident managers of smaller buildings simply do not qualify as exempt employees because of the job duties, which tend to be clerical and routine.

MISCELLANEOUS ISSUES

Posting of Notices

Check with local state regulations to determine which notices must be provided to your employees. For instance, in California the following notices are required to be posted in a conspicuous place (usually in the rest room or supply room):

1. Name of carrier and expiration date of workers' compensation policy.
2. Address and phone number of labor commissioner's office.
3. Right to receive workers' compensation benefits.
4. Notice of regular payday and time (unless automatically deposited to employee's account). Employees are to be paid at least twice a month unless they are exempt employees or subject to a collective bargaining agreement.
5. Wage and Hour Order 5-80.
6. State disability insurance benefits.
7. Unemployment insurance benefits.
8. Fair employment practices and equal opportunity information.

Payroll Deductions

Many states have complicated formulas for determining state payroll deductions on the value of an apartment given to a resident manager. If a manager is only given an apartment in lieu of cash for custodial duties, he is still your employee, and if there are no cash wages from which to make deductions, you, the employer, will have to pay them on behalf of the employee.

Payroll Records

Determine what type, in what format, and for how long payroll records are to be maintained according to local regulations.

Casual Labor

Casual labor is often thought of as the incidental labor used occasionally on the property site for which wages are usually paid in cash or "under the table." This is a very dangerous policy to follow. Casual laborers are still your employees and subject to payroll deductions and workers' compensation coverage.

The overlap between state and federal labor requirements may appear to be very complicated, and the hours of on-site employees difficult to control properly and document. However, failure to understand and apply the law correctly and to maintain proper payroll records will result in expensive lawsuits and back wage claims.

PART 3

Leasing

CHAPTER 5

Leasing residential property

William C. Weaver
North Texas State University
Denton, Texas

This chapter is written especially for people who are involved with the day-to-day leasing of residential real estate (apartment units or single-family homes). Owner/managers should find much practical information here.

The material is oriented toward the owner/manager with small- to medium-sized holdings and the beginning resident manager. The following areas are discussed in detail:

Advertising and promotion

Tenants (sources and qualifying criteria)

Property presentation

Rent control

Renting of houses

Included is much down-to-earth, practical information people need to have immediately to lease their own property successfully or to be on-site managers for property management companies.

KNOW YOUR PROPERTY

To market residential rentals properly, you must know your property! This means knowing your property's strengths and weaknesses. You don't need to know all the construction details, but you certainly should know about practical items such as soundproofing. Are the common walls constructed to avoid the transmission of sound from one apartment to the next? The following information should be "on the tip of your tongue":

1. Size of apartments and of each room*
2. Number, type, and size of closets
3. Number of bathrooms and equipment
4. Floor plans
5. Types and brands of equipment such as stove, refrigerator, disposal, heating/air conditioning, and furnishings
6. Amenities such as pool, laundry facilities, club rooms, saunas, extra soundproofing, burglar and fire alarms, self-cleaning ovens, ice makers, and trash compactors; in short, all the possible "extras" in your apartment complex
7. Whether cablevision is available or not
8. Types and colors of carpet available
9. Whether pest control service is provided
10. Policies on pets
11. Policies on children
12. Apartment security

You should know every possible advantage your property has, and for each advantage you should be able to relate several benefits to your prospective tenant. Remember to stress benefits to your prospective tenant, not "facts."

KNOW YOUR COMPETITION

The best way to gain knowledge of your competition is to visit competing properties. Take a look, not once, but regularly. Your competition can

*Small apartments may have an advantage over big complexes because of their very smallness. If designed and managed well, they may be able to offer the resident more privacy, a more "homey" atmosphere, and a better location. You should maximize this very valuable amenity if it's present. Plan the landscaping, decking, porches, and so on to take maximum advantage of privacy and quietness!

be divided into two types—direct and indirect. *Direct competition* includes apartments much like yours that offer basically the same accommodations at about the same price. The direct competition should be "shopped" regularly. Any advertising material used by your competitors as well as their newspaper ads should be collected and saved for reference.

Properties that do not try to attract the same market as yours are classified as *indirect competitors*. The units are priced quite a bit higher or lower than yours, or they appeal to other types of people. You may be able to arrange a "working relationship" with managers whose properties are in indirect competition with yours. You can swap leads—even swap names of repair persons and other workers.

Shopping of competitors should start with the collection of data, such as advertising material and ads in the newspapers, followed by a visit. This marketing approach may not seem too important when the market is firm, with few vacancies. But when the trends change, as they inevitably do, resulting in unoccupied units, you will find that to be competitive you need to know what else is on the market. If you keep up-to-date, you'll know when prices change and be able to react at once. Another advantage of an exhaustive survey is that it prepares you psychologically to meet the prospective tenant; you know your strong points and weak points and just what your competition offers.

KNOW THE COMMUNITY

Besides knowing your property and your competition, you need a thorough knowledge of your community. Apartment owners or managers who can tell a prospective tenant all about the community—especially in relation to the complex—have a much better chance of leasing up quickly and remaining 100 percent full. Usually the leasing decision is not made on the basis of any one point but as the result of several small items. The more professional you seem in your management, the more assured your prospective tenant will be concerning good management. Many people with a good deal of experience in apartment living place more and more importance on adequate management.

Community Survey

The best way to approach a community survey is to have a map of your area posted on a bulletin board in a common room or area of your complex. If this is not possible, you should memorize the distances to various community services. The following list, by no means exhaustive, tells some of the data you need to know:

1. Income level and type of people in area
2. View
3. Shopping
4. Transportation
5. Schools
6. Churches
7. Employment
8. Fire and police services
9. Medical and dental emergency services
10. Recreation
11. Child-care services
12. Local government offices with a list of specifics (e.g., drivers' licenses, voting registrations)
13. Utility services
14. Liabilities of area
15. Points of interest and amenities
16. Noise level

Immediate Community

What kind of people live in your immediate area—students, families, older people? Is it a residential area (apartments, houses, or mixed) or a commercial area? Is it close to a university? What is the average person in your area like? Remember, people usually prefer to live around people similar to themselves.

TENANT SELECTION

Property Marketing

Renting apartments should be approached with a great deal of thought regarding marketing. The first step in this process is to decide to whom you want to rent. It is usually not wise to say, simply, "Here it is; the rent is $525 per month." It is far better to pick the type of resident you want to attract and design a marketing campaign aimed at that group of people. Technically this is called *market segmentation.* All it really means is that you feel you can more effectively market your complex to a smaller group of people who have some common characteristics.

For example, you may decide to appeal to students, older retired couples, or young married couples with small children. Depending on which group you choose, your advertising copy would be different, it would appear in different places, and your rent schedules may be set differently. All successful managers of apartment complexes aim their marketing at specific groups of people rather than taking a "shotgun" approach. An apartment can't be all things to all people. You must design it with one, or at most, a few groups or types of people in mind.

PROMOTION AND ADVERTISING

Once you have decided whom you want to rent to, you immediately simplify the task. You can't design effective advertising without knowing the target. Another vital point to keep in mind when writing any advertising copy—for newspapers, bulletins, radio, TV, or other—is the difference between features and benefits.

Features and Benefits

All apartments have features: 14-foot by 15-foot bedrooms, tiled baths, carpet, 9-foot by 6-foot storage rooms, attic storage; the unit is brand new and well lighted, and so on. Features are details, usually physical, about your complex. Features do not sell! Benefits sell. And benefits result from features.

Take one of the examples given: "14-foot by 15-foot bedroom." This in itself does not sell your apartment. Change that to "Lovely 14-foot by 15-foot bedrooms to allow plenty of space for your king-sized bedroom suite." Similarly, "tiled baths" is just a statement of fact. Your apartment sells better when you say, "The beautiful ceramic tile is easily cleaned." Convert your features into benefits for your customers.

Now that you have an idea of whom you are selling to and what (features and benefits) you are selling, it's time to go to work!

GOAL OF ADVERTISING

Advertising does not sell apartments! No ad in any paper ever rented an apartment. Advertising merely brings people to your property or causes them to phone for more information so that *you* have an opportunity to sell them your apartment.

Attention, interest, desire, action—these are the four words to live by. Any ad must attract a prospect's *attention*; it must cause him or her to become *interested* after that. If the ad is good enough it will generate a *desire* for more information and cause the prospect to take *action*—a phone call or a visit.

Attention

Your headline grabs the prospect's attention via a wanted and believable benefit. (Remember—you looked at your market to decide whom you wanted to sell to. This knowledge of *who* makes it easier to pick a benefit that is wanted.) When good layout, correct use of white space, and proper positioning are used, the headline reaches out and grabs the reader's attention. A picture or line drawing sometimes helps.

Interest and Desire

Your message, or "copy," should provoke interest first and then desire. It should prove your headline benefit and "translate" the benefit to your reader's interest. If possible, additional benefits should be presented in the same way—strong subheads followed by the expansion of the statement. Be careful not to put too much data in the advertisement. Remember, ads don't rent apartments—they only help to get a prospect to those who do—*you.*

Action

The action element of the model can be very specific—"Call Mr. Bill Weaver at 262-2147 today!"—or it may be implied by merely listing the address and phone number.

For this attention/interest/desire/action model to work for you, the copy should use emotionally motivating words. Each benefit must be described in such a way that your reader feels a strong emotional pull to your property. The following list of words used in ads is intended to be a guide in your thinking; see how many more words or phrases you can add:

Atmosphere

Luxury, deluxe
Quiet
Artistic
Fine view
Attractive
Sunny
Set in garden
Charming neighborhood
Resort
Luxurious
Spotlessly clean
Cheerful
Picture window
View of bay, ocean, lake
Secluded
Professional people
New area
Residential
Friendly
Unusually large
Casual luxury

Atmosphere *(continued)*

Convenient
Lovely
Executive
Pleasant
Restful
Desirable
Exciting
Delightful
Excellent planning
Quiet and countrylike
Picturesque and exclusive
Many luxury extras
Efficient management
Seclusion and quiet
Individual privacy
Gracious living
Uniquely designed
True adult living
Centrally located
Space and quality
Newly landscaped
Easy, relaxed living
Homey feeling
Charming setting
Quiet adult living
Restful and secluded
New fashion in modern living
Desirable quiet
Peaceful
Carefully planned
Flexible living room
Security patrol

Location

Easy commuting
Easy access to freeway
Bus at door
Near shops
Near schools
Hillside view
Above reproach
Accessible to shopping
Near university or college

Condition

Newly furnished
Redecorated
New building
Sound conditioning
Newly painted
Very clean
Sparkling

Luxuries

Private balcony, terrace, or patio
Enclosed garage
Maid service
Dressing room
Air conditioned
FM music
Switchboard
Elevator
Built-in stove and oven
Phone jacks
Parking attendant
Heated swimming pool
Garden patio
Play area fully equipped

Decor

Chinese modern
Artist studio
Smartly furnished
Modern oriental
Open beam
Beam
French modern
Smart
Wood-paneled
Nylon carpeting
Custom drapes
Custom furniture
Knotty pine
Decorate to suit

Luxuries *(continued)*
Near recreation
Game room
Recreation room
Color TV in lobby

Recreation

Overlooks pool
Sports minded
Patio
Barbecue
Sunny area
Exercise room
Billiards
Sauna bath
Putting greens
Social activities
Private entrance
Double entrance

Decor *(continued)*
Provincial
Interior decorator styled
Sliding glass door
Like home

Conveniences

Forced air heat
Electric kitchen
Gas kitchen
Automatic washer-dryer
Telephone service
Free parking
Off-street parking
Private garage
Extra closets
Built-in TV antenna
Private storage
Extra telephone outlet

Others

Spacious
Split level
View

ADVERTISING MEDIA

In most market areas there are many available advertising media. The professional must choose the most effective medium for the lowest cost. Your prospective resident profile can help you to select the medium that will reach the people you want as residents in your apartment. The following is a sample list of advertising media available to apartment owners and managers:

1. Newspaper
2. Apartment signs
3. Highway signs
4. Apartment-locating services
5. Banners
6. Flags and streamers
7. Directories
8. Brochures
9. Outdoor and directional signs

10. Shopper publications
11. House organs
12. Radio and TV
13. Magazines
14. Car cards
15. Bench cards
16. Flyers
17. Postcards
18. Advertising cards
19. Manager's card
20. Letterheads and sales letters
21. Word of mouth

No matter which medium or combination of media you choose, your copy should follow the model of attention, interest, desire, and action: After attracting attention, it should create interest and desire by citing specific benefits that will appeal to the market segment. The use of emotionally motivating adjectives will assist you in gaining interest. The design and structure of the advertisement will do the rest. Following is a closer look at some of these media.

Newspapers

There are two general types of newspaper advertising: classified sections and display advertising. The classifieds are the single most useful and popular medium in use today. They are confined basically to the geographic area you are trying to reach and they are repeated every day. In addition, people are accustomed to looking there when they are in search of an apartment. Thus your message gets to the people you want to communicate with. Prospective renters use this medium as their no. 1 source of available units.

Although classified advertising is usually inexpensive relative to the exposure, an apartment complex can sink a goodly sum into this area in a short time with little to show for it. One way to cut cost is to make use of discounts.

Most newspapers offer three types of discounts: quantity, frequency, and cash. Generally speaking, the more space you use, the less expensive each column inch is. The same idea applies with the discount for frequency: The more a particular ad is inserted, the less expensive the ad is. A cash discount expressed as 2 percent 10 net 30, for example, simply means that if you pay your bill during the first 10 days you receive a 2 percent discount. The full amount of the bill is due within 30 days.

The amount of the discounts can be determined from the publisher's advertising rate card, available at the newspaper advertising office, along with data concerning deadlines for receiving copy and extra charges for special services. Sometimes they can even give you data about readership. *Be sure you refer to the current rates.*

How do you write a good ad? What kind of design aid do you need? These are common questions that should be asked. The first step in writing an ad is to get the reader's attention. This is the single most important factor in *any* classified ad. Your copy is competing with hundreds of others. You must have some method of directing the reader to your copy rather than to the competition.

Attracting the reader's attention. The three basic methods of gaining attention are through size of type, white space, and headlines. Although these elements can be listed and discussed separately, they should always be used together. Making your type size different from that of adjacent advertisements, using attention-getting headlines, and the thoughtful use of white or blank space on the top, bottom, and sides work together to grab the reader's attention.

Why is it so important for your ad to stand out? Research has shown that the average apartment hunter picks out only a few ads that look especially attractive to follow up with a phone call. If, after the phone conversation, these people are still interested, they go and see the apartments. Make sure yours is one of the first they call!

One way to ensure that you get called is the wise use of the three previously discussed methods of gaining attention. It is also advised that you be very careful with the use of abbreviations. Take a look at most classified ads—too many ar's, br's, rms, tl, fl's, and so on. Many times an ad can be made totally incomprehensible with the use of abbreviations. BR for bedroom is about the most commonly accepted abbreviation and should be the *only* one used. Why save a few cents and possibly lose your reader?

One last point to remember in classified ad design is that it's not good to advertise several apartments in the same ad. Much research has been done that shows that when two or more apartments of different sizes are listed together, the ad loses much of its impact. People may wonder why you have so many vacancies. Many people respond negatively to multiple apartment ads. Take a look at the advertising of really successful large complexes. Most run *separate* ads for each apartment size and in separate locations (down the page or in another column altogether).

Display ads. Display ads can be found throughout the newspaper. They can be any size up to two facing pages and often have a great variety of type and illustration. While the display ad can be quite expensive, it has a much better chance of gaining attention due to its placement (away from competing copy) and its size and copy. Display ads are not used in everyday promotion unless problems are encountered in renting units. Openings, new units on the market, or attempts to reposition a complex in the market, however, are good reasons for using display ads.

Professional help is suggested for display ad composition, especially if artwork is going to be used. An advertising agency is usually a helpful source. Many take a commission from the media and are thus free, and some charge a small amount for the actual art layout. Many newspapers employ people to give you assistance in this area; check both agencies and newspapers before making a decision.

A constant check should be made on competitive advertising, especially display ads. They may serve as a tip-off to important changes in policies, rent schedules, market strategies, and so on.

Housing section in newspapers. Many newspapers have special sections that feature housing or even apartment housing. This is usually a good section to use because the people reading it are preselected. They are interested in housing or they would not be reading that section. It's best to place display ads in this section if possible for the same reason. Positioning your display ad is important, and the professionals should be able to give you helpful advice. Sometimes it's more expensive to have special placement rather than letting the editor choose where to insert your copy, but if you are going to the trouble and expense of purchasing a display ad, the extra placement charge is worth every cent.

Signs

One of the most important media for advertising apartments, large or small, is the sign. The sign on the premises states emphatically, "This is an apartment house." The message must be short, distinctive, and understood quickly. Good design of an apartment sign is difficult and should be approached with much thought if not done by a professional.

Your sign should transmit an image that fits with the previously developed customer profile. Probably 70 percent of the signs now used are tasteless, ineffective, and unattractive, and besides—*they don't work.*

It is surprising that a developer will spend millions on a large complex and then use the cheapest, most ineffective sign obtainable. Signs should be refurbished or replaced *at the first sign of wear.* Cheap, weather-worn signs turn off prospects just at the time that they need reinforcement—the first sight of your property.

All signs should be, but usually are not, integrated into the property.

A sign should look built-in rather than tacked on. Your signs should look as if they belonged. One of the most effective ways to accomplish this is by the use of a structure—a clock tower kind of building. If the property is large enough, some sort of entrance gate or structure can serve as an excellent location for a well-designed sign. The sign structure should be architecturally integrated into the style of the buildings or building that it advertises.

Good, effective lighting can and should be used to highlight your signs. No flashing neon lights but tasteful spots tied in with landscaping efforts can create a sign that is even more effective at night than during the day. Any sign should be designed with enough flexibility to allow changes and updates to be done easily.

One point that *must* be remembered: Always check with your local zoning board and research the sign ordinances before ordering a sign. It can be expensive enough to have a sign erected without having an official drop by with a request to remove it.

Another type of sign is the highway sign. It can be a large billboard or a smaller sign alongside a local highway. The billboard is usually too expensive for an apartment complex—too expensive for the results it can generate. Smaller signs, however, can be extremely useful. Commonly known as *directional signs,* these smaller signs can be a help in directing traffic to your location. It's not uncommon for people looking for another property to stop at a complex whose directional signs are clear and effective. Usually these signs are owned by the complex; space is rented or purchased near main travel routes and intersections. The sign should be professionally done, weather resistant, and very clear regarding directions.

Banners and Streamers

Banners are rarely used in the apartment business, for a very good reason. They usually do not fit into the image that you are trying to establish. Banners tend to be cheap looking and should be used, if at all, for initial openings only. Streamers are much like banners; they should be used only at openings or up-gradings when you are trying to convey the idea that what you are offering is new. They do attract attention—especially with a breeze—and can be useful in special situations.

Directories

There are two kinds of directories: the familiar yellow pages and special apartment guides published to help people locate apartments. For the apartment guides, you are usually asked to purchase space. The guide is filled with useful information about the community and distributed free from area motels, restaurants, and other locations. This can be a good buy if the advertising cost is low enough.

Although you rarely gain new prospects from a listing in the yellow pages, such a listing aids in establishing your property in the market. Although a display ad is relatively expensive, it can be a good choice in a very competitive market. You are entitled to a one-line listing in the yellow pages if the complex has a *business* telephone number. For a small extra charge, you can have your ad placed in bold-face type—a good buy.

Brochures

One of the most useful advertising media is the brochure, which may be defined as any printed material about an apartment. The most popular size for a brochure is 8½ by 11 inches (standard letter size), although almost every size imaginable has been successfully used. The letter size will fit into standard envelopes, packets, and racks with ease and usually offers enough space to get your message across. One other advantage is that it's the least expensive size to print.

Like any advertising medium, the brochure must convey features and benefits about your property in a tasteful way. Any image can be produced; professional advice may be needed if you desire a very special image a cut above the competition. Photographs of common areas will say more about your property than any copy. Pools, tennis courts, and other recreational areas can be marketed far more effectively with a photograph. Save the written material for benefits inherent to each apartment (e.g., ice makers, self-cleaning ovens, dishwashers).

Always include a map on a brochure to show your location. Your name, phone number, and address should also appear on any brochure.

Remember to supply every prospect with a brochure. Never let a "looker" leave without taking one—lookers often become buyers later on. They often can influence others to consider your property just by showing them the brochure. People often shop several locations and then sit quietly at home and discuss the advantages and disadvantages of each before making a decision. A good brochure will help them to remember all the advantages of your property.

Shopper Publications

Little research has been done in the area of shopper publications. Our suggestion is to give the medium a try and see what kind of results come from it. Be sure that you use the same guidelines in writing copy that you would use for any newspaper advertisement.

Radio and Television

Normally neither of these two media serve our purpose; they do not reach the specific audience that we want to reach: people searching for a home. They reach too large an audience over too large an area and require too large an outlay from our advertising budgets. In smaller towns with lower air costs, a local radio station may be of considerable help. If the copy is well written, the image of your property may be improved significantly.

Always use radio on weekends; it's much more effective than midweek. Also, use it for the last 2 weeks of the month, not the first 2. People who shop for an apartment usually do so during this last 2-week period.

Magazines

Magazines are very rarely used for apartment advertising. Like TV, they reach too broad an audience.

Flyers

A flyer is a less expensive brochure designed to be distributed in quantity—an announcement medium. These are usually small handouts designed to be spread around in all sorts of places—gasoline stations, laundry facilities, motels, hotels—any high-traffic area. If you decide to use this medium, make sure your flyer is printed rather than mimeographed. Printed flyers look much better and cost only pennies more. Flyers, however, should not be used for high-image properties!

Managers' Cards

Managers' business cards can be very effective in promoting your property. All resident managers should have cards with their name, the name of the property, address, and phone number. If you use a fold-out card you have plenty of room left for a message—a map, if needed, a list of benefits, and so on. Be sure to have the cards designed by a professional and to use a *quality* printer.

Letterhead and Sales Letters

Depending on the type of market you are trying to reach, letterhead stationery can be of tremendous value. If you are oriented toward the top end of the market, *tasteful, well-designed* letterhead stationery distributed to your present residents can be one of the best media available. Every time a resident writes a letter to a friend in town you receive good advertising; advertising to the very group of people that you want to reach—people like your present residents.

Printing letterhead stationery in large quantities costs relatively little and will make a very impressive holiday gift from the management to the residents. This will assist in word-of-mouth advertising. It's a public relations effort on your part that will pay off in better resident relations and, at the same time, presents great promotion possibilities. The same letterhead can be used to develop a sales letter to send to groups of people: newlyweds, companies, professionals. This medium can be extremely useful if well done.

Word of Mouth

In the long run, word of mouth is one of the most powerful advertising media available to anyone. Positive word of mouth can persuade people more effectively to move into your property than any other medium. People believe other people, especially friends, above anything else. If you can make sure your present residents are out there plugging for you, rest assured that you will have a step-up on any competition. Many complexes reward their residents for bringing in their friends by rental reductions, cash, or prizes. Whatever method you choose, if any, make sure that your residents are *for* rather than *against* you.

Apartment-Locating Services

In some regions, especially urban areas, there are firms that specialize in helping people find suitable housing. They operate on a "no charge" basis to the tenant and are paid by the apartment owners. If services of this type are available in your area, make sure that you know each and every one of them. What's more important, make sure that each and every one of them knows you! Sell them on your apartments. The more sold they are on your property, the better they will be able to send their clients to you.

It's hard to overestimate the value of these services to the average apartment complex. Apartment managers usually are only too anxious to cooperate in hard times with apartment-locating services, but they often tend to become less than cooperative when occupancy rates are high. In the long run, it is best to remain on good terms all the time.

OTHER SOURCES OF TENANTS

Professional apartment owners or managers come to know many people in the process of managing their property. The following is only a partial list of persons who may be called on to help in renting:

Personnel Directors of Area Companies

Anyone involved in relocation services for local industries and businesses should be contacted. The professional manager should have a planned program of *personal* calls to meet and develop these contacts. *Sell* your property to these people. Work with them. If they need an apartment for one of their new executives for a month or two, provide it if possible. Bend a little for them and they may help you quite a bit.

Have you ever met a couple who were just going to stay in an apartment a few months while house hunting and, a year later, were still looking? And still renting? It happens!

Many companies have training programs in which they bring several people to town for months at a time. When the first group leaves, a new crew arrives. It may even be possible to rent several units at a time for a long period at higher than normal rates to groups like this. A bit more trouble, but a lot more profitable.

Hotel-Motel Personnel
New people come into town and stay at area motels. If the management has advertising materials available, they can often refer prospects to you. Return the favor by keeping their brochures on hand.

Moving Companies and Neighborhood Merchants
These people should have a personal call from the professional manager. If approached properly, they often can put in a good word for you. It may be possible to work out advertising deals with local merchants so that you distribute special promotions from them to your residents. If merchants are properly selected image-wise, the relationship can add to the image of your property.

Military Base Personnel
If your properties are near military reservations or bases, it's wise to meet the base officer in charge of housing. Many times off-base housing is required, and if you have built up a good relationship with the housing officer, you may get more than your share of the business. You need a "military" lease for this. It is simply a conventional lease that allows lessees to break the lease with no penalty if their orders move them from the city. A reasonable enough provision.

Proper use of the various media in your particular situation depends on knowing how well they perform for you. You should always find out how well each ad works by asking all persons that come to you how they found out about your apartments. Keep tabs on the answers. They tell you how well you are spending your advertising budget.

"SELLING" THE PROPERTY

Provided you use good copy in effective media, you will cause a prospect either to visit your property or to call for more information. A phone call is your chance to "sell" the prospect, not on your apartment but on a *visit* to your property. Rarely, if ever, will you rent an apartment over the phone. You must convince prospects to visit your property and, in the process, gain some information concerning their needs. The Bell Telephone Company has developed a set of helpful hints for conducting business over the telephone:

1. *Be alert.* Do not act sleepy or uninterested.
2. *Be pleasant.* No grumpy "Hello, who is this?" *Smile*—it will show up in your voice.
3. *Be natural.* Use normal words—no slang or technical terms.
4. *Be expressive.* Don't speak in a monotone; vary the pitch and volume of your speech.
5. *Be distinct.* Try not to slur words or speak with too much of an accent.
6. *Be polite.* "Please," "thank you," "you are welcome," and so on. Even if a prospect declines a visit, end the conversation on a polite note: "Thank you for calling."

Always answer the phone with the name of your apartments and your name. For example, "Good morning, Old Town Apartments, Bill Weaver speaking." If you end this greeting with a rising inflection in your voice, it will almost always generate a very positive response. You have given the caller information he or she needs: the name of your apartment house and your name. You will find it easy, now, to ask his name. Ask it.

Always have paper, pencils, a map, and your latest advertisement control form by your phone. Write callers' names down, and as the conversation develops, jot down any additional information about them that you get: where they are from, names of children, who is the employer—anything; you might even have a small pad preprinted with a short form.

Selling

Once you have the prospect at your property, you have the opportunity to go to work. All our discussion up until now has been geared toward getting you ready: knowing your product, learning about your competition, learning about the community and the media. Now it's selling time! But how do you "sell" an apartment? Answer: You don't. An apartment should "sell" itself—with a little help from you.

First, sit down and list *every* feature of your property: pools, tennis, laundry facilities, putting greens, barbecues, children's play areas, adult play areas (e.g., bar), parking spaces per unit, landscaping, decor, size of rooms, number and size of closets, any extra storage outside or inside, kitchen equipment—*everything*!

After examining each feature, place a +, a 0, or a − beside each, or use the instructions and form shown in Fig. 5-1. In short, is this feature

FEATURES

Instructions

Place a heavy dot under the appropriate +, 0, or – beside each feature. Place a dot in the plus column when you have a feature that most of your competition does not have, place a dot in the minus column when your competition has a feature that you do not have, and put a dot in the neutral (0) column when both you and your competition have the same feature. Once you have finished, add up the pluses and the minuses to see your relationship to competition. You may want to complete one of these forms for *each* major competitor. This will give you a very firm idea of where you stand compared to the competition. Be honest—this information must be known before you can do a good selling job. It may also be helpful if you plan on making your property more competitive. A few changes can make a substantial difference, and this method will help identify the changes that need to be made.

For a really effective comparison of your property with your few (usually under 10) strong competitors, prepare one analysis form for each. Put your score in red and your competitor's score in black on each form. Take a ruler and connect all the red dots and then all the black dots. You will then have a profile of your complex and a single competitor. Once you do this for each competitor, you can do one more form to represent an average of all the competition.

With these data, you can analyze your property in comparison with any single strong, competitive unit. The last step, averaging each of the separate analyses into one competitive profile and comparing it to yours, reveals your strengths and weaknesses. It's then up to you to emphasize the strong points and make them stronger. It's also useful for deciding (on a cost-effective basis) if it would be worthwhile to upgrade the property and in just what area to make it more competitive.

Form 11

Feature	+	0	–
Pool			
Private patio, balcony, or terrace			
Tennis court			
Laundry facilities			
Enclosed garage			
Maid service			
Putting greens			
Dressing rooms for pool			
Air conditioning			
FM music system			
Switchboard			
Elevators			

Figure 5-1 Listing the features of your property.

Barbecues			
Children's play areas			
Baby-sitting service			
Child development center			
Refrigerator (+ for large; − for small)			
Stove (+ for deluxe, − for less than average)			
Dishwasher			
Garbage disposal			
Trash compactor			
Game room for adults			
Recreation room (e.g., bar)			
Exercise room			
Saunas			
Open-beam construction			
Carpets			
Closets (+ for larger than average, − for smaller)			
Bedrooms			
Living rooms			
Dining rooms			
Kitchen			
Built-in TV antenna cable			
Double entrance			
Private storage			
Security patrol			
Others:			

Figure 5-1 *(Continued)*

better than, less than, or equal to what your competition has to offer? By looking down this list and adding up the pluses, minuses, and neutrals, you can get a quick idea of how your property compares with its competition.

Once you have a really complete list of your features, the next step is to develop a series of benefits associated with each feature. Benefits, as you remember, are expansions of features. For example, an ice maker is a feature, the benefits of which may be stated as follows: (1) Plenty of ice for parties, (2) Never buy ice for home made ice cream—make your own, or (3) Ice always available with no messy breaking of cubes out of

BENEFITS

Feature: ______________________________

Benefit 1. ______________________________
____
____

Benefit 2. ______________________________
____
____

Benefit 3. ______________________________
____
____

Feature: ______________________________

Benefit 1. ______________________________
____
____

Benefit 2. ______________________________
____
____

Benefit 3. ______________________________
____
____

Figure 5-2 Listing the benefits of each feature.

ice trays. You should additionally expand each benefit by telling just what the benefit will mean to the prospect. Use the sample form in Fig. 5-2 to come up with several (at least three) benefits for each feature. Know these benefits, and use them in describing your property.

While there are always some good features to expand on, there usually are some bad ones as well. You *must* be able to play down the negative features just as well as or better than you sell the good ones. List your "bad" features just as you did the positive ones and think of at least three logical ways of handling questions about each. It is vital to anticipate tough questions and have a ready answer.

How you minimize your negative features is critical. Try to turn a negative into a positive: "No, Mr. Prospect, we do not have townhouses. All of our apartments are designed without steep stairs. No stairs to climb a dozen times a day and no worry about falling."

Closing

While there are many different closing methods, perhaps one of the most effective and easiest is to assume the sale is made. Once you have shown the grounds and the model, pick up a copy of your lease, hand it to your prospect, and say, "Why don't you look this over while I get the application form filled out?" If you say it as if it were commonplace, in a casual, low-keyed way, it will work wonderfully well.

This method is a low-key, high-pressure close! It is low key because the prospect does not feel that you are pressuring him or her, but high pressure in that you are forcing the prospect to decide one way or another. If he says nothing, continue with your personal-data questions and have him sign the lease. If he objects, act surprised and ask what the problem is. The prospect will then come up with an objection—a reason for not renting. If it is an easy objection, such as one arising out of a misunderstanding or from a fact that you failed to discuss, answer it directly and return to the close. If it is a difficult objection, try to minimize it by stating some advantages that offset the objection and then return to the close. If your prospect comes up with several objections, handle them all in this way, always returning to the close. Eventually his or her real reason for not renting will surface. If you are able to recognize the fact that it is a really important objection, concentrate especially hard on your answer. Recap the features and benefits that seemed to appeal to your prospect and go on to close in the same manner.

QUALIFICATIONS FOR TENANTS

Once a prospect is sold, there is but one last step—that of processing his or her application. You've never heard of an application . . . you've always filled out the lease right on the spot? How much money has your property lost due to poor tenant selection, including money lost directly due to unpaid rents and money lost indirectly due to legal fees and time spent? Tenant selection is as important to profits as is the sales process or more so. It does not do much good to fill up your property and go around evicting people right and left for one reason or another. Not only is it costly in terms of money, it is costly to your image. It is *far better* to concentrate on selecting responsible people to start with.

The tenant selection process is a three-stage effort: (1) A prospective resident signs the lease (you don't), fills out a personal credit and data form, pays a deposit, and receives a receipt; (2) you or a credit agency checks out the person's background as thoroughly as possible; (3) you notify the prospective resident whether or not she is accepted and give her either a signed lease or the deposit back.

In following these steps you are, first of all, using your lease as a closing tool. You hand the prospect the lease and ask her to read it while you fill out a rental application. You should have a printed lease that looks professional and is legally correct. As you might surmise, the lease should be tight and binding. Also, it's much better for the lessee and lessor to sit down together and go over each section carefully than to have to hire a lawyer later to take care of a misunderstanding that was caused by either a weak form or your failure to cover something that should have been covered at the time the lease was signed.

While the prospect is looking over the lease, you should be filling out the tenant information sheet. You can fill out the prospect's name, last address, bank, employer, and so on. Just go down the form asking questions and printing the answers. Once you have completed the form, hand it to the prospect and let him or her verify the correctness of the data and sign it. While he is involved in this, you can proceed to fill out the lease itself. After completing the lease, go over each basic item entered by hand and explain just what is there and why. Then go over each section of the lease. Explain in plain terms what the lease says. Hand the prospect the lease and a pen and shut up! Don't talk at all until he either signs or asks a question. Answer the question and again shut up. This approach forces prospects to make a decision; if you approach this closing technique with confidence, it will be successful 90 percent of the time.

When your new residents sign the lease, give them a receipt for the deposit and whatever prorated rental is agreed on. Be sure to ask them to write on the check: "For $______ deposit on apartment #______ and for prorated rental from ______ to ______." Tell them that this is the best receipt possible once you have cashed their check.

Once you have a signed lease—signed by both husband and wife or all adults who will live there—a properly completed application form, and a deposit check, you may proceed to check on the applicant.

Your credit and "behavioral pattern" check is the most important step in the process. This is when you weed the undesirable out—not via an eviction suit. There are basically two methods: Do it yourself or have it done. You may want to investigate the local credit agencies to see if they can furnish the information that you require. You not only need some idea of your prospective tenants' credit-worthiness, but also you want to know of their past behavior. If an agency can supply all the data you need to make a decision, it may be less expensive in the long run to hire one to do the job. If the credit agencies either can't do the job or are not available, the job falls on you. You can use the following list as a guide:

1. You need to know what debts are outstanding. Can your prospective tenant afford to pay you rent in addition to other debts?

2. Look at the sources of income. Are all parties employed? Where? Can you verify employment? Are their jobs short term or long term? How long have they been employed there? What is the gross income?
3. Check bank references. What kind of account do they have (checking and savings)? Have they ever had insufficient funds to cover a check? What is the average balance in the account?
4. Look at where they are living now and where they lived before that. A previous manager may give a more accurate report of their behavior than the present one.
5. Check out their personal references. Who are they? What kind of people?

Caution—never use this behavioral/credit check to discriminate against any minority group, no matter how easy it appears to be to do so. If you are going to use this resident selection concept at all, it *must* be applied across the board. You should have a definite list of requirements to be met. You may want to attach a small form to each receipt given to a prospective resident saying: All applications will be checked and may not be accepted for the following reasons:

1. No job
2. Job less than one year
3. Income less than four times monthly rent
4. More than four in the family
5. Poor credit report
6. No credit at all
7. Incorrect information on application
8. Poor references

This is just a sample list; you can make your own up. The thing to remember is that you must treat everyone alike. If you turn away one family due to a poor credit rating, you must turn away all those who have poor credit ratings.

Realistically, it is a value judgment on your part when you consider a rating poor. With a systematic approach, however (keeping records on *everyone*), if and when you have a discussion with the Department of Housing and Urban Development (HUD) or other agencies, you will have documentation that you follow the open housing law to the letter.

The last step in the tenant selection process is the ratification of acceptance or rejection. This should be via a form letter. You can write a simple note saying that all the paper work has been completed and the application for apartment #______ has been approved. In the letter you should mention the date the tenants are to take occupancy, the amount they have paid as a deposit, and the rent and its due date. In rejecting an application you must protect yourself from legal action if at all possible. The form letter should be short and to the point:

> Dear ______________,
> The information we have obtained does not qualify you for tenancy in our units at this time. We are enclosing your deposit, which was made by your check #__________, dated __________, in the amount of __________.

Don't include the reason unless the applicant requests it. If possible, discuss reasons in person rather than in writing.

Two points to remember in the resident selection process: Keep copies of *everything*, and keep all information *confidential*. Never give out specifics about a prospective resident to anyone. For that matter, never give out specifics about a present resident to anyone. If someone (a credit bureau, for example) inquires about a resident, present or past, give only general details: Tell the agency that the person either has or has not lived up to the lease agreement. Don't give specific details.

RENT CONTROL

Rent control is one of those issues that tends to evoke the fiercest of emotions—both positive and negative. Generally, tenant-oriented people tend to be positive about rent control, and owners or owners' agents tend to think of it as a negative influence.

From a purely economic point of view, most economists would probably agree that rent control has negative long-term effects. New York City has had rent control, in some form or another, since World War II. National rent controls expired in 1946, but the state of New York continued a modified system until 1962. When the state got out of the rent control business, the city of New York again modified the system; it was turned back to the state in 1984. Most observers of the New York experience feel that, in the long run, rent control has resulted in shortages of rental housing, poor maintenance, and generally inequitable treatment for tenants. A mayor of New York City, Edward Koch, remained in his private apartment for awhile rather than live in the official mayoral residence for fear of losing his rent-controlled apartment!

But what does rent control mean to the property manager? If you manage property in a rent-controlled area (parts of Boston, and Berkeley, Santa Monica, Los Angeles, Davis, and Beverly Hills in California, for example), you don't really have much choice. The local rules prevail.

These vary as to place and you must carefully read and come to understand all the regulations.

Generally, most systems provide for controlled increases in rent: increases tied, for the most part, to some index such as the Consumer Price Index (CPI). As the index increases, landlords may increase the rent, either on a one-for-one basis or using some percentage of the increase. Each local system varies somewhat.

Some communities allow new residential properties to be excluded from the system. Others only exclude properties with rents above a certain level. If you are in a rent-controlled area, *be certain* to follow the local guidelines; some communities have severe penalties for failing to comply.

If you own rental property in an area that is considering rent control, it will be to your long-term advantage to help educate tenants about its long-term negative effects. These effects include a general lowering of quality of rental stock, reductions in construction of new rental housing stock, difficulty in finding vacant units (demand often exceeds supply), and ultimately, urban blight. Also, since investors generally avoid investing in rent-controlled areas (even building non-rent-controlled buildings for fear that they may come under future rent control laws), resale values are usually depressed. Your property does not appreciate as fast as it otherwise might—another incentive for you to take the time and effort to fight against new rent-control legislation.

SINGLE-FAMILY HOUSES

The similarities in renting single-family homes and apartments are far greater than the differences. With both markets you should target your potential audience (tenants), and plan your marketing campaign accordingly. However, marketing the single-family home is different with respect to tenant selection.

As you might imagine, you must be *extremely* careful in selecting tenants for single-family houses. The typical apartment unit may cost $20,000 to $60,000, but it's rare to find a single-family house within that price range. Since you are renting a more expensive unit, the risk of loss due to tenant damage is higher. Credit and, more important, behavioral checks are critical.

The same suggestions provided previously for these processes apply to the single-family market. However, greater care must be taken when deciding on families. (You can count on children when you rent a single-family house.) The family with several small children can produce greater wear and tear than expected; balance this with greater security/

damage deposits. If you allow pets, be certain to collect a *nonrefundable* pet deposit large enough to pay for, at a minimum, carpet cleaning and deodorizing and pest control both inside and out (e.g., fleas, ticks). You may run into additional expense if the pet damages the carpets, which is not unusual, or the structure. I recall a property in New Orleans that I managed with a puppy—a sheepdog, if I remember correctly. It went through the teething process using the wooden trim on every windowsill in the place! It cost about $600 to repair and repaint all the windows; needless to say, the pet deposit did not cover this expense!

Just as in apartment rental, be certain to include in the lease the right to inspect the property. You want to be able to inspect all properties periodically to make certain that your tenants are taking care of them. Be sure to include in the lease the same clause concerning number of occupants that you have in your apartment leases. It's not unusual for single-family rentals to attract groups of nonrelated adults, especially in university towns! The best way to control this is to insist that *all* persons who will live in the house sign the lease. If the lease limits the number and time period that "visitors" may stay, you have some control over "commune-style" tenants.

CONCLUSIONS

We have discussed the very basics of what is necessary to market rental property successfully. You must know not only your own property and surrounding community but your competitors' property as well. Once you have this basic knowledge, you can start developing a profile or "picture" of the ideal resident. The more you know about this "person," the more effective your marketing efforts can be. This is called *segmenting* the market: deciding on a certain type of person and "going after them." It's important to know your "target" market so that you can correctly orient your advertising with the rest of the marketing effort. This is of prime importance in new complex development and design. Pick a target market, design the amenities just for the segment, and prerent 90 percent of your units!

The discussion of advertising media touched on a few practical points to remember about the various media. Make certain that your use of media matches your resident profile. That is, be sure that you advertise in places that are most likely to reach the type of person you want as a resident.

Finally, have a good, legally binding lease written, explain it *thoroughly* to your residents, and *live by it*!

CHAPTER 6

Leasing and managing commercial and office buildings

Joseph W. DeCarlo, CPM
J. D. Property Management Company
Costa Mesa, California

This chapter gives the reader a nuts and bolts overview of commercial property management: a subject of such complexity a detailed discussion would require a whole book.

Laws and regulations vary from city to city and state to state. These same laws and regulations are constantly being modified and changed. Readers should, therefore, use this chapter as a beginning reference and obtain legal counsel to provide up-to-date interpretations of laws and regulations in their local community for commercial real estate.

Our definition of property management is "a professional approach to operate property in such a manner as to maximize net operating income (NOI) while increasing appreciation." The two goals inherent in this definition, maximizing NOI and increasing appreciation, do not necessarily go hand in hand. For instance, while deferred maintenance will increase income, it is a detriment to the value and appreciation of the property.

Good property managers, in order to fulfill their defined obligation, will increase the NOI and enhance appreciation through astute lease negotiation, maintenance programs, and financial controls. Specifics are discussed later in this chapter.

HISTORICAL PERSPECTIVE

The field of real estate management is both evolving and rapidly changing. To understand future trends better, we need to examine the evolution of commercial real estate management. During colonial times, the development of American cities tended to occur at seaports and on major waterways. The primary reason for this was the ease of shipment of goods. The early cities, such as Boston, New York, and Philadelphia, had downtown (public square) areas which served as both trading and shopping areas. During the 1800s, the American population grew and cities expanded. Office and commercial buildings were attracted to these developing downtown areas.

In the early 1900s significant changes were beginning to take place. The advent of the automobile allowed both businesspersons and consumers to start to move away from the now congested downtown area. Technologic building advancements, such as steel-framed buildings and elevators, allowed taller buildings and increased the density of commercial areas. In turn, a trend away from single-family homes to multifamily apartment buildings allowed residential population density to increase.

After World War II, returning soldiers were aided by Veterans Administration (VA) and Federal Housing Administration (FHA) loans to buy their own homes. Many of these new homes were located in suburbia. Following the population migration, developers built offices and shopping centers convenient to the suburban population. In suburbia, shopping centers at first tended to be small and convenience oriented, tenanted by small retailers and grocers. As the population continued to migrate from the city to the suburbs in the 1960s and 1970s, so did commercial developers. Larger centers were built, incorporating the traditional downtown stores which offered one-stop shopping, free parking, and climate-controlled malls. The postwar baby boomers also helped fuel this tremendous growth, providing many retail and office employers to work in suburbia.

Future trends may again reverse this migration pattern. Many areas of the country are now saturated with large shopping centers, and those presently being built are frequently smaller in size. The population in some areas has begun to show a trend toward smaller sized families who are moving back to the cities. We also see an increase in shopping centers in areas which were initially passed over. Specialty centers in the cities, such as Ghirardelli Square in San Francisco, a factory rehabilitated into a specialty shopping mart, are being developed. Present suburban centers are being "recycled" and rehabilitated to increase their customer appeal. New facades and high-traffic businesses (florists, coffee shops) are being developed on previously unused corners of shopping center parking lots.

The property manager must keep abreast of changing demographics—locations, sizes of families, and ages—as well as consumer buying habits. America is changing from a nation that produces a product to one that provides services. By 1990 80 percent of our population will be engaged in providing services. It is projected that by the year 2030, only 5 percent of the population will be engaged in manufacturing. This means less industrial building growth and more office building development. Living in a nation with a population of more than 225 million people and an area of greater than 3.6 million square miles, we must be cognizant of regional conditions, needs, and trends that differ from the national norm.

PROFESSIONAL PROPERTY MANAGEMENT

The title *professional property manager* has been misused and abused for many years. There is no college degree offered in this area, but there are several professional designations. The three types we will discuss are certified property manager (CPM), certified shopping center manager (CSM), and real property administrator (RPA).

The first designation, CPM, is conferred by the Institute of Real Estate Management (IREM), a branch of the National Association of Realtors. To earn the designation, the candidate must complete three courses and pass an examination following each course. The candidate must also have 5 years experience (reduced to 3 if supervised by a CPM) managing at least 300 apartment units, 120,000 square feet of office space, or 150,000 square feet of retail space. The candidate must also write a long-range management plan, usually 100 pages or more in length. More information and additional CPM designation criteria can be obtained by writing to:

Institute of Real Estate Management
430 N. Michigan Avenue
Chicago, IL 60611

The International Council of Shopping Centers bestows the CSM designation. The requirements include experience of 4 years plus a passing score on a written examination. There are no required courses, but two courses are available to help prepare for the examination. Regarding actual management, there is no minimum square footage requirement. Additional information can be obtained by writing to:

International Council of Shopping Centers
665 Fifth Avenue
New York, NY 10022

The RPA is issued by the Building Owners Management Association (BOMA). The RPA designation does not set minimum experience levels or a square footage requirement. The candidate must, however, successfully complete a seven-course program to receive the RPA designation. Additional information can be obtained by contacting:

BOMA International
1250 Eye Street, N.W.
Washington, DC 20005

THE MANAGEMENT PLAN

One of the most important property management tools is the management plan. It establishes property management objectives and outlines the means of attaining these objectives. It is important that owners, partners, management agents, and on-site managers understand and agree on the plan. A detailed analysis of a management plan is contained in chapter 4 of *Principles of Real Estate Management*, by James C. Downs, Jr.

A basic overview of the management plan is as follows:

1. *Regional analysis.* Are growth factors positive?
2. *Neighborhood analysis.* Examine the neighborhood population growth and income levels (available through census figures). Are these factors increasing?
3. *Subject analysis*
    a. *Physical condition.* Is any functional obsolescence present?
    b. *Management level.* How is property presently being managed?
    c. *Financial condition.* Examine expenses and income.
4. *Market analysis.* What are leasing rates and vacancy rates within the trade or competition areas and submarkets?

5. *Recommended plan*
   a. Proposed physical renovations and budget for cost of improvements.
   b. Management—new systems to be implemented and changes in staff.
   c. Financial—discounted cash-flow analysis.
6. *Financing*
   a. Internal—by present owner.
   b. External—by outside financial sources.
7. *Evaluation*
   a. Present market value.
   b. Estimated future market value.
8. *Summary and recommendation*

   After implementation, the management plan should be reviewed at least on a quarterly basis and revised on an annual basis. It is important that all the persons affected by the plan be involved in its formulation if the plan is to be successful. The management plan is the yardstick or reference point for measuring performance.

ON-SITE MANAGEMENT

Whether or not on-site management is used will depend on the size of the facility. A regional shopping center, for example, would entail both an on-site manager and a leasing agent. A neighborhood center would use off-site management and leasing, either by the owner or by an independent management company. In many cases the owner will appoint one tenant as a "quasi-manager" to call the plumber or electrician if a problem in the common area arises. (As most leases are "net," tenants usually handle their own repairs within their suite or store.) Some owners use their janitorial contractors as their eyes and ears to report potential problems. There should, however, always be an emergency number posted so that the tenants, fire department, police department, and so on, can call if the need arises. A 24-hour answering service can screen the calls and contact you only in the event of a true emergency.

SELECTION OF A PROPERTY-MANAGEMENT COMPANY

If an outside company is to be used for property management, the question often asked is, "How do we select that company?" Since the management firm will be entrusted with several thousand dollars in rent collections each month, it is prudent to inquire carefully before selecting a firm. Some questions which should be asked include:

What is the company's size?

How long has it been in business?

Is it bonded?

Do the managers have a real estate license (essential in California)?

Is the company involved primarily in property management or real estate sales?

Does it have a trust account?

Just as there are different types of properties, management companies have expertise in specific types of properties. For example, a management company that specializes in residential units would be a poor selection to manage a medical building. When selecting a management company, ask for a written proposal providing information about fees, who has responsibility for hiring and training on-site resident managers, payment of bills, leasing proposals, inspection frequency, and supervision criteria; ask also for a copy of the management agreement, references, and a history of the firm. Visit the management company's office and meet the people who will be in charge of your property. Do their executive managers have a CPM designation? Ask to see a sample of the monthly financial statement you will receive.

In summary, the property manager should bring diversified talents, experience, controls, and computer reporting systems all in one package to help the property perform to its maximum potential. According to an old cliché, the owner should benefit: "Property management doesn't cost—it pays."

REPORTS TO OWNERS

Depending on the degree of sophistication and detail required, reports for commercial property management vary but usually include:

Net income and expenses—generated monthly with year-to-year totals

Check register—showing to whom each check is drawn and the amount

Rent roll—listing the amount of rent actually collected from each tenant with corresponding "paid-to" dates

Bills—copies of the actual invoices for the month

Other reports include periodic leasing, vacancy, delinquency, and budget comparison summaries, with variances from the management plan explained.

When the management entity is an outside firm or a partnership, a trust account is usually required for deposit of rent collections. If accounting is computerized with adequate account balance controls, a separate checking account is not needed for each owner. Each owner must, however, receive separate accounting reports. Never may owner's funds be "commingled," that is, one owner allowed to have a negative balance, thus using other owners' funds. Sophisticated property management computer systems which run a general ledger can provide this accounting on a daily basis.

TENANT SELECTION

In our analysis of tenant selection, we consider credit-screening methods, leasing techniques, advertising, promotional perks, and on-site leasing agents.

When dealing with major tenants, a Dun & Bradstreet report and rating should be obtained. Contact their vendors and other landlords to check on their payment record. Ask for copies of their latest financial statements and review them carefully with your CPA.

When dealing with smaller "ma and pa" merchants and businesses that are not rated, the task is more difficult. With smaller tenants, concentrate more on the individual rather than the business, running credit reports on the principals. As with larger firms, contact their bank and talk to their bank branch manager. In many instances, when the small entity is a corporation, we require the principals to sign a personal guarantee as individuals as well as corporate officers. A conscientious effort by the owner or manager in tenant selection will save considerable time, money, expense, and aggravation at a later date. As a word of caution, many states have privacy laws making it necessary to obtain written permission from the prospective tenant before starting credit-checking procedures.

ADVERTISING AND PROMOTIONAL TECHNIQUES

For you to obtain tenants, prospective renters must be made aware of your building. Create a favorable image by tying in desirable features of your complex to your promotion efforts. For example, newer office buildings are being built with courtyards or small lakes in the common area. Your building name, "The Lakes Medical Building," will draw attention to this desirable feature.

Promotional techniques, called "perks," take forms beyond the well-used free month's rent. Prestigious buildings may, for example, capitalize on today's health consciousness by offering a small in-building gym or membership in a local health center to their tenants' executives.

The point to remember is that cost alone is not always the deciding factor in a tenant's location selection. Target your potential market and think of creative ways to entice that market to your facility and away from your competition.

Some specific advertising techniques include:

Newspaper advertising. Advertisements should be placed in a paper that businesspeople read. *The Wall Street Journal,* for example, has editions for different parts of the country.

Brochures. These should create desire and identify the building's location, amenities, access to transportation, and safety or security features, as well as contain photographs of the building.

Direct mail. After identifying prospective tenants and using the local yellow pages for their addresses, a word processor can be used to send individual letters to members of the specific market you want to attract. This can be your most effective tool if you properly select your targeted markets.

Other media. Radio and television are expensive and usually not as effective as the printed media. Local business magazines are a good means of placing institutional advertisements to draw attention to your complex. Select a magazine specifically geared toward your targeted market. For example, if you have a medical building you might consider advertising in a local medical association magazine.

Publicity. Grand openings and open houses for potential tenants (influential businesspeople such as bankers, attorneys, and real estate agents) are effective. It is also advantageous to involve the local mayor or other dignitaries in ribbon-cutting ceremonies to get free newspaper coverage of your event.

Perks. Items such as free rent for a month, extra tenant improvements (TI's), free parking, tenant amenities such as gyms, and secretarial services are excellent tenant motivators.

Signage. Visible signs should be on the building for identification including a phone number. Every building should have a name (e.g., "The Lakes Medical Building").

SHOPPING CENTERS

In this section we present practical discussions of center size and characteristics, types of leases, tenant mix, merchant associations, common area maintenance, and general legal issues.

Shopping centers are normally categorized into six types by size:

Strip centers are small in size, consisting of two to fifteen stores. Usually they include 24-hour convenience stores, and the trading area depends on location.

Neighborhood centers are 25,000 to 125,000 square feet in size, and normally consist of at least one anchor tenant (a large food or discount store). The trading area is only within a 1½- to 2-mile radius.

Community centers are 125,000 to 300,000 square feet in size and contain more than one anchor. Types of stores include hardware, junior department, home furnishing, and discount. The trading area encompasses up to a 3-mile radius.

Regional centers are up to 800,000 square feet in size. They contain department stores, specialty apparel stores, jewelry stores, and the like, and often are in an enclosed mall. Their trading area is within a 7- to 10-mile radius.

Super regional centers are 1,000,000 square feet in size or larger. Usually they are in enclosed malls and have several anchor department stores and an assortment of specialty shops, plus clothing stores, shoe stores, and so on. They usually contain several restaurants. Some super regional centers house community libraries and music and cultural centers to attract shoppers to the center. The trading area can be within a radius of 15 or more miles.

Specialty centers vary in size up to 80,000 square feet and have no anchor tenants. Usually located near high-income areas and major tourist-attraction centers, they contain unique stores and, frequently, theme restaurants.

The trading areas given in these descriptions are for metropolitan areas. In outlying regions, a community center may fulfill the shopping needs of a 300-square-mile area or greater.

TYPES OF LEASES

There are three basic types of leases:

Gross lease. The tenant pays a set monthly rental sum which includes taxes, maintenance, insurance, utilities, and so on in the gross figure.

Net lease. The tenant pays a minimal rental rate and pays extra for taxes, insurance, common area maintenance, and utilities. A *triple net lease* is one in which the tenant pays all the extra costs.

Percentage of sales. The tenant pays a minimal rent or a percentage of his or her total sales each month. Most leases are written so that the tenant always pays the higher amount.

Commercial property rent is usually paid in advance, except in the case of percentage rent. Shopping center and restaurant building owners frequently favor percentage rents as they tend to increase faster as the result of good merchandising and inflation. Caution must be used when writing a percentage lease: The tenant must be a good merchandiser with a growing business. Most gross and net leases, or modifications of gross and net leases, have escalation clauses. The consumer price index (CPI) and minimum and maximum increases are frequently cited.

Lease terms are as hotly negotiated as the basic rental rate. The savvy tenant will try to negotiate out acceleration and cost of living clauses as quickly as the center owner trys to get them in. Shorter term leases are most beneficial to the center, especially for the ma and pa tenants who usually pay the highest rent per square foot. These tenants are usually not on percentage leases or, if they are, frequently fail to reach the percentage "break point." Unless conscientious attention to inflation guards is given on long-term leases, owners may find themselves in an untenable situation of below market rents. One center for which we took over management had 20-year-old leases at twelve cents per square foot per month with additional options at the existing scheduled rent. Market rent in the area was one dollar per square foot per month.

Concessions in term length are usually given major anchor tenants because of their benefit to center traffic. Again, however, the lease should be loaded with "catch up" clauses allowing the center to maintain a fair market rent. Options, when given, should be at the current market rent.

When purchasing a commercial property, it is always prudent to look beyond the presently scheduled rental income to the lease itself. Does it have provisions for future rental increases? Will those increases at least match the rate of inflation? Another serious consideration is the schedule of expirations. A new center may find itself faced with many vacancies at rollover of the first leases if all were scheduled to expire in 5 years. A scattering of lease due dates among the first tenants will avoid this problem.

ON-SITE LEASING AGENTS

The need for an on-site leasing agent depends on the size of the center and its vacancy level. For a new, vacant 100,000-square-foot shopping center, an on-site leasing agent is desirable. If the center is 95 percent full after 1 year, however, leasing can be handled from a main leasing office.

There is no pat answer as to whether it is appropriate for the leasing agent and manager to be from the same or different companies. Circumstances and conditions can point to different conclusions. Since property managers have to live with the end results of leasing, they are able to see long-term implications of leasing endeavors. They may be a little more diligent in ensuring good long-term results from those endeavors. A leasing agent who steps out when the commission is paid may not have the same incentive.

Another consideration is whether the leasing agent should be from a large national firm or a smaller local firm. Many owners have found compromise to be the best solution: A large firm is retained to solicit the major anchor tenants with whom the national agents have contact, and a smaller firm is used to solicit the local incubator (ma and pa) tenants. While the larger leasing agents may not be as diligent regarding these smaller tenants (for whom there is a smaller commission), the ma and pa placements will be an important part of the smaller agents' portfolio and they will be given high priority in their marketing program. Regardless of what size firm is used, the individual agent, not the company, usually determines the success or failure of the leasing program.

LEASING TECHNIQUES

Many leasing techniques have been discussed in the section on advertising and promotion; some additional methods involve use of cold call and telephone canvassing, model offices, space layout, special rental rates or lease terms, status tenants, and lease renewal programs.

Canvassing

One of the most effective, but most difficult and discouraging, techniques is cold canvassing of potential users by telephone and personal visits. It is discouraging because the "turn down" ratio is high, but it is effective because tenants are obtained who might otherwise not be reached. Because the tenant may not be looking, you look for the tenant. Again, emphasis must be placed on targeting your market, limiting your intense efforts to areas from which you are most likely to gain results.

For example, our firm was able to attract two desirable merchants to our smaller center from a nearby shopping center undergoing extensive remodeling. Our cold call canvassing identified the merchants, long established in their trade area, as potential tenants. Until we contacted them, they were not in the market for a new location. Rather, they were just fretting about their present situation and, from their point of view, unnecessary changes. We created the market by showing the tenants the potential for less downtime and lower rents in moving to our center.

Model Offices and Space Layout

In newer office buildings and medical buildings, a project's potential is frequently enhanced through the use of model suites. The model helps potential tenants to visualize their business or practice in the building. Having an architect or space planner available to work with a prospective tenant is an additional aid in leasing. While lower rental rates are always an attraction to tenants, professional advice on how to maximize use of the square footage leased frequently overcomes objections to a higher rental rate. Tenants, for the most part, do not budget dollars per square foot; they budget a set figure per month for rent. If their needs are filled through correct space utilization, the 50 or 500 square feet they are not taking means little to them. What matters is the end dollar figure.

Special Rental Rates

Although we have just discussed a method by which a higher rental rate can be obtained through proper space planning, lower rental rates remain a very viable selling point, especially in older, already improved facilities. One method of maintaining a higher rental figure for such buildings is through provision of free rent for a period of time. Tenants may be willing to pay higher figures if they receive free rent for an initial period in the lease. While the rent may average out to be the same after a while, the period of free rent allows tenants a break at the beginning when their start-up costs are being expended. The owner has the advantage of a higher scheduled rent with its ensuing effect on future market value. A word of caution: Rents for a new tenant should never be lower than those for existing tenants unless you are willing to take the serious discord and potential vacancies which will occur when your present tenants find out.

Lease Terms

Owners should consider that tenants don't look only at the quoted rental rate to make their decision. They consider lease terms such as cost pass-through clauses and options to renew. These conditions seriously affect marketability and can be used as incentive perks in the leasing of property. A successful leasing agent will find ways to satisfy the tenant's needs rather than simply quoting a cost and showing a vacant space.

Status Tenants

Another very effective leasing technique is securing a "status" tenant. Commonly used when obtaining anchor tenants in shopping centers, a status tenant will draw other tenants to an office or medical building. For example, offering a "deal which can't be refused" to a local prestigious law firm will draw smaller, less prestigious firms who wish to share the status identity and the limelight by being in the same building.

In a medical building, concessions to family practitioners and pediatricians pay off in increased leasing to the specialists who hope to obtain referrals from the general practitioners.

Lease Renewal

The last, but probably most effective, leasing technique is the retention of your existing tenants. Constant attention to the success and contentment of existing tenants through good management is the best method of tenant retention. Remember, your building's success is directly related to your tenant's success—your tenants are, after all, your customers. Acting accordingly throughout the lease term will greatly increase your percentage of renewals.

PARKING AND ZONING

As part of the management game plan, a prudent owner or manager checks with the local municipality regarding parking, zoning, and use restrictions before purchasing the property. Failing to establish a written management plan which considers local ordinances such as parking requirements, novice owners may find themselves with a tenant mix requiring more parking than they can provide. Parking codes vary from city to city. An example of a code follows:

Medical: six spaces per 1000 square feet.

Office and retail: four spaces per 1000 square feet.

Furniture store: two spaces per 1000 square feet.

Restaurant: ten spaces per 1000 square feet for the first 3000 square feet.

As can be seen from the above chart, too many restaurants in a center could easily result in a parking shortage. As a planning commissioner, I witnessed a case in which an owner, not doing his homework, used up his entire parking allocation with 5000 square feet left to lease. Consequently, a prospective tenant was not able to secure a business license. The owner had to rent the remaining space at a lower rental rate to a less desirable tenant who did not require as much parking.

Managers should also check the types of businesses the city will allow in the zoning for their center. It is embarrassing and could be costly to lease to a prohibited user.

DESIRABLE TENANTS

High-traffic tenants are usually the most desirable to a shopping center, although they must blend into the total tenant mix plan. These tenants frequently can be put on percentage leases, which are usually the most desirable for the owner if the tenant is a high grossing retailer. A large merchant, however, is not always more desirable than a small ma and pa merchant. The most important factors to consider are the following:

1. The tenant is a good merchandiser.
2. The tenant is compatible and complementary with other tenants in parking needs and type and quality of merchandise.
3. The tenant is able and willing to pay fair market rent.

Signage

Many tenants have signage criteria which must be met before they will consider locating in your project. A signage clause spelling out sign rights is a *must* in your lease. Most cities now have sign ordinances limiting the amount of signage allowed per facility. Just as with parking codes, check with your local municipality regarding signage restrictions. Remember, signage is a valuable leasing tool. It should be analyzed carefully and a planned signage program designed. A planned program will not only give you greater control of the final results, but also improve the aesthetic quality of the project.

LEGAL ISSUES

This section does not dwell on specific legal issues, because they vary according to jurisprudence and location. The assistance of an attorney who concentrates on commercial real estate is a must to review and/or develop the lease agreement, handle evictions, and provide counsel regarding the legality of issues involved in the operation of the center. Some current issues of which commercial managers must be aware include:

1. *Soliciting.* *Robbins* v. *Punard* (U.S. Supreme Court) prevents the manager from forbidding groups to solicit in the center. Reasonable rules and requirements may, however, be imposed.
2. *Eviction.* The U.S. Bankruptcy Act Revision, 1984, changed the law regarding time allowed for a trustee to accept a lease and eviction proceeding.
3. *Insurance*
   a. Employees and vendors (who do not have their own coverage) should be covered under workers' compensation insurance.
   b. Sufficient liability and coinsurance should be maintained.
   c. Management firms should have an "additionally insured clause" in their management agreement.
4. *1099 forms.* All contractors who are paid more than $600 per year must supply a federal identification or social security number. A 1099 form must be sent every January to both the IRS and the contractor. Check with your CPA for specific guidelines regarding current procedures.

Merchant Associations

Merchant associations are formed to allow retailers to work together on promotions, thus increasing the traffic of the center and the individual stores. In many cases agreement and participation among the merchants is hard to get. If handled improperly, the association meeting can turn into a tenant complaint session.

There are basically three approaches the manager can take when participating in a merchant association. They are:

1. Contributing money for special promotions of the association
2. Taking an active part in the association
3. Hiring an employee to manage and run the association if economically feasible

Merchant associations are funded by dues and assessments from the tenants. In some larger centers, membership is mandatory and specified in the lease. The smaller center associations are more difficult to administer. The owner usually makes a contribution to the association's fund.

Common Area Maintenance

The retail net lease usually contains a clause that spells out who pays the costs of common area maintenance (CAM). The typical CAM cost includes:

Taxes—should specify who pays increase or reassessment on sale

Insurance—covers outside liability and fire insurance only; tenants normally required to have separate policy on interior liability and contents

Electricity—outside lighting in common area

Gas—common area only or prorated for nonindividually metered units

Water—common area only or prorated for nonindividually metered units

Landscaping—common area only

Exterior security—common area only

Cleaning—common area only

Repairs—outside of store in common area

Special assessments—for example, parking lot repaving

The CAM prorata is usually determined in the following manner, although each lease should be checked:

1. Individual tenant space is calculated as a percentage of total space in the center (e.g., a 5000-square-foot store in a 100,000-square-foot center takes up 5 percent of the space).
2. Total bills are added up for the reporting period (monthly, quarterly, or yearly).
3. The tenant's percentage is multiplied by the total and the result is his or her CAM charge. For example, if the total monthly bill were $10,000 and the tenant's percentage of the total space was 5 percent, his CAM charge would be $500.

These calculations can be time-consuming and difficult to do by hand. Normally, a blank chart is prepared and the figures written in monthly (Figure 6-1). This chart can be totaled across the top and bottom to give a double check. We have developed a computer program to do the CAM on a monthly basis as well as generate an invoice to each merchant including both CAM and base rent (Figure 6-2).

STORE NUMBER		NAME	RENT	SQ FT	KWH	ELECT	GAS	WATER	TRASH	CAM	TAX	INS	CAM TOTAL	CAM PCT	CAM CHARGE	SPECIAL ASSESS	TOTAL CHARGE
08/25/84						BILLING SUMMARY FOR PROPERTY 60001							FROM 09/01/84 TO 09/30/84				
	BILLED AMOUNT:				50620	4104.69	91.54	122.60	338.91	1121.83	1020.88	553.75				945.50	
	RATIO:					.08109	.00292	.00341	.01030	.03116	.02835	.01538				.02626	
2037	10	(24)	3861.00	3100	0	0.00	0.00	10.57	0.00	96.60	87.89	47.68	242.74	24.27	120.87	81.41	4209.42
2093–95	10	(7)	0.00	2000	1338	108.50	5.84	6.82	20.60	62.32	56.70	30.76	291.54	29.15	91.47	52.52	373.21
2097	10	(2)	555.00	925	1787	144.91	2.70	3.15	9.53	28.82	26.22	14.23	229.56	22.95	51.77	24.29	831.80
2099	5	(3)	600.00	1500	2335	189.35	4.33	5.12	15.45	46.74	42.53	23.07	326.64	16.33	63.07	39.39	982.36
2101	10	(4)	735.00	1050	3855	312.60	3.07	3.58	10.82	32.72	29.77	16.15	408.71	40.87	73.59	27.57	1212.15
2103	10	(5)	650.00	1200	2203	178.64	3.50	4.09	12.36	37.39	34.02	18.46	288.46	28.84	66.23	31.51	998.81
2105	5	(6)	802.80	1200	2491	202.00	3.50	4.09	12.36	37.39	34.02	18.46	311.82	15.59	52.98	31.51	1161.72
2107	10	(7)	1056.00	1200	2013	163.23	3.50	4.09	12.36	37.39	34.02	18.46	273.05	27.30	64.69	31.51	1387.86
2109	5	(9)	726.97	1200	1877	152.21	3.50	4.09	12.36	37.39	34.02	18.46	262.03	13.10	50.49	31.51	1033.61
2111	10	(10)	621.00	1380	1569	127.23	4.03	4.71	14.21	43.00	39.12	21.22	253.52	25.35	68.35	36.24	936.11
2113	10	(11)	666.00	1110	2520	204.35	3.24	3.79	11.43	34.59	31.47	17.07	305.94	30.59	65.18	29.15	1031.68
2115–17	5	(12)	1422.14	2400	0	0.00	7.01	8.18	24.72	74.78	0.00	36.91	151.60	7.58	82.36	63.02	1644.44
2119	5	(13)	698.00	1200	5810	471.13	3.50	4.09	12.36	37.39	34.02	18.46	580.95	29.04	66.43	31.51	1339.50
2121	10	(14)	660.00	1200	3685	298.82	3.50	4.09	12.36	37.39	34.02	18.46	408.64	40.86	78.25	31.51	1141.01
2123	10	(15)	540.00	1200	2133	172.96	3.50	4.09	12.36	37.39	34.02	18.46	282.78	28.27	65.66	31.51	882.56
2125	10	(16)	540.00	1200	2377	192.75	3.50	4.09	12.36	37.39	34.02	18.46	302.57	30.25	67.64	31.51	904.33
2127	5	(17)	591.82	1200	0	0.00	3.50	4.09	12.36	37.39	34.02	18.46	109.82	5.49	42.88	31.51	738.64
2129	5	(18)	434.50	1580	0	0.00	0.00	5.39	16.27	49.23	0.00	0.00	70.89	3.54	52.77	41.49	550.42
2131–5	10	(19)	1740.00	2960	4664	378.20	8.64	10.09	30.49	92.23	83.92	45.52	649.09	64.90	157.13	77.73	2531.72
2137	10	(8)	500.00	1200	932	75.58	3.50	4.09	12.36	37.39	34.02	18.46	185.40	18.54	55.93	31.51	735.45
2139	5	(20)	575.30	1000	1997	161.94	2.92	3.41	10.30	31.16	28.35	15.38	253.46	12.67	43.83	26.26	867.69
2141	10	(21)	567.00	1027	1058	85.79	3.00	3.50	10.58	32.00	29.12	15.80	179.79	17.97	49.97	26.97	791.73
2143	10	(22)	635.00	973	2361	191.45	2.84	3.32	10.02	30.32	27.58	14.96	280.49	28.04	58.36	25.55	1019.08
2145	5	(23)	0.00	3000	0	0.00	8.76	10.23	30.90	93.48	0.00	0.00	143.37	7.16	100.64	78.78	229.31
			19227.53	36005	47005	3811.64	91.43	122.76	338.92	1121.89	822.87	483.35	6792.86	568.75	1690.64	945.47	27534.61

SQ FT FOR GAS RATIO =	31325	OTHER CAM EXPENSES	828.78	TAX DIFFERENCE..........	198.01
SQ FT FOR WATER RATIO =	36005	+ ELECTRICAL DIFFERENCE	293.05	+ INSURANCE DIFFERENCE..	70.40
SQ FT FOR TRASH RATIO =	32905	= TOTAL CAM BILLED AMOUNT	1121.83	= ABSORBED BY OWNER.....	268.41

Figure 6-1 Determining common area maintenance (CAM) costs.

J. D. PROPERTY MANAGEMENT
3520 Cadillac Avenue, Suite B
Costa Mesa, California 92626
(714) 751-2787

FROM 09/01/84 TO 09/30/84

ABC Hardware
1000 Main Street
Anaheim, CA 92805

SQUARE FEET	1500	
BASE RENT		600.00
ELECTRIC		183.35
GAS		4.38
WATER		5.02
TRASH		15.55
COMMON AREA MAINTENANCE		63.07
REAL ESTATE TAXES		42.53
INSURANCE		28.07
SPECIAL ASSESSMENT		39.39
TOTAL AMOUNT DUE		982.36

PLEASE MAKE CHECKS PAYABLE TO J. D. PROPERTY MANAGEMENT CO.

Figure 6-2 Computer-generated invoice including both CAM and base rent.

OFFICE BUILDINGS

The office building can be defined as a property which provides facilities to a service-oriented tenant—contrasted with a place where goods are sold (shopping center) or manufactured (industrial building). As discussed earlier in this chapter, the growth trend in the United States is toward service industries (e.g., insurance, financial, government, information processing) and away from manufacturing. A similar change occurred a hundred years ago with the move from agriculture to manufacturing. These new services require office space to function. Developers are providing more and more buildings each year to meet this demand.

Discussing office buildings separately does not mean that they always exist as islands by themselves. Several of the most prestigious buildings, such as Rockefeller Center in New York and the Water Tower Place in Chicago, provide retailing within the structure. This "mixed-use concept," existing in Europe for generations, has also extended to provision of residential space in the top floors of some business complexes. Management of these mixed-use complexes must be multifaceted, and managers must be able to deal with a variety of leases, tenants, and problems.

Size and Characteristics of Office Buildings

Office buildings range from one-story buildings to skyscrapers such as the Sears Tower in Chicago, which is 110 stories and rises 1454 feet. New technologic advances in design, energy management, and elevators allow for the construction of these "cities within the city."

The two major types of office buildings—downtown and suburban—are characterized in the Institute of Real Estate Management publication *Income and Expense Analysis: Office Buildings.* This analysis of office buildings, published yearly, divides them into:

Building types—one to two stories, three to four stories, and so on, up to thirty-six stories or more

Age groups—built before 1920, between 1920 and 1929, and so on, up to 1971 to present

Rental range—$5.99 per square foot per year or less, $6.00 to $7.99, and so on up to $22.00 per square foot and up

Building size—5000 to 19,900 square feet, 20,000 to 49,999 square feet, and so on up to 500,000 square feet and above

Using the above criteria, a manager can compare a building to a sample of over 9000 buildings divided by national, regional, and metropolitan areas.

The comparison chart of accounts covers such areas as income (offices, retail stores, parking, vacancies) and expenses (electricity, water, heating, janitorial service, maintenance and repair, administration, payroll, landscaping, and other services).

The number of buildings compared are given in each sample and the figures averaged to reveal "dollars per gross area," "dollars per rentable office area," and "dollars per net rentable office area." The amount of each expense and income item is categorized as high, low, or medium in terms of dollars.

These figures, used as benchmarks, make analyses of operation and performance more meaningful. This information can also be compared to a seller's records when one is considering purchasing an office building. Rents are quoted per square foot per month in some areas of the country, but annual cost per square foot is normally the standard.

Tenant Mix

Office buildings, like shopping centers, need to have a balanced and predetermined tenant makeup. A prestigious office building that caters to legal and financial firms probably will not solicit as a tenant a "hypnotist."

In a medical building, a good tenant mix would include use of the first floor for auxiliary services such as a pharmacy and radiology laboratory. Securing several general practice doctors is very desirable as they are a constant source of referrals to the optometrists, podiatrists, surgeons, and other specialists, who will then be attracted to the building. Leasing to an alternative practitioner such as a chiropractor might cause resentment on the part of the medical doctors.

Careful analysis of tenant parking requirements is also a necessity for two reasons: First, city or municipal parking codes must be followed, and second, an overparked building will result in vacancies and unrest by present tenants. For example, renting a large space to an insurance company with a large clerical staff might make it difficult for your other tenants and their clients to find a parking space.

Measuring the Building

Methods of calculating the size of office space differ among owners and among regions in the country. We will use the Institute of Real Estate Management (IREM) method in our discussion.

Gross area of entire building. The sum of the areas at each floor, including corridors, lobbies, and garages within the building that are included within the principal outside faces of the exterior walls.

Gross rentable area. Computed by measuring inside finish of permanent outer building walls. Includes all area within outside walls less stairs, elevator shafts, flues, pipe shafts, vertical ducts, and balconies.

Net rentable area. Computed by measuring inside finish of permanent outer building walls or glass line where at least 50 percent of outer wall is glass. No deductions are made for columns and projections necessary to the building. Excluded are stairs, elevator shafts, flues, pipe shafts, vertical ducts, balconies, air conditioning rooms, janitor and electrical closets, washrooms, public corridors, and other rooms not available to the tenants' personnel and their enclosing walls.

As can be seen, the tenant may incur a loss by being charged for columns and corridors not used as office space. For example, if the net rentable area were 50,000 square feet, but only 45,000 square feet were usable, the loss factor (net rentable area divided by usable area) would be 1.11. As a general rule, the higher the loss factor the lower the rent because the space becomes less desirable.

Break-Even Rental Rate

One of the most common questions asked is how rental rates are determined. In the next section, Market Analysis, we discuss doing a survey of competitors. We should, however, be aware of the minimum rent needed to cause the building to break even. The formula to determine the break-even (B/E) point is as follows:

$$\text{B/E rent} = \frac{\text{expense} + \text{mortgage} + \text{return}}{\text{square footage of building}}$$

$$\text{B/E} = \frac{425{,}000 + 750{,}000 + 96{,}000^{*}}{100{,}000 \text{ square feet}} = \frac{1{,}271{,}000}{100{,}000} = \$12.71$$

The break even rental is $12.71 per square foot. The manager must be able to charge a rent of at least $12.71 per square foot per year to allow the owner to break even on his or her cash flow.

Market Analysis

James Downs, in his book *Principles of Real Estate Management,* has set forth twelve criteria for comparing office buildings:

Location. Is the building close to other business facilities, financial centers, and so on? Is it in an area that has a positive growth trend?

Neighborhood. Are there attractive surrounding buildings? Does the area have a good image?

Transportation. If in a central business district, is the building near public transportation, highways, airports, and so on?

Appearance. Does the building have good curb appeal? (Older buildings can be made more attractive.)

Lobby. What are the style, appearance, cleanliness, and character of the central lobby? Is the directory neat and organized?

Elevators. Are they well located within the building and of good capacity, appearance, and speed?

*Owner has equity of $800,000 and expects a 12 percent return, which is $96,000.

Corridors. Are they tastefully decorated, well illuminated, and of adequate size?

Office interiors. Is there sufficient column spacing and ceiling height for good layout design?

Tenant services. How is the janitorial service, security, after-hours access, and air conditioning?

Maintenance. Is the level of maintenance sufficient to project a desirable image?

Tenant mix. What are the reputations and professional standings of existing tenants?

Rental schedule. Consider the type of building, competition, economic conditions, owner break-even points, amenities, and so on.

Energy Management

The largest single expense category in office buildings is utilities, representing more than 30 percent of the total operating costs. The property manager must, therefore, initiate an energy management program as a means of reducing expenses and increasing net income. Such a program will also increase the value of the building; however, managers must not freeze out tenants in the winter by reducing the temperature level to 50°.

A successful energy management program involves the following steps:

1. *Gathering information*—past utility bills, energy-saving features now in place, and so on
2. *Analyzing information*—fuel usage per square foot
3. *Developing alternative measures*—cost efficiency and the pay-back period for new equipment, such as a boiler
4. *Implementing selected measures*—budgeting and purchase
5. *Following up and controlling*—periodic review of fuel bills and operating costs and use of a performance ratio

Performance ratio. The performance ratio is calculated by converting the fuel usage figure into BTU and dividing by the square footage of the building and then by the total heating and cooling degree-days. The lower the performance ratio, the less energy the building consumes per square foot per degree-day. A chart containing heating and cooling days in different regions is found on page 212 of *Managing the Office Building*, published by the Institute of Real Estate Management.

Energy conservation measures (nuts and bolts). The following are useful practices for conserving energy in office buildings:

1. Put outside and inside lighting on timers (security factors should be considered in their use).
2. Make sure hot water recirculating pumps are working properly and the hot water temperature set (usually at 105°) for proposed use. (In medical buildings, it should be 140°.)
3. Keep all machinery in good working condition and well maintained on a regularly scheduled basis.
4. Convert air conditioning systems to recycle air rather than pull in 100 percent fresh air.
5. Preset thermostat controls in public areas (summer, 78°; winter, 60°).
6. If possible, separate or submeter tenants' electrical usage. Studies show usage decreases by over 20 percent when tenants pay.
7. Repair any plumbing leaks such as dripping faucets—especially hot water drips.
8. Replace an incandescent light with fluorescent lighting, and use only two bulbs in a four-bulb fixture. Dummy bulbs are available that appear as if they are giving light while utilizing little electricity.
9. Charge tenants for air conditioning used after 6 p.m. and on Sundays if this is after normal business hours for the building. (This should be stated in the lease.)
10. Properly insulate your building to prevent heat loss in winter and cooling loss in summer.

Life-Support Systems Plan

When managing an office building it is necessary to develop a security and emergency procedure plan. It may be beneficial to have an outside consultant evaluate your building and help you develop such a plan. Liability resulting from negligence should be foremost in a manager's mind when developing this plan. Some of the items in a life-support systems plan are as follows:

1. *Perimeter security*—entrances, exits, windows, parking lot, landscaping, guard patrol, and outside lighting
2. *Interior security*—alarms, security guards, closed-circuit television monitors, public-area lighting, and rest rooms
3. *Traffic control*—traffic patterns of your tenants and their customers and vendors

4. *Fire and bomb control plan*—coordinated with local police and fire departments
5. *Power failure plan*—such as emergency diesel power generators to provide emergency lighting and bring elevators to ground floor, found in many buildings and especially important in medical buildings

It is important to get the tenants involved and familiar with these plans for them to be effective. No building is ever totally fireproof or secure. (Foolproof security cannot even be provided for the President of the United States.) We can, however, point out the measures we have implemented to prospective tenants as a leasing aid.

Maintenance

Proper maintenance is necessary for the successful management of office buildings. Maintenance is either routine or in response to request.

Routine maintenance includes the following:

Janitorial service—sweeping, cleaning, and so on

Regular repairs—such as replacing broken windows

Preventive service—scheduled maintenance on furnace, boiler, air conditioning system, roof, elevators, and so on

Some helpful suggestions for maintaining office buildings include the following:

1. Use a purchase order system (consecutively numbered) to record and control repairs.
2. Make sure vendors and contractors are insured and licensed.
3. Obtain and have readily available plans of the building's plumbing and electrical systems as well as operating and maintenance manuals for equipment such as air conditioning systems and boilers.
4. Encourage use of centralized janitorial vendors even when the tenants pay for their own service. A centralized janitorial service will be cheaper and security easier to control.

INDUSTRIAL BUILDINGS

Historically industrial buildings have been owned and managed by manufacturers, who located close to the source of their raw materials. As our economy moves from production of goods to provision of services, the location, type, and size of industrial buildings are changing. Newer buildings tend to be smaller in size and located in industrial parks near the source of more highly skilled employees and closer to the market to be served rather than the raw material used.

Characteristics of Industrial Buildings

Types of Buildings

1. *Single tenant.* These are larger in size, and involve a long-term lease.
2. *Multitenant*
   a. Older buildings in urban areas usually are leased by manufacturing tenants.
   b. Older industrial buildings in suburban industrial parks attract ma and pa incubator-type tenants with short leases.
   c. New research and development firms have 30 to 40 percent of their total space as offices.

Parking and traffic requirements. Unlike office buildings, in which employees come and go at peak periods (8 to 9 a.m. and 4 to 5 p.m.), and shopping centers, which have a dispersed traffic flow, the industrial building can be used for two or three shifts, thus partially dispersing the traffic flow. The parking requirements (three cars per 1000 square feet) are typically less than those for office buildings and shopping centers.

The location should be near major highways, allowing workers easier access to their jobs. Affordable housing, for some of the lower scale employee positions, is a problem developing in areas of high land prices.

Types of leases. Industrial leases include gross and net leases in addition to sale lease-back agreements to free up capital for the user and give additional tax benefits to the new owner.

SUMMARY

In this chapter we cover the basics of commercial property management. It is a challenging, demanding field to which a property manager must bring various talents, experience, expertise, and creativity. No chapter or book can give the answers, as common sense and willingness to seek out and accept change are not learned in a textbook. Managers should discover the highest and best use for their properties.

In conclusion, the manager should view the property as a business entity and run it as a business rather than a tax shelter. As tax laws change, the economics of using good management to operate the property and increase net income will become of paramount importance. The role of the property manager will be enhanced.

SELECTED REFERENCES

Building Owners Management Association. *BOMA Experience Exchange Report.* Washington, D.C., 1984.

Downs, James, Jr. *Principles of Real Estate Management* (12th ed.). Chicago: Institute of Real Estate Management, 1980.

Kyle, Robert, & Kennehan, Ann. *Property Management.* Chicago: Real Estate Education Co., 1979.

Institute of Real Estate Management. *Income and Expense Analysis: Office Buildings.* Chicago: Institute of Real Estate Management, 1984.

Institute of Real Estate Management. *Managing the Office Building.* Chicago: Institute of Real Estate Management, 1981.

Institute of Real Estate Management. *Managing the Shopping Center.* Chicago: Institute of Real Estate Management, 1983.

R. S. Mears Co. *Mean Square Foot Costs.* Kingston, Mass.: R. S. Mears Co., 1985.

Urban Land Institute. *Dollars and Cents of Shopping Centers.* Washington, D.C.: Urban Land Institute, 1982.

Urban Land Institute. *Shopping Center Development Handbook.* Washington, D.C.: Urban Land Institute, 1982.

Walters, William, Jr. *The Practice of Real Estate Management.* Chicago: Institute of Real Estate Management, 1983.

CHAPTER 7

Marketing decisions in commercial property management

Thomas D. Pearson, Ph.D.
Lomas & Nettleton Mortgage Banking
North Texas State University
Denton, Texas

The field of commercial real estate involves use of land for wholesale, retail, and service activities and combinations of these activities. For example, office-warehouse space may be used for wholesaling, while office-showroom space typically is retail-use-oriented. With the blurring of lines of demarcation between different types of business activities, a high-tech computer company may operate from an office-showroom building yet be involved in both wholesale and retail sales while simultaneously servicing the hardware and developing and selling software. Thus it is hard to define precisely what commercial property is.

With this caveat, this chapter focuses on marketing decisions for commercial property, which will be defined as planned shopping centers. However, the suggestions offered may be modified easily to accommodate other types of commercial property.

The marketing decisions in commercial real estate must begin prior to development of the property and continue during the operations phase of the investment. Even before the ground is broken for construction purposes, the developer must make choices concerning location, design, and image. It is through the locational decision that the property services are "distributed" to customers; it is through the architectural design decisions that the property is "packaged" in a form to appeal to the customer; the choice of anchor, or key, tenants helps to establish the image of the center. Distribution, packaging, and image decisions are functions of marketing.

Once the structure is built, the management of a shopping center must be concerned with melding a community of merchants into a unit with the express purpose of enhancing sales, reducing costs and risks, and maximizing profits. Thus marketing decisions must also be made during the ongoing operations of the property. To accomplish these ends, decisions are made to optimize sales by appropriate tenant selection and mix and by proper spacing and placement of tenants within the center. It is the decisions made during the operations phase of the property that this chapter deals with.

The remainder of the chapter includes a discussion of the functions of property management regarding the typical planned shopping center. After defining management's obligations, we discuss tenant selection and placement for productivity and sales maximization. Finally, tenant placement and selection practices are examined.

PROPERTY MANAGEMENT FUNCTIONS

A commercial property is simultaneously a real estate investment and a business investment. The quality of property management will greatly influence how well the property performs as an economic unit. Commercial property managers have, fundamentally, three sets of functions: (1) operating and maintaining the physical facilities, (2) negotiating tenant leases, and (3) managing a community of merchants. In executing these functions, the property manager has an obligation to mesh operations with the investor's overall investment strategy, planning, and portfolio of assets. Therefore, it is important for the manager to define investor objectives clearly and precisely.

The basic interest is in obtaining owner satisfaction and benefits, which may come in a variety of forms. The most commonly stated owner objectives are cash flow, tax shelter, estate (wealth) buildup, and psychological (pride of ownership) benefits. These vary from one owner to another depending on circumstances. For example, a private, individual owner may be interested in cash flow, whereas a corporate owner may want to maximize taxable income because it translates into earnings per share, thereby enhancing the company's stock value.

To maximize owner benefits, the commercial property manager must maximize gross revenues and minimize operating costs, resulting in an optimum net income. These objectives involve marketing decisions to promote the shopping center, attract customers, and enhance sales. Given the market area, demographic makeup, and income of the population, the property manager must tailor tenant selection to provide merchandise which will satisfy market needs, tastes, and preferences. Additionally, the management of the center must decide where tenants should be placed in the center to maximize sales. This role of tenant selection, mix, and placement is crucial to shopping center profitability and rate of return on investment.

TENANT SELECTION FOR PRODUCTIVITY

Commercial property productivity is measured by profit-loss statements. The desire is to select the combination of tenants which results in the highest net rents to the property owner. Management therefore must be aware of retailers' merchandising principles and select a mixture of complementary tenants to the greatest extent possible.

Retail Store Compatibility and Cumulative Attraction[1]

Some businesses are compatible and others are not. The question is whether store A, located next to store B, is an aid, a hindrance, or neutral to store B. Developers, leasing agents, and managers should take into account the compatibility and cumulative attraction of retail shops when planning the image and merchandising mixture of a center. Similarly, an individual retailer should give consideration to store compatibility when selecting a location.

The major generators of customer traffic in a shopping center are the anchor tenants, which typically are supermarkets and drug stores in neighborhood centers, and department stores in regional centers. Ancillary stores within the center should be complementary to the anchor tenants and to each other. The greater the complementarity and compatibility of the stores and merchandise, the stronger will be the attractiveness of the center to customers. For example, a variety store next to a department store may not cause customers to come to a center. However, a center that has a variety store next to a department store will

[1] Richard L. Nelson, *The Selection of Retail Locations,* F. W. Dodge Corp., New York, 1958, chapters 6, 7, 8.

attract more customers than a freestanding department store. This also is true for stores with weak generative powers such as shoe stores, boutiques, and so on. However, if stores with weak generative powers and similar merchandise cluster, they can benefit from cumulative attraction.

Theory of Cumulative Attraction

Nelson[2] proposed that a cluster of four stores providing the same merchandise (e.g., four shoe stores) will expand the total market area, have greater market penetration, and generate a larger sales volume than will the same four stores if they are widely dispersed. By grouping together, the retail outlets form a type of "mini shoe mart" or "shoe center," thereby increasing market share and volume because of their compatibility.

Rule of Retail Compatibility[3]

Two or more businesses are highly compatible if the volume of business for both (or all) is increased because of their proximity to each other. They are compatible because of customer interchange. Without technically stating the rule of compatibility, Nelson studied more than 10,000 customer shopping trips and discovered a direct relationship between customer interchange among retail outlets and business volume. The increase in total volume of two stores may be computed by using the following formula, which demonstrates the rule of retail compatibility:

$$V = P_I\,(V_A + V_B)\left(\frac{V_B}{V_A}\right)\left(\frac{G_A}{V_A} + \frac{G_B}{V_B}\right)$$

where: V = increase in total volume of sales in dollars

P_I = percentage of customers who visit both store A and B—i.e., percentage of customer interchange

V_A = volume of sales for store A

V_B = volume of sales for store B

G_A = generative purchases in store A—i.e., store A generated the customer shopping trip and purchase

G_B = generative purchase in store B constrained by $V_A > V_B$—i.e., store A is the larger of the two stores

Example: V_A = \$500,000 P_I = 35 percent

V_B = \$100,000 G_A = \$350,000

G_B = \$ 40,000

[2] Nelson, *op. cit.,* especially chapter 7.

[3] Nelson, *op. cit.,* chapters 6, 7, 8.

$$V = .35(\$500{,}000 + \$100{,}000)\left(\frac{\$100{,}000}{\$500{,}000}\right)\left(\frac{350{,}000}{500{,}000} + \frac{40{,}000}{100{,}000}\right)$$

$$= 210{,}000\ (.20)(.70 + .40)$$

$$= \$46{,}200$$

Not only may four shoe stores be compatible, but ten or twenty may be also. Whether there should be only one, four, ten, or twenty stores selling similar merchandise must be determined by the market potential; thus the preceding equation demonstrates the increase in business volume for compatible stores, other things equal. It is left to the property manager to determine whether the center's market area will support four shoe shops, ten, or twenty.

Tenant Mix for Productivity

Another factor the shopping center property manager will have to consider is the composition of tenants, or tenant mix. Questions must be answered about the number of stores providing a similar line of merchandise: How many shoe (or dress, or men's suit) stores can the market support? Should there be a wide range in quality and prices, such as a Neiman-Marcus and a Sears, or should quality and prices be more uniform between stores—Sears and J. C. Penney (or Neiman-Marcus and Lord & Taylor)? Finally, questions concerning the number of stores selling women's apparel, men's apparel, candy, ice cream, sandwiches, phonographs, and so on must be addressed. These questions can be generalized by categorizing the different merchandise and store types into generative, susceptive, and shared business types.[4]

A store that generates business for a shopping center is extremely important. Generative business occurs because of the reputation of the store, because of unique or varied merchandise lines carried, or because of heavy advertising and promotion. Department stores have much generative power due to their wide range of merchandise, including jewelry, clothing, appliances, and furniture, and usually serve as anchor tenants for regional centers. Supermarkets sell day-to-day essentials and provide generative power for neighborhood centers. Stores that deal in comparable goods or promote brand-name products, such as Hickey-Freeman suits or Nikon cameras, may also generate a substantial amount of business.

At the other extreme are stores whose business derives primarily from people who happen to be at the site for purposes other than to make a purchase at that store. In a shopping center, stores of this type include tobacco stands and sandwich and ice cream shops. The store

[4] Nelson, *op. cit.*, pp. 52–54.

undertakes no advertising and almost exclusively provides a service to customers who have come to purchase items from other stores. This type of store is called a susceptive business by Nelson.

The most common type of store is the one that shares business because of the generative power of neighboring stores. It may have generative power of its own, but it is a weak generative power. Most of its business comes from people whose primary purpose for being in the vicinity is to visit another store, perhaps a department or grocery store.

In sum, a shopping center manager who is familiar with the market area, customer shopping habits, merchandising principles, store advertising policies, and product lines can group stores into generative, susceptive, and shared categories and make judgments about their generative powers, compatibility, and complementarity. Through analysis, the manager should be able to identify the types of stores and merchandise lines needed to improve tenant selection for maximizing shopping center productivity.

TENANT PLACEMENT FOR PRODUCTIVITY

There are two fundamental underlying approaches to tenant placement in a shopping center: the rent theory approach and the merchandising theory approach. They are not mutually exclusive and have overlapping elements. The fundamental difference between them is the thrust, or focus of emphasis. In the first approach, it is the underlying rent that is paid that explains placement; in the second approach, distribution of tenants and merchandise to maximize center sales explains placement.

Rent Theory and Tenant Placement

Central place theory and the hierarchy of urban service centers have been studied extensively by Brian Berry and others.[5] These concepts when coupled with elementary rent theory also have much power for explaining the distribution of retail services within urban areas.[6] There is no known research relating these factors to the internal structure, or placement of tenants, in a planned shopping center, but it seems logical that there is a relationship. The following discussion describes this perceived relationship.

Central place theory and the hierarchy of retail centers within an

[5] B. J. L. Berry, *Geography of Market Centers and Retail Distribution,* Prentice-Hall, Englewood Cliffs, N.J., 1967. Berry has an extremely impressive list of articles and books pertaining to this subject; the book cited is simply one of many.

[6] Berry, *op. cit.*

urban area results in land values that peak at major intersections. Rent theory suggests that peak value intersections should have retail services that are distributed outward, with the highest rents being paid at sites closest to the intersection where maximum density of pedestrian and vehicular traffic occurs. For a regional, unplanned shopping center, regional functions with higher market thresholds should pay the highest rents and be located at the intersection, with community and neighborhood functions pushed farther away from the intersection. For community and neighborhood level retail nucleations, community and neighborhood functions should be located adjacent to the peak value intersection.

The data suggest that agglomeration economies, space demands, and product differentiation cause divergences between theory and reality.[7] However, when the data provided by Berry and Tennant[8] are coupled with rent theory and Nelson's concepts of susceptive, shared, and generative business types, the nature of the internal placement of tenants emerges. Susceptive businesses such as ice cream parlors, candy stores, and fast food facilities tend to be placed at peak value intersections within a planned shopping center, as Berry and Tennant found. Shared businesses with weak generative powers, but which are highly complementary to the generative anchor tenants, tend to be placed in a fashion that maximizes exposure of customers as they move from one generative business to another. These shared businesses will be pushed away from the peak value intersection and will pay somewhat lower rents than the susceptive enterprises. Finally, the large, space-consuming anchor tenants—the generative businesses—are located at the periphery of the shopping centers, pay the lowest rents, and are placed to encourage customers to traverse the mall. Thus, as rent theory suggests, areas with high-density pedestrian traffic have the highest rents in a center, and large space-consuming stores locate at the periphery where rents are lower. Agglomeration economies and product differentiation influence the placement of shared business types.

Merchandising Theory and Tenant Placement

Department stores have developed merchandising principles that serve their purposes well. Placement of merchandise in a large, full-line department store is designed to move customer traffic through different departments of the store, thereby exposing customers to a wide array of

[7] For an excellent discussion of these points, see Maurice Yeates & Barry Garner, *The North American City* (2nd ed.), Harper and Row, New York, 1976, chapter 13, especially pp. 316–323.

[8] B. J. L. Berry & R. Tennant, *Chicago Commercial Reference Handbook,* Research Paper 86, Department of Geography, University of Chicago Press, Chicago, 1963, p. 3.

goods and services. These merchandising principles can be successfully applied to tenant placement in a shopping center by following two axioms: (1) Locate anchor tenants and parking areas to induce customer traffic to flow past the storefronts of as many supplementary tenants as possible and (2) arrange tenants to take maximum advantage of the rule of compatibility.

To obtain maximum benefits from the first rule, key tenants should be separated rather than placed adjacent to each other. For example, a supermarket and drugstore in a neighborhood center might be placed at each end rather than side by side in the center of the mall.

The rule of compatibility states that tenants should be arranged to generate the greatest amount of interchange among them. The property manager may follow a "mix" or a "match" strategy depending on tenants, merchandise quality, and other variables. For example, shops selling men's apparel, sporting goods, and shoes may be clustered together to provide some cumulative attraction power within the center. However, strong arguments may also be made that these functions should be dispersed to generate additional traffic throughout the center. At this time, there is no literature that addresses the effect of clustering versus dispersal of similar or complementary tenants on the overall productivity of the center.

In sum, tenant placement to enhance shopping center productivity may follow the rent theory rule or the merchandising theory rule. The two rules will result in a similar placement of tenants even though the underlying rationales differ.

EVALUATING TENANTS FOR PRODUCTIVITY

Principles of tenant selection and placement have been presented. The next step is to evaluate tenants in light of these principles, keeping in mind that the desire is to maximize shopping center sales and productivity.

The Key Tenant

The key tenant is the major generator of shopping center traffic. Selecting the proper anchor tenant or tenants cannot be overemphasized because these tenants will set the tone and image of the center. They will influence the layout, design, and even the financial negotiations of the center. Thus the role and significance of the key tenants are critical: without them there will be no shopping center.

One of the functions of the property manager oftentimes is to negotiate the lease, or occupancy agreement, with the key tenant. To negotiate from strength in the interests of the owners, the management must have a good grasp of the market characteristics of the center and the merchandising philosophy of the anchor tenants in the region. The tenant and the market must be matched and fitted. Additionally, there must be an understanding of the tenants' philosophy regarding expansion, occupancy commitments, and other subtle features that may make a tenant highly compatible with a wide range of secondary tenants. A high degree of interchange and compatibility can be an important feature for attracting a list of strong secondary tenants.

Once the key tenants have been signed up, the property manager must monitor their productivity. These tenants are evaluated on the basis of two features: They must be successful in attracting customers to the site, and they must have the ability to induce customers to walk through the center. It is the expectation that the key tenants will deliver a significant share of the customer count to other tenants in the center, and they should be selected and evaluated on this basis.

Fundamentally, there are four key tenant types: supermarkets, drugstores, junior department stores, and full-line department stores. Supermarkets and drugstores are traditional anchors for neighborhood and community centers. Supermarkets typically are not major tenants for regional centers and, if associated with one, are usually freestanding outlets. Drugstores, however, are highly desirable in all centers. Whereas a drugstore may be permitted to sell a wide range of merchandise and take on characteristics of a junior department or variety store, a supermarket usually is restricted from departing into nonfood merchandise to any great extent.

Junior department stores are not capable of careful definition. The term generally refers to a store that does not carry a full line of goods. Traditionally, the junior department store has been an anchor for community centers and is rarely found in a neighborhood center. In recent years, because customers wish to shop closer to home, community centers have been upgrading the size of junior department stores and increasing the merchandise lines. In some cases, these stores are beginning to take on characteristics of small, but full-line, department stores.

The full-line department store is found in regional and superregional shopping centers. The management of such centers will want from two to four or more of these stores. The major problem is to design the physical layout of the center to spread the department stores apart to generate customer traffic in the mall, yet permit easy, direct access to the stores from the parking lot. Careful attention must be given to make sure the department store fits the image the property manager wishes to create for the center. In doing so, consideration should be given to customer loyalties, market segment, pricing policies, merchandise lines, and store image.

Other Tenants

The purpose of other tenants in a shopping center is to provide the variety of merchandise, entertainment, or food necessary to appeal to the customer population in the market area. Also, these secondary tenants should be selected based on their generative and shared business capacities. The list of tenant types may be quite long and will include the following: restaurants; gourmet food markets; variety stores; discount stores; apparel stores; shoe stores; furniture and home furnishings outlets; home repair and hardware centers; service shops such as beauty salons, barber shops, laundries, and key makers; toy stores; and book stores.

SUMMARY

For this chapter commercial property has been defined as planned shopping centers, and marketing decisions discussed have been restricted to tenant selection, composition, and placement for maximizing center productivity and investor rate of return.

Using the rules of retail compatibility and cumulative attraction as guides, the property manager can improve the selection of tenants for sales maximization, relative to costs. Similarly, by recognizing the generative, shared, or susceptive nature of a tenant's business, the manager can enhance the mix to improve sales revenues.

Two approaches to tenant placement have been cited: the rent theory and the merchandising theory approaches. The two approaches should result in a similar placement, or dispersal, of tenants throughout a shopping center. The rent theory approach suggests how tenants will be distributed based on their different rent-paying capacities. The merchandising approach recognizes that anchor tenants are the traffic generators of the center; these must be placed to pull, or induce, customers to travel through the center, thereby exposing secondary tenants to the customers.

CHAPTER 8

The lease

K. Reed Harrison
Attorney
Westlake Village, California

The purpose of this chapter is to give the reader an overview of the landlord-tenant relationship. The reader will also be given an overview and explanation of the inherent differences in requisite formalities of leases for residential, commercial/retail, and industrial properties, and of tenants' remedies and duties on breach of express or implied covenants.

CONVEYANCE VERSUS CONTRACT

Historically, the lease of real property was regarded as a conveyance of an interest in land. More recently, however, the trend is to apply modern contract principles to the landlord-tenant relationship. The relationship of the landlord and tenant is based on contract, express or implied, and their respective rights and duties are determined by such contract. Usually the contract is in the form of a lease, together with the law of the jurisdiction within which the real property is located, which may be read into the contract.

NECESSARY FORMALITIES

Oral leases are normally valid and binding on the landlord and tenant if the period specified in the oral agreement does not exceed the local statute of frauds. In most jurisdictions, under the statute of frauds an oral lease is not enforceable if it exceeds the period of 1 year.

A written lease is preferable to an oral lease because the term may exceed 1 year and because the parties more clearly understand their respective rights and duties under a written lease. At a minimum, a written lease should contain a correct designation and identification of the parties and/or their respective agents, an accurate description of the premises (including parking arrangements, if applicable), the term of the lease, the landlord's duty in delivering the premises to the tenant at commencement of the term, the party responsible for paying various expenses and repairs associated with the property, and who may use the property and for what purposes; the lease should be signed by the parties. A complete checklist for reviewing leases is provided at the end of this chapter.

An oral modification of a lease is invalid if both the original and remaining periods of the lease exceed the local statute of frauds. For example, in most jurisdictions a lease which exceeds 10 years cannot be validly orally modified. Similarly, an agreement to make a lease would be valid (if the lease is for a period greater than 1 year) when the agreement is in writing and contains the essential elements set forth in the preceding paragraph.

AGENCY-PRINCIPAL RELATIONSHIP

Both the landlord and tenant may authorize a third party to act as an agent for the purposes of negotiation and/or entry into a lease. The authorized party thereby becomes a principal, and an agency-principal relationship is established.

In most jurisdictions, if the law requires the lease to be in writing, the authorization of an agent to exercise discretion to enter into the lease on behalf of the principal must also be in writing. This is known as the "equal dignities rule."

If the authority of the agent is not in writing, the terms of the lease cannot be enforced against the principal; however, since the principal is the only person with standing to raise this defect, the lease can be ratified by him or her. When entry into the lease by the agent is nondiscretionary or mechanical, however, or the principal gives oral authorization with full knowledge of the circumstances and receives clear benefit from the lease, the principal may not repudiate the lease.

EFFECT OF INVALID LEASE

The parties may inadvertently create an invalid lease. If the tenant pays rent to the landlord pursuant to an invalid lease, the tenant may create a periodic tenancy, that is, a tenancy which is valid for the period during which the landlord accepted rent. Such a lease will remain in effect for successive periods until one of the parties gives notice of the lease's termination for a period equal to the period for which the tenant paid rent. If the tenant enters into possession without paying rent, a tenancy at will is created, and the landlord may immediately bring an action to evict the tenant. If the parties to the lease fully perform as if the lease were valid, some authorities argue that the lease should be given full force and effect.

PERMITTED USES

A tenant has the right to use and occupy the premises described in the lease and to use any personal property included therein. In absence of a restriction in the lease, the tenant has the right to occupy and use the land demised in the same manner that the owner might have done for any lawful purpose or business which does not injure the landlord's interest in the property. The parties to a lease may, however, by express provisions in the lease, restrict the uses to which the tenant may put the leased premises, so long as such restrictions are not for the purpose of creating a monopoly or restraining trade, or otherwise contrary to public law or policy.

CONDITIONS AND COVENANTS

A tenant generally has no right to remove, destroy, or alter buildings or other improvements on the leased premises without the express consent of the lessor. In modern times, however, alterations or improvements of the premises in commercial or industrial settings are often required during the normal course of business. Rights and limitations of the parties may be expressly stated by provisions in a written lease, known as conditions and covenants. A *condition* is something that must occur or be done before a reciprocal obligation of performance arises *for the other party*. A *covenant* is a promise to do or refrain from doing a specific act. The breach of a covenant may give rise to an action for damages (in dollars) or an equitable right to enforce the covenant specifically or prevent (enjoin) its violation. The breach of a covenant usually does not operate to terminate the lease, while the breach of a condition may.

Whether the breach of a condition will operate to terminate the lease is usually left to the nonbreaching party. If the nonbreaching party ignores or does not take action on the breach of either a covenant or a condition, he or she may effectively waive action regarding the nonperformance of the breaching party.

Parties have broad discretion to bargain and negotiate for conditions or covenants as long as they do not violate public law or policy.

Implied Covenants

A covenant may be implied from the language of the lease when there is legal necessity or when it is indispensable to give effect to the intention of the parties. In most leases, unless expressly stated otherwise, there is an implied covenant that the landlord has valid title to the property and that the tenant shall have the quiet enjoyment and possession of the premises during the term of the lease.

In modern times, it is implied that a residential landlord covenants that the premises are habitable, or fit for human habitation. When the covenant of implied habitability is recognized, it cannot be bargained away or waived by a tenant in writing or otherwise. This implied covenant does not extend to commercial and industrial leases.

With the exception of the implied covenant of habitability, if the subject is expressly and completely covered by the terms of the lease, a covenant cannot be implied.

Covenants by Tenant to Continue in Business

A general statement in the lease referring to the purpose for which the premises are leased does not usually limit the tenant to use the premises for that purpose. Tenants remain free to change or discontinue their business as long as they comply with the express terms of the lease. However, a covenant to remain in and not to alter the business materially may be implied when rent is based on a percentage of the proceeds of the tenant's business and an adequate minimum base rent is not reserved. If a substantial, adequate minimum base rent is reserved, a covenant will not be implied.

Covenant Not to Compete

Parties may expressly or by implication covenant that the landlord will not compete with, and/or allow other tenants to compete with, the tenant's business on the property.

A noncompetition covenant may be implied from the language of the lease, although this implication is strictly construed. The basis of the implication must be the lease itself. The inference cannot rest solely on the surrounding circumstances.

An express covenant not to compete will be enforced. The breach of this covenant may give the tenant an election of remedies. He or she may be entitled to prevent (enjoin) the violation of the covenant and/or to receive damages. The measure of damages usually is the difference in rental value of the premises without the covenant or the loss of profits resulting from the breach.

LANDLORDS' DUTIES TO TENANTS

Unless specified in the lease, the residential landlord has an obligation to maintain the property in a reasonable manner. Agreements placing the burden on the tenant are binding on the parties unless there is an overriding social policy which would prohibit placing the obligation to maintain and repair on the tenant.

Normally the tenant has the right of quiet use and enjoyment of the demised premises, and the landlord (unless it is specified otherwise) has the duty and obligation to maintain the premises. An actual or constructive eviction of a tenant occurs when any act of the landlord deprives the tenant of his or her right to quiet use and possession of the demised premises, when the tenant is expelled from the premises, or when the tenant is denied the use thereof. An eviction of the tenant must be distinguished from a voluntary abandonment of the premises by the tenant. Any disturbance of the tenant's right to quiet use and possession by the landlord, or by someone acting under his or her authority, which renders the premises unfit for their intended occupancy or which deprives the tenant of the beneficial enjoyment of the demised premises, causing the tenant to abandon the premises, amounts to a constructive eviction. Thus the failure of the landlord to perform her obligation to furnish heat, light, water, elevator service, sewage services, or means of ingress and/or egress, or any other act which deprives the tenant of the beneficial enjoyment of the premises in the manner contemplated by the parties, may amount to a constructive eviction.

For the tenant to claim constructive eviction the tenant must (1) cease paying rent, (2) immediately vacate the property, and (3) notify the landlord that she is terminating the lease. If the tenant fails to perform any of these three steps, the tenant effectively waives the landlord's breach of covenant and any right to legal action against the landlord which she may have.

It should be remembered that an eviction of a tenant may also occur when there is a breach of a covenant to title or quiet enjoyment. Normally, a covenant of title and quiet enjoyment exists in a lease expressly or is implied to exist in the lease by law. Therefore, when the landlord either intentionally or negligently disturbs the quiet use and possession of the tenant or when a third person who claims a paramount or superior title to the landlord in the property disturbs the tenant's right to possession, an unlawful eviction occurs and the tenant has the right to make legal claims against the landlord.

When the landlord is obligated to make repairs and an unsuitable condition arises after the tenant enters into possession, the landlord has an obligation to repair the demised premises promptly. In such a situation, the tenant should notify the landlord promptly and in writing of the required repairs.

The wrongful eviction of a tenant by a landlord, whether actual or constructive, may terminate the tenant's obligations under the lease and, in certain situations, may also entitle the tenant to recover damages against the landlord. Such damages may include the actual or rental value of the unexpired lease term, costs of leasehold improvements, costs of moving to new premises, and other expenses associated with the landlord's breach. Additionally, the tenant may have the right to discontinue paying rent or terminate the lease and move, and may be entitled to an abatement of the rent based on the fair market value of the lease, to use the rent to eliminate or repair the default (in residential leases), to place the rent in escrow pending the abatement of the offending condition, or as indicated above, to sue the landlord for damages.

Many jurisdictions have now enacted ordinances which impose on the landlord a duty to maintain the property "in a reasonably good state of repair," "in a clean and sanitary condition," or "in reasonably good working condition," statements which leave a great deal of discretion to the agency enforcing the local codes and ordinances. Certain local codes and ordinances provide monetary penalties, imprisonment, or other penalties for the violation of the foregoing types of laws. Additionally, some laws confer on the tenant the right to withhold payment of rent, terminate the lease, sue for damages, or make repairs and deduct the cost from the rental payment.

GUARANTY OF LEASE

In modern times many commercial and industrial landlords require that the proposed tenant acquire a financially sound third party to act as guarantor of the lease. The guarantor acts to guarantee payment and performance of the terms of the lease on breach or default by the tenant.

Generally, guarantors can require that landlords exhaust the enforcement of their rights under the lease against tenants before proceeding against the guarantors. This means landlords must pursue their action against the tenants' security before proceeding against the guarantors. Guarantors generally retain all defenses available to tenants.

The guarantor may also, in some instances, hold subrogation rights in the event of a breach of covenant or condition by the landlord. That is, the guarantor may reimburse the landlord for her loss and commence his own action for damages against the tenant. It should be noted that these rights can be waived by agreement of the parties.

ASSIGNMENT AND SUBLETTING

Questions frequently arise in the landlord-tenant relationship as to whether the tenant has the right to assign or sublet the demised premises. An assignment of a leasehold interest is a transaction whereby the tenant transfers his or her entire interest in the demised premises, or a part thereof, for the entire unexpired term of the original lease. A sublease contemplates that the tenant retain some interest in the demised premises even though she has in turn leased to a third party. In the absence of a statutory provision to the contrary or, as is more normally the case, a restriction on the right of assignment in the lease, a tenant has a right to assign her leasehold interest in the demised premises without the consent of the lessor.

Leases frequently contain a provision indicating that the tenant may not assign or sublet the lease without the consent of the landlord, "which consent shall not be unreasonably withheld." If such a provision is contained in the lease, the landlord may deny assignment or subletting only for a good-faith business reason. If, however, the lease gives the landlord unfettered and absolute discretion to prohibit assignment or subletting, the landlord may prohibit assignment or subletting even though he has no good-faith or justifiable reason for denying permission to assign or sublet.

Most jurisdictions hold that the owner or landlord may validly impose a restriction against the assignment of the term or any part thereof by the tenant. Additionally, in some jurisdictions the right of a tenant to assign is restricted by statutory provisions.

The assignee of a lease receives all the benefits that the tenant would otherwise have enjoyed in the property. Additionally, the law implies a promise on the part of the assignee to perform all the duties which had been previously imposed on the former tenant. The former tenant, or assignor, retains her obligation to the landlord to perform all the terms and conditions of the lease. If the assignee fails or refuses to perform the conditions of the lease and the original tenant or assignor is obligated to pay rent, taxes, or other sums of money to the original lessor under the covenants and promises in the lease, the original tenant or assignor may pay such sums and recover from the assignee. Normally, however, the duties of an assignee terminate when she assigns the lease to a third party. In such a situation, the original tenant, or assignor, remains liable for all the terms and conditions in the lease.

RETALIATORY EVICTION

Many jurisdictions have by statute or common law developed laws prohibiting the "retaliatory eviction" of residential tenants. The dominant purpose of the prohibitions against retaliatory eviction is to prevent the landlord from evicting a tenant because of the tenant's complaint to an appropriate governmental agency as to the tenantability of a dwelling when the tenant is *not* in default in the payment of rent. Such anti-retaliatory eviction laws normally also apply when the tenant has made repairs to the demised premises and deducted the amount of such repairs from the amount of the rental due the landlord. Additionally, the landlord normally may not retaliate by increasing the rent or decreasing services to the tenant when the tenant has, in addition to complaining to a governmental agency with regard to housing or health code violations, complained to the landlord of violations or organized to become a member of a tenants' union.

Such laws are not totally one-sided, and the landlord may bring an action for possession if the violation was caused by the tenant or some other person in her household or on the request of the tenant, if the tenant is in default of rent, or if the landlord evicts the tenant to comply with applicable building or housing code ordinances requiring alteration, remodeling, or demolition which would deprive the tenant of the use of the dwelling unit.

Retaliatory eviction is based primarily on the landlord's breach of the implied covenant of habitability; therefore it is generally available only to residential tenants.

RENT

Leases generally require the payment of rent. *Rent* may be defined as the usual price or consideration paid by a tenant to a landlord for the use and occupation of real property under a lease. If the lease or contract between the parties fixes the amount in terms of payment of rent, such provisions will control. When the relation of landlord and tenant is established without any express agreement as to the amount of rent to be paid, the law will imply a promise by the tenant or occupant to pay the reasonable value of the use and occupation of the premises. Unless there is a provision in the lease or custom is to the contrary, the rent is payable at the end of the term by which the rent is measured. However, the lease will usually provide for payment of rent at the beginning of the term and that is when the rent is due.

EMINENT DOMAIN

An eviction of the tenant by the landlord, whether actual or constructive, normally relieves the tenant of the duty to pay all or part of the rent during the time the tenant has been actually or constructively evicted. The taking of the demised premises under the power of eminent domain likewise terminates the liability for future rents. A well-drawn commercial lease will specify the respective rights and liabilities of the parties in the event the property is taken by eminent domain.

DESTRUCTION OF THE PREMISES

Most commercial leases today contain a covenant requiring either the tenant or landlord to repair or rebuild the leased premises if they are totally or partially destroyed. In such cases, the party's obligations and liabilities are determined by the terms of the lease. If the landlord has the express obligation to repair or rebuild the demised premises partially or totally destroyed, the tenant cannot terminate the lease. A general covenant to repair, distinguished from a covenant to rebuild, does not deprive the tenant of her right to terminate the lease when the property is totally destroyed.

In the absence of an express covenant stating the obligations of the parties in the event of destruction of the premises, the tenant is relieved of his obligation to pay rent when the premises are totally destroyed. If there is a partial destruction of a substantial portion, or of that portion which is material to the tenant's use, the tenant may elect to terminate the lease. If the tenant exercises his election to terminate the lease, his covenant to pay rent also terminates.

Even if the landlord does have the obligation to repair or rebuild, if the destruction is caused by the tenant's negligence, he is liable to the landlord for damages.

INJURIES TO THIRD PERSONS

Landlords are not generally liable for acts of tenants when injuries result to others from tenants' negligent use of the premises. However, landlords may be liable to persons outside the demised premises for injury or damage resulting from their own negligent maintenance of the premises or from a nuisance existing thereon at the time of the lease. This liability may extend to owners or occupants of adjoining or neighboring premises or to users of adjacent public ways.

The duties and liabilities of a landlord to persons on the leased premises by the consent of the tenant are the same as those owed to the tenant. This rule applies to members of the tenant's family as well as invitees and subtenants. When the property is leased for use by the public and such property is not safe for the purpose intended, and the owner knew, or by the exercise of reasonable diligence should have known, of such dangerous conditions, the owner will be liable to patrons or customers on the premises for injuries resulting from such conditions. Additionally, when the owner leases premises to different tenants and expressly or by implication reserves common areas such as entrances, halls, stairs, elevators, and walkways for the common use of the various tenants, it is the duty of the landlord to exercise reasonable care to keep such places safe, and the landlord will be liable to a tenant or an invitee on the premises who is injured.

EXPIRATION OF TERM

The parties to a lease may, either in the original lease or by a subsequent agreement, agree to renew or extend a lease after the expiration of the original term. Such provisions for renewal or extension are frequently in the form of an option to the tenant. If a general covenant to renew or extend the lease makes no provision regarding the terms of renewal or extension, the covenant will be construed as providing renewal or extension on the same terms as provided in the original lease, including the amount and terms of payment of the rental and the duration of the lease. Under such a covenant to renew, the tenant is not entitled to have inserted in the renewal lease a covenant for additional renewal. In the absence of a statute to the contrary, it is generally held that a provision in a lease clearly giving the lessee and his assignees the right to perpetual renewals is valid. Most leases contain a notice procedure whereby tenants must give landlords notice of intent to renew. Tenants, to avail themselves of the right or option to renew or extend the lease, must give the landlord proper notice of their demand for renewal or extension.

The tenant has no right to hold over or remain in possession of the demised premises after the termination of the lease without the agreement of the landlord. Landlords have the option to bring an action for ejectment against tenants who wrongfully hold over after the termination of a lease or may elect to treat them as periodic tenants. The tenant may become a tenant at sufferance, at will, month-to-month, year-to-year, or through some other definite term depending on the circumstances of the case and the statutes involved.

A tenancy for a fixed term terminates without notice to the tenant. The fixed-term tenancy automatically expires at the end of the specified term. If the tenant fails to vacate the demised premises, the landlord may commence a summary proceeding to recover possession from the tenant.

OPTIONS

An option to purchase the demised premises is often contained in a lease. An option contained in a lease is subject to the same rules applicable to options generally. The option is an irrevocable offer by the landlord to sell the property which may be accepted by the tenant's exercise of the option. The payment of rent required by the lease and the performance of the other lease covenants serve as consideration for the option.

The option itself does not alter the landlord-tenant relationship until it has been exercised. On exercise of the option by tender of all or part of the purchase price, the option becomes a binding contract for sale. At this time, the landlord-tenant relationship ceases, and the status of the parties becomes vendor-purchaser. Until such time as performance is tendered by the tenant by payment of all or part of the purchase price, the tenant remains wholly liable for rent. On the other hand, once the tenant has made a down payment toward the purchase price as required by the terms of the option, his or her obligation to pay rent ceases. Therefore, the option must contain the complete terms of purchase with definiteness and certainty. As a minimum, the option should contain an adequate description of the parties, an adequate description of the property, the purchase and loan terms, any warranties of seller, any conditions of buyer's obligation to purchase, and buyer's rights on failing to pay rent.

Some leases also give the tenant the right of first refusal to purchase the demised premises. If the tenant has the right of first refusal, such right is conditional on the landlord's willingness to sell. The tenant merely has a preference over other prospective purchases if the landlord decides to sell the demised premises. Should the landlord decide to sell the demised premises, either to a third party or to the tenant, the tenant's right of refusal ripens into an option.

TERMINATION

A tenancy at will is terminated by either party giving the notice required by local statute. A tenancy for an unspecified term is deemed to be renewed for the period for which the tenant pays rent (periodic tenancy). The periodic tenancy may be terminated by giving notice equal to the period or as required by the local jurisdiction. The most common type of periodic tenancy is the month-to-month tenancy. The month-to-month tenancy is terminated by either party giving 30 days written notice to the other party.

When this notice must be given varies from jurisdiction to jurisdiction. Traditionally it was necessary to give notice of termination of the lease precisely on the last day of the preceding 30-day period. In modern times many jurisdictions are relaxing this requirement, and as long as a minimum of 30 days notice is given, it is not necessary to give such notice exactly on the last day of the preceding period.

EVICTION

Most jurisdictions provide for a summary remedy when the landlord becomes entitled to possession of the premises because of termination of the lease, passage of time, forfeiture, conditions subsequent to foreclosure or sale by trustee, failure to pay rent, breach of a condition or covenant in the lease, or other reason. The statutory remedy provided in most jurisdictions is usually summary in nature; that is, it is designed to simplify and expedite the proceeding by which the landlord may recover possession of his property. Typically the summary proceeding available to the landlord may recover possession of the property and unpaid rent, as well as sue for damages to the property and other related claims.

The summary procedure for possession and damages by the landlord may be maintained against a tenant only when the conventional relationship of landlord and tenant exists between the plaintiff and the person sought to be evicted from the premises. The summary procedure cannot normally be maintained when the landlord-tenant relationship no longer exists.

The normal summary procedure requires as a condition precedent to bringing the action that the landlord serve the tenant with a notice to perform the covenants or conditions contained in the lease, pay rent, perform some other act, or quit the premises. The notice should state that the landlord elects to terminate the lease. A defect in the notice will normally be a valid defense to the summary dispossession action.

The action can normally be brought by the landlord, the landlord's personal representative, a co-lessor, a co-tenant, a successor to the landlord, and a tenant who has assigned or sublet the demised premises. No person other than the tenant, subtenant, or assignee of the demised premises need be made a party defendant to the lawsuit.

The normal statute providing for the summary dispossession procedure requires that the complaint in unlawful detainer allege the existence of the landlord-tenant relationship; contain an adequate description of the premises; determine termination date of the tenancy, exact amount of rent alleged to be due from tenant, or neglect or failure to perform some covenant or condition of the lease agreement other than the payment of rent, an unauthorized assignment or subletting of the demised premises, the maintenance of a nuisance or use of the premises for an unlawful purpose, or failure by the tenant to deliver possession as specified in the written notice of termination or offer to surrender which is accepted in writing by the landlord. Additionally, the complaint must allege that the defendant has been served the necessary notice requiring him or her to pay rent or perform covenants or conditions for possession of the premises and has refused to comply. Certain statutes also allow the landlord to seek treble damages.

Most jurisdictions provide a shortened period of time for the defendant to answer the suit and provide for preference in setting the case for trial. After trial of the matter the court will, if plaintiff is entitled thereto, give judgment for possession, rent, and damages due to the plaintiff. Treble damages may be available if there has been waste or destruction to the property. Generally, for treble damages to be available it must appear from the circumstances and extent of the damages that such damage was committed knowingly, maliciously, wantonly, and willfully. After obtaining judgment, the landlord may obtain a writ of possession which authorizes the sheriff to move the tenant forcibly from the property.

As affirmative defenses to the landlord's suit, the tenant may allege that the landlord has breached a covenant in the lease, the property is uninhabitable (residential lease), or the tenant has complied with all terms and conditions of the lease, or may undertake other authorized affirmative defenses. The landlord may not engage in any self-help in restoring himself to possession unless a local statute specifically authorizes him to do so.

MITIGATION OF DAMAGES

In a majority of jurisdictions, landlords are not required to make a reasonable effort to minimize their damages (loss of rental income) by leasing the property to another after the lease is executed by the parties and subsequently breached by the tenant. The reason for the rule is the theory that the lease of real property is a sale of an interest in land and not merely a contract, and, therefore, the tenant's breach does not terminate the lease but gives rise to the landlord's cause of actions for damages. Should the landlord elect to stand by and do nothing, he may sue the lessee as each installment of rent matures or for the whole amount when it becomes due. The landlord also has the option of retaking possession and treating the lease as terminated or may retake possession for the account of the tenant and hold the tenant liable for general damages for the difference between the rental stipulated to be paid and what in good faith the landlord is able to recover from reletting.

The expanding minority of jurisdictions, applying modern contract principles, provide by statute that a tenant's breach of the lease and abandonment of the property operates to terminate the lease automatically if there is no provision to the contrary in the lease agreement. The present law in the minority jurisdictions additionally provides the landlord with the affirmative obligation to make a reasonable and good-faith attempt to mitigate damages by subletting the property at the fair market rate. As a result, the tenant is entitled to offset against the unpaid rent which accrues after the date of termination the amount of rent actually received by the landlord from subletting, as well as the amount of rents the tenant is able to prove the landlord could have obtained by acting reasonably in subletting the property.

In the minority jurisdictions, the landlord may be able to stand by and collect rent from the breaching tenant if the lease so provides, as long as the landlord does not terminate the tenant's right to possession, and only if the lease expressly permits the tenant to mitigate his damages by subletting or assigning his leasehold estate. The affirmative obligation is thereby shifted from the landlord to the tenant, who has the duty to mitigate personally his own damages. Should the landlord relet the property, his right to recover rent from the original tenant is terminated at the time he terminates the tenant's right to possession.

It should be noted that wrongful termination of a commercial or industrial lease may result in additional actions for damages to the business.

CHECKLIST FOR REVIEWING LEASES

1. Parties

a. Are the parties named correctly? ( )

b. If the landlord or tenant is an agent, is evidence of authority indicated in writing? ( )

c. Is either party's performance guaranteed? Should it be? ( )

2. Premises

a. Is the description of the premises adequate? ( )

b. Is a plot plan necessary? ( ) Should a legal description be included? ( )

c. Is parking provided for? ( )

3. Term of lease

a. Are the commencement and termination dates specified or determinable? ( )

b. Is the date on which tenant is bound by the terms of the lease specified or determinable? ( )

c. Is there a renewal provision? ( ) If so, are the provisions the same as in the original? ( ) Is the method for determining rent on renewal adequate? ( ) May tenant renew if in default? ( )

d. Is there a holding over provision? ( ) Are the terms and rent the same? ( )

4. Delivery of premises

a. Is the building completed? ( )

b. Is work to be done in readying the premises? ( ) Is such work described in the lease or letter agreement in sufficient detail? ( )

c. Must landlord proceed with due diligence in completing work on the premises? ( )

d. If tenant requests or does work, must the plans be approved? ( )

e. Is the lease void or voidable if not ready on the commencement date? ( ) If not, is the rent adjusted? ( )

f. Does the lease terminate if occupancy does not commence within a specified time? ( )

g. Is a certificate of occupancy required? ( )

5. Rent

a. Is the amount of rent clearly set forth? ( )

b. Is proration provided for? ( ) For what purpose?

c. Is it clear where the rent is to be paid? ( )

d. Are setoffs permissible? ( )

e. Are interest and penalties payable on late payments? ( ) How much? ( )

f. Is there a deposit? ( )

(1) If so, is interest payable on the deposit? ( )

(2) Is the deposit to be returned? ( )

(3) Applied against rent? ( )

(4) In the event of a transfer of landlord's interest, does the lease specify what happens to the deposit? ( )

6. Rent adjustment—expenses

a. Is there a rent adjustment clause? ( )

b. Is the determination of expenses a function of the first year of operation of the building? ( ) Is the base year adequately defined? ( )

c. Is the statement of expenses prepared by a CPA? ( ) If not, may tenant examine the books? ( )

d. Does tenant have a right to object to such statement? ( )

e. Is the tenant's pro rata share the same as the floor space occupied? ( ) Is this percentage specified in the lease? ( )

f. Are the expense factors specified? ( ) Which of the following are expenses of the building for this purpose:

(1) Real estate taxes ( )

(2) Personal property taxes ( )

(3) Building employees' wages ( )

(4) Assessments ( )

(5) Utilities ( )

(6) Repairs ( )

(7) Remodeling ( )

g. If increased taxes are paid on a pro rata basis, are the base assessment and tax fiscal year adequately specified? ( ) If the building may be remodeled, are provisions adequate? ( )

7. Taxes

a. Is tenant liable to pay real estate taxes on the premises ( ) Personal property taxes? ( )

b. Is tenant required to pay the taxes attributable to his or her improvements or fixtures? (   ) If so, must tenant request separate billing? (   )

c. Is tenant required to pay taxes on any other areas of the building? (   )

d. Must tenant pay assessments? (   )

e. Does landlord have the right to pay taxes for tenant and require repayment from tenant? (   ) Is this payment designated as additional rent? (   )

f. If tenant pays taxes or assessments, may he or she challenge assessment in name of landlord? (   )

8. Use of premises

a. Is tenant's use of premises sufficiently broad or sufficiently restricted? (   )

b. Must tenant comply with laws and public regulations? (   )

c. Does tenant's business involve any risk of violating such laws or regulations? (   )

d. Is there a "no competition" business clause? (   )

9. Repairs and alterations

a. Does tenant accept the unit "as is"? (   )

b. Who must repair? (   ) Must tenant repair for damage not caused by misuse or neglect? (   ) Must landlord repair:

(1) Plumbing? (   )

(2) Heating and air conditioning? (   )

(3) Windows? (   )

(4) Roof? (   )

c. Are repairs distinct from restoration after casualty? (   )

d. Must repairs be made if insurance proceeds are insufficient? (   ) Must reconstruction be made? (   )

e. If so, who pays the difference? (   )

f. After a casualty, is landlord responsible for any repairs other than reconstruction? (   )

(1) Must landlord repair or replace tenant's alterations or fixtures? (   ) Reconstruct? (   )

(2) Are the circumstances requiring reconstruction sufficiently defined? (   )

(3) Does landlord have the option to terminate if reconstruction is not possible? (   ) If it is not desired? (   )

(4) Does tenant have the option to terminate if reconstruction is not completed within a specified time period? (   )

(5) Is the rent adjusted pending reconstruction? (   )

g. May tenant make any alterations? (   )

h. Does tenant's business suggest that alterations are necessary? (   ) If so, are they to be made prior to tenancy? (   ) If they are to be made after tenancy:

(1) Must tenant pay for alterations? (   )

(2) Do alterations belong to landlord? (   )

(3) Must landlord or contractor approve the plans? (   )

(4) Are there restrictions on tenant's right to alter? (   )

(5) Are prior notice and landlord's "stop notice" required? (   )

i. Must the tenant restore the premises at the conclusion of the tenancy? (   ) Is fair wear and tear excepted? (   )

j. Does the tenant have trade fixtures? (   ) May they be removed after the surrender of the premises? (   ) Must they be removed? (   )

10. Assignment and subletting

a. Is landlord's consent required? (   )

b. Does landlord agree not to withhold consent unreasonably? (   )

c. Are standards for assignment or subletting specified? (   ) Does landlord have the option to terminate the lease if consent for assignment or sublease is requested? (   )

d. Can assignment or subletting take place by operation of law? (   ) By mortgage (   ), pledge (   ), hypothecation (   ), encumbrance (   ), bankruptcy (   ), death? (   )

e. Is the sale of stock in a corporate tenant covered by this provision? (   ) Is a merger (   ), sale of assets (   ), attachment (   ), execution (   )?

f. Does landlord share in any increased rent under subletting? (   )

11. Transfer of landlord's interest

a. Is landlord relieved of liability on the lease? (   )

b. Is there a clause requiring attornment to landlord's successor? (   )

c. Must landlord's transferee assume the obligations of the lease in writing? (   )

d. May transferee terminate the lease? (   )

12. Indemnification of landlord

a. Must tenant indemnify landlord for causes other than tenant's negligence? (   ) Are injuries caused by landlord's negligence or willful misconduct excluded? (   ) Is there a waiver of subrogation? (   )

b. Must tenant indemnify landlord for injuries sustained by third parties in common areas? (   ) For breach of its obligations under the lease? (   )

13. Services and utilities

a. Is landlord's duty to supply utilities to the premises sufficiently defined? (   )

(1) Must utilities be supplied on weekends? (   )

(2) Nights? (   )

(3) Include elevators? (   ) Air conditioning? (   )

(4) Janitorial services? (   )

b. Is tenant required to pay for the utilities either directly or by reimbursing landlord? (   )

c. Is tenant's use of certain apparatus on the premises restricted? (   ) Is it anticipated that tenant will use apparatus which will require large amounts of utility services? (   )

d. Is landlord liable for damage caused to anyone by operation or nonoperation of services and utilities? (   )

e. Is rent abated if services or utilities are not provided? (   ) For interruption due to labor disputes? (   ) For casualties? (   )

f. Are utility services adequate for intended use? (   )

14. Common areas

a. Are there common areas? (   )

b. Are there restrictions on tenant's right to make use of a common area? (   )

c. Are the common areas sufficiently defined? (   )

d. Does tenant bear any costs in the operation or maintenance of the common areas? (   )

15. Reentry by landlord

a. Is reentry by landlord specifically permitted? (   )

(1) To carry out landlord's obligations? (   )

(2) To show the premises? (   ) Is this limited to a specified period before the end of the term? (   )

(3) To make repairs? (   )

b. Does tenant specifically waive claims for damages caused by reentry? ( ) For use of scaffolding, and so on? ( ) Is blockage of entrance or unreasonable interference with business excepted? ( )

c. Is unlawful entry, detainer, or eviction excepted? ( )

d. Are there any areas landlord does not have a right to enter? ( ) Should not have a right to enter? ( )

16. Default

a. Are defaults adequately specified? ( )

b. Is abandonment a default? ( )

c. In the event of abandonment does landlord have the right to remove and store personal property for tenant's account? ( ) To appoint a receiver? ( )

d. May landlord use tenant's fixtures in the event tenant abandons the premises? ( )

e. May landlord reenter on default? ( ) Lease the premises for the account of the tenant? ( ) Terminate the lease? ( ) Are liquidated damages provided? ( )

17. Eminent domain

a. Does landlord have the option to terminate the lease for a taking of less than all the premises? ( ) Does the tenant? ( )

b. Does tenant share in the condemnation award if the entire premises are condemned? ( ) For a partial taking? ( ) For improvements and moving expenses? ( )

c. Does tenant waive all claims against the landlord for the value of the unexpired term? ( )

d. In the event of a partial taking is there a proportionate reduction in the rent? ( )

18. Attorneys' fees

a. Are they provided? ( )

b. Are they limited to court action? ( ) To actions resulting in judgment? ( )

c. Do both parties have a right to attorneys' fees? ( )

d. Does tenant have a right to? ( )

e. Must the amount be reasonable? ( ) Determined by court? ( )

19. Waiver

a. May a waiver by landlord constitute a later waiver on identical matters? ( )

b. Does subsequent acceptance of rent by landlord constitute a waiver of anything but that rental payment? ( )

c. Is it provided that a surrender of the premises can be accepted only in writing? ( )

20. Insurance

a. Does tenant have a duty to maintain insurance in specified types and amounts? ( ) If so, specify amounts and types:

___

Are amounts adequate to protect landlord? ( )

b. Is approval of insurer by landlord required, or are standards set forth in the lease? ( )

c. Do landlord and tenant waive subrogation? ( ) Does tenant waive subrogation regarding other tenants? ( ) Are these waivers conditioned on not incurring an additional premium? ( )

d. Should landlord be named an additional insured on tenant's policies? ( )

21. Notices

a. Must all notices be written? ( )

b. Must all notices be served by registered or certified mail, postage paid, return receipt requested? ( )

c. May notices be served on tenant by leaving them at the premises? ( )

22. Abandonment

a. Is abandonment a breach of the lease? ( )

b. Does abandonment terminate the lease? ( )

23. Subordination

a. Are the lease and tenant's interest therein expressly subordinated to mortgages and deeds of trust? ( ) To other leases? ( )

b. Does tenant have a duty to execute instruments evidencing the lease? ( )

c. Is there a requirement that mortgagees or master lessors execute nondisturbance agreements? ( )

d. Does the purchaser have the right to attornment? ( ) To terminate the lease? To require a new lease? ( )

24. Miscellaneous

a. Does invalidity of one section affect the remainder of the issue? ( )

b. Does the lease constitute the entire agreement between the parties? (   )
Are there other agreements? (   ) If so, state:

___

___

c. Is the manner of amending specified? (   )

d. Is time of the essence? (   )

e. Is the lease binding on successors and assignees of one of the parties? (   ) Both? (   )

f. Is the landlord's performance excused by labor disputes? (   )

g. Is a governing law specified? (   )

h. Are the signatures properly executed and notarized when required? (   )

See samples of leases, Figures 8-1 to 8-8.

RESIDENTIAL LEASE

THIS IS INTENDED TO BE A LEGALLY BINDING AGREEMENT—READ IT CAREFULLY.

CALIFORNIA ASSOCIATION OF REALTORS® STANDARD FORM

________________________, California ________________________ 19______

____, Landlord, and

____, Tenant, agrees as follows:

1. Landlord leases to Tenant and Tenant hires from Landlord those premises described as: ________________________

____

together with the following furniture, and appliances, if any, and fixtures: ________________________

(Insert "as shown on Exhibit A attached hereto" and attach the exhibit if the list is extensive.)

2. The term of this lease shall be for a period of ________________ months, ________ years commencing ________________ 19______ and terminating ________________ 19______

3. Tenant is to pay a total rent of $ ________________, payable as follows: ________________________

____

The rent shall be paid at ________________________
or at any address designated by the Landlord in writing.

4. $ ________________ as security has been deposited. Landlord may use therefrom such amounts as are reasonably necessary to remedy Tenant's defaults in the payment of rent, to repair damages caused by Tenant, and to clean the premises upon termination of tenancy. If used toward rent or damages during the term of tenancy, Tenant agrees to reinstate said total security deposit upon five days written notice delivered to Tenant in person or by mailing. Balance of security deposit, if any, together with a written itemized accounting shall be mailed to Tenant's last known address within 14 days of surrender of premises.

5. Tenant agrees to pay for all utilities and services based upon occupancy of the premises and the following charges: ________________

____

except ________________________
which shall be paid for by Landlord.

6. Tenant has examined the premises and all furniture, furnishings and appliances if any, and fixtures contained therein, and accepts the same as being clean, in good order, condition, and repair, with the following exceptions: ________________________

7. The premises are leased for use as a residence by the following named persons: ________________________

No animal, bird, or pet except ________________________
shall be kept on or about the premises without Landlord's prior written consent.

8. Any holding over at the expiration of this lease shall create a month to month tenancy at a monthly rent of $ ________________ payable in advance. All other terms and conditions herein shall remain in full force and effect.

9. Tenant shall not disturb, annoy, endanger or interfere with other Tenants of the building or neighbors, nor use the premises for any unlawful purposes, nor violate any law or ordinance, nor commit waste or nuisance upon or about the premises.

10. Tenant agrees to comply with all reasonable rules or regulations posted on the premises or delivered to Tenant by Landlord.

11. Tenant shall keep the premises and furniture, furnishings and appliances, if any, and fixtures which are leased for his exclusive use in good order and condition and pay for any repairs to the property caused by Tenant's negligence or misuse or that of Tenant's invitees. Landlord shall otherwise maintain the property. Tenant's personal property is not insured by Landlord.

12. Tenant shall not paint, wallpaper, nor make alterations to the property without Landlord's prior written consent.

13. Upon not less than 24 hours advance notice, Tenant shall make the demised premises available during normal business hours to Landlord or his authorized agent or representative, for the purpose of entering (a) to make necessary agreed repairs, decorations, alterations or improvements or to supply necessary or agreed services, and (b) to show the premises to prospective or actual purchasers, mortgagees, tenants, workmen or contractors. In an emergency, Landlord, his agent or authorized representative may enter the premises at any time without securing prior permission from Tenant for the purpose of making corrections or repairs to alleviate such emergency.

14. Tenant shall not let or sublet all or any part of the premises nor assign this lease or any interest in it without the prior written consent of Landlord.

15. If Tenant abandons or vacates the premises, Landlord may at his option terminate this lease, and regain possession in the manner prescribed by law.

16. If any legal action or proceeding be brought by either party to enforce any part of this lease, the prevailing party shall recover in addition to all other relief, reasonable attorney's fees and costs.

17. Time is of the essence. The waiver by Landlord or Tenant of any breach shall not be construed to be a continuing waiver of any subsequent breach.

18. Notice upon Tenant shall be served as provided by law. Notice upon Landlord may be served upon Manager of the demised premises ________________________
at ________________________. Said Manager is authorized to accept service on behalf of Landlord.

19. Within 10 days after written notice, Tenant agrees to execute and deliver a certificate as submitted by Landlord acknowledging that this agreement is unmodified and in full force and effect or in full force and effect as modified and stating the modifications. Failure to comply shall be deemed Tenant's acknowledgement that the certificate as submitted by Landlord is true and correct and may be relied upon by any lender or purchaser.

20. The undersigned Tenant acknowledges having read the foregoing prior to execution and receipt of a copy hereof.

Landlord ________________________ Tenant ________________________

Landlord ________________________ Tenant ________________________

NO REPRESENTATION IS MADE AS TO THE LEGAL VALIDITY OF ANY PROVISION OR THE ADEQUACY OF ANY PROVISION IN ANY SPECIFIC TRANSACTION. A REAL ESTATE BROKER IS THE PERSON QUALIFIED TO ADVISE ON REAL ESTATE. IF YOU DESIRE LEGAL ADVICE CONSULT YOUR ATTORNEY.

To order, contact—California Association of Realtors®
525 South Virgil Avenue, Los Angeles, California 90020

(Revised, 1978)

FORM LR-14

EQUAL HOUSING OPPORTUNITY

Figure 8-1 Residential lease. (*Reprinted by courtesy of the California Association of Realtors®.*)

TENANT APPLICATION

Property Address: ______ Apt. No. ______

Name(s) of Applicant(s): ______

Other Name(s) used within last 3 years: ______

Names and Age of other Occupants: ______

Pets (Number & Type): ______

Present Address: ______ City-State ______ zip ______

How long? ______ Reason for leaving: ______

Name and Address of Owner or Owner's Agent: ______

Previous Address (Past 3 Years): ______ City-State ______ zip ______

How long? ______ Reason for leaving: ______

Name and Address of Owner or Owner's Agent: ______

Previous Address (Past 3 Years): ______

How long? ______ Reason for leaving: ______

Name and Address of Owner or Owner's Agent: ______

Employment:
Social Security Number [ ][ ][ ] – [ ][ ] – [ ][ ][ ][ ] Drivers License Number [ ][ ][ ][ ][ ][ ][ ]

Birth Date (Mo.-Day-Yr.) ______ (State and Expiration Date) ______

Present Employer: ______ How long? ______

Address: ______ Telephone: ______

Employed as: ______ Salary: $ ______ per ______

Other Occupant:
Social Security Number [ ][ ][ ] – [ ][ ] – [ ][ ][ ][ ] Drivers License Number [ ][ ][ ][ ][ ][ ][ ]

Birth Date (Mo.-Day-Yr.) ______ (State and Expiration Date) ______

Present Employer ______ How long? ______

Address: ______ Telephone: ______

Employed as: ______ Salary: $ ______ per ______

Other Income: $ ______ Source: ______

Credit References (2): ______

Credit Cards: Issuer ______ Acct. No. [ ][ ][ ][ ][ ][ ][ ][ ][ ][ ][ ][ ][ ][ ][ ][ ] Issuer ______ Acct. No. [ ][ ][ ][ ][ ][ ][ ][ ][ ][ ][ ][ ][ ][ ][ ][ ]

Name of Bank	Branch Address

Automobile License No. ______ State of Registry: ______

Make & Model: ______ Year: ______ Color: ______

IN CASE OF EMERGENCY:
Name of Person to be Informed: ______ Relationship: ______

Address: ______ Telephone: ______

AUTHORIZATION TO VERIFY INFORMATION

I Authorize Landlord or his Authorized Agents to Verify the above information, including but not limited to obtaining a Credit Report and if this application is accepted I agree to execute the residential lease or rental agreement as set forth on the reverse side hereof.

Date ______ 19 ______ Applicant: ______

Telephone No. ______ Applicant: ______

RECEIPT FOR DEPOSIT

The undersigned acknowledges receipt of $ ______ in the form of ( ) Cash, ( ) Personal Check or ( ) ______ payable to ______ as deposit on the above described property.

Date ______ Agent ______

Figure 8-1 (*Continued*)

Southern California Chapter of the Society of Industrial Realtors,® Inc.

INDUSTRIAL REAL ESTATE LEASE

ARTICLE ONE: **BASIC TERMS**

This Article One contains the Basic Terms of this Lease between the Landlord and Tenant named below. Other Articles, Sections and Paragraphs of the Lease referred to in this Article One explain and define the Basic Terms and are to be read in conjunction with the Basic Terms.

Section 1.01. **Date of Lease:** ____________________

Section 1.02. **Landlord:** ____________________

Address of Landlord: ____________________

Section 1.03. **Tenant:** ____________________

Address of Tenant: ____________________

Section 1.04. **Property:** (Include street address, approximate square footage and description) ____________________

Section 1.05. **Lease Term:** __________ **beginning on** __________ or such other date as is specified in this Lease, and **ending on** __________

Section 1.06. **Permitted Uses:** (See Section 5.01) ____________________

Section 1.07. **Tenant's Guarantor:** (If none, so state) ____________________

Section 1.08. **Landlord's Broker:** (See Article Fourteen)(If none, so state) ____________________

Section 1.09. **Tenant's Broker:** (If none, so state) ____________________

Section 1.10. **Commission Payable to Landlord's Broker:** (See Article Fourteen) $ __________

Section 1.11. **Initial Security Deposit:** (See Paragraphs 3.03 and 13.03(c)) $ __________

Section 1.12. **Vehicle Parking Spaces Allocated to Tenant:** (See Multi-Tenant Facility Lease Rider, if attached) __________

Section 1.13. **Rent and Other Charges Payable by Tenant:**

(a) BASE RENT: ____________________($__________) per month for the first __________ months, as provided in Section 3.01, and shall be increased on the __________ months after the Commencement Date, either (i) in accordance with the increase in the United States Department of Labor, Bureau of Labor Statistics, Consumer Price Index for Urban Wage Earners and Clerical Workers (all Items for the __________ Statistical Area on the basis of 1967 = 100 [the "Index"]), as provided in Section 3.02, or (ii) ____________________. If (ii) is completed, then (i) and Section 3.02 are inapplicable.

(b) OTHER PERIODIC PAYMENTS: (i) Real Property Taxes above the "Base Real Property Taxes" (See Section 4.02); (ii) Utilities (See Section 4.03); (iii) Increased Insurance Premiums above "Base Premiums" (See Section 4.04); (iv) Common Area Charges (See Section 4.05 or Multi-Tenant Facility Lease Rider, if attached). The initial monthly common area charge is $__________; (v) Maintenance, Repairs and Alterations (See Article Six).

Section 1.14. **Costs and Charges Payable by Landlord:**

(a) BASE REAL PROPERTY TAXES (See Section 4.02),

(b) BASE INSURANCE PREMIUMS (See Section 4.04(c)),

(c) MAINTENANCE AND REPAIR (See Article Six).

Section 1.15 **Riders:** The following Riders are attached to and made a part of this Lease: (If none, so state) ____________________

1

Initials __________

(Gross Form)

Figure 8-2 Industrial real estate lease. (*Reprinted by courtesy of the Southern California Chapter of the Society of Industrial Realtors,® Inc.*)

ARTICLE TWO: **LEASE TERM**

Section 2.01. **Lease of Property For Lease Term.** Landlord leases the Property to Tenant and Tenant leases the Property from Landlord for the Lease Term. The Lease Term is for the period stated in Section 1.05 above and shall begin and end on the dates specified in Section 1.05 above, unless the beginning or end of the Lease Term is changed under any provision of this Lease. The "Commencement Date" shall be the date specified in Section 1.05 above for the beginning of the Lease Term, unless advanced or delayed under any provision of this Lease.

Section 2.02. **Delay in Commencement.** Landlord shall not be liable to Tenant if Landlord does not deliver possession of the Property to Tenant on the first date specified in Section 1.05 above. Landlord's non-delivery of the Property to Tenant on that date shall not affect this Lease or the obligations of Tenant under this Lease. However, the Commencement Date shall be delayed until possession of the Property is delivered to Tenant. The Lease Term shall be extended for a period equal to the delay in delivery of possession of the Property to Tenant, plus the number of days necessary to end the Lease Term on the last day of a month. If Landlord does not deliver possession of the Property to Tenant within sixty (60) days after the first date specified in Section 1.05 above, Tenant may elect to cancel this Lease by giving written notice to Landlord within ten (10) days after the 60-day period ends. If Tenant gives such notice, the Lease shall be cancelled and neither Landlord nor Tenant shall have any further obligations to the other. If Tenant does not give such notice, Tenant's right to cancel the Lease shall expire and the Lease Term shall commence upon the delivery of possession of the Property to Tenant. If delivery of possession of the Property to Tenant is delayed, Landlord and Tenant shall, upon such delivery, execute an amendment to this Lease setting forth the Commencement Date and expiration date of the Lease.

Section 2.03. **Early Occupancy.** If Tenant occupies the Property prior to the Commencement Date, Tenant's occupancy of the Property shall be subject to all of the provisions of this Lease. Early occupancy of the Property shall not advance the expiration date of this Lease. Tenant shall pay Base Rent and all other charges specified in this Lease for the early occupancy period.

Section 2.04. **Holding Over.** Tenant shall vacate the Property upon the expiration or earlier termination of this Lease. Tenant shall reimburse Landlord for and indemnify Landlord against all damages incurred by Landlord from any delay by Tenant in vacating the Property. If Tenant does not vacate the Property upon the expiration or earlier termination of the Lease and Landlord thereafter accepts rent from Tenant, Tenant's occupancy of the Property shall be a "month-to-month" tenancy, subject to all of the terms of this Lease applicable to a month-to-month tenancy, except that the Base Rent then in effect shall be increased by twenty-five percent (25%).

ARTICLE THREE: **BASE RENT**

Section 3.01. **Time and Manner of Payment.** Upon execution of this Lease, Tenant shall pay Landlord the Base Rent in the amount stated in Paragraph 1.13(a) above for the first month of the Lease Term. On the first day of the second month of the Lease Term and each month thereafter, Tenant shall pay Landlord the Base Rent, in advance, without offset, deduction or prior demand. The Base Rent shall be payable at Landlord's address or at such other place as Landlord may designate in writing.

Section 3.02. **Cost of Living Increases.** The Base Rent shall be increased at the times specified in Paragraph 1.13(a) above, in proportion to the increase in the Index which has occurred between the first month of the Lease Term and the month in which the rent is to be increased. Landlord shall notify Tenant of each increase by delivering a written statement setting forth the Index for the first month of the Lease Term, the Index for the month in which the Base Rent is to be increased, the percentage increase between those two Indices, and the new amount of the Base Rent. The Base Rent shall not be reduced from the last previous adjusted Base Rent by reason of any decrease in the Index. Tenant shall pay the new Base Rent from its effective date until the next periodic increase. Landlord's notice may be given after the effective date of the increase since the Index for the appropriate month may be unavailable on the effective date. In such event, Tenant shall pay Landlord the necessary rental adjustment for the months elapsed between the effective date of the increase and Landlord's notice of such increase within ten (10) days after Landlord's notice. If the format or components of the Index are materially changed after the Date of Lease, Landlord shall substitute an index which is published by the Bureau of Labor Statistics or similar agency and which is most nearly equivalent to the Index in effect on the Date of Lease. Landlord shall notify Tenant of the substituted index, which shall be used to calculate the increase in the Base Rent unless Tenant objects in writing within fifteen (15) days after receipt of Landlord's notice. If Tenant objects, the substitute Index shall be determined in accordance with the rules and regulations of the American Arbitration Association. The cost of such arbitration shall be borne equally by Landlord and Tenant.

Section 3.03. **Security Deposit Increases.** Each time the Base Rent is increased, Tenant shall deposit additional funds with Landlord sufficient to increase the Security Deposit to an amount which bears the same relationship to the adjusted Base Rent as the initial Security Deposit bore to the initial Base Rent.

Section 3.04. **Termination; Advance Payments.** Upon termination of this Lease under Article Seven (Damage or Destruction), Article Eight (Condemnation) or any other termination not resulting from Tenant's default, and after Tenant has vacated the Property in the manner required by this Lease, an equitable adjustment shall be made concerning advance rent, any other advance payments made by Tenant to Landlord, and accrued real property taxes, and Landlord shall refund the unused portion of the Security Deposit to Tenant or Tenant's successor.

2 Initials ____________

 (Net Form) ____________

Figure 8-2 (*Continued*)

ARTICLE FOUR: **OTHER CHARGES PAYABLE BY TENANT**

Section 4.01. **Additional Rent.** All charges payable by Tenant other than Base Rent are called "Additional Rent." Unless this Lease provides otherwise, all Additional Rent shall be paid with the next monthly installment of Base Rent. The term "rent" shall mean Base Rent and Additional Rent.

Section 4.02. **Real Property Taxes.**

(a) **Payment of Taxes.** Landlord shall pay the "Base Real Property Taxes" on the Property during the Lease Term. Base Real Property Taxes are real property taxes applicable to the Property as shown on the tax bill for the most recent tax fiscal year ending prior to the Commencement Date. However, if the structures on the Property are not completed by the tax lien date of such tax fiscal year, the Base Real Property Taxes are the taxes shown on the first tax bill showing the full assessed value of the Property after completion of the structures. Tenant shall pay Landlord the amount, if any, by which the real property taxes during the Lease Term exceed the Base Real Property Taxes. Subject to Paragraph 4.02(c), Tenant shall make such payments within fifteen (15) days after receipt of Landlord's statement showing the amount and computation of such increase. Landlord shall reimburse Tenant for any real property taxes paid by Tenant covering any period of time prior to or after the Lease Term.

(b) **Definition of "Real Property Tax."** "Real property tax" means: (i) any fee, license fee, license tax, business license fee, commercial rental tax, levy, charge, assessment, penalty or tax imposed by any taxing authority against the Property; (ii) any tax on the Landlord's right to receive, or the receipt of, rent or income from the Property or against Landlord's business of leasing the Property; (iii) any tax or charge for fire protection, streets, sidewalks, road maintenance, refuse or other services provided to the Property by any governmental agency; (iv) any tax imposed upon this transaction, or based upon a re-assessment of the Property due to a change in ownership or transfer of all or part of Landlord's interest in the Property; and (v) any charge or fee replacing any tax previously included within the definition of real property tax. "Real property tax" does not, however, include Landlord's federal or state income, franchise, inheritance or estate taxes.

(c) **Joint Assessment.** If the Property is not separately assessed, Tenant's share of the real property tax payable by Tenant under Paragraph 4.02(a) shall be determined from the assessor's worksheets or other reasonably available information. Landlord shall make a reasonable determination of Tenant's proportionate share of such real property tax and Tenant shall pay such share to Landlord within fifteen (15) days after receipt of Landlord's written statement.

(d) **Personal Property Taxes.**

(i) Tenant shall pay all taxes charged against trade fixtures, furnishings, equipment or any other personal property belonging to Tenant. Tenant shall try to have personal property taxed separately from the Property.

(ii) If any of Tenant's personal property is taxed with the Property, Tenant shall pay Landlord the taxes for the personal property within fifteen (15) days after Tenant receives a written statement from Landlord for such personal property taxes.

Section 4.03. **Utilities.** Tenant shall pay, directly to the appropriate supplier, the cost of all natural gas, heat, light, power, sewer service, telephone, water, refuse disposal and other utilities and services supplied to the Property. However, if any services or utilities are jointly metered with other property, Landlord shall make a reasonable determination of Tenant's proportionate share of the cost of such utilities and services and Tenant shall pay such share to Landlord within fifteen (15) days after receipt of Landlord's written statement.

Section 4.04. **Insurance Premiums.**

(a) **Liability Insurance.** During the Lease Term, Tenant shall maintain a policy of comprehensive public liability insurance, at Tenant's expense, insuring Landlord against liability arising out of the ownership, use, occupancy or maintenance of the Property. The initial amount of such insurance shall be at least $1,000,000, and shall be subject to periodic increase based upon inflation, increased liability awards, recommendation of professional insurance advisers, and other relevant factors. However, the amount of such insurance shall not limit Tenant's liability nor relieve Tenant of any obligation hereunder. The policy shall contain cross-liability endorsements, if applicable, and shall insure Tenant's performance of the indemnity provisions of Section 5.04. Such policy shall contain a provision which prohibits cancellation or modification of the policy except upon thirty (30) days' prior written notice to Landlord. Tenant may discharge its obligations under this Paragraph by naming Landlord as an additional insured under a policy of comprehensive liability insurance maintained by Tenant and containing the coverage and provisions described in this Paragraph. Tenant shall deliver a copy of such policy or certificate (or a renewal thereof) to Landlord prior to the Commencement Date and prior to the expiration of any such policy during the Lease Term. If Tenant fails to maintain such policy, Landlord may elect to maintain such insurance at Tenant's expense. Landlord may also elect to maintain, at Landlord's expense, a Landlord's protective liability endorsement with respect to the Property. Tenant shall, at Tenant's expense, maintain such other liability insurance as Tenant deems necessary to protect Tenant.

3 Initials ______________

 (Gross Form) ______________

Figure 8-2 (*Continued*)

(b) **Hazard and Rental Income Insurance.** During the Lease Term, Landlord shall maintain policies of insurance at Tenant's expense, covering loss of or damage to the Property in the full amount of its replacement value. Such policies shall provide protection against all perils included within the classification of fire, extended coverage, vandalism, malicious mischief, special extended perils (all risk), sprinkler leakage, earthquake sprinkler leakage, and Inflation Guard endorsement, and any other perils (except flood and earthquake) which Landlord deems necessary. Landlord may obtain insurance coverage for Tenant's fixtures, equipment or building improvements installed by Tenant in or on the Property. Tenant shall, at Tenant's expense, maintain such primary or additional insurance on its fixtures, equipment and building improvements as Tenant deems necessary to protect its interest. During the Lease Term, Landlord shall also maintain a rental income insurance policy at Tenant's expense, with loss payable to Landlord in an amount equal to one year's Base Rent, estimated real property taxes and insurance premiums. Tenant shall not do or permit to be done anything which invalidates any such insurance policies.

(c) **Payment of Premiums; Insurance Policies.** Subject to Section 4.05 and any Multi-Tenant Facility Lease Rider attached to this Lease, Tenant shall pay all premiums for the insurance policies covering the Property described in Paragraphs 4.04 (a) and (b) within fifteen (15) days after receipt by Tenant of a copy of the premium statement or other evidence of the amount due. If the insurance policies maintained by Landlord cover improvements or real property other than the Property, Landlord shall also deliver to Tenant a statement of the amount of the premiums applicable to the Property showing, in reasonable detail, how such amount was computed. If the Lease Term expires before the expiration of the insurance policy period, Tenant's liability for insurance premiums shall be prorated on an annual basis. All insurance shall be maintained with companies holding a "General Policyholder's Rating" of B+ or better, as set forth in the most current issue of "Best's Insurance Guide." Tenant shall be liable for the payment of any deductible amount under Landlord's insurance policies.

Section 4.05. **Multiple Tenant Buildings; Rules and Regulations.** If the Property is part of a larger building or group of buildings, Tenant shall pay monthly, in advance, its pro rata share of common area maintenance and repair costs as reasonably determined by Landlord. Tenant shall also comply with Landlord's rules and regulations respecting the management, care and safety of the common areas of such buildings and grounds, including parking areas, landscaped areas, walkways, hallways and other facilities provided for the common use and convenience of other occupants. Notice of such rules and regulations will be posted or given to Tenant. Tenant shall pay for any increase in the property insurance premiums for such buildings caused by Tenant's acts, omissions, use or occupancy of the Property.

Section 4.06. **Late Charges.** Tenant's failure to pay rent promptly may cause Landlord to incur unanticipated costs. The exact amount of such costs are impractical or extremely difficult to ascertain. Such costs may include, but are not limited to, processing and accounting charges and late charges which may be imposed on Landlord by any ground lease, mortgage or trust deed encumbering the Property. Therefore, if Landlord does not receive any rent payment within ten (10) days after it becomes due, Tenant shall pay Landlord a late charge equal to ten percent (10%) of the overdue amount. The parties agree that such late charge represents a fair and reasonable estimate of the costs Landlord will incur by reason of such late payment.

Section 4.07. **Interest on Past Due Obligations.** Any amount owed by Tenant to Landlord which is not paid when due shall bear interest at the rate of fifteen percent (15%) per annum from the due date of such amount. However, interest shall not be payable on late charges to be paid by Tenant under this Lease. The payment of interest on such amounts shall not excuse or cure any default by Tenant under this Lease. If the interest rate specified in this Lease is higher than the rate permitted by law, the interest rate is hereby decreased to the maximum legal interest rate permitted by law.

Section 4.08. **Impounds for Insurance Premiums and Real Property Taxes.** If requested by any ground lessor or lender to whom Landlord has granted a security interest in the Property, or if Tenant is more than ten (10) days late in the payment of rent more than once in any consecutive twelve (12) month period, Tenant shall pay Landlord a sum equal to one-twelfth (1/12) of the annual real property taxes and/or insurance premiums payable by Tenant under this Lease, together with each payment of Base Rent. Such payments shall be held by Landlord in a non-interest bearing impound account. The amount of real property taxes and insurance premiums when unknown shall be reasonably estimated by Landlord. Funds in the impound account shall be applied by Landlord to the payment of real property taxes and insurance premiums when due. Any deficiency of funds in the impound account shall be paid by Tenant to Landlord upon written request. If Tenant defaults under this Lease, Landlord may apply any funds in the impound account to any obligation then due under this Lease.

4

Initials ______________

(Net Form) ______________

Figure 8-2 *(Continued)*

ARTICLE FIVE: **USE OF PROPERTY**

Section 5.01. **Permitted Uses.** Tenant may use the Property only for the Permitted Uses set forth in Section 1.06 above.

Section 5.02. **Manner of Use.** Tenant shall not cause or permit the Property to be used in any way which constitutes a violation of any law, ordinance, or governmental regulation or order, which annoys or interferes with the rights of tenants of the development of which the Property is part, or which constitutes a nuisance or waste. Tenant shall obtain and pay for all permits, including a Certificate of Occupancy, required for Tenant's occupancy of the Property and shall promptly take all substantial and non-substantial actions necessary to comply with all applicable statutes, ordinances, rules, regulations, orders and requirements regulating the use by Tenant of the Property, including the Occupational Safety and Health Act.

Section 5.03. **Signs and Auctions.** Tenant shall not place any signs on the Property without Landlord's prior written consent. Tenant shall not conduct or permit any auctions or sheriff's sales at the Property.

Section 5.04. **Indemnity.** Tenant shall indemnify Landlord against and hold Landlord harmless from any and all costs, claims or liability arising from: (a) Tenant's use of the Property; (b) the conduct of Tenant's business or anything else done or permitted by Tenant to be done in or about the Property; (c) any breach or default in the performance of Tenant's obligations under this Lease; (d) any misrepresentation or breach of warranty by Tenant under this Lease; or (e) other acts or omissions of Tenant. Tenant shall defend Landlord against any such cost, claim or liability at Tenant's expense with counsel reasonably acceptable to Landlord or, at Landlord's election, Tenant shall reimburse Landlord for any legal fees or costs incurred by Landlord in connection with any such claim. As a material part of the consideration to Landlord, Tenant hereby assumes all risk of damage to property or injury to persons in or about the Property arising from any cause, and Tenant hereby waives all claims in respect thereof against Landlord, except for any claim arising out of Landlord's gross negligence or willful misconduct.

Section 5.05. **Landlord's Access.** Landlord or its agents may enter the Property at all reasonable times to show the Property to potential buyers, investors or tenants or other parties, or for any other purpose Landlord deems necessary. Landlord shall give Tenant prior notice of such entry, except in the case of an emergency. Landlord may place customary "For Sale" or "For Lease" signs on the Property.

Section 5.06. **Quiet Possession.** If Tenant pays the rent and complies with all other terms of this Lease, Tenant may occupy and enjoy the Property for the full Lease Term, subject to the provisions of this Lease.

ARTICLE SIX: **CONDITION OF PROPERTY; MAINTENANCE, REPAIRS AND ALTERATIONS**

Section 6.01. **Existing Conditions.** Tenant accepts the Property in its condition as of the execution of the Lease, subject to all recorded matters, laws, ordinances, and governmental regulations and orders. Tenant acknowledges that neither Landlord nor any agent of Landlord has made any representation as to the condition of the Property or the suitability of the Property for Tenant's intended use.

Section 6.02. **Exemption of Landlord from Liability.** Landlord shall not be liable for any damage or injury to the person, business (or any loss of income therefrom), goods, wares, merchandise or other property of Tenant, Tenant's employees, invitees, customers or any other person in or about the Property, whether such damage or injury is caused by or results from: (a) fire, steam, electricity, water, gas or rain; (b) the breakage, leakage, obstruction or other defects of pipes, sprinklers, wires, appliances, plumbing, air conditioning or lighting fixtures or any other cause; (c) conditions arising in or about the Property or upon other portions of any building of which the Property is a part, or from other sources or places; or (d) any act or omission of any other tenant of any building of which the Property is a part. Landlord shall not be liable for any such damage or injury even though the cause of or the means of repairing such damage or injury are not accessible to Tenant. The provisions of this Section 6.02 shall not, however, exempt Landlord from liability for Landlord's gross negligence or willful misconduct.

5

(Gross Form)

Initials ______________

____

Figure 8-2 (*Continued*)

(b) All of Tenant's obligations to maintain and repair shall be accomplished at Tenant's sole expense. If Tenant fails to maintain and repair the Property, Landlord may, on ten (10) days' prior notice (except that no notice shall be required in case of emergency) enter the Property and perform such repair and maintenance on behalf of Tenant. In such case, Tenant shall reimburse Landlord for all costs so incurred immediately upon demand.

Section 6.04. **Landlord's Obligations.** Subject to the provisions of Article Seven (Damage or Destruction) and Article Eight (Condemnation), Landlord shall have absolutely no responsibility to repair, maintain or replace any portion of the Property at any time. Tenant waives the benefit of any present or future law which might give Tenant the right to repair the Property at Landlord's expense or to terminate the Lease due to the condition of the Property.

Section 6.05. **Alterations, Additions, and Improvements.**

(a) Tenant shall not make any alterations, additions, or improvements to the Property without Landlord's prior written consent, except for non-structural alterations which do not exceed Five Thousand Dollars ($5,000) in cost cumulatively over the Lease Term and which are not visible from the outside of any building of which the Property is part. Landlord may require Tenant to provide demolition and/or lien and completion bonds in form and amount satisfactory to Landlord. Tenant shall promptly remove any alterations, additions, or improvements constructed in violation of this Paragraph 6.05(a) upon Landlord's written request. All alterations, additions, and improvements will be accomplished in a good and workmanlike manner, in conformity with all applicable laws and regulations, and by a contractor approved by Landlord. Upon completion of any such work, Tenant shall provide Landlord with "as built" plans, copies of all construction contracts, and proof of payment for all labor and materials.

(b) Tenant shall pay when due all claims for labor and material furnished to the Property. Tenant shall give Landlord at least ten (10) days' prior written notice of the commencement of any work on the Property. Landlord may elect to record and post notices of non-responsibility on the Property.

Section 6.06. **Condition upon Termination.** Upon the termination of the Lease, Tenant shall surrender the Property to Landlord, broom clean and in the same condition as received except for ordinary wear and tear which Tenant was not otherwise obligated to remedy under any provision of this Lease. However, Tenant shall not be obligated to repair any damage which Landlord is required to repair under Article Seven (Damage or Destruction). In addition, Landlord may require Tenant to remove any alterations, additions or improvements (whether or not made with Landlord's consent) prior to the termination of the Lease and to restore the Property to its prior condition, all at Tenant's expense. All alterations, additions and improvements which Landlord has not required Tenant to remove shall become Landlord's property and shall be surrendered to Landlord upon the termination of the Lease, except that Tenant may remove any of Tenant's machinery or equipment which can be removed without material damage to the Property. Tenant shall repair, at Tenant's expense, any damage to the Property caused by the removal of any such machinery or equipment. In no event, however, shall Tenant remove any of the following materials or equipment without Landlord's prior written consent: any power wiring or power panels; lighting or lighting fixtures; wall coverings; drapes, blinds or other window coverings; carpets or other floor coverings; heaters, air conditioners or any other heating or air conditioning equipment; fencing or security gates; or other similar building operating equipment and decorations.

ARTICLE SEVEN: **DAMAGE OR DESTRUCTION**

Section 7.01. **Partial Damage to Property.** Tenant shall notify Landlord in writing immediately upon the occurrence of any damage to the Property. If the Property is only partially damaged and if the proceeds received by Landlord from the insurance policies described in Paragraph 4.04 (b) are sufficient to pay for the necessary repairs, this Lease shall remain in effect and Landlord shall repair the damage as soon as reasonably possible. Landlord may elect to repair any damage to Tenant's fixtures, equipment, or improvements. If the insurance proceeds received by Landlord are not sufficient to pay the entire cost of repair, or if the cause of the damage is not covered by the insurance policies which Landlord maintains under Paragraph 4.04(b), Landlord may elect either to (a) repair the damage as soon as reasonably possible, in which case this Lease shall remain in full force and effect, or (b) terminate this Lease as of the date the damage occurred. Landlord shall notify Tenant within thirty (30) days after receipt of notice of the occurrence of the damage, whether Landlord elects to repair the damage or terminate the Lease. If Landlord elects to repair the damage, Tenant shall pay Landlord the "deductible amount" (if any) under Landlord's insurance policies, and, if the damage was due to an act or omission of Tenant, the difference between the actual cost of repair and any insurance proceeds received by Landlord. If Landlord elects to terminate this Lease, Tenant may elect to continue this Lease in full force and effect, in which case Tenant shall repair any damage to the Property and any building in which the Property is located. Tenant shall pay the cost of such repairs, except that, upon satisfactory completion of such repairs, Landlord shall deliver to Tenant any insurance proceeds received by Landlord for the damage repaired by Tenant. Tenant shall give Landlord written notice of such election within ten (10) days after receiving Landlord's termination notice. If the damage to the Property occurs during the last six (6) months of the Lease Term, Landlord may elect to terminate this Lease as of the date the damage occurred, regardless of the sufficiency of any insurance proceeds. In such event, Landlord shall not be obligated to repair or restore the Property and Tenant shall have no right to continue this Lease. Landlord shall notify Tenant of its election within thirty (30) days after receipt of notice of the occurrence of the damage.

6

(Net Form)

Initials ____________________

____

Figure 8-2 (*Continued*)

elect to repair any damage to Tenant's fixtures, equipment, or improvements. If the insurance proceeds received by Landlord are not sufficient to pay the entire cost of repair, or if the damage was due to a cause not covered by the insurance policies which Landlord maintains under Paragraph 4.04(b), Landlord may elect either to (a) repair the damage as soon as reasonably possible in which case this Lease shall remain in full force and effect, or (b) terminate this Lease as of the date the damage occurred. Landlord shall notify Tenant within thirty (30) days after receipt of notice of the occurrence of the damage, whether Landlord elects to repair the damage or terminate the Lease. If Landlord elects to repair the damage and if the damage was due to an act or omission of Tenant, Tenant shall pay Landlord upon demand the difference between the actual cost of repair and any insurance proceeds received by Landlord. If Landlord elects to terminate the Lease, Tenant may elect to continue this Lease in full force and effect, in which case Tenant shall repair any damage to the Property and any building in which the Property is located. Tenant shall pay the cost of such repairs, except that, upon satisfactory completion of such repairs, Landlord shall deliver to Tenant any insurance proceeds received by Landlord for the damage repaired by Tenant. Tenant shall give Landlord written notice of such election within ten (10) days after receiving Landlord's termination notice. If the damage to the Property occurs during the last six (6) months of the Lease Term, Landlord may elect to terminate this Lease as of the date the damage occurred regardless of the sufficiency of any insurance proceeds. In such event, Landlord shall not be obligated to repair or restore the Property and Tenant shall have no right to continue this Lease. Landlord shall notify Tenant of its election within thirty (30) days after receipt of notice of the occurrence of the damage.

Section 7.02. **Total or Substantial Destruction.** If the Property is totally or substantially destroyed by any cause whatsoever, or if the Property is in a building which is substantially destroyed (even though the Property is not totally or substantially destroyed), this Lease shall terminate as of the date the destruction occurred regardless of whether Landlord receives any insurance proceeds. However, if the Property can be rebuilt within one (1) year after the date of destruction, Landlord may elect to rebuild the Property at Landlord's own expense, in which case, this Lease shall remain in full force and effect. Landlord shall notify Tenant of such election within thirty (30) days after the occurrence of total or substantial destruction. If the destruction was caused by an act or omission of Tenant, Tenant shall pay Landlord the difference between the actual cost of rebuilding and any insurance proceeds received by Landlord.

Section 7.03. **Temporary Reduction of Rent.** If the Property is destroyed or damaged and Landlord or Tenant repairs or restores the Property pursuant to the provisions of this Article Seven, the Base Rent payable during the period of such damage, repair and/or restoration shall be reduced according to the degree, if any, to which Tenant's use of the Property is impaired. However, the reduction shall not exceed the sum of one year's payment of Base Rent. Except for such possible reduction in Base Rent, Tenant shall not be entitled to any compensation, reduction, or reimbursement from Landlord as a result of any damage, destruction, repair, or restoration of or to the Property.

Section 7.04. **Waiver.** Tenant waives the protection of any statute, code or judicial decision which grants a tenant the right to terminate a lease in the event of the substantial destruction of the leased property. Tenant agrees that the provisions of Section 7.02 above shall govern the rights and obligations of Landlord and Tenant in the event of any substantial or total destruction to the Property.

ARTICLE EIGHT: **CONDEMNATION**

If all or any portion of the Property is taken under the power of eminent domain or sold under the threat of that power (all of which are called "Condemnation"), this Lease shall terminate as to the part taken or sold on the date the condemning authority takes title or possession, whichever occurs first. If more than twenty percent (20%) of the floor area of the building in which the Property is located, or which is located on the Property, is taken, either Landlord or Tenant may terminate this Lease as of the date the condemning authority takes title or possession, by delivering written notice to the other within ten (10) days after receipt of written notice of such taking (or in the absence of such notice, within ten (10) days after the condemning authority takes possession). If neither Landlord nor Tenant terminates this Lease, this Lease shall remain in effect as to the portion of the Property not taken, except that the Base Rent shall be reduced in proportion to the reduction in the floor area of the Property. Any Condemnation award or payment shall be distributed in the following order: (a) first, to any ground lessor, mortgagee or beneficiary under a deed of trust encumbering the Property, the amount of its interest in the Property; (b) second, to Tenant, only the amount of any award specifically designated for loss of or damage to Tenant's trade fixtures or removable personal property; and (c) third, to Landlord, the remainder of such award, whether as compensation for reduction in the value of the leasehold, the taking of the fee, or otherwise. If this Lease is not terminated, Landlord shall repair any damage to the Property caused by the Condemnation, except that Landlord shall not be obligated to repair any damage for which Tenant has been reimbursed by the condemning authority. If the severance damages received by Landlord are not sufficient to pay for such repair, Landlord shall have the right to either terminate this Lease or make such repair at Landlord's expense.

Initials ______________

____

(Gross Form)

Figure 8-2 (*Continued*)

transferee defaults under this Lease, Landlord may proceed directly against Tenant without pursuing remedies against the transferee. Landlord may consent to subsequent assignments or modifications of this Lease by Tenant's transferee, without notifying Tenant or obtaining its consent. Such action shall not relieve Tenant's liability under this Lease.

Section 9.04. **Landlord's Election.** Tenant's request for consent to any transfer described in Section 9.01 above shall be accompanied by a written statement setting forth the details of the proposed transfer, including the name, business and financial condition of the prospective transferee, financial details of the proposed transfer (e.g., the term of and rent and security deposit payable under any assignment or sublease), and any other information Landlord deems relevant. Landlord shall have the right (a) to withhold consent, if reasonable; (b) to grant consent; or (c) if the transfer is a sublease of the Property or an assignment of this Lease, to terminate this Lease as of the effective date of such sublease or assignment, in which case Landlord may elect to enter into a direct lease with the proposed assignee or subtenant.

Section 9.05. **No Merger.** No merger shall result from Tenant's sublease of the Property under this Article Nine, Tenant's surrender of this Lease or the termination of this Lease in any other manner. In any such event, Landlord may terminate any or all subtenancies or succeed to the interest of Tenant as sublandlord thereunder.

ARTICLE TEN: **DEFAULTS; REMEDIES**

Section 10.01. **Covenants and Conditions.** Tenant's performance of each of Tenant's obligations under this Lease is a condition as well as a covenant. Tenant's right to continue in possession of the Property is conditioned upon such performance. Time is of the essence in the performance of all covenants and conditions.

Section 10.02. **Defaults.** Tenant shall be in material default under this Lease:

(a) If Tenant abandons the Property or if Tenant's vacation of the Property results in the cancellation of any insurance described in Section 4.04;

(b) If Tenant fails to pay rent or any other charge required to be paid by Tenant, as and when due;

(c) If Tenant fails to perform any of Tenant's non-monetary obligations under this Lease for a period of thirty (30) days after written notice from Landlord; provided that if more than thirty (30) days are required to complete such performance, Tenant shall not be in default if Tenant commences such performance within the thirty (30) day period and thereafter diligently pursues its completion. However, Landlord shall not be required to give such notice if Tenant's failure to perform constitutes a non-curable breach of this Lease. The notice required by this Paragraph is intended to satisfy any and all notice requirements imposed by law on Landlord and is not in addition to any such requirement.

(d) (i) If Tenant makes a general assignment or general arrangement for the benefit of creditors; (ii) if a petition for adjudication of bankruptcy or for reorganization or rearrangement is filed by or against Tenant and is not dismissed within thirty (30) days; (iii) if a trustee or receiver is appointed to take possession of substantially all of Tenant's assets located at the Property or of Tenant's interest in this Lease and possession is not restored to Tenant within thirty (30) days; or (iv) if substantially all of Tenant's assets located at the Property or of Tenant's interest in this Lease is subjected to attachment, execution or other judicial seizure which is not discharged within thirty (30) days. If a court of competent jurisdiction determines that any of the acts described in this subparagraph (d) is not a default under this Lease, and a trustee is appointed to take possession (or if Tenant remains a debtor in possession) and such trustee or Tenant transfers Tenant's interest hereunder, then Landlord shall receive, as Additional Rent, the difference between the rent (or any other consideration) paid in connection with such assignment or sublease and the rent payable by Tenant hereunder.

Section 10.03. **Remedies.** On the occurrence of any material default by Tenant, Landlord may, at any time thereafter, with or without notice or demand and without limiting Landlord in the exercise of any right or remedy which Landlord may have:

(a) Terminate Tenant's right to possession of the Property by any lawful means, in which case this Lease shall terminate and Tenant shall immediately surrender possession of the Property to Landlord. In such event, Landlord shall be entitled to recover from Tenant all damages incurred by Landlord by reason of Tenant's default, including (i) the worth at the time of the award of the unpaid Base Rent, Additional Rent and other charges which had been earned at the time of the termination; (ii) the worth at the time of the award of the amount by which the unpaid Base Rent, Additional Rent and other charges which would have been earned after termination until the time of the award exceeds the amount of such rental loss that Tenant proves could have been reasonably avoided; (iii) the worth at the time of the award of the amount by which the unpaid Base Rent, Additional Rent and other charges which would have been paid for the balance of the term after the time of award exceeds the amount of such rental loss that Tenant proves could have been reasonably avoided; and (iv) any other amount necessary to compensate Landlord for all the detriment proximately caused by Tenant's failure to perform its obligations under the Lease or which in the ordinary course of things would be likely to result therefrom, including, but not limited to, any costs or expenses incurred by Landlord in maintaining or preserving the Property after such default, the cost of recovering possession of the

(Net Form)

Initials ______________

____

Figure 8-2 (*Continued*)

(a) Terminate Tenant's right to possession of the Property by any lawful means, in which case this Lease shall terminate and Tenant shall immediately surrender possession of the Property to Landlord. In such event, Landlord shall be entitled to recover from Tenant all damages incurred by Landlord by reason of Tenant's default, including (i) the worth at the time of the award of the unpaid Base Rent, Additional Rent and other charges which had been earned at the time of the termination; (ii) the worth at the time of the award of the amount by which the unpaid Base Rent, Additional Rent and other charges which would have been earned after termination until the time of the award exceeds the amount of such rental loss that Tenant proves could have been reasonably avoided; (iii) the worth at the time of the award of the amount by which the unpaid Base Rent, Additional Rent and other charges which would have been paid for the balance of the term after the time of award exceeds the amount of such rental loss that Tenant proves could have been reasonably avoided; and (iv) any other amount necessary to compensate Landlord for all the detriment proximately caused by Tenant's failure to perform its obligations under the Lease or which in the ordinary course of things would be likely to result therefrom, including, but not limited to, any costs or expenses incurred by Landlord in maintaining or preserving the Property after such default, the cost of recovering possession of the Property, expenses of reletting, including necessary renovation or alteration of the Property, Landlord's reasonable attorneys' fees incurred in connection therewith, and any real estate commission paid or payable. As used in subparts (i) and (ii) above, the "worth at the time of the award" is computed by allowing interest on unpaid amounts at the rate of fifteen percent (15%) per annum, or such lesser amount as may then be the maximum lawful rate. As used in subpart (iii) above, the "worth at the time of the award" is computed by discounting such amount at the discount rate of the Federal Reserve Bank of San Francisco at the time of the award, plus 1%. If Tenant shall have abandoned the Property, Landlord shall have the option of (i) retaking possession of the Property and recovering from Tenant the amount specified in this Paragraph 10.03(a), or (ii) proceeding under Paragraph 10.03(b);

(b) Maintain Tenant's right to possession, in which case this Lease shall continue in effect whether or not Tenant shall have abandoned the Property. In such event, Landlord shall be entitled to enforce all of Landlord's rights and remedies under this Lease, including the right to recover the rent as it becomes due hereunder;

(c) Pursue any other remedy now or hereafter available to Landlord under the laws or judicial decisions of the state in which the Property is located.

Section 10.04. **Cumulative Remedies.** Landlord's exercise of any right or remedy shall not prevent it from exercising any other right or remedy.

ARTICLE ELEVEN: **PROTECTION OF LENDERS**

Section 11.01. **Subordination.** Landlord shall have the right to subordinate this Lease to any ground lease, deed of trust or mortgage encumbering the Property, any advances made on the security thereof and any renewals, modifications, consolidations, replacements or extensions thereof, whenever made or recorded. However, Tenant's right to quiet possession of the Property during the Lease Term shall not be disturbed if Tenant pays the rent and performs all of Tenant's obligations under this Lease and is not otherwise in default. If any ground lessor, beneficiary or mortgagee elects to have this Lease prior to the lien of its ground lease, deed of trust or mortgage and gives written notice thereof to Tenant, this Lease shall be deemed prior to such ground lease, deed of trust or mortgage whether this Lease is dated prior or subsequent to the date of said ground lease, deed of trust or mortgage or the date of recording thereof.

Section 11.02. **Attornment.** If Landlord's interest in the Property is acquired by any ground lessor, beneficiary under a deed of trust, mortgagee, or purchaser at a foreclosure sale, Tenant shall attorn to the transferee of or successor to Landlord's interest in the Property and recognize such transferee or successor as Landlord under this Lease. Tenant waives the protection of any statute or rule of law which gives or purports to give Tenant any right to terminate this Lease or surrender possession of the Property upon the transfer of Landlord's interest.

Section 11.03. **Signing of Documents.** Tenant shall sign and deliver any instrument or documents necessary or appropriate to evidence any such attornment or subordination or agreement to do so. If Tenant fails to do so within ten (10) days after written request, Tenant hereby makes, constitutes and irrevocably appoints Landlord, or any transferee or successor of Landlord, the attorney-in-fact of Tenant to execute and deliver any such instrument or document.

Section 11.04. **Estoppel Certificates.**

(a) Upon Landlord's written request, Tenant shall execute, acknowledge and deliver to Landlord a written statement certifying: (i) that none of the terms or provisions of this Lease have been changed (or if they have been changed, stating how they have been changed); (ii) that this Lease has not been cancelled or terminated; (iii) that the last date of payment of the Base Rent and other charges and the time period covered by such payment; and (iv) that Landlord is not in default under this Lease (or, if Landlord is claimed to be in default, stating why). Tenant shall deliver such statement to Landlord within ten (10) days after Landlord's request. Any such statement by Tenant may be given by Landlord to any prospective purchaser or encumbrancer of the Property. Such purchaser or encumbrancer may rely conclusively upon such statement as true and correct.

(b) If Tenant does not deliver such statement to Landlord within such ten (10) day period, Landlord, and any prospective purchaser or encumbrancer, may conclusively presume and rely upon the following facts: (i) that the terms and provisions of this Lease have not been changed except as otherwise represented by Landlord; (ii) that this Lease has not been cancelled or terminated except as otherwise represented by Landlord; (iii) that not more than one month's Base Rent or other charges have been paid in advance; and (iv) that Landlord is not in default under the Lease. In such event, Tenant shall be estopped from denying the truth of such facts.

9 Initials ______________________

 (Gross Form) ______________________

Figure 8-2 (*Continued*)

ARTICLE TWELVE: **LEGAL COSTS**

Section 12.01 **Legal Proceedings.** Tenant shall reimburse Landlord, upon demand, for any costs or expenses incurred by Landlord in connection with any breach or default of Tenant under this Lease, whether or not suit is commenced or judgment entered. Such costs shall include legal fees and costs incurred for the negotiation of a settlement, enforcement of rights or otherwise. Furthermore, if any action for breach of or to enforce the provisions of this Lease is commenced, the court in such action shall award to the party in whose favor a judgment is entered, a reasonable sum as attorneys' fees and costs. Such attorneys' fees and costs shall be paid by the losing party in such action. Tenant shall also indemnify Landlord against and hold Landlord harmless from all costs, expenses, demands and liability incurred by Landlord if Landlord becomes or is made a party to any claim or action (a) instituted by Tenant, or by any third party against Tenant, or by or against any person holding any interest under or using the Property by license of or agreement with Tenant; (b) for foreclosure of any lien for labor or material furnished to or for Tenant or such other person; (c) otherwise arising out of or resulting from any act or transaction of Tenant or such other person; or (d) necessary to protect Landlord's interest under this Lease in a bankruptcy proceeding, or other proceeding under Title 11 of the United States Code, as amended. Tenant shall defend Landlord against any such claim or action at Tenant's expense with counsel reasonably acceptable to Landlord or, at Landlord's election, Tenant shall reimburse Landlord for any legal fees or costs incurred by Landlord in any such claim or action.

Section 12.02. **Landlord's Consent.** Tenant shall pay Landlord's reasonable attorneys' fees incurred in connection with Tenant's request for Landlord's consent under Article Nine (Assignment and Subletting), or in connection with any other act which Tenant proposes to do and which requires Landlord's consent.

ARTICLE THIRTEEN: **MISCELLANEOUS PROVISIONS**

Section 13.01. **Non-Discrimination.** Tenant promises, and it is a condition to the continuance of this Lease, that there will be no discrimination against, or segregation of, any person or group of persons on the basis of race, color, sex, creed, national origin or ancestry in the leasing, subleasing, transferring, occupancy, tenure or use of the Property or any portion thereof.

Section 13.02. **Waiver of Subrogation.** Landlord and Tenant each hereby waive any and all rights of recovery against the other, or against the officers, employees, agents or representatives of the other, for loss of or damage to its property or the property of others under its control, if such loss or damage is covered by any insurance policy in force (whether or not described in this Lease) at the time of such loss or damage. Upon obtaining the policies of insurance described herein, Landlord and Tenant shall give notice to the insurance carrier or carriers of the foregoing mutual waiver of subrogation.

Section 13.03. **Landlord's Liability; Certain Duties.**

(a) As used in this Lease, the term "Landlord" means only the current owner or owners of the fee title to the Property or the leasehold estate under a ground lease of the Property at the time in question. Each Landlord is obligated to perform the obligations of Landlord under this Lease only during the time such Landlord owns such interest or title. Any Landlord who transfers its title or interest is relieved of all liability with respect to the obligations of Landlord under this Lease to be performed on or after the date of transfer. However, each Landlord shall deliver to its transferee all funds previously paid by Tenant if such funds have not yet been applied under the terms of this Lease.

(b) Tenant shall give written notice of any failure by Landlord to perform any of its obligations under this Lease to Landlord and to any ground lessor, mortgagee or beneficiary under any deed of trust encumbering the Property whose name and address have been furnished to Tenant in writing. Landlord shall not be in default under this Lease unless Landlord (or such ground lessor, mortgagee or beneficiary) fails to cure such non-performance within thirty (30) days after receipt of Tenant's notice. However, if such non-performance reasonably requires more than thirty (30) days to cure, Landlord shall not be in default if such cure is commenced within such thirty (30) day period and thereafter diligently pursued to completion.

(c) Upon the execution of this Lease, Tenant shall deposit with Landlord a cash Security Deposit in the amount set forth in Section 1.11 above. Landlord may apply all or part of the Security Deposit to any unpaid rent or other charges due from Tenant or to cure any other defaults of Tenant. If Landlord uses any part of the Security Deposit, Tenant shall restore the Security Deposit to its full amount within ten (10) days after Landlord's written request. Tenant's failure to do so shall be a material default under this Lease. No interest shall be paid on the Security Deposit. Landlord shall not be required to keep the Security Deposit separate from its other accounts and no trust relationship is created with respect to the Security Deposit.

Section 13.04. **Severability.** A determination by a court of competent jurisdiction that any provision of this Lease or any part thereof is illegal or unenforceable shall not cancel or invalidate the remainder of such provision or this Lease, which shall remain in full force and effect.

10 Initials ______________

 (Net Form) ______________

Figure 8-2 *(Continued)*

Section 13.04. **Severability.** A determination by a court of competent jurisdiction that any provision of this Lease or any part thereof is illegal or unenforceable shall not cancel or invalidate the remainder of such provision or this Lease, which shall remain in full force and effect.

Section 13.05. **Interpretation.** The captions of the Articles or Sections of this Lease are to assist the parties in reading this Lease and are not a part of the terms or provisions of this Lease. Whenever required by the context of this Lease, the singular shall include the plural and the plural shall include the singular. The masculine, feminine and neuter genders shall each include the other. In any provision relating to the conduct, acts or omissions of Tenant, the term "Tenant" shall include Tenant's agents, employees, contractors, invitees, successors or others using the Property with Tenant's expressed or implied permission.

Section 13.06. **Incorporation of Prior Agreements; Modifications.** This Lease is the only agreement between the parties pertaining to the lease of the Property and no other agreements are effective. All amendments to this Lease shall be in writing and signed by all parties. Any other attempted amendment shall be void.

Section 13.07. **Notices.** All notices required or permitted under this Lease shall be in writing and shall be personally delivered or sent by certified mail, return receipt requested, postage prepaid. Notices to Tenant shall be delivered to the address specified in Section 1.03 above, except that upon Tenant's taking possession of the Property, the Property shall be Tenant's address for notice purposes. Notices to Landlord shall be delivered to the address specified in Section 1.02 above. All notices shall be effective upon delivery. Either party may change its notice address upon written notice to the other party.

Section 13.08. **Waivers.** All waivers must be in writing and signed by the waiving party. Landlord's failure to enforce any provision of this Lease or its acceptance of rent shall not be a waiver and shall not prevent Landlord from enforcing that provision or any other provision of this Lease in the future. No statement on a payment check from Tenant or in a letter accompanying a payment check shall be binding on Landlord. Landlord may, with or without notice to Tenant, negotiate such check without being bound to the conditions of such statement.

Section 13.09. **No Recordation.** Tenant shall not record this Lease without prior written consent from Landlord. However, either Landlord or Tenant may require that a "Short Form" memorandum of this Lease executed by both parties be recorded.

Section 13.10. **Binding Effect; Choice of Law.** This Lease binds any party who legally acquires any rights or interest in this Lease from Landlord or Tenant. However, Landlord shall have no obligation to Tenant's successor unless the rights or interests of Tenant's successor are acquired in accordance with the terms of this Lease. The laws of the state in which the Property is located shall govern this Lease.

Section 13.11. **Corporate Authority; Partnership Authority.** If Tenant is a corporation, each person signing this Lease on behalf of Tenant represents and warrants that he has full authority to do so and that this Lease binds the corporation. Within thirty (30) days after this Lease is signed, Tenant shall deliver to Landlord a certified copy of a resolution of Tenant's Board of Directors authorizing the execution of this Lease or other evidence of such authority reasonably acceptable to Landlord. If Tenant is a partnership, each person signing this Lease for Tenant represents and warrants that he is a general partner of the partnership, that he has full authority to sign for the partnership and that this Lease binds the partnership and all general partners of the partnership. Tenant shall give written notice to Landlord of any general partner's withdrawal or addition. Within thirty (30) days after this Lease is signed, Tenant shall deliver to Landlord a copy of Tenant's recorded statement of partnership or certificate of limited partnership.

Section 13.12. **Joint and Several Liability.** All parties signing this Lease as Tenant shall be jointly and severally liable for all obligations of Tenant.

Section 13.13. **Force Majeure.** If Landlord cannot perform any of its obligations due to events beyond Landlord's control, the time provided for performing such obligations shall be extended by a period of time equal to the duration of such events. Events beyond Landlord's control include, but are not limited to, acts of God, war, civil commotion, labor disputes, strikes, fire, flood or other casualty, shortages of labor or material, government regulation or restriction and weather conditions.

ARTICLE FOURTEEN: **BROKERS**

Section 14.01. **Broker's Fee.** When this Lease is signed by and delivered to both Landlord and Tenant, Landlord shall pay a real estate commission to Landlord's Broker named in Section 1.08 above, if any, as provided in a written agreement between Landlord and Landlord's Broker. If there is no such written agreement, Landlord shall pay the sum stated in Section 1.10 above for services rendered to Landlord by Landlord's Broker in this transaction. Landlord shall pay Landlord's Broker a commission if Tenant exercises any option to extend the Lease Term or to buy the Property, or any similar option or right which Landlord may grant to Tenant, or if Landlord's Broker is the procuring cause of any other lease or sale entered into between Landlord and Tenant covering the Property. Such commission shall be the amount set forth in Landlord's Broker's commission schedule in effect as of the execution of this Lease. If a Tenant's Broker is named in Section 1.09 above, Landlord's Broker shall pay an appropriate portion of its commission to Tenant's Broker if so provided in any agreement between Landlord's Broker and Tenant's Broker. Nothing contained in this Lease shall impose any obligation on Landlord to pay a commission or fee to any party other than Landlord's Broker.

11

(Gross Form)

Initials ______________________

____

Figure 8-2 (*Continued*)

Article Fourteen. Landlord's Broker shall have the right to bring a legal action to enforce or declare rights under this provision. The prevailing party in such action shall be entitled to reasonable attorneys' fees to be paid by the losing party. Such attorneys' fees shall be fixed by the court in such action. This Paragraph is included in this Lease for the benefit of Landlord's Broker.

Section 14.03 **No Other Brokers.** Tenant represents and warrants to Landlord that the brokers named in Sections 1.08 and 1.09 above are the only agents, brokers, finders or other parties with whom Tenant has dealt who are or may be entitled to any commission or fee with respect to this Lease or the Property.

ADDITIONAL PROVISIONS MAY BE SET FORTH IN A RIDER OR RIDERS ATTACHED HERETO OR IN THE BLANK SPACE BELOW. IF NO ADDITIONAL PROVISONS ARE INSERTED, PLEASE DRAW A LINE THROUGH THE SPACE BELOW.

Landlord and Tenant have signed this Lease at the place and on the dates specified adjacent to their signatures below and have initialled all Riders which are attached to or incorporated by reference in this Lease.

Signed on ______________________, 19____ ______________________________

at ______________________________. ______________________________

By: ______________________________

Its: ______________________________

By: ______________________________

Its: ______________________________

"LANDLORD"

Signed on ______________________, 19____ ______________________________

at ______________________________. ______________________________

By: ______________________________

Its: ______________________________

By: ______________________________

Its: ______________________________

"TENANT"

THIS PRINTED FORM LEASE HAS BEEN DRAFTED BY LEGAL COUNSEL AT THE DIRECTION OF THE SOUTHERN CALIFORNIA CHAPTER OF THE SOCIETY OF INDUSTRIAL REALTORS,® INC. NO REPRESENTATION OR RECOMMENDATION IS MADE BY THE SOUTHERN CALIFORNIA CHAPTER OF THE SOCIETY OF INDUSTRIAL REALTORS,® INC., ITS LEGAL COUNSEL, THE REAL ESTATE BROKERS NAMED HEREIN, OR THEIR EMPLOYEES OR AGENTS, AS TO THE LEGAL SUFFICIENCY, LEGAL EFFECT OR TAX CONSEQUENCES OF THIS LEASE OR OF THIS TRANSACTION. LANDLORD AND TENANT SHOULD RETAIN LEGAL COUNSEL TO ADVISE THEM ON SUCH MATTERS AND SHOULD RELY UPON THE ADVICE OF SUCH LEGAL COUNSEL.

12

(Net Form)

Figure 8-2 *(Continued)*

GUARANTY OF LEASE

This Guaranty of Lease (the "Guaranty") is attached to and made part of that certain real estate Lease (the "Lease") dated ______________________, between ____
______________________, as Landlord, and ____
______________________, as Tenant, covering the Property commonly known as ______________________
__________________________. The terms used in this Guaranty shall have the same definitions as set forth in the Lease. In order to induce Landlord to enter into the Lease with Tenant, ______________________
____ ("Guarantors"), have agreed to execute and deliver this Guaranty to Landlord. Each Guarantor acknowledges that Landlord would not enter into the Lease if each Guarantor did not execute and deliver this Guaranty to Landlord.

1. **Guaranty.** In consideration of the execution of the Lease by Landlord and as a material inducement to Landlord to execute the Lease, each Guarantor hereby irrevocably, unconditionally, jointly and severally guarantees the full, timely and complete (a) payment of all rent and other sums payable by Tenant to Landlord under the Lease, and any amendments or modifications thereto by agreement or course of conduct, and (b) performance of all covenants, representations and warranties made by Tenant and all obligations to be performed by Tenant pursuant to the Lease, and any amendments or modifications thereto by agreement or course of conduct. The payment of those amounts and performance of those obligations shall be conducted in accordance with all terms, covenants and conditions set forth in the Lease, without deduction, offset or excuse of any nature and without regard to the enforceability or validity of the Lease, or any part thereof, or any disability of Tenant.

2. **Landlord's Rights.** Landlord may perform any of the following acts at any time during the Lease Term, without notice to or assent of any Guarantor and without in any way releasing, affecting or impairing any of Guarantor's obligations or liabilities under this Guaranty: (a) alter, modify or amend the Lease by agreement or course of conduct, (b) grant extensions or renewals of the Lease, (c) assign or otherwise transfer its interest in the Lease, the Property, or this Guaranty, (d) consent to any transfer or assignment of Tenant's or any future tenant's interest under the Lease, (e) release one or more Guarantor, or amend or modify this Guaranty with respect to any Guarantor, without releasing or discharging any other Guarantor from any of such Guarantor's obligations or liabilities under this Guaranty, (f) take and hold security for the payment of this Guaranty and exchange, enforce, waive and release any such security, (g) apply such security and direct the order or manner of sale thereof as Landlord, in its sole discretion, deems appropriate, and (h) foreclose upon any such security by judicial or nonjudicial sale, without affecting or impairing in any way the liability of Guarantor under this Guaranty, except to the extent the indebtedness has been paid.

3. **Tenant's Default.** This Guaranty is a guaranty of payment and performance, and not of collection. Upon any breach or default by Tenant under the Lease, Landlord may proceed immediately against Tenant and/or any Guarantor to enforce any of Landlord's rights or remedies against Tenant or any Guarantor pursuant to this Guaranty, the Lease, or at law or in equity without notice to or demand upon either Tenant or any Guarantor. This Guaranty shall not be released, modified or affected by any failure or delay by Landlord to enforce any of its rights or remedies under the Lease or this Guaranty, or at law or in equity.

4. **Guarantor's Waivers.** Each Guarantor hereby waives (a) presentment, demand for payment and protest of non-performance under the Lease, (b) notice of any kind including, without limitation, notice of acceptance of this Guaranty, protest, presentment, demand for payment, default, nonpayment, or the creation or incurring of new or additional obligations of Tenant to Landlord, (c) any right to require Landlord to enforce its rights or remedies against Tenant under the Lease, or otherwise, or against any other Guarantor, (d) any right to require Landlord to proceed against any security held from Tenant or any other party, (e) any right of subrogation and (f) any defense arising out of the absence, impairment or loss of any right of reimbursement or subrogation or other right or remedy of Guarantors against Landlord or any such security, whether resulting from an election by Landlord, or otherwise. Any part payment by Tenant or other circumstance which operates to toll any statute of limitations as to Tenant shall operate to toll the statute of limitations as to Guarantor.

5. **Separate and Distinct Obligations.** Each Guarantor acknowledges and agrees that such Guarantor's obligations to Landlord under this Guaranty are separate and distinct from Tenant's obligations to Landlord under the Lease. The occurrence of any of the following events shall not have any effect whatsoever on any Guarantor's obligations to Landlord hereunder, each of which obligations shall continue in full force or effect as though such event had not occurred: (a) the commencement by Tenant of a voluntary case under the federal bankruptcy laws, as now constituted or hereafter amended or replaced, or any other applicable federal or state bankruptcy, insolvency or other similar law (collectively, the "Bankruptcy Laws"), (b) the consent by Tenant to the appointment of or taking possession by a receiver, liquidator, assignee, trustee, custodian, sequestrator or similar official of Tenant or for any substantial part of its property, (c) any assignment by Tenant for the benefit of creditors, (d) the failure of Tenant generally to pay its debts as such debts become due, (e) the taking of corporate action by Tenant in the furtherance of any of the foregoing; or (f) the entry of a decree or order for relief by a court having jurisdiction in respect of Tenant in any involuntary case under the Bankruptcy Laws, or appointing a receiver, liquidator, assignee, custodian, trustee, sequestrator (or similar official) of Tenant or for any substantial part of its property, or ordering the winding-up or liquidation of any of its affairs and the continuance of any such decree or order unstayed and in effect for a period of sixty (60) consecutive days. The liability of Guarantors under this Guaranty is not and shall not be affected or

Initials ______________________

____

Figure 8-3 Guaranty of lease. (*Reprinted by courtesy of the Southern California Chapter of the Society of Industrial Realtors,® Inc.*)

impaired by any payment made to Landlord under or related to the Lease for which Landlord is required to reimburse Tenant pursuant to any court order or in settlement of any dispute, controversy or litigation in any bankruptcy, reorganization, arrangement, moratorium or other federal or state debtor relief proceeding. If, during any such proceeding, the Lease is assumed by Tenant or any trustee, or thereafter assigned by Tenant or any trustee to a third party, this Guaranty shall remain in full force and effect with respect to the full performance of Tenant, any such trustee or any such third party's obligations under the Lease. If the Lease is terminated or rejected during any such proceeding, or if any of the events described in Subparagraphs (a) through (f) of this Paragraph 5 occur, as between Landlord and each Guarantor, Landlord shall have the right to accelerate all of Tenant's obligations under the Lease and each Guarantor's obligations under this Guaranty. In such event, all such obligations shall become immediately due and payable by Guarantors to Landlord. Guarantors waive any defense arising by reason of any disability or other defense of Tenant or by reason of the cessation from any cause whatsoever of the liability of Tenant.

6. **Subordination.** All existing and future advances by Guarantor to Tenant, and all existing and future debts of Tenant to any Guarantor, shall be subordinated to all obligations owed to Landlord under the Lease and this Guaranty.

7. **Successors and Assigns.** This Guaranty binds each Guarantor's personal representatives, successors and assigns.

8. **Encumbrances.** If Landlord's interest in the Property or the Lease, or the rents, issues or profits therefrom, are subject to any deed of trust, mortgage or assignment for security, any Guarantor's acquisition of Landlord's interest in the Property or Lease shall not affect any of Guarantor's obligations under this Guaranty. In such event, this Guaranty shall nevertheless continue in full force and effect for the benefit of any mortgagee, beneficiary, trustee or assignee or any purchaser at any sale by judicial foreclosure or under any private power of sale, and their successors and assigns. Any married Guarantor expressly agrees that Landlord has recourse against any Guarantor's separate property for all of such Guarantor's obligations hereunder.

9. **Guarantor's Duty.** Guarantors assumes the responsibility to remain informed of the financial condition of Tenant and of all other circumstances bearing upon the risk of Tenant's default, which reasonable inquiry would reveal, and agree that Landlord shall have no duty to advise Guarantors of information known to it regarding such condition or any such circumstance.

10. **Landlord's Reliance.** Landlord shall not be required to inquire into the powers of Tenant or the officers, employees, partners or agents acting or purporting to act on its behalf, and any indebtedness made or created in reliance upon the professed exercise of such powers shall be guaranteed under this Guaranty.

11. **Incorporation of Certain Lease Provisions.** Each Guarantor hereby represents and warrants to Landlord that such Guarantor has received a copy of the Lease, has read or had the opportunity to read the Lease, and understands the terms of the Lease. The provisions in the Lease relating to the execution of additional documents, legal proceedings by Landlord against Tenant, severability of the provisions of the Lease, interpretation of the Lease, notices, waivers, the applicable laws which govern the interpretation of the Lease and the authority of the Tenant to execute the Lease are incorporated herein in their entirety by this reference and made a part hereof. Any reference in those provisions to "Tenant" shall mean each Guarantor and any reference in those provisions to the "Lease" shall mean this Guaranty, except that (a) any notice which any Guarantor desires or is required to provide to Landlord shall be effective only if signed by all Guarantors and (b) any notice which Landlord desires or is required to provide to any Guarantor shall be sent to such Guarantor at such Guarantor's address indicated below, or if no address is indicated below, at the address for notices to be sent to Tenant under the Lease.

Signed on ______________________, 19____ ______________________________

____

______________________________ By: ______________________________

______________________________ Its: ______________________________

Address

Signed on ______________________, 19____ ______________________________

____

______________________________ By: ______________________________

______________________________ Its: ______________________________

Address

THIS PRINTED FORM GUARANTY HAS BEEN DRAFTED BY LEGAL COUNSEL AT THE DIRECTION OF THE SOUTHERN CALIFORNIA CHAPTER OF THE SOCIETY OF INDUSTRIAL REALTORS, INC. NO REPRESENTATION OR RECOMMENDATION IS MADE BY THE SOUTHERN CALIFORNIA CHAPTER OF THE SOCIETY OF INDUSTRIAL REALTORS, INC., ITS LEGAL COUNSEL, OR THEIR EMPLOYEES OR AGENTS, AS TO THE LEGAL SUFFICIENCY, LEGAL EFFECT OR TAX CONSEQUENCES OF THIS GUARANTY OR OF THIS TRANSACTION. EACH GUARANTOR SHOULD RETAIN LEGAL COUNSEL TO ADVISE SUCH GUARANTOR ON SUCH MATTERS AND SHOULD RELY UPON THE ADVICE OF SUCH LEGAL COUNSEL.

Figure 8-3 (*Continued*)

OPTION TO PURCHASE PROPERTY
LEASE RIDER

This Rider is attached to and made part of that certain Lease (the "Lease") dated ______________________
between ____, as Landlord,
and ____, as Tenant,
covering the Property commonly known as ____
____ (the "Property").
The terms used in this Rider shall have the same meanings as in the Lease. This Rider shall supersede any inconsistent or conflicting provisions of the Lease.

A. **Grant and Exercise of Option**

Landlord hereby grants to Tenant the sole and exclusive right and option (the "Option") to purchase the Property, together with all real property improvements located thereon (except as otherwise provided in any attached exhibit), at the price and on the terms and conditions set forth below. To exercise the Option, Tenant shall deliver written notice (the "Notice of Exercise") to Landlord not earlier than 210 days nor later than 150 days prior to the date of Closing set forth in Paragraph B(6) (the "Notice Period"). If the Notice of Exercise is not given during the Notice Period, the Option shall lapse and Tenant shall have no further rights under this Rider.

B. **Summary of Basic Terms of Option To Purchase Property**

This Paragraph B contains the Basic Terms concerning the Option. These Basic Terms are to be read together with the remainder of this Rider:

1. Purchase Price ("Purchase Price") for the Property on exercise of the Option: ______________________ (words)
____ Dollars ($______________).
If the Purchase Price is not filled in, then the Purchase Price shall be determined by appraisal as provided in Paragraph D below, but shall not be less than the minimum price (the "Minimum Price") of ______________________
____ Dollars ($______________).

2. Amount of the Deposit to be delivered upon exercise of the Option pursuant to Paragraph C(1): ______________ (words)
____ Dollars ($______________).
The Deposit shall be credited against any cash payable pursuant to Paragraph B(3).

3. Payment of Purchase Price:
The Purchase Price shall be paid as indicated below (check appropriate boxes and fill in appropriate blanks):

☐ (a) Purchase is to be payable all cash.

☐ (b) The unpaid balance of any promissory note secured by a deed of trust or mortgage (referred to as "deeds of trust") encumbering the Property both before and after Closing (an "Existing Note") shall be credited against the Purchase Price. The balance of the Purchase Price shall be paid in cash.

☐ (c) There shall be a cash down payment of $______________ [or] __________% of the Purchase Price and the balance of the Purchase Price, less the outstanding balance of any Existing Note, shall be paid by a note (the "Purchase Money Note") payable to Landlord. The terms and provisions of the Purchase Money Note are as follows:
 (i) Interest rate: __________% per annum
 (ii) Payable either:
  ☐ (A) interest only OR
  ☐ (B) Principal and interest amortized over a __________ year period.
 (iii) Due date: ______________________.
 (iv) Note payments shall be monthly on the __________ day of the month.

☐ (d) ____
____
____
____
____
____
____

4. Name and address of the escrow company through which the purchase and sale of the Property is to be closed:
____
____

5. Name and address of the Title Company to issue the Title Policy on the Closing:
____
____

6. Date of Closing: ______________________

Initials ______________________
____

Figure 8-4 Option to purchase property—lease rider. (*Reprinted by courtesy of the Southern California Chapter of the Society of Industrial Realtors,® Inc.*)

C. **Conditions to The Exercise of The Option**

The following are conditions to the obligation of Landlord to sell the Property to Tenant. If any of the following conditions are not satisfied, Landlord shall have no obligation to sell the Property to Tenant, whether or not Tenant exercises the Option.

1. Tenant shall deliver to Landlord, together with the Notice of Exercise, a cashier's or certified check, payable to Escrow, in the amount of the Deposit. The Deposit shall be credited to the Purchase Price on the Closing.

2. The Lease shall be in full force and effect and Tenant shall not be in default under the Lease at the time of the exercise of the Option or at any time thereafter.

3. The Option is personal to the Tenant named in the Lease (or any Tenant's Affiliate). The Option may not be exercised if (a) Tenant or a Tenant's Affiliate does not occupy at least fifty (50%) percent of the Property during the entire Lease Term; (b) Tenant has subleased more than fifty (50%) percent of the area of the Property during any part of the Lease Term to an entity other than a Tenant's Affiliate, or (c) Tenant has assigned or otherwise transferred its interest under this Lease to an entity other than a Tenant's Affiliate. The Option shall not be severable from the Leasehold estate created under the Lease.

D. **Computation of Purchase Price if Price Not Stated**

If the Purchase Price is not stated in Paragraph B(1) above, then the Purchase Price shall be the "fair market value" of the Property, determined as follows:

1. Promptly after Landlord's receipt of the Notice of Exercise, Landlord and Tenant shall meet in an effort to negotiate, in good faith, the fair market value of the Property as of the expiration of the Lease Term. If Landlord and Tenant have not agreed upon such fair market value within 30 days after the Notice of Exercise, then Landlord and Tenant shall attempt to agree in good faith upon a single appraiser not later than 40 days after the Notice of Exercise. If Landlord and Tenant are unable to agree upon a single appraiser within such time period, then Landlord and Tenant shall each appoint one appraiser not later than 50 days after the Notice of Exercise. Within 10 days after the appointment of such appraisers, the two appointed appraisers shall appoint a third appraiser. If either Landlord or Tenant fails to appoint its appraiser within the prescribed time period, the single appraiser appointed shall determine the fair market value of the Property. If any party fails to appoint an appraiser within the prescribed time period, then the first appraiser thereafter appointed by a party shall determine the fair market value of the Property. Each party shall bear the cost of its own appraiser, and the parties shall bear equally the cost of the third or single appraiser. All appraisers shall be independent, shall have at least five years' experience in the appraisal of commercial/industrial real property substantially similar to the Property, and shall be members of professional organizations such as MAI or equivalent.

2. For the purpose of such appraisal, the term "fair market value" shall mean the price that a ready and willing buyer would pay to a ready and willing seller of the Property, as of the date of the appraisal, if the Property were exposed for sale on the open market for a reasonable period of time, taking into account all purposes for which the Property may be used and as if the Property were not encumbered by the Lease or any other actually existing tenant leases. If three appraisals are submitted, the fair market value of the Property shall be the arithmetic average of the two appraisals closest in value to each other and the third appraisal shall be disregarded. Otherwise, the appraisal of the single appraiser so appointed shall be conclusive and binding on both Landlord and Tenant. If the appraisers determine that the fair market value of the Property is less than the Minimum Price, then the Purchase Price shall be the Minimum Price in Paragraph B(1). Landlord and Tenant shall instruct the appraisers to complete the determination of fair market value within 60 days after appointment of such appraisers. When the fair market value of the Property has been determined, Landlord shall deliver notice thereof to Tenant. If the fair market value of the Property is not determined in accordance with the time schedule set forth above, the date of Closing shall be postponed to the date which is 20 days after the final determination of fair market value.

E. **Existing Financing; Subordination**

1. If the payment of the Purchase Price contemplates that Tenant shall have credit against the Purchase Price for the unpaid balance of any Existing Note, such provision shall be effective only if Tenant has the right under such Existing Note (and any such deed of trust securing such note) to take title to the Property "subject to" the Existing Note or to assume the Existing Note and deed of trust. Otherwise, the Tenant shall pay the principal amount of the Existing Note, in cash, through Escrow. If Tenant takes title subject to or assumes the Existing Note and deed of trust, Tenant shall pay all assumption fees, "points" and other costs associated therewith, and shall be bound by changes in the interest rate, prepayment provisions or other terms required by the holder of any Existing Note, if the consent of such holder is required. If any Existing Note is not paid in full at the Closing, Tenant shall also execute all such further documents and instruments as may be necessary to maintain the security of the holder of the Existing Note, including, without limitation, assignments of leases, UCC financing statements and estoppel certificates.

2. This Option is and shall be subject and subordinate to (a) the lien of any mortgage, deeds of trust or other encumbrance ("Loan Instrument") encumbering the Property on the date of this Rider, and (b) any consolidation, renewal, replacement or extension ("Replacement Loan Instrument") of such Loan Instrument which meets the criteria set out in Paragraph (3) below. Within ten (10) days after receipt of written request, Tenant shall sign any subordination agreement or other document requested by any lender to establish the priority of any Loan Instrument which encumbers the Property as of the date of this Rider, or any document requested by any lender to establish the priority of any Replacement Loan Instrument which meets such criteria. If Tenant fails to sign any such subordination agreement or other document within ten (10) days after receipt of written request therefor, this Option shall lapse and Tenant shall have no further rights under this Rider.

3. The criteria which must be met before Tenant is obligated to subordinate this Option to any Replacement Loan Instrument are as follows: The terms and provisions of any Replacement Loan Instrument which will encumber the Property after Closing cannot be materially less favorable than the terms of the Loan Instrument replaced by such Replacement Loan Instrument. The terms will be deemed to be materially less favorable and Tenant shall not be obligated to subordinate this Option to such Replacement Loan Instrument if the principal amount of the Replacement Loan Instrument is higher than the replaced Existing Note; the interest rate is greater; the monthly debt service payments are greater; the "due date" is sooner; the prepayment penalty is higher, or the lock-in period is longer. However, the Replacement Loan Instrument may include more stringent late payment charges and insurance requirements, shorter "cure periods" and other similar provisions, and such provisions shall not be

Initials ______________________

____

Figure 8-4 *(Continued)*

deemed to be materially less favorable to Tenant. If there is a dispute whether the terms of a Replacement Loan Instrument are materially less favorable than the terms of the Existing Note or Loan Instrument which it replaces, such dispute shall be submitted to conclusive and binding arbitration under the commercial arbitration rules of the American Arbitration Association at the American Arbitration Association office closest to the Property, and both Landlord and Tenant shall be bound by the results of such arbitration.

F. **Escrow**

1. Within ten (10) days after receipt of the Notice of Exercise, Landlord and Tenant shall deliver into Escrow (or to such other escrow company acceptable to both Landlord and Tenant) executed counterparts of this Option, and such other supplemental escrow instructions as are customarily and reasonably required by the Escrow Agent, which shall be the escrow instructions for the closing of the purchase and sale contemplated hereunder. Landlord shall deliver the Deposit to Escrow Agent upon opening of Escrow.

2. Promptly upon the opening of Escrow, the Escrow Agent shall order and deliver to Landlord and Tenant a preliminary title report (the "PTR") for the Property, together with copies of all instruments referred to in the PTR, from the Title Company. The PTR shall be conclusively deemed approved by Tenant unless, within ten (10) days after the delivery of the PTR and the last of the instruments referred to therein, Tenant has disapproved any matter set forth in the PTR by written notice to Landlord and the Title Company. If Tenant disapproves any such matter within the ten (10) day period, Landlord may agree to remove such disapproved title exception within 45 days after receipt of Tenant's notice of disapproval. If Landlord has not agreed in writing within such 45 day period to remove such disapproved title exception, Tenant may, by written notice to Landlord and Escrow Agent, given within ten (10) days after the expiration of such 45 day period, either (a) terminate Escrow or (b) waive such defect and proceed with the purchase and sale contemplated hereunder. If Tenant fails to give such notice within the prescribed period, Tenant shall be conclusively deemed to have waived such defect and to have elected to proceed with the purchase and sale of the Property. If Tenant elects to terminate Escrow, the Escrow shall return the Deposit to Tenant, less any escrow fees, title fees, Landlord's appraisal fees, or any other costs incurred by Landlord in connection with Tenant's exercise of the Option. If Tenant elects to proceed, Tenant shall be conclusively deemed to have approved the PTR subject to the removal of any disapproved title exception which Landlord has agreed to remove, and shall take title to the Property in the condition described in the PTR. Once Tenant has approved or been deemed to have approved the PTR, Landlord shall, at its cost, remove any exceptions to title thereafter appearing of record, other than those which were created or permitted by Tenant. In any event, Landlord shall cause any liens covering the Property securing monetary obligations to be released or reconveyed from the Property, if under this Rider, title is to be conveyed free of any such lien.

3. Except as otherwise provided in the approved PTR, Tenant acknowledges that Tenant accepts the Property "AS IS" in its physical condition existing at the Closing. Tenant acknowledges that neither Landlord nor its employees or agents has made any representations or warranties to Tenant regarding the Property, except as specifically set forth in the Lease, and only to the extent that any such representations or warranties still exist as of the date of Closing.

G. **Closing**

The close of Escrow (the "Closing") shall take place on or before the date specified in Paragraph B(6). Title to the Property shall be conveyed to Tenant at the Closing, and the Closing shall be accomplished as follows:

1. The Purchase Price shall be paid by Tenant through Escrow in the manner provided in Paragraph B(2). All funds required to be paid by Tenant at the Closing shall be deposited in Escrow by Tenant in the form of a cashier's check drawn on, or wire transfer from, a bank doing business in the county in which the Property is located, not later than the day prior to the day set for the Closing. If, as part of the Purchase Price, Tenant makes and executes a Purchase Money Note, such note shall be secured by a deed of trust on the Property (the "Purchase Money Trust Deed"). The Purchase Money Note and the Purchase Money Trust Deed shall be on forms then used for such purposes by the Title Company. The Purchase Money Trust Deed shall be subordinate to any deed(s) of trust securing Existing Note(s) which are to remain after the Closing. If there shall be no Existing Notes which remain after the Closing, the Purchase Money Trust Deed shall be a first lien deed of trust.

2. Unless otherwise indicated by Tenant in writing to Landlord and Escrow, the Lease shall terminate as of Closing.

3. If the Lease is a gross lease, then real property taxes, insurance premiums and rents shall be prorated as of Closing. Real Property taxes shall be prorated based upon the latest available tax bill. If the Lease is a net lease, then only rents shall be prorated as of Closing. Interest on any Existing Notes which remain after the Closing shall be prorated as of the Closing. Any unused security deposit held by Landlord under the Lease shall be credited to the Purchase Price. Landlord shall pay all documentary transfer taxes required as a result of the sale. Except as provided in Paragraph (4) below, Landlord and Tenant shall pay equally all escrow costs. All other costs shall be borne by Landlord and Tenant in accordance with the standard practices of the county in which the Property is located, except as otherwise stated herein.

4. Landlord shall provide to Tenant, at Landlord's expense, a standard coverage owner's policy of title insurance insuring title to the Property in Tenant in an amount equal to the Purchase Price, subject to all matters set forth in the approved PTR, any Purchase Money Trust Deed given to Landlord or to a third party lender, and any other title exceptions created or permitted by Tenant. The parties shall execute such other documents as are reasonably requested by Escrow in order to complete the purchase of the Property as provided by this Rider.

5. If a real estate commission has been earned by Landlord's Broker by reason of the exercise of the Option, such commission shall be paid to Landlord's Broker at the Closing out of the funds otherwise payable to Landlord. Landlord shall instruct Escrow to pay the commission directly to Landlord's Broker from the funds in Escrow.

H. **Exchange**

Notwithstanding the date of Closing set forth in Paragraph B(6) above, Landlord shall have the right to delay Closing for up to 180 days to accomplish a tax-deferred exchange of real property pursuant to Internal Revenue Code Section 1031. If Landlord elects to accomplish such exchange, Tenant shall cooperate with Landlord, as long as Tenant shall not be liable for any cash consideration or expense greater than that which Tenant would have incurred had Tenant purchased the Property by a direct sale from Landlord at the Purchase Price. All such additional expenses and consideration shall be paid by Landlord. If an exchange

Initials ______________________

____

3

Figure 8-4 *(Continued)*

transaction is established which requires cash consideration less than required pursuant to Paragraph B(3) above, the balance of the Purchase Price shall be payable by Tenant to Landlord through Escrow as provided herein. If Landlord fails to complete such exchange within such extended time period, the Escrow shall close as a direct sale by Landlord to Tenant under the terms set forth in Paragraph B(2) above.

NOTE: THIS FORM DOES NOT COVER THE TAX EFFECTS UPON EITHER LANDLORD OR TENANT RESULTING FROM ANY TAX-DEFERRED EXCHANGE. THE PARTIES SHOULD CONSULT THEIR PERSONAL TAX ADVISORS REGARDING SUCH TAX CONSEQUENCES.

I. **Breach of Agreement; Liquidated Damages**

If Tenant breaches any agreement contained in this Option or defaults in its obligations to close Escrow, Landlord may either (1) be released from all obligations to sell the Property to Tenant or (2) proceed against Tenant upon any claim or remedy which Landlord may have at law or in equity; provided however, that, BY PLACING THEIR INITIALS HERE, TENANT ________ AND LANDLORD ________ AGREE THAT LANDLORD SHALL HAVE THE RIGHT TO RETAIN THE LESSER OF THE DEPOSIT DESCRIBED IN PARAGRAPH B(2) OR 3% OF THE PURCHASE PRICE, AS LIQUIDATED DAMAGES. THE BALANCE OF THE DEPOSIT, IF ANY, SHALL BE PROMPTLY RETURNED TO TENANT (LESS ANY ESCROW FEES, TITLE FEES, APPRAISAL FEES, ATTORNEY FEES, OR OTHER COSTS INCURRED BY LANDLORD IN CONNECTION WITH THE TRANSACTION CONTEMPLATED HEREUNDER). BY PLACING THEIR INITIALS ABOVE, LANDLORD AND TENANT AGREE THAT THE DAMAGES TO LANDLORD RESULTING FROM TENANT'S DEFAULT ARE DIFFICULT AND IMPRACTICAL TO ASCERTAIN, THAT THE LIQUIDATED DAMAGES SPECIFIED HEREIN ARE A REASONABLE ESTIMATE OF LANDLORD'S DAMAGES IN SUCH EVENT, AND THAT THE RETENTION OF SUCH LIQUIDATED DAMAGES AND THE OTHER DIRECT COSTS DESCRIBED ABOVE SHALL CONSTITUTE LANDLORD'S SOLE AND EXCLUSIVE REMEDY FOR SUCH BREACH.

J. **Closing After Lease Expiration**

If, for any reason, Closing occurs after the expiration of the Lease Term, Tenant shall be deemed to be a holdover tenant at the monthly rent payable as of the last month of the stated Lease Term (notwithstanding any contradictory provisions of the Lease), and all obligations of Tenant hereunder shall continue in full force and effect until Closing (or until either party fails to fulfill its obligations set forth herein, in which case this Lease shall become a month-to-month tenancy terminable by the non-defaulting party upon 30 days' prior written notice to the other).

K. **Other Provisions**

____

____

____

____

____

____

____

____.

____

____

By: ____________________________

Its: ____________________________

By: ____________________________

Its: ____________________________

"LANDLORD"

____

____

By: ____________________________

Its: ____________________________

By: ____________________________

Its: ____________________________

"TENANT"

THIS RIDER HAS BEEN DRAFTED BY LEGAL COUNSEL AT THE DIRECTION OF THE SOUTHERN CALIFORNIA CHAPTER OF THE SOCIETY OF INDUSTRIAL REALTORS,® INC. NO REPRESENTATION OR RECOMMENDATION IS MADE BY THE SOUTHERN CALIFORNIA CHAPTER OF THE SOCIETY OF INDUSTRIAL REALTORS,® INC., ITS LEGAL COUNSEL, ANY REAL ESTATE BROKER NAMED IN THE LEASE TO WHICH THIS RIDER IS ATTACHED, OR THEIR EMPLOYEES OR AGENTS, AS TO THE LEGAL SUFFICIENCY, LEGAL EFFECT, OR TAX CONSEQUENCES OF THIS RIDER OR OF THIS TRANSACTION. ALL REAL PROPERTY PURCHASE TRANSACTIONS ARE COMPLICATED. THIS RIDER HAS BEEN PREPARED ONLY FOR RELATIVELY STANDARD TRANSACTIONS AND SHOULD NOT BE USED IN ALL SITUATIONS. LANDLORD AND TENANT SHOULD RETAIN LEGAL COUNSEL TO ADVISE THEM ON SUCH MATTERS AND SHOULD RELY UPON THE ADVICE OF SUCH COUNSEL.

4

Figure 8-4 (*Continued*)

MULTI-TENANT FACILITY

LEASE RIDER

This Rider is attached to and made part of that certain lease dated ______________________ between ____, as Landlord, and ____, as Tenant, covering the Property commonly known as ____ ____ (the "Lease"). The terms used in this Rider shall have the same definitions as set forth in the Lease. The provisions of this Rider shall prevail over any inconsistent or conflicting provisions of the Lease.

A. **Amendment to Section 1.04 of the Lease.**

The following is hereby added at the end of Section 1.04 of the Lease:

"The Property is part of a multi-tenant industrial/commercial real property development of Landlord described in an exhibit attached hereto and incorporated herein by this reference (the "Project"). The Project includes the land, the buildings and all other improvements located thereon, and the common areas described in Paragraph 4.05(a) below."

B. **Amendment to Section 4.05 of the Lease.**

Section 4.05 of the Lease is hereby deleted and the following is inserted in its place:

"4.05 **Common Areas; Use, Maintenance and Costs.**"

(a) **Common Areas.** As used in this Lease, "Common Areas" shall mean all areas within the Project which are available for the common use of tenants of the Project and which are not leased or held for the exclusive use of Tenant or other tenants, including, but not limited to, parking areas, driveways, sidewalks, loading areas, access roads, corridors, landscaping and planted areas. Landlord may from time to time change the size, location, nature and use of any of the Common Areas, including converting Common Areas into leasable areas, constructing additional parking facilities (including parking structures) in the Common Areas, and increasing or decreasing Common Area land and/or facilities. Tenant acknowledges that such activities may result in occasional inconvenience to Tenant from time to time. Such activities and changes shall be expressly permitted if they do not materially affect Tenant's use of the Property.

(b) **Use of Common Areas.** Tenant shall have the nonexclusive right (in common with other tenants and all others to whom Landlord has granted or may grant such rights) to use the Common Areas for the purposes intended, subject to such reasonable rules and regulations as Landlord may establish from time to time. Tenant shall abide by such rules and regulations and shall use its best effort to cause others who use the Common Areas with Tenant's expressed or implied permission to abide by Landlords' rules and regulations. At any time, Landlord may close any Common Areas to perform any acts in and to the Common Areas as, in Landlord's judgment, may be desirable to improve the Project. Tenant shall not, at any time, interfere with the rights of Landlord, other tenants, or any other person entitled to use the Common Areas.

(c) **Specific Provision re: Vehicle Parking.** Tenant shall be entitled to use the vehicle parking spaces in the Project allocated to Tenant in Section 1.12 of the Lease without paying any additional rent. Tenant's parking shall not be reserved and shall be limited to vehicles no larger than standard size automobiles or pickup utility vehicles. Tenant shall not cause large trucks or other large vehicles to be parked within the Project or on the adjacent public streets. Temporary parking of large delivery vehicles in the Project may be permitted by the rules and regulations established by Landlord. Vehicles shall be parked only in striped parking spaces and not in driveways, loading areas or other locations not specifically designated for parking. If Tenant parks more vehicles in the parking area than the number set forth in Section 1.12 of the Lease, such conduct shall be a material breach of the Lease. In addition to Landlord's other remedies under the Lease, Tenant shall pay a reasonable daily charge for each such additional vehicle.

(d) **Maintenance of Common Areas.** Landlord shall maintain the Common Areas in good order, condition and repair and shall operate the Project, in Landlord's sole discretion, as a first class industrial/commercial real property development. Tenant shall pay Tenant's pro rata share (as defined below) of all costs incurred by Landlord for the operation and maintenance of the Common Areas. Common Area costs include, but are not limited to, costs and expenses for the following: gardening and landscaping; utilities, water and sewage charges; maintenance of signs (other than Tenants' signs); premiums for liability, property damage, fire and other types of casualty insurance on the Common Areas and worker's compensation insurance; all real property taxes and assessments levied on or attributable to the Common Areas and all Common Areas improvements; all personal property taxes levied on or attributable to personal property used in connection with the Common Areas; straight-line depreciation on personal property owned by Landlord which is consumed in the operation or maintenance of the Common Areas; rental or lease payments paid by Landlord for rented or leased personal property used in the operation or maintenance of the Common Areas; fees for required licenses and permits; repairing, resurfacing, repaving, maintaining, painting, lighting, cleaning, refuse removal, security and similar items; reserves for roof replacement and exterior painting and other appropriate reserves; and a reasonable allowance to Landlord for Landlord's supervision of the Common Areas (not to exceed five percent (5%) of the total of all other Common Area costs for the calendar year). Landlord may cause any or all of such services to be provided by third parties. Common Area costs shall not include depreciation of real property which forms part

Figure 8-5 Multitenant facility—lease rider. (*Reprinted by courtesy of the Southern California Chapter of the Society of Industrial Realtors,® Inc.*)

of the Common Areas. Landlord may, at Landlord's election, estimate in advance and charge to Tenant monthly as Common Area costs, all real property taxes for which Tenant is liable under Paragraph 4.02 of the Lease, all insurance premiums for which Tenant is liable under Paragraph 4.04 of the Lease, and all maintenance and repair costs for which Tenant is liable under Section 6.03 of the Lease.

(e) **Tenant's Share and Payment.** Tenant shall pay Tenant's annual pro rata share of all estimated Common Area costs, in advance, in monthly installments on the first day of each month during the Lease Term (pro rated for any fractional month). Tenant's pro rata share shall be calculated by dividing the square foot area of the Property, as set forth in Section 1.04 of the Lease, by the aggregate square foot area of the Project which is leased or held for lease for the exclusive use by tenants upon the date the computation is made. Landlord may adjust such estimates at any time and from time to time based upon Landlord's experience and reasonable anticipation of costs. Such adjustments shall be effective as of the next rent payment date after notice to Tenant. Within thirty (30) days after the end of each calendar year of the Lease Term, Landlord shall deliver to Tenant a statement prepared in accordance with generally accepted accounting principles setting forth, in reasonable detail, the actual Common Area costs paid or incurred by Landlord during the preceding calendar year and Tenant's pro rata share. Upon receipt of such statement, there shall be an adjustment between Landlord and Tenant with payment to or credit given by Landlord (as the case may be) so that Landlord shall receive the entire amount of Tenant's share of such costs and expenses for such period. Any changes in the Common Area costs and/or the aggregate area leased or held for lease for the exclusive use of all tenants of the Project during the Lease Term shall be effective on the first day of the month after such change occurs.

C. **Amendment to Article Six of Lease**

Sections 6.03 and 6.04 of the Lease are hereby deleted and the following inserted in their place:

"Section 6.03 **Landlord's Obligations.**

(a) Except as provided in Article Seven (Damage and Destruction) and Article Eight (Condemnation), Landlord shall keep the following in good order, condition and repair: the foundations, exterior walls and exterior roof of the Property (including painting the exterior walls of the Property not more often than once every five (5) years, if necessary) and all components of electrical, mechanical, plumbing, heating and air conditioning systems and facilities located in the Property which are concealed or used in common by tenants of the building in which the Property is located. However, Landlord shall not be obligated to maintain or repair windows, doors, plate glass or the interior surfaces of exterior walls. Landlord shall have no obligation to make repairs under this Section 6.03 until a reasonable time after receipt of written notice from Tenant for the need for such repairs.

(b) If the Lease to which this Rider is attached is an SIR GROSS LEASE or any other form of gross lease, then Landlord shall pay only the cost of maintaining and repairing the foundations, the structural portions of walls, and the roof of the Property, unless the need for such repair was caused by Tenant's acts or omissions. Tenant shall pay all costs and expenses incurred by Landlord under Paragraph 6.03(a) above which Landlord is not specifically obligated to pay under this Paragraph 6.03(b).

(c) If the Lease to which this Rider is attached is an SIR NET LEASE or any other form of net lease, Tenant shall pay or reimburse Landlord for all costs incurred by Landlord under Section 6.03(a) above.

(d) Landlord may either (i) estimate in advance all costs and expenses of maintenance and repair for which Tenant is liable and charge such costs and expenses to Tenant monthly as Common Area costs in the manner described in Sections 4.05 of the Lease or (ii) bill Tenant for the costs and expenses for which Tenant is liable as such costs are incurred by Landlord. Tenant expressly waives the benefit of any statute in effect now or in the future which might give Tenant the right to make repairs at Landlord's expense or to terminate this Lease due to Landlord's failure to keep the Property in good order, condition and repair.

Section 6.04 **Tenant's Obligations.**

(a) Except as provided in Section 6.03, Article Seven (Damage or Destruction) and Article Eight (Condemnation), Tenant shall keep all portions of the Property (including structural, nonstructural, interior, exterior and landscaped areas, portions, systems and equipment) in good order, condition and repair. If any portion of the Property or any system or equipment in the Property which Tenant is obligated to repair cannot be fully repaired, Tenant shall promptly replace such portion of or system or equipment in the Property, regardless of whether the benefit of such replacement extends beyond the Lease Term. Tenant shall maintain a preventative maintenance contract providing for the regular inspection and maintenance of the heating and air conditioning system by a licensed heating and air conditioning contractor, unless such equipment is maintained by Landlord pursuant to Section 6.03 above. If any part of the Property or the Project is damaged by any act or omission of Tenant, Tenant shall pay Landlord the cost of repairing or replacing such damaged property, whether or not Landlord would otherwise be obligated to pay the cost of maintaining or repairing such property. It is the intention of Landlord and Tenant that, at all times during the Lease Term, Tenant shall maintain the portions of the Property, which it is obligated to maintain, in an attractive, first-class and fully operative condition.

(b) All of Tenant's obligations under this Section 6.04 shall be accomplished at Tenant's sole expense. If Tenant fails to maintain or repair the Property as required by this Section 6.04, Landlord may, upon ten (10) days' prior notice to Tenant (except that no notice shall be required in the case of an emergency), enter the Property and perform such maintenance or repair on behalf of Tenant. In such case, Tenant shall reimburse Landlord for all costs incurred in performing such maintenance or repair immediately upon demand."

Attach site plan of Project as an exhibit. Cross-hatch the Property leased on such exhibit or attach a separate exhibit showing the Property leased.

Initials ____________________

____

Figure 8-5 (*Continued*)

CONSTRUCTION OF IMPROVEMENTS BY LANDLORD

LEASE RIDER

This Rider is attached to and made part of that certain lease dated ____________________
between ____, as Landlord,
and ____, as Tenant,
covering the Property commonly known as ____________________________
____
____("the Lease").
The terms used in this Rider shall have the same definitions as set forth in the Lease. The provisions of this Rider shall prevail over any inconsistent or conflicting provisions of the Lease.

A. **Description of Improvements.** Landlord shall, at Landlord's expense, construct certain improvements on or about the Property (the "Work") in accordance with certain plans and specifications attached hereto as Exhibit "1" and incorporated herein by this reference. Tenant hereby approves the plans and specifications attached hereto as Exhibit "1".

B. **Preliminary Plans.** If the plans and specifications attached hereto are final plans and specifications, such final plans and specifications are hereinafter referred to as the "Final Plans", and the remainder of this Paragraph shall be inoperative. If the plans and specifications attached hereto are preliminary plans, Landlord shall prepare final working drawings and outlined specifications for the Work and submit such plans and specifications to Tenant for its approval on or before ____________________. Tenant shall approve or disapprove such drawings and specifications within ______________ days after receipt from Landlord. Tenant shall have the right to disapprove such drawings and specifications only if they materially differ from the plans and specifications attached hereto. If Tenant disapproves such drawings and specifications, Landlord and Tenant shall promptly meet in an attempt to resolve any dispute regarding such drawings and specifications. If the parties are unable to agree upon the final working drawings and specifications for the Work on or before ____________________, Landlord may, at Landlord's option, either (1) terminate this Lease upon seven (7) days' prior written notice to Tenant, in which case neither Landlord nor Tenant shall have further liability to the other, or (2) submit the matter to conclusive and binding arbitration in accordance with the Commercial Arbitration Rules of the American Arbitration Association. Final working drawings and specifications prepared in accordance with this Paragraph B and approved by Landlord and Tenant are hereinafter referred to as the "Final Plans".

C. **Completion of the Work.** Landlord shall use its best efforts to complete the Work described in the Final Plans prior to the scheduled Commencement Date set forth in Section 1.05 of the Lease. Notwithstanding the date set forth in Section 1.05, the Commencement Date shall be the date upon which the Work is substantially completed and the Property is delivered to Tenant. For the purposes of this Paragraph C, the Work shall be conclusively deemed to be substantially completed when all Work described in the Final Plans is completed, except for minor items of work (e.g., "pick-up work") which can be completed with only minor interference with Tenant's conduct of business on the Property.

D. **Changes.** Landlord's obligation to prepare the Property for Tenant's occupancy is limited to the completion of the Work set forth in the plans and specifications attached hereto as Exhibit "1". Landlord shall not be required to furnish, construct or install any items not shown thereon. If Tenant requests any change, addition or alteration ("Changes") in such plans and specifications or in the construction of the Work, Landlord shall promptly give Tenant an estimate of the cost of such Changes and the resulting delay in the delivery of the Property to Tenant. Within three (3) days after receipt of such estimate, Tenant shall give Landlord written notice whether Tenant elects to proceed with such Changes. If Tenant notifies Landlord in writing that Tenant elects to proceed with such Changes and if Landlord approves such Changes, Landlord shall, at Tenant's expense, promptly make such Changes. If Tenant fails to notify Landlord of its election within the three (3) day period, Landlord may either (1) make such Changes at Tenant's expense or (2) complete the Work without making such Changes. Tenant shall pay or reimburse Landlord for the costs of such Changes within fifteen (15) days after billing. Any delay caused by Tenant's request for any Changes or from the construction of any Changes shall not, in any event, delay the Commencement Date, which shall occur on the date it would have occurred but for such Changes. The Work shall be the property of Landlord and shall remain upon and be surrendered with the Property upon the expiration of the Lease Term.

Attach plans and specifications as Exhibit "1".

Initials ____________________

____

Figure 8-6 Construction of improvements by landlord—lease rider. (*Reprinted by courtesy of the Southern California Chapter of the Society of Industrial Realtors,® Inc.*)

OPTION TO EXTEND TERM

LEASE RIDER

This Rider is attached to and made part of that certain Lease (the "Lease") dated ______________
between ____, as Landlord,
and ____, as Tenant,
covering the Property commonly known as ____
____ (the "Property").
The terms used herein shall have the same definitions as set forth in the Lease. The provisions of this Rider shall supersede any inconsistent or conflicting provisions of the Lease.

A. **Option(s) to Extend Term.**

1. Landlord hereby grants to Tenant __________ option(s) (the "Option(s)") to extend the Lease Term for additional term(s) of ______________________ years each (the "Extension(s)"), on the same terms and conditions as set forth in the Lease, but at an increased rent as set forth below. Each Option shall be exercised only by written notice delivered to Landlord at least one hundred twenty (120) days before the expiration of the Lease Term or the preceding Extension of the Lease Term, respectively. If Tenant fails to deliver Landlord written notice of the exercise of an Option within the prescribed time period, such Option and any succeeding Options shall lapse, and there shall be no further right to extend the Lease Term. Each Option shall be exercisable by Tenant on the express conditions that (a) at the time of the exercise, and at all times prior to the commencement of such Extension, Tenant shall not be in default under any of the provisions of this Lease and (b) Tenant has not been ten (10) or more days late in the payment of rent more than a total of three (3) times during the Lease Term and all preceding Extensions.

2. **Personal Options.**

The Option(s) are personal to the Tenant named in Section 1.03 of the Lease or any Tenant's Affiliate described in Section 9.02 of the Lease. If Tenant subleases any portion of the Property or assigns or otherwise transfers any interest under the Lease to an entity other than a Tenant Affiliate prior to the exercise of an Option (whether with or without Landlord's consent), such Option and any succeeding Options shall lapse. If Tenant subleases any portion of the Property or assigns or otherwise transfers any interest of Tenant under the Lease to an entity other than a Tenant Affiliate after the exercise of an Option but prior to the commencement of the respective Extension (whether with or without Landlord's consent), such Option and any succeeding Options shall lapse and the Lease Term shall expire as if such Option were not exercised. If Tenant subleases any portion of the Property or assigns or otherwise transfers any interest of Tenant under the Lease in accordance with Article 9 of the Lease after the exercise of an Option and after the commencement of the Extension related to such Option, then the term of the Lease shall expire upon the expiration of the Extension during which such sublease or transfer occurred and only the succeeding Options shall lapse.

B. **Calculation of Rent.**

The Base Rent during the Extension(s) shall be determined by one or a combination of the following methods (INDICATE YOUR CHOICE UPON EXECUTION OF THE LEASE):

1. Cost of Living Adjustment (Section B(1), below) ☐
2. Fair Rental Value Adjustment (Section B(2), below) ☐
3. Fixed Adjustment (Section B(3), below) ☐

1. **Cost of Living Adjustment.**

The Base Rent shall be increased on the first day of the ______________________ month(s) of the ______________________ Extension(s) of the Lease Term (the "Rental Adjustment Date") by reference to the Index defined in Section 1.13(a) of the Lease or the substitute index described in Section 3.02 of the Lease, as follows: The Base Rent in effect immediately prior to the applicable Rental Adjustment Date (the "Comparison Base Rent") shall be increased by the percentage that the Index has increased from the month in which the payment of the Comparison Base Rent commenced through the month in which the applicable Rental Adjustment Date occurs. In no event shall the Base Rent be reduced by reason of such computation.

Initials ______________________

____

Figure 8-7 Option to extend term—lease rider. (*Reprinted by courtesy of the Southern California Chapter of the Society of Industrial Realtors,® Inc.*)

2. **Fair Rental Value Adjustment.**

The Base Rent shall be increased on the first day of the ______________________ month(s) of the ______________________ Extension(s) of the Lease Term (the "Rental Adjustment Date(s)") to the "fair rental value" of the Property, determined in the following manner:

(a) Not later than one hundred (100) days prior to any applicable Rental Adjustment Date, Landlord and Tenant shall meet in an effort to negotiate, in good faith, the fair rental value of the Property as of such Rental Adjustment Date. If Landlord and Tenant have not agreed upon the fair rental value of the Property at least ninety (90) days prior to the applicable Rental Adjustment Date, the fair rental value shall be determined by appraisal, as follows (INDICATE YOUR CHOICE UPON EXECUTION OF THE LEASE):

Appraisal by Appraisers. ☐ Appraisal by Brokers. ☐

(b) If Landlord and Tenant are not able to agree upon the fair rental value of the Property within the prescribed time period, then Landlord and Tenant shall attempt to agree in good faith upon a single appraiser or broker, as indicated above, not later than seventy-five (75) days prior the applicable Rental Adjustment Date. If Landlord and Tenant are unable to agree upon a single appraiser/broker within such time period, then Landlord and Tenant shall each appoint one appraiser or broker, as indicated above, not later than sixty-five (65) days prior to the applicable Rental Adjustment Date. Within (10) days thereafter, the two appointed appraisers/brokers shall appoint a third appraiser or broker, as indicated above. If either Landlord or Tenant fails to appoint its appraiser/broker within the prescribed time period, the single appraiser/broker appointed shall determine the fair rental value of the Property. If both parties fail to appoint appraisers/brokers within the prescribed time periods, then the first appraiser/broker thereafter selected by a party shall determine the fair rental value of the Property. Each party shall bear the cost of its own appraiser or broker and the parties shall share equally the cost of the single or third appraiser or broker, if applicable. If appraisers are used, such appraisers shall have at least five (5) years' experience in the appraisal of commercial/industrial real property in the area in which the Property is located and shall be members of professional organizations such as MAI or equivalent. If brokers are used, such brokers shall have at least five (5) years' experience in the sales and leasing of commercial/industrial real property in the area in which the Property is located and shall be members of professional organizations such as the Society of Industrial Realtors or equivalent.

(c) For the purposes of such appraisal, the term "fair market value" shall mean the price that a ready and willing tenant would pay, as of the applicable Rental Adjustment Date, as monthly rent to a ready and willing landlord of property comparable to the Property if such property were exposed for lease on the open market for a reasonable period of time and taking into account all of the purposes for which such property may be used. If a single appraiser/broker is chosen, then such appraiser/broker shall determine the fair rental value of the Property. Otherwise, the fair rental value of the Property shall be the arithmetic average of the two (2) of the three (3) appraisals which are closest in amount, and the third appraisal shall be disregarded. In no event, however, shall the Base Rent be reduced by reason of such computation. Landlord and Tenant shall instruct the appraiser(s)/broker(s) to complete their determination of the fair rental value not later than thirty (30) days prior to the applicable Rental Adjustment Date. If the fair rental value is not determined prior to the applicable Rental Adjustment Date, then Tenant shall continue to pay to Landlord the Base Rent applicable to the Property immediately prior to such Extension, until the fair rental value is determined. When the fair rental value of the Property is determined, Landlord shall deliver notice thereof to Tenant, and Tenant shall pay to Landlord, within (10) days after receipt of such notice, the difference between the Base Rent actually paid by Tenant to Landlord and the new Base Rent determined hereunder.

3. **Fixed Adjustment.**

The Base Rent shall be increased to the following amounts on the following dates: ______________

____

____

____

____

____

Initials ______________________

____

Figure 8-7 (*Continued*)

RIGHT OF FIRST OFFER

LEASE RIDER

This Rider is attached to and made part of that certain lease dated ____________________
between ____, as Landlord,
and ____, as Tenant,
covering the Property commonly known as ______________________________________
____
____(the "Lease").
The terms used in this Rider shall have the same definitions as set forth in the Lease. The provisions of this Rider shall prevail over any inconsistent or conflicting provisions of the Lease.

Right of First Offer.

If at any time during the Lease Term, Landlord intends to offer the Property for sale to third parties or to accept an offer of a third party to purchase the Property, Landlord shall first give written notice to Tenant of the purchase price and other material terms upon which Landlord is willing to sell the Property ("Landlord's Sale Notice"). Landlord's Sale Notice shall constitute an offer to sell the Property to Tenant at the price and upon the terms and conditions contained in Landlord's Sale Notice. Tenant shall have ten (10) days after receipt of Landlord's Sale Notice in which to accept such offer. Tenant shall accept such offer, if at all, only by written notice to Landlord in which Tenant shall agree to purchase the Property from Landlord at the price and upon the terms and conditions contained in Landlord's Sale Notice. If Tenant accepts such offer within the ten (10) day period, Landlord and Tenant shall open an escrow, within five (5) days thereafter, for the purchase and sale of the Property. Tenant shall purchase the Property from Landlord through such escrow at the price and in accordance with the terms and conditions contained in Landlord's Sale Notice. If Tenant fails to give Landlord notice of Tenant's acceptance of the offer contained in Landlord's Sale Notice within the ten (10) day period, then all rights of Tenant to purchase the Property under this Rider shall terminate and Landlord shall have no further obligation to notify Tenant of any other proposed purchase or sale of the Property. Landlord shall thereafter have the unconditional right to sell the Property to third parties or to accept the offers from third parties to purchase the Property without further obligation to Tenant. The preceding Right of First Offer shall not apply to (a) sales or transfers among entities or persons related to Landlord, including, but not limited to: partners, if Landlord is a partnership; shareholders, if Landlord is a corporation; or family members of any individual Landlord or any such partner or shareholder; (b) any transfer or disposition by assignment, gift, devise, testamentary transfer, intestate successions; or (c) any transfer to a trust for the benefit of any heir at law of Landlord (or any heir at law of any partner or shareholder of Landlord) or for the benefit of Landlord.

Initials ____________________

____

Figure 8-8 Right of first offer—lease rider. (*Reprinted by courtesy of the Southern California Chapter of the Society of Industrial Realtors,® Inc.*)

CHAPTER 9

Eviction

Louis B. Hansotte
Hansotte, Nostrand & Lange
San Diego, California

THE PROPERTY MANAGER'S ROLE

A property manager probably has no more distasteful duty to perform than the involuntary recovery of an apartment unit from a nonpaying tenant or from one who has breached one or more of the covenants of a lease. Yet there is probably nothing more important than the prompt and businesslike removal of such a tenant from the premises when the time has come to do so, for the following reasons:

1. The unit will not generate any income until the malfeasant is removed and replaced with a paying tenant.
2. The owner wants a cash return based on the scheduled income that the property should produce.
3. The manner and promptness with which the ouster is performed will be noted by other tenants, especially those who are likely to take advantage of a lax management system.
4. A large number of problems may stem from the improper removal of a tenant, some of which may be more difficult to deal with than the problems requiring the tenant's removal in the first place.

It is therefore extremely important for the property manager to know what action is proper under varying sets of circumstances and at what point legal action in obtaining compliance with or termination of the lease should be instituted.

REVIEW OF EXISTING LEASE OR RENTAL AGREEMENT

Any tenant in possession of real property should be on the premises pursuant to a valid lease or rental agreement. Should the property manager take over management of a property and find no formal lease or rental agreement in force, the creation and execution of such an agreement with the existing tenant should be the first order of business. If there are existing agreements that are deficient with respect to provisions for the removal of a tenant, the deficiencies should be corrected and new agreements executed. If there are long-term leases in existence, the manager will not be able to require execution of any modifications, although the tenant might be requested to do so voluntarily. In any event, the file should be marked to provide for a new agreement at the expiration of the current term of each such lease. If month-to-month rental agreements are deficient, they should be replaced with proper agreements as soon as any applicable notice requirements can be met.

QUIET ENJOYMENT

Before considering the methods by which a tenant may be removed from the premises, it is important that the property manager keep one common-law concept firmly in mind: There is, in *every* lease, an implied covenant from the lessor to the tenant, allowing the tenant the right of *quiet enjoyment* of the premises during the term of the lease. This covenant exists in the lease without any expressed statement to that effect, thus the term *implied covenant.* This stipulation means that the tenant's right of possession of the leased premises during the term of the lease (and absent any wrongdoing on the tenant's part) is absolute and, in fact and in law, is greater than the lessor's right to the possession of his or her own property.

The law jealously guards the tenant's right to this implied covenant of quiet enjoyment, and for this reason it is always the burden of the owner to show a proper reason for dispossessing the tenant, rather than the other way around.

The property manager who keeps this common-law rule in mind will clearly recognize the need to justify the actions taken to remove the tenant from possession of the premises and will be able to document those actions to ensure compliance with all technical requirements of the law. It is not enough to know the law, or even to follow it. In any litigation which flows from an action for possession, it will be necessary to *prove* that there has been strict compliance with the technicalities of the law.

RECOVERY OF POSSESSION

American Jurisprudence, a leading authority on law in the United States, spells out five methods of obtaining possession of property when there has been a default in the terms of an occupancy agreement (32 *AmJur* 845):

1. *Peaceable reentry,* which is obtaining possession of the premises without the use of any force, and without physically barring the former tenant from the premises
2. *Use of reasonably necessary force,* remembering that deadly force in protecting property is never justified, and that only that force which is reasonable under the circumstances may ever be justified
3. *Writ of entry,* or *action of ejectment,* which involves court action and which was the usual common-law remedy for recovery of possession
4. *Forcible detainer,* involving the use of force or emotional distress to recover possession—risky at best and highly inadvisable in today's consumer-oriented society
5. *Summary eviction,* known now in most jurisdictions as *unlawful detainer*

These remedies of eviction will be discussed at some length in subsequent sections.

BREACH OF LEASE

A breach of the lease usually involves either or both of the following conditions:

1. Rent is not paid, or is not paid in a timely and appropriate fashion.
2. Rent is paid as required by the terms of the lease, but there are one or more other breaches of covenants contained in the lease.

The procedures to correct the deficiencies may vary according to which of the foregoing situations exist. The most common problem area of default with tenants involves tenants who do not pay rent at all or who are consistently late in paying rent. Actions for rent do not differ materially from those involving other types of breaches, except of course in the proof of the facts alleged. Our discussion will therefore be limited primarily to defaults in the payment of rent.

TERMINATION OF LEASE WITHOUT LITIGATION

It is axiomatic in law that litigation is always a *last* resort. When faced with a nonpaying tenant, it is better to recover possession of the premises peacefully and without litigation, even if it means making concessions not required by law.

For example, tenants might be forgiven all or a portion of back rent on the condition that they vacate the premises within a short period of time *and* leave the premises in a clean and undamaged condition. It is important to make the forgiveness conditional so that if it becomes necessary to bring legal action for eviction, the tenant cannot successfully argue that payment of the rent was waived by the actions of the lessor or lessor's agent.

It is not unheard of for an owner or property manager to offer to pay a portion of the tenant's moving expenses as an inducement to the tenant to leave quickly and peaceably. Actual payment should not be made, of course, until the premises have been physically vacated and left in good condition.

TERMINATION OF LEASE WITH NOTICE

If the term of the lease is near an end, or if the tenancy is on a month-to-month rental agreement, the lease should be terminated by giving formal notice in accordance with the provisions of the lease itself and state law.

Notice requirements must be strictly complied with, and usually call for *personal* service on *each adult occupant* of the premises (not just those who have signed or are referred to in the lease or rental agreement). Even if the law permits the owner or agent to make such service, good practice dictates that it be made instead by a disinterested third person. Proof of the time and manner of service of notice is critical to any litigation which may follow, and the objective testimony of a third person can make the difference between winning and losing in court. Some states also require that a copy of the notice be posted conspicuously on the premises, with a copy mailed (certified or registered) to the tenant shortly thereafter. For example, Section 13-40-107 of Colorado's Revised Statutes provides that

> A tenancy may be terminated by notice in writing, served not less than the respective period fixed before the end of the applicable tenancy, as follows:
>
> (a) A tenancy for one year or longer, three months;
>
> (b) A tenancy of six months or longer but less than a year, one month;
>
> (c) A tenancy of one month or longer but less than six months, ten days;
>
> (d) A tenancy of one week or longer but less than one month, or a tenancy at will, three days;
>
> (e) A tenancy for less than one week, one day.

Under Section 13-40-108, the statute continues:

> A notice to quit or demand for possession of real property may be served by delivering a copy thereof to the tenant or other person occupying such premises, or by leaving such copy with some person, a member of the tenant's family above the age of fifteen years, residing on or in charge of the premises, or in case no one is on the premises at the time service is attempted, then by posting such copy in some conspicuous place on the premises.

It may appear that the methods of service are interchangeable and that no one method is preferred over another. In fact, when using a method other than personal service, it is usually necessary to establish that the alternative method of service was required because personal service could not be made after a due and diligent attempt. Be prepared to make such a showing if personal service cannot be made.

An interesting provision of Maryland's statutes provides:

> *8-501 Time of Notice to Terminate Tenancy*
>
> No written agreement between a landlord and tenant shall provide for a longer notice period to be furnished by the tenant to the landlord in order to terminate the tenancy than that required of the landlord to the tenant in order to terminate the tenancy (1974, ch. 699).

If these measures fail, it becomes necessary to consider legal or other action to remove the tenant.

Some states permit a property owner a limited amount of self-help, including the use of a degree of force that may be reasonably necessary under the circumstances to permit recovery of possession of the real property. Even when permitted by law, however, evicting a tenant in this manner is strongly frowned on because it can easily lead to the use of excess force, sometimes called *forcible detainer,* which is universally prohibited.

Colorado's statute (Section 13-40-101) defines forcible entry and detainer as follows:

> (1) If any person enters upon or into any lands, tenements, mining claims, or other possessions with force or strong hand or multitude of people, whether any person is actually upon or in the same at the time of such entry, or if any person by threats of violence or injury to the party in possession or by such words or actions as have a natural tendency to excite fear or apprehension of danger gains possession of any lands, tenements, mining claims, or other possessions and detains and holds the same, such person so offending is guilty of a forcible entry and detainer within the meaning of this article.
>
> (2) If any person enters peaceably upon any lands, tenements, mining claims, or other possessions, whether any person is actually in or upon the same at the time of such entry and by force turns the party in possession out or, by threats or by words or actions which have a natural tendency to excite fear or apprehension of danger, frightens the party out of possession and detains and holds the same, such person so offending is guilty of a forcible detainer within the meaning of this article.
>
> (3) If any person enters upon or into any lands, tenements, mining claims, or other possessions by force or by threats of violence, or words, or actions which have a natural tendency to excite fear or apprehension of danger, and intimidates the party entitled to possession from returning upon or possessing the same, such person so offending is guilty of a forcible entry within the meaning of this article.

A notice to quit, such as shown in Figure 9-1, need not be given in the alternative, such as a notice to quit *or* pay rent. This is because the lease is at an end, or the tenancy can be terminated by appropriate notice. This form *cannot* be used if the term of the lease is not over. In that event, an alternative notice, shown in a subsequent section, *must* be used.

LITIGATION

It litigation is required, it may take several forms and will vary in procedure from state to state. Notwithstanding the variations, the actions generally fall into two categories:

1. Formal evictions, frequently called *actions in ejectment*
2. Summary evictions, known as *unlawful detainer*

NOTICE OF TERMINATION OF TENANCY

To: (enter name of all tenants, subtenants, and anyone else in possession of the following premises)

Address of premises: (enter the street addres of the premises)

YOU ARE HEREBY NOTIFIED THAT YOUR TENANCY IN THE ABOVE DESCRIBED PREMISES IS TERMINATED, EFFECTIVE ON: ____________________. (Enter date, not less than 30 days after service of notice on the last person served.)

Failure to vacate the premises on or before the effective date of this notice may result in legal proceedings against you, including a judgment and costs for your failure to comply with the terms of this notice.

Keys should be returned to the undersigned (lessor or agent) at the time you vacate the premises. You will be liable for any damage to the premises caused during your possession or after you vacate if you do not give prior notice to the undersigned of the date and time you intend to vacate the premises.

Dated:______________________ at ____________________

____

(signature of lessor or agent)

Figure 9-1 Notice of termination of tenancy.

EJECTMENT

Any breach of a condition of a lease is grounds for its termination by the lessor, and failure to pay rent is but one of the reasons for such termination.

It the lease term is not at an end, or close enough to the end to suggest waiting to commence eviction proceedings until it is at an end, it is usually necessary to give the tenant an opportunity to cure any default before the lease can actually be terminated.

This requirement stems from the fact that even minor breaches of a lease have permitted lessors to evict a tenant summarily, only to discover later that, in fact, the lease was not breached. By the time the tenant has been removed, however, the question of proper grounds for such removal may be moot. The tenant has been dispossessed, forced to find other accommodations, and incurred moving expenses, and may not be economically able to support legal action against the lessor for wrongful dispossession. Therefore, notice of intent to terminate the tenancy for breach of a condition, including the payment of rent, should, and in those jurisdictions requiring it, must be given in the alternative.

An alternative notice, as the name suggests, advises the tenant to either cure the breach (pay the rent or cease the objectionable activities) *or* quit the premises. In this sense, compliance with the notice requirement is a condition precedent to the actual removal of the tenant. The tenant may be allowed, or the law may require, a specific period of time within which to cure the breach. In California, for example, it is necessary to serve the tenant with a 3-day notice before actual eviction proceedings may be initiated. Figure 9-2 is a sample notice to quit or pay rent.

Following service of the notice on the tenant (and any others residing in the premises) in one of the ways discussed, the tenant has the period

NOTICE TO QUIT OR PAY RENT

To: (enter name of all tenants, subtenants, and anyone else in possession of the following premises)

Address of premises: (enter the street address of the premises)

YOU ARE HEREBY NOTIFIED THAT YOUR TENANCY IN THE ABOVE DESCRIBED PREMISES WILL BE TERMINATED, unless within THREE (3) DAYS after the service of this notice upon you, you pay to undersigned (lessor or agent) the sum of $____________, being the rent due from you under the lease or rental agreement pursuant to which you occupy the premises. This sum is computed as follows:

Rental for the period __________ to __________ $________;
Rental for the period __________ to __________ $________;
Rental for the period __________ to __________ $________;
PLUS late fees of $________;
For a TOTAL of $________.

If you fail to pay the amounts indicated, your lease or rental agreement will be terminated and you will be subject to legal proceedings for recovery of possession of the premises, and damages (including legal fees and costs) as may be awarded by the court. Damages may be trebled (multiplied by three) at the discretion of the court.

Dated:____________ at ____________

____
(signature of lessor or agent)

Figure 9-2 Three-day notice to quit or pay rent.

given to cure the default. If the default is cured, the tenant is restored to all the rights granted under the lease or rental agreement, and the eviction process is ended.

If payment of rent or the curing of other defaults is accepted by the lessor, and the lessor later discovers that another breach of the lease remains, it is necessary to commence eviction proceedings again from the beginning. *Never* attempt to continue the eviction process once the proceedings have been interrupted, or a default waived, without service of a new and timely notice.

If the default is not cured within the time allowed, the eviction process continues with the filing and service of a formal complaint in the appropriate court. This is the first time the court actually becomes involved in the eviction process.

After a formal complaint is filed by the plaintiff (lessor), the defendant (tenant) has a time period within which to answer the complaint. Except for a summary proceeding such as unlawful detainer, the time allowed to answer an eviction complaint is usually the same as that to answer any other type of lawsuit.

If the tenant files an answer within the time period permitted by statute, the case is set for hearing. Some states give a preference to matters in ejectment on the trial calendar, permitting an earlier hearing than one for other matters filed at the same time. If the state doesn't give preference, the scheduling of such a matter becomes a part of the strategy of filing the case in ejectment in the first place—an unlawful detainer action may be heard much more quickly.

One function of an action in ejectment is to allow all matters affecting the tenancy to be heard at the same time. If there are collateral issues, such as trying title to the property involved, or substantive defenses which the tenant wants to raise, they are heard in conjunction with the formal eviction action. This allows all issues to be settled in one court proceeding; this usually cannot be done at summary hearings in unlawful detainer.

The trial of the matter determines whether the plaintiff or defendant will be the prevailing party in the action. If the defendant successfully raises and proves one or more defenses, the lease will not be terminated and possession of the premises will remain with the tenant. Damages may be awarded to the tenant, depending on the outcome of the trial. If the lease provides for attorneys' fees in the event legal action is instituted, some states allow the tenant to be awarded attorneys' fees even if the lease expressly provides such fees are only awardable to the successful lessor. In virtually all states, an award of attorneys' fees is discretionary with the court, unless there is a specific statute requiring such fees to be awarded.

DEFAULT

If the tenant fails to answer the complaint within the allowable time period, a judgment by default may be obtained. Some courts are predisposed to set aside a default judgment and allow the matter to be tried on its merits if any plausible excuse for doing so is presented. Except for this tendency, a default judgment is just as good as any other. In some states it is more difficult to set a default judgment aside after a specified period of time has elapsed, and if the time is not too lengthy, it may be best to allow this period to expire before attempting to obtain possession of the premises. It then becomes much more difficult for the tenant to undo the effect of the default judgment.

OBTAINING POSSESSION

If the lessor prevails in the action, the court will order the premises to be surrendered by the tenant, together with an award of back rent and damages, if appropriate. If the tenant does not vacate the premises voluntarily, the lessor may obtain a *writ of possession,* also known as a *writ of entry,* or the equivalent, to oust the tenant physically and be restored to possession.

Statutes may require the sheriff or marshal under order of the writ of possession to give the tenant additional notice and an opportunity to vacate the premises peacefully, and many such officers offer additional time to vacate whether or not the court orders it or the law requires it.

If at the end of such time as the peace officers have allowed, the premises are still occupied by the tenants, they will be physically removed and their possessions placed either on the street or in storage, according to the requirements of the law in that jurisdiction. The statutes may require the lessor to post a deposit guaranteeing storage fees during the time the tenant is allowed by law to pay for, and reclaim, the property. If not reclaimed, the property may be sold, usually at public auction, the sales price being applied to the costs of sale and then to the plaintiff's judgment.

SUMMARY REMEDIES

A substantial disadvantage of filing a lawsuit is the time it usually takes to get a matter to trial. In some jurisdictions it can take 4 or 5 years after a case is filed before getting to the hearing stage. In the case of rental properties, the tenant is allowed to remain in possession during this period. Although rental payments should ultimately be ordered by the court, the insolvent tenant will have had the benefit of the use of the premises during the time it took to get to trial without then having the money with which to pay the judgment—clearly a hapless situation for the lessor.

In many cases, these time delays occur because of the complex legal issues presented in a contested matter. The main concern of an unpaid lessor is usually either getting paid or getting possession of the premises so that a proper tenant may be found. Other issues, however important to the parties, are often collateral to the problems of payment or possession and can be dealt with by more traditional litigation procedures.

The law provides ways to achieve faster results, however—the use of what are known as *summary remedies.* In the case of lessor-tenant problems, these remedies address the issues of payment and possession *only,* leaving the other issues for a different forum. The summary remedy for possession of real property is called *unlawful detainer.*

UNLAWFUL DETAINER

Some of the differences between conventional and summary remedies may be illustrated by the following distinctions between actions in ejectment and unlawful detainer.

The time period for responding to the filing of a regular lawsuit may be 30 days or more. In unlawful detainer actions, that time is frequently shortened to a period of between 3 and 5 days. This means that the tenant has only that time to consult with a legal adviser, have an answer to the complaint prepared and filed, and appear in court for the hearing.

As in regular eviction actions, failure to answer the complaint will allow the plaintiff to take a judgment by default and obtain a writ from the court authorizing the sheriff or other public official to obtain physical possession of the premises.

Initially, courts did not allow the tenant to raise any defenses or issues other than those relating to proof of payment of rent. The theory was that if rent were in default the tenant should vacate the premises forthwith and could sue later for whatever other damages or remedies might be appropriate; this gave the lessor timely possession of the premises for reletting.

Problems developed in providing such speedy relief to the lessor, including infringement on the tenant's constitutional rights. A tenant could be dispossessed by substantially unsupported allegations made by the lessor, without having an opportunity for a hearing on the merits of those allegations. If later proof showed that the lessor was not in fact entitled to possession, it frequently was too late; the damage (to the tenant) was already done.

At the same time, in order to protect the tenant's constitutional right to due process, it became necessary not only to guarantee to the tenant the right to a hearing, but also to allow one or more defenses to be raised in the unlawful detainer action itself. Two important issues with have a bearing on the tenant's right to defend against summary eviction are *habitability* and *retaliatory eviction.*

HABITABILITY OR TENANTABILITY

Most jurisdictions now require that premises designed or offered for human residential occupancy be habitable or tenantable.

In California, for example, this means that the premises must be relatively free from rodent infestation; that there must be an adequate hot and cold water supply to the premises; that doors, windows, and roofs must not leak; that there be adequate heating and ventilation; and that refuse collection and hygienic facilities be available.

If the premises fail to meet minimum statutory requirements, the tenant may expend an amount up to 1 month's rental payment to make necessary repairs or improvements, or may terminate the lease, although both actions require the tenant to give the lessor timely notice of the defects.

If the tenant takes advantage of this provision of the law (which may not be done more than once in any 12-month period), the lessor cannot evict the tenant for failure to use these same funds to pay the rent. This defense must be (and is) allowed to be raised by the tenant in a summary eviction action; otherwise the right of habitability would be meaningless.

RETALIATORY EVICTION

A relative newcomer to the eviction scene, and gaining legal strength and increased use throughout the country, is the doctrine of *retaliatory eviction.*

In allowing tenants to raise defenses other than proof of payment of rent, courts are recognizing that a right isn't a right if it is not protected and upheld. If the law upholds a lease provision waiving the tenant's right to habitable premises, all leases would soon contain such a waiver and the "right" to habitable premises would disappear.

In very similar cases reported on both coasts, tenants exercised their right to report their lessors for failing to meet standards of health and habitation required by the local housing agencies. Under these health laws, such failures constituted criminal conduct.

When the lessors were cited for their unlawful conduct, one took action to evict the reporting tenant and the other raised the tenant's rent to a prohibitive figure, which the tenant could not pay.

Courts at the trial level questioned the lessors' improper behavior, but allowed the unlawful detainer proceedings to go to judgments for eviction on the grounds, under existing law, that periodic tenancies could be terminated by the lessors (with proper notice) for any reason or for no reason at all. Although the lessors may have acted unconscionably, they were not required to do otherwise.

Higher courts in both jurisdictions carved out a new exception to the rule prohibiting substantive defenses to be raised in unlawful detainer proceedings. They introduced the concept of what is now called retaliatory eviction. They held that if the dominant purpose of the lessor in terminating a tenancy is to retaliate for some lawful conduct on the part of the tenant, the eviction action cannot be maintained.

Subsequent case and statutory law have more specifically defined what action or conduct constitutes retaliatory eviction, requiring that the actions be "infused with the public interest." Specific acts which have met this test judicially include the reporting of violations of health or safety standards to appropriate public agencies, since it is a citizen's duty to report the commission of a crime and the state's duty to protect the citizen for having done so, and engaging in lawful collective bargaining activities on the leasehold interest of a tenant farmer which result in an attempt by the lessor to terminate the lease.

CONSTRUCTIVE EVICTION

The lessor is permitted to recover possession of the premises if it can be done peaceably. Use of reasonable force, although permitted in some jurisdictions, can result in a judgment of *forcible detainer,* exposing the lessor to liability for improper termination of the tenancy. Closely akin to forcible detainer is the removal of the tenant, not by actual force, but by such action as to make continued occupancy by the tenant impractical. The result is the same as if physical force is used. The tenant may thus be constructively, if not actually, evicted. Like forcible detainer, constructive eviction is improper in most jurisdictions.

Examples of constructive eviction include such actions by the lessor as changing all the locks on the outside doors so that the tenant can gain access only by the use of force; removing doors, partitions, or portions of the roof so that the tenant is exposed to the elements even while indoors; and cutting off essential services such as gas, water, and electricity.

The lessor's contention may be that since no force was used to remove the tenant, the lessor's actions are justifiable, especially since it is the tenant who is really violating the lease by failing to make rent payments. The law does not sympathize with the lessor's reasoning in these cases, and attempts to evict the tenant by such actions will result in severe penalties against the lessor.

Many of the problems involved in litigation over tenant breaches occur regardless of which method is used to recover possession. Following are some of the more frequently encountered concerns.

DAMAGES

Recovery of possession is usually the lessor's primary objective when a lease is breached, but recovery of unpaid rental or other monetary damages runs a very close second. The lessor usually has three primary economic goals in litigating a dispute with a tenant:

1. Recovery of past due rent
2. Recovery of damages inflicted on the premises by the tenant
3. Recovery of future damages over the remaining lease term, particularly if the premises cannot easily be re-let, or cannot be rented for an amount at least equal to the rental called for under the original lease

PAST DUE RENT

There should be no doubt about the lessor's entitlement to past due rent in any jurisdiction, subject only to defenses which the tenant may successfully interpose. As long as the tenant has the exclusive right to possess the property, and the lessor does not interfere with that right, the tenant should be liable for the cost thereof as set forth in the lease.

Most jurisdictions permit the lessor to sue for unpaid rent at the end of each rental period (e.g., every month the rent is in arrears, or at least after the day the rent is due). Under common law, rent was traditionally paid at the end of the lease term, usually out of the profits earned by the tenant (farmer) during the lease. Modern practice usually calls for payment of rent in advance, but even if payable in advance the rent is not due until the date set in the lease for payment.

The lessor may instead wait until the lease runs its course and then bring one lawsuit for the entire amount due. This avoids a multiplicity of lawsuits, but also requires the lessor to do without any income during the remaining term of the lease and then face the likely prospect that the tenant will be unable to pay a judgment awarded by the court. There is also a conflict with a well-established concept of the law requiring the nonbreaching party to a contract to mitigate, or lessen the damages, if it is reasonably possible to do so. The tenant, if still available and solvent at the end of the lease period, may well argue that the lessor should have terminated the lease soon after the tenant's default and attempted to find another tenant, whose rent to that extent would offset the damages accruing to the tenant.

DAMAGES OTHER THAN RENT

If there are damages attributable to the tenant other than or in addition to back rent, the lessor will seek reimbursement for those as well. A common problem here is that the lessor may not have proper receipts, may not be making a reasonable charge for services performed by the lessor, or may not be able to prove that the damages were in fact caused by the acts or omissions of the tenant.

The property manager must carefully document both the condition of the premises (at the commencement and end of the period of occupancy) and the nature and cost of all repairs made or required, and must be able to prove such to the satisfaction of the court should legal action become necessary to recover those costs.

Documentation is especially important if a damage or security deposit was taken from the tenant at the inception of the lease. Some states require the tenant to be given a prompt accounting following termination of the lease, and allow a penalty assessment against the lessor if he or she fails either to account for or to return the excess of the tenant's deposit.

FUTURE DAMAGES

Allowing the lessor recovery for future damages—those occurring after the tenant abandons or breaches the lease—is relatively new in the law. A theory which was held for many years was that until rent became due, an action for it could not be taken. Also, any act by the lessor which was inconsistent with the tenant's right of occupancy, such as bringing legal action for past due rent, constituted a termination of the lease by operation of law. When the lessor thereafter sought to recover additional rent, the court was quick to find that the lease had been terminated and no rent could therefore be due.

To avoid the prospect of being sued periodically, or being liable for the entire unpaid rent at the conclusion of the lease, some tenants induced their lessors into conduct which the tenants felt would cause a forfeiture or termination of the lease. And many times it did; the lessor had to be very careful to ensure that action taken to preserve a right under the lease would not result in an unintentional termination of the lease.

Many leases, and some jurisdictions, still contain or require specific language in the lease to the effect that certain actions or remedies taken under the lease will not terminate it unless the intent to terminate is expressed. If the lessor desires to re-let the premises without terminating the lease, the re-letting may only be done by the lessor as the *agent* for the tenant. This creates the anomalous situation of the unpaid lessor working for the defaulting tenant! In these cases the lessor must anticipate the likelihood of being able to re-let the premises for more rent than the original tenant was paying. If this happens, the excess belongs to the defaulting tenant! The solution is to terminate the lease expressly and re-let the premises for the lessor's own account. Should the new tenant default, however, the former tenant will no longer be liable for any unpaid rent because the legal basis for collecting that rent is canceled.

The more modern view is to allow for a single action to be brought by the lessor at the time of the default, and to allow a claim for future rent even though it is technically not yet due or payable.

California law permits a provision to be included in a lease containing language such as the following:

> In event of a breach of this lease the LESSOR may recover:
>
> 1. The worth at the time of award of the unpaid rent which has been earned at the time of termination; [e.g., past due rent]
>
> 2. The worth at the time of award of the amount by which the unpaid rent which would have been earned after termination until the time of award exceeds the amount of such rental loss that LESSEE proves could have been reasonably avoided; [e.g., mitigation prior to time of award]
>
> 3. The worth at the time of award of the amount by which the unpaid rent for the balance of the term after the time of award exceeds the amount of such rental loss for such period that LESSEE proves could reasonably be avoided; [e.g., mitigation after time of award]
>
> 4. Any other amount necessary to compensate LESSOR for all the detriment proximately caused by LESSEE'S failure to perform any obligation under this lease, or which in the ordinary course of things would be likely to result therefrom. [e.g., damages other than unpaid rent]

5. The "worth at the time of award" of the amounts referred to herein is computed by discounting such amount at the discount rate of the Federal Reserve Bank in San Francisco at the time of award plus 1%.

References to discounting the amount which may be recovered for future damages are taken from the California statutes. Their intent is to allow calculation of an amount of damages which represents the present value of all future damages discounted over the remaining term of the lease. The discount rate is published monthly and is readily available to the general public. This theory is very similar to the accepted practice of computing the present value of a right to receive future payments, which is used extensively in real property financing and appraising.

It is important to note that the California statutes do not make the lessor's right to receive future damages automatic; provisions similar to the foregoing must be expressly included in the lease.

TREBLE DAMAGES

The law occasionally provides for the equivalent of a penalty when there is a breach of certain types of agreements. In some states, leases are included in that group. When they are, an arbitrary award of treble damages—three times the damages actually proved by the lessor—may be allowed by the court. The purpose is to punish the tenant for intentional wrongdoing, while at the same time permitting a quick calculation of total damages. Arguments over what amount is reasonable are thereby avoided, without denying the lessor some amount in excess of the actual damages proved.

Treble damages are not automatic in most instances and are left to the sound discretion of the court. Unless mandated by law, they are awarded only in cases in which the tenant has demonstrated a substantial disregard for the obligations contained in the lease. If the lessor does not expressly request treble damages when the complaint is filed, they will not be awarded.

ABANDONMENT

The tenant may cease paying rent but remain in occupancy, or may cease paying rent and abandon the premises. It may be some time after the failure to receive rent that the owner or property manager learns that the tenant has abandoned the premises. One eviction problem is made much easier by abandonment: There is no one there to evict.

Another problem that presents itself, however, is that it is difficult to determine when abandonment actually occurs. A temporary, or even extended, absence from the premises is not an abandonment, and if the rent is current and there are no other breaches of the lease, there is no valid reason for the lessor to complain.

Does absence *and* a failure to pay rent constitute an abandonment? Not necessarily. The tenant may intend to return, but for some reason beyond the tenant's control be unable to communicate that fact to the lessor or the property manager, or to make a timely rent payment. Failure to make timely payment of rent *is* a breach of the lease, but it is not necessarily an abandonment of the premises.

In the law relating to abandonments generally, the definition of abandonment contemplates some act or omission coupled with an intent to surrender possession or some other right, permanently. An easement, for example, can be lost by abandonment. But mere nonuse of the easement (other than one acquired prescriptively) will not be sufficient to work an abandonment, absent some other evidence of an intent to surrender all additional use of it.

California resolves this dilemma for the lessor by providing a statutory procedure when abandonment is suspected. The lessor must give the tenant written notice of the lessor's belief of abandonment, and the tenant must, in turn, respond thereto prior to the time set for termination of the lease in the notice. If the lessor gives the required notice and the tenant does not respond, there is a conclusive (irrefutable) presumption of abandonment.

Notice may be given by the lessor anytime after rent has been due and unpaid for a period of 14 days, provided the lessor is acting in good faith and has no reason to know or believe that the tenant has not, in fact, abandoned the premises. Figure 9-3 is a sample notice of belief of abandonment taken from the form used in California.

ABANDONED PROPERTY

It may not be the premises but the tenant's personal property that is abandoned. Of course, it can be both. Just as it is never safe to assume the tenant has abandoned the premises, it is not proper to appropriate any of the tenant's belongings which may remain on the premises until a judicial determination of the tenant's status has been made.

Property of a defaulting tenant is still the tenant's property, not the lessor's. More than one tenant has successfully maintained legal action for recovery of property allegedly damaged, destroyed, or stolen after the lessor took custody of the premises. The diamond ring in the top drawer of the dresser; the cash under the mattress; and the irreplaceable

NOTICE OF BELIEF OF ABANDONMENT

TO: (Tenant's Name and Address)

This notice is given pursuant to Section 1951.3 of the Civil Code concerning the real property leased by you at (address of property). The rent on this property has been due and unpaid for 14 consecutive days and the lessor believes that you have abandoned the property.

The real property will be deemed abandoned within the meaning of Section 1951.2 of the Civil Code and your lease will terminate on (insert date not less than 15 days after personal service of this notice, or 18 days if mailed) unless before such date the undersigned received at the address indicated below a written notice from you stating both of the following:

(1) Your intent not to abandon the real property.

(2) An address at which you may be served by certified mail in any action for unlawful detainer of the real property.

You are required to pay the rent due and unpaid under the lease, and your failure to do so can lead to a court proceeding against you.

Dated: ____________________ at ____________________, California.

____

(signature of lessor or agent)

Figure 9-3 Notice of belief of abandonment.

world leaders autograph collection all have a tendency to disappear mysteriously when the lessor retakes possession of the premises.

The lessor must take physical possession of all property belonging to the tenant or found in the tenant's apartment, carefully and completely inventory it, safeguard it, insure it, and store it—or be liable for the consequences. One of the property manager's most important duties is to see to it that these responsibilities are effectively and efficiently met when an eviction action is maintained.

The lessor may look to this property for reimbursement for rent and other damages to which the lessor is entitled. But any such action must be taken in accordance with the strict requirements of law. When personal property remains on the premises after a tenancy has been terminated and the premises have been vacated by the tenant, the lessor must give written notice to the tenant and to any other person whom the lessor reasonably believes may be the owner of the property.

The notice should describe the property in a manner reasonably adequate to permit the owner of the property to identify it. If the lessor does not describe the property in its entirety, the notice is not defective but does not protect the lessor regarding any property not specifically de-

NOTICE OF RIGHT TO RECLAIM ABANDONED PROPERTY

TO: (Name and Address of Former Tenant or other Owner)

When you vacated the premises at (address), the following personal property remained: (describe the property).

You may claim this property at (address).

Unless you pay the reasonable cost of storage for all the above-described property, and take possession of the property which you claim, not later than (insert a date not less than 15 days from the date of personal service, or 18 days from the date of mailing) the property may be disposed of pursuant to Civil Code Section 1988.

If you fail to redeem the property, it will be sold at a public sale after notice of the sale has been given by publication. You have the right to bid on the property at this sale. After the property is sold and the cost of storage, advertising, and sale is deducted, the remaining money will be paid over to the county. You may claim the remaining money at any time within one year after the county receives the money.

Dated: ____________________ at ____________________, California.

Signed: ____
(signature of lessor or agent)

Figure 9-4 Notice of right to reclaim abandoned property.

scribed. Locked containers may be identified as such without breaking them open to determine their contents.

Statutes will usually prescribe the contents of the notice. One prescribed form of such notice is shown in Figure 9-4.

The form of notice is slightly different if it is to be sent to the reputed owner of the property rather than the former tenant.

If the property has a value less than a stated amount (e.g., \$100), the statutes may permit disposing of it without public sale after notice of the right to redeem has been given.

Actual sale of the property is also handled according to statute. The typical procedure for selling abandoned personal property is outlined in the notice.

Compliance with the foregoing requirements exonerates the lessor from any additional liability to the tenant by reason of the property so abandoned.

WAIVER OF RIGHT TO PROMPT PAYMENT

Many times a lessor or property manager will accept late payments from a tenant, albeit with some unkind thoughts. Or perhaps other breaches of the lease will be known to the lessor but tolerated. Subsequently, the lessor or property manager may decide he or she has been too lenient and commence action to terminate the lease because of the late payments or other violations.

It is very possible that, by his tolerance of the tenant's conduct, he has waived the right to prompt payment or the right to terminate the lease because of the previous violations.

This is a difficult concept for lessors and property managers to accept. They will point to the provable breaches of the lease and complain that the lease ". . . isn't worth the paper it's printed on . . ." because the terms cannot be enforced.

The blame may be misplaced.

By condoning the previous breaches, the tenant was allowed to infer that the questionable conduct was acceptable. It would more likely be unfair to lull the tenant into a false sense of security by such conduct and then permit the tenant to be arbitrarily deprived of the rights vested by the lease.

The restraint on enforcement of the lease provisions is not serious from the lessor's standpoint. What the law requires is simply that the right to prompt payment, or strict compliance with other provisions in the lease, be *restored.* This is done by notifying the tenant that, past conduct notwithstanding, the exact covenants of the lease will hereafter be strictly enforced. Having restored the right to prompt payment, if the next payment is not timely, the lessor's right to commence eviction proceedings is once again an enforceable one.

LATE PAYMENTS

Some leases provide a penalty if the tenant fails to make payment within the first 10 or 15 days after the rent is due. The penalty should be reasonable and not in the nature of a forfeiture. If the state's statutes do not expressly allow or limit the amount of the late payment allowable under a lease, the owner or manager should consult the statutes related to late payments under a promissory note. Most courts would accept the amount of late payment charges in notes as being reasonable if included in a lease, absent a specific statute covering leases.

It is most probable that once a tenant has been charged a late fee, future rent payments will be made promptly. Paying a late fee merely raises the effective rent for the premises. However, the tenant may take the position that because there is a late payment provision in the lease, rent payments are not actually due until just before the late charge is about to be incurred. The law does not reach the same conclusion. It should be made clear to the tenant that a late charge is a penalty, not a privilege. Late payments may subject the tenant to attorneys' fees, court costs, and other damages if legal action is instituted to enforce the terms of the lease (assuming the lease so provides) and might even cause the lease itself to be terminated.

CONCLUSION

An understanding of the statutes in the jurisdiction in which the property manager is operating is essential to the proper performance of the manager's duties. Inexpensive, soft-bound copies of codes or statutes are available in most states and should be a part of the property manager's reference library.

Following the procedures outlined here, adapted to the specific location, will allow the manager to take effective action aimed at avoiding litigation whenever possible. When litigation is required, and inevitably at some time it will be, these steps will help ensure a favorable outcome of that litigation.

PART 4

Skills and techniques of property management

CHAPTER 10

On-site office administration and recordkeeping

Ruth I. Frishman, J.D., M.B.A.
Attorney at Law and Property Management Consultant
Emeryville, California

Property management, more so than most service businesses, involves an incredible amount of paperwork, record keeping, and documentation to the extent that if you don't get a handle on these functions, they will bury you in a morass of confusion, frustration, and unnecessary lawsuits.

WHY KEEP RECORDS IN THE FIRST PLACE?

Records are important in property management for several reasons. First of all, your client has turned over a substantial piece of investment property to you with a sizable cash flow. Records must be kept to control and account for the cash and other property on-site.

Good records enable you to evaluate new maintenance techniques and operating procedures. For instance, how do you determine whether the claims made by the person selling you long-life light bulbs indicate a legitimate cost-effective investment rather than marketing hype? Without good records to determine your operating costs before and after the new technique is implemented, you simply cannot tell.

Good records, consistently maintained, are necessary to compare the operating efficiency of one building with other buildings in your portfolio or against industry standards, so that the return on investment can be maximized.

Good records are an absolute necessity in preparing for or defending a lawsuit such as an unlawful detainer, security deposit refund action, discrimination complaint, or disgruntled employee claim. All things being equal, if it is your word against the word of the resident, employee, or rejected applicant and you have inadequate documentation or no documentation at all, you stand a good chance of losing: The benefit of the doubt, as a practical matter, is given to the "little guy." You are in a business, you are held to a higher standard, and part of that higher standard is to maintain adequate business records and documentation.

The head office is also dependent on the records that are submitted from the resident managers on a daily, weekly, and monthly basis to prepare income tax returns and payroll reports as well as the next year's budget.

Finally, you have a fiduciary responsibility to the property's owners and investors to account for the investment which has been entrusted to you. This is more than just a moral obligation, it is a legal obligation, breach of which can jeopardize your real estate broker's license and, therefore, your livelihood.

BASIC PRINCIPLES

When organizing your system and designing or purchasing forms, consider the following principles. First of all, a well-organized system is simple to understand and follow. If it is not, no one will follow it or use it.

The forms should be readable and understandable as well as simple to fill out and use. Frequently, the forms are understandable to the person who designed them but incomprehensible to the staff who must use them. If the forms are not understandable to the people who have to fill them out, you will not get adequate or accurate data needed to make good management decisions.

If a notice has to be given to any resident more than two or three times, make a form out of it. That way you only have to fill in the blank or check off the appropriate box. It also increases the efficiency of your operations, because there is less to procrastinate over in filling out a form than in writing a formal letter.

Keep a sample of each form filled out in red ink in a clear plastic sheet protector in the back of each folder for the manager to refer to quickly. Also, keep one blank copy of the form on the other side of the sheet protector so that you always have a clean original from which to make photocopies. Fifth- or tenth-generation photocopies are sloppy and unprofessional.

Second, the system should be uniform and consistent: There should be a logical theme which flows through it. Forms which are purchased from various sources are often contradictory or inconsistent. Procedures designed by different staff people for different purposes may be redundant rather than providing additional information. Haphazardly designed bookkeeping systems often leave no audit trail or system of checks and balances.

Third, record-keeping and reporting systems must have deadlines built in and honored. If your staff is continually late in submitting reports, you may have good grounds to suspect not only its efficiency and competency, but its honesty as well. One of the first clues that a manager is stealing is consistently delinquent monthly reports. A common technique to cover the theft is to roll the current month's rent collections into the last month's report to make it balance.

Fourth, whatever bookkeeping and accounting systems you use, make sure that they balance, crossfoot, and leave an audit trail.

OFFICE ORGANIZATION

Where are the records to be kept? Most large apartment complexes have a rental office where the records and on-site files are kept. But what about smaller developments in which the resident manager's dining room table doubles as your rental office, that is, between breakfast, lunch, dinner, and Johnny's after-school snack? In such situations, make sure that your resident manager has a small desk and file drawer set aside in one corner which is to be used strictly for the operation of your business, because that is what you are operating—a business. This is not a ma and pa custodial operation anymore. The liability is too great for you to fail to operate even the smallest building properly and professionally.

In the larger complexes, the rental office in each building should be set up identically to the other buildings in your portfolio so that if you have a manager who quits in the middle of the night with no notice, becomes ill, has to leave temporarily because of a family emergency, or is fired, you can send in a backup person from another site who only needs an hour or two to become oriented with minimal disruptions to the project operations.

Although it may seem rude or presumptuous to organize resident managers' files and offices for them, you must remember that as the property manager, you are the one who is ultimately responsible for those records, not the resident manager.

Finally, by setting up a comprehensive system, it is ensured that everything has its place. Large files labeled "miscellaneous," correspondence not in chronologic order, and large stacks of unsorted papers on the desks and filing cabinets are evidence of an unorganized system, even if the manager claims to know where everything is.

FILING SYSTEM

The filing system is set up topically rather than alphabetically because it is logically easier to find a file or document that someone else has filed by topic. If your system is set up alphabetically, you will find a great deal of confusion and redundancy because there is not a form or file in your office that cannot go by three or four different names depending on who did the filing and when.

For instance, a rental agreement could be filed under any of the following:

L—lease

M—month-to-month agreement

O—occupancy agreement

R—rental agreement or resident agreement

T—tenant agreement

The blank forms are kept in the resident manager's desk file drawer for easy access when preparing reports and processing new rental applications. The administration files are kept in a file cabinet.

The general topics (e.g., resident forms, monthly reports, legal notices) are inserted in the plastic tabs of the legal-sized hanging folders. If the desk drawer does not have a built-in frame for holding the hanging files, an adjustable frame can be purchased from the stationery store. Hanging files are used because they keep the files in a permanent order and facilitate access since they slide back and forth easily.

The topics should be organized in a logical sequence that follows your daily operations. Below is a recommended guideline, although the system can be reduced or expanded according to the size and needs of the building. Items marked with an asterisk have explanatory comments following the sample filing-system guidelines.

1. Blank form file (desk file drawer)
   a. Office administration—three-part memo
   b. Marketing
      (1) Market comparison survey
      (2) Traffic control report
      (3) Rental agent performance report
      (4) Occupancy and turnover report
      (5) Unit availability list
   c. Resident forms
      (1) Rental application
      (2) Rental and occupancy policies
      (3) Rental agreement
      (4) House rules
      (5) Pool rules
      (6) Move-in/move-out inspection
      (7) Statement of security deposit policies
      (8) Resident orientation form
      (9) Notice of intent to vacate
      (10) Move-out checklist
      (11) Letter of instructions to departing residents
      (12) Exit interview
      (13) Statement of security deposit account
      (14) Request for payment of excess damages
      (15) Resident questionnaire
   d. Bookkeeping and rent collections
      (1) Notice of returned check
      (2) Delinquent rent reminder
      (3) Rent roll
      (4) Occupancy and delinquency report
      (5) Former residents' accounts receivable
      (6) Security deposit account reconciliation
      (7) Petty cash envelope*
      (8) Petty cash voucher
   e. Legal notices
      (1) Three-day notice to pay rent or quit

(2) Three-day notice to correct breach of covenant or quit
(3) Three-day notice for breach of covenant
(4) Thirty-day notice
(5) Notice of abandonment of real property
(6) Notice to reclaim abandoned personal property
(7) Notice of rent increase
(8) Notice of change of terms of tenancy
(9) Proof of service

f. Employee forms
(1) Employment applications
(2) Employee letter of welcome
(3) Employment contract
(4) Job description: general employee qualifications
(5) Job description: resident manager
(6) Job description: maintenance person
(7) Job description: groundsperson
(8) Job description: rental clerk
(9) Withholding allowance certificate (W-4)
(10) Fidelity bond application
(11) Health insurance application
(12) New employee–employee termination checklist
(13) Time cards
(14) Employee absentee record
(15) Employee evaluation
(16) Master vacation schedule
(17) Injury report forms
(18) State, federal, and insurance notices

g. Maintenance
(1) Daily-weekly preventive maintenance schedule
(2) Yearly preventive maintenance schedule
(3) Painting schedule
(4) Equipment and appliance information sheet
(5) Mechanical equipment service record
(6) Tool and equipment inventory*
(7) Purchase orders

(8) Work orders
(9) Unit maintenance record
(10) Quarterly property inspection report
(11) Unit inspection report
(12) Notice of unit inspection
(13) Warning notice to resident re housekeeping problems
(14) Unit make-ready report
(15) Landscape maintenance schedule
(16) Contractor's indemnity agreement

h. Safety and security
(1) Accident-incident notice
(2) Key receipt card
(3) Instructions for fire evacuation
(4) Fire plan layout

2. Administration files (first drawer of file cabinet)

a. Emergency information (*red folder*)
(1) Turn-off valve diagram
(2) Alarm system description
(3) Key chart*
(4) Emergency phone numbers
(5) Emergency procedures

b. Correspondence*
(1) General correspondence
(2) Interoffice memos and directives
(3) Specific correspondence
(4) Chronologic reading file

c. Suppliers-contractors-vendors
(1) Correspondence
(2) Contracts
(3) Warranties
(4) Indemnity agreement
(5) Working notes and memos*

d. Miscellaneous reports (copies of completed reports which have been sent to the head office)
(1) Traffic-advertising

(2) Budgets
(3) Inventories
(4) Security log*
(5) Maintenance log
(6) Inspection reports

e. Monthly financial reports*

(1) Entire report filed by month including rent roll, disbursements, payables, and so on
(2) Purchase orders (third copy)*

f. Employees (individual file)*

(1) Employment contract
(2) Job description
(3) Time cards
(4) Correspondence, warnings, evaluations, and so on

g. Maintenance and inspection reports

(1) Quarterly property inspection reports
(2) Tool and equipment inventories
(3) Unit maintenance file
(Each unit should have a permanent folder filed in numerical order. The unit maintenance record should go on the left side of the file, and the completed work orders and unit make-ready report on the right side.)

h. Backup alphabetic files (miscellaneous items)*

(1) Community services and agencies
(2) Informational items
(3) Newsletters
(4) Other

3. Resident files (second and third drawers of file cabinet)*

a. Hanging files by unit number

b. Individual resident file jacket

(1) Application
(2) Emergency information
(3) Move-in/move-out inspection
(4) Maintenance service requests*
(5) Correspondence to and from residents
(6) Copies of legal notices and warnings

4. Dead files (fourth drawer file cabinet)*
   a. Former residents
   b. Rejected and withdrawn applications

TIPS ON MAINTAINING FILES

When opening a new file, punch it with two holes; insert brads; and secure with tape so that the brads do not fall out, catch on other files, or scratch the desk top. Insert several sheets of legal-sized tablet paper on either one or both sides upside down so that they fold over the top of any new papers added; use these for your working notes and memo log sheet.

Keep all files and documents in chronological order. Also, make sure that all papers are notated with a complete date (e.g., 7/6/84). If a resident has occupied your unit for 5 years, a loose slip of paper dated "7/6" is simply not very informative. These two procedures will save you hours of wasted time trying to piece together the history of something that has happened over a period of months or years.

In addition, systematically and consistently filing papers in the proper file and in the proper order will prevent paperwork from getting out of control and reduce the chances of misfiling or losing important documents.

PETTY CASH

Petty cash is for inexpensive purchases—five- to seven-dollar items. A petty cash fund should not be any larger than necessary. A fund of $50 to $100 is usually adequate for most developments.

All expenditures should be substantiated by a receipt and itemized on the face of the petty cash envelope. The receipts on hand plus cash should equal the total amount in the petty cash fund at all times.

INVENTORIES

Inventories should be completed for maintenance supplies, equipment and tools, and office equipment, with the name, model and serial number, purchase price, and date of purchase.

Review your inventories whenever changing staff or management companies so that the person (or company) leaving parts with a clean record, and the person (or company) coming on starts with a clean record.

SECURITY LOG

A security log is a notebook in which all accidents and security incidents are logged regardless of whether or not they have been reported to the police or insurance company. A short notation as to name, date, time, witnesses, and details of the incident may save you hours of aggravation and litigation down the road. The log will also provide a reference point for improving security procedures and reducing accidents.

KEYS AND KEY CHART

Keys should be kept in a locked steel key box which is mounted to a stud in the back of a closet that can be locked. The keys should not be left in open view, nor should they be identified by the address of the building or unit. Keys are to be coded and the "key" to the code filed away from the keys themselves (e.g., in the emergency file).

Carefully consider whether you want the building provided with a master key, because as a managing agent you may be liable for any thefts and for the subsequent rekeying of the entire building if the master key is stolen or disappears and it can be proved that you maintained sloppy or inadequate key control.

EMERGENCY PHONE NUMBERS AND PROCEDURES

A list of emergency numbers and procedures should be kept in the same place for each project (e.g., the emergency file), in a three-ring binder on the receptionist's desk in the main office and with each property manager at home. The list of emergency numbers should include all on-site employees and service people, such as the plumber, roofer, boiler maintenance company, and landscaper. This information should be reviewed and updated periodically (see Figure 10-1).

In many offices, the property managers take turns at on-call duty for after-hour calls during the week and on the weekends and are able to handle emergency calls on their associates' projects which they may never have seen.

CORRESPONDENCE

Copies of all correspondence are filed in the appropriate file (general or specific; resident, vendor, employee, and so on) and a second copy in the chronological reading file, which is reviewed and initialed by the area supervisor each time she visits the site.

WORKING NOTES AND MEMOS

All verbal communications should be confirmed in a follow-up letter or on a three-part memo, or notated in the file, indicating the details of the conversation. If a three-part memo is used, the top copy goes to the recipient, the second copy is filed in the appropriate file, and the third copy is filed in the chronological reading file.

Get in the habit of making working notes and memos of conversations, interviews, inspections, and so on. Jot down the date, time, name of person to whom you spoke, and nature of the discussion, and place the information in the appropriate file. A good habit to develop is to have the file pulled and in front of you when speaking to a resident or vendor so that the notes can be made directly in the file instead of on slips of paper which can be lost or misfiled. You need only ask the caller or visitor to wait a brief moment while the file is being retrieved.

Recollections of discussions that are recorded long after the fact and for the purposes of going to trial are not acceptable evidence in a court of law. However, if you can show that you habitually and routinely make working notes, these notes become the business records exception to the hearsay rule and are acceptable as legal evidence. In fact, the better documented your affairs are, the more likely you are to stay out of court in the first place.

ON-SITE COPIES

On-site managers should keep copies of every report sent to the head office. They should never send the only copy, which may be lost in the mail or misplaced, in which event the entire report would have to be reconstructed from scratch.

FINANCIAL REPORTS

Copies of financial reports are sent to resident managers so that they can see where the rent monies they collect are going. To give managers little

PROPERTY DESCRIPTION & EMERGENCY INFORMATION

Prepared as of ______/______/______

PROPERTY NAME ________________________________ UNITS ____________

ADDRESS ____

AGE OF PROPERTY ____________ CONDITION ______________ MILES FROM OFFICE ________

PROPERTY MANAGER ______________________________ PHONE (______) ________

I. EMPLOYEES

	Name	Unit #	Phone	Salary
A. Resident Manager				
B. Assistant				
C. Maintenance				
D. Janitor				
E.				
F.				
G.				

II. VENDORS & EMERGENCY NUMBERS

	Name	Address	Phone	Rate
A. Police				
B. Fire				
C. Answering Service				
D. Boiler/HVAC				
E. Cable TV				
F. Elevator				
G. Electrician				
H. Landscape				
I. Laundry				
J. Pool Service				
K. Plumber				
L. Rooter Service				
M. Roof Repair				
N. Towing Service				
O.				
P.				
Q.				

III. OTHER

	Name/Contact Person	Address	Phone
A. Owner			
B. Attorney			
C. Accountant			
D. Insurance Broker			
E.			

IV. SUMMARY OF CONTRACT TERMS

A. Term from ______ to ______. Fee $ ________ or ________%.
B. Maximum expenditure limit $ ________.
C. Maximum lease term authorized __________.
D. Maximum service contract authorized __________.
E. Special Terms ____

____

____

Figure 10-1 Property description and emergency information form. (Reprinted from *Property Management Camera Ready Forms* by Ruth I. Frishman, J.D., M.B.A.)

V. RENTAL SCHEDULE

No. of Units	Size	Rent Range (__/__/__)		Gross Rent Total
( )	____BR/____B	$______	to ______	= $______
( )	____BR/____B	$______	to ______	= $______
( )	____BR/____B	$______	to ______	= $______
( )	____BR/____B	$______	to ______	= $______
( )	____BR/____B	$______	to ______	= $______
( )				$______

VI. AMENITIES

______	Pool	______	Community Center	______	Extra Storage
______	Jacuzzi	______	Recreation Program	______	Security Building
______	Sauna	______	Garages	______	Fireplaces
______	Racquetball	______	Carports	______	Cable TV
______	Tennis Courts	______	Laundry Rooms	______	Master TV Antenna
______	______	______	______	______	______

VII. RENTAL POLICIES

A. Lease or M/M ____________
B. Security Deposit ____________
C. Other Charges ____________
D. Pets ____________
E. Utilities Included ____________
F. Resident Qualifications ____________
G. ____________
H. ____________
I. ____________
J. ____________

VIII. APPLIANCES & OTHER SPECIFICATIONS Make Model No. Description

A. Refrigerator ____________
B. Range ____________
C. Dishwasher ____________
D. Disposal ____________
E. Compactor ____________
F. Water Heater ____________
G. Furnace/Heater ____________
H. Air Conditioner ____________
I. Locks ____________
J. Carpets ____________
K. Drapes ____________
L. Paint ____________
M. ____________
N. ____________

IX. INSURANCE Name/Contact Person Maximum Coverage Annual Premium Deductible Period Covered

A. Fire ____________
B. Liability ____________
C. Rent Loss ____________
D. Workers Comp. ____________
E. Fidelity Bond ____________
F. ____________
G. ____________

X. OTHER COMMENTS ____________

____

Figure 10-1 *(Continued)*

or no information is to ask them to do their jobs with one hand tied behind their backs. If you don't want the manager to know the specifics about the entire financial picture of the project, at least give her the numbers on the operating expenses that she controls on-site.

PURCHASE ORDERS

Charge accounts are to be set up for all other recurring expenses. If accounts are set up for stationery, paint, hardware, and janitorial supplies, you have your daily operations generally well covered.

Shop around for the best service with the best prices. The area supervisor, rather than the on-site manager, should set up the account to maintain control of the purchasing.

Managers usually have the authority to purchase items up to $50 to $100 without previous approval. Any purchase above that limit is approved with a purchase order at the time of ordering the supplies or services.

Purchase orders should contain the following information:

1. Description of the item or service ordered
2. Quantity ordered or terms of service
3. Unit price and total amount charged less any discounts
4. Supervisor's approval

Preparation of the purchase order can be delegated to the resident manager who notes the supervisor's approval per phone call across the bottom of the form. A three-part purchase order is then distributed to the following persons:

1. Vendor
2. Supervisor in head office
3. On-site manager

Purchase orders should also be sequentially numbered so that control is maintained. The number of the purchase order approved by phone should be notated on a master log by the supervisor and matched against the purchase orders and invoices as they come into the head office.

The use of purchase orders also gets your managers in the habit of requesting approval before incurring financial liabilities for poorly priced products, services or items that are beyond the development's budget, or "under the counter" deals.

EMPLOYEES

Resident managers are always employees, never independent contractors. Therefore, proper attention should be given to make sure that state and federal payroll reporting and wage requirements are met. Each on-site employee should have an employment contract, a job description, a W-4 form, and signed time sheets for each payroll period. Letters of recommendation, evaluations, and warnings also should be kept in the individual employee's file.

BACKUP ALPHABETICAL FILES

The backup files are where all the miscellaneous information (sometimes known as junk) we tend to collect is filed, thus leaving the administration files, which are much more important, pared to the bare essentials.

RESIDENT FILES

Resident files are permanently organized by unit or address number in the hanging files (e.g., 101, 102, 103). Each resident will have an individual manila folder labeled as follows:

DOE, John S. & Mary E. (move-in date)

385 Woodside Drive #24

On the right side of each folder is filed the rental application, credit check, resident's emergency information, move-in/move-out inspection, rental agreement, and addendums, if any, in chronological order.

On the left side is filed any maintenance service requests, correspondence to and from the resident, copies of legal notices, warnings, and so on, again in chronological order.

MAINTENANCE SERVICE REQUESTS

All resident service requests are put in writing with the date, time, nature of request, and name of the person making the request. (See Safeguard Maintenance Control System, Figure 10-2.)

The top copy goes to the maintenance person, who fills the back out with time, labor, and materials when then job is completed; this copy is filed in the resident's folder.

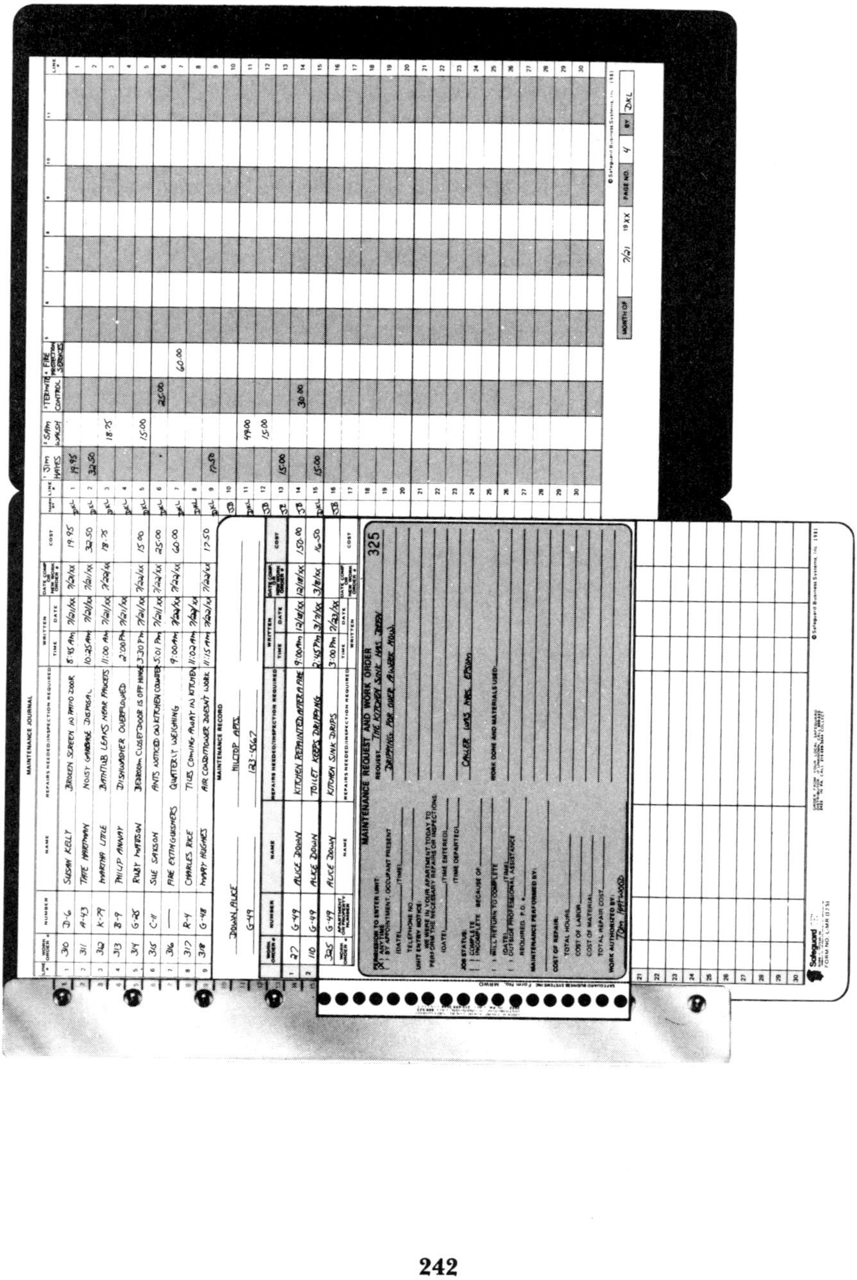

Figure 10-2 Safeguard Maintenance Control System.

The second copy becomes the following:

1. A chronological maintenance log
2. A program for scheduling employee job duties
3. The business records exception to the hearsay rule should you have to go to court to defend a claim of breach of the implied warranty of habitability

By the way, these are called "service requests" not "maintenance complaints." It's all a matter of attitude!

"DEAD" FILES

The dead files do not have to be set up in hanging folders. Alphabetical cardboard index separators are adequate and much cheaper since these files are not used frequently, although they still are necessary.

All former resident files and rejected and withdrawn applications are to be filed in the bottom drawer. Indicate the move-out date by hand in red ink on the label of the former resident's file before filing. Once a year go through the dead files and remove all files that are 5 years old. (The statute of limitations is 4 years for written contracts.)

Also, keeping rejected and withdrawn applications for at least a year will provide you with good documentation regarding how you select and reject applicants in the event of a discrimination complaint—but only if you have made appropriate notations on the back of each application. Simply writing "credit not approved" in the corner of the application, for instance, is not sufficient documentation. The date, time, name of person to whom you spoke, what was said, and initials of the person taking down the information should be on the back of each application for your selection process to be adequately documented.

RENT COLLECTION SYSTEMS

Three-Part Receipt Book

A three-part receipt book (found in any business stationery store) is perfectly adequate for most small properties. The original or top copy goes to the residents whether they want a receipt or not because what you are doing is creating an audit trail from your original entry in the receipt book.

The second copy is attached with an adding machine tape to the duplicate bank deposit slip which is sent to the head office to document or substantiate the deposit. The deposit slip is checked against the bank statement at the end of the month, thus creating your audit trail.

The third copy stays in the receipt book in chronological order for reference in the event that there are any questions or posting errors in the subsequent reports generated from the original.

No matter which rent collection system is used, make sure that all receipts are preprinted with sequential receipt numbers. Receipts are just as important as checks. You don't use temporary checks indefinitely any more than you would throw away a voided check when you make a mistake. The same careful control is used with receipts as well.

The bookkeeper in the head office checks to make sure that the last receipt number of the last month corresponds with the first receipt number for the present month. All receipts are to be accounted for. Voided receipts are sent up to the head office.

There should never be two receipt books at a time on-site, which is a common way for managers to collect rent from allegedly vacant units without the owner, property manager, or resident suspecting anything is amiss. (That is also why you should spot-check vacant units periodically.)

One-Write System (Pegboard)

In the one-write system, five entries are made with one posting. (See the Safeguard Rent Receipts System in Figure 10-3.)

When residents pay their rent, their ledger cards are pulled from the storage tray and placed under the receipts, which are clipped to the pegboard in shingled sheets of twenty-five over two carbon-sensitized cash journal pages and a bank deposit slip. At the same time that you write the resident's receipt, you should also post the cash journal pages for the head office and the on-site copy, as well as the bank deposit slip with the check transit numbers.

The system saves time, reduces transposition and mathematical errors, and, if used properly, helps to reduce the chances for acts of dishonesty by employees.

The ledgers are filed alphabetically in the storage tray, which has two sets of alphabetical indexes. As each resident pays his or her rent, his ledger card is moved to the back set of alphabetical indexes. You can tell at a glance by the fifth or sixth of the month which residents are delinquent because theirs will be the only ledgers remaining in the front of the tray.

Whatever system is used, make sure that it leaves an audit trail. An audit trail is not an esoteric accounting concept. All it means is that you can trace any single entry on any report all the way back to the original entry. If you cannot do that with your bookkeeping and financial reports, you are probably losing money—either inadvertently or through outright theft.

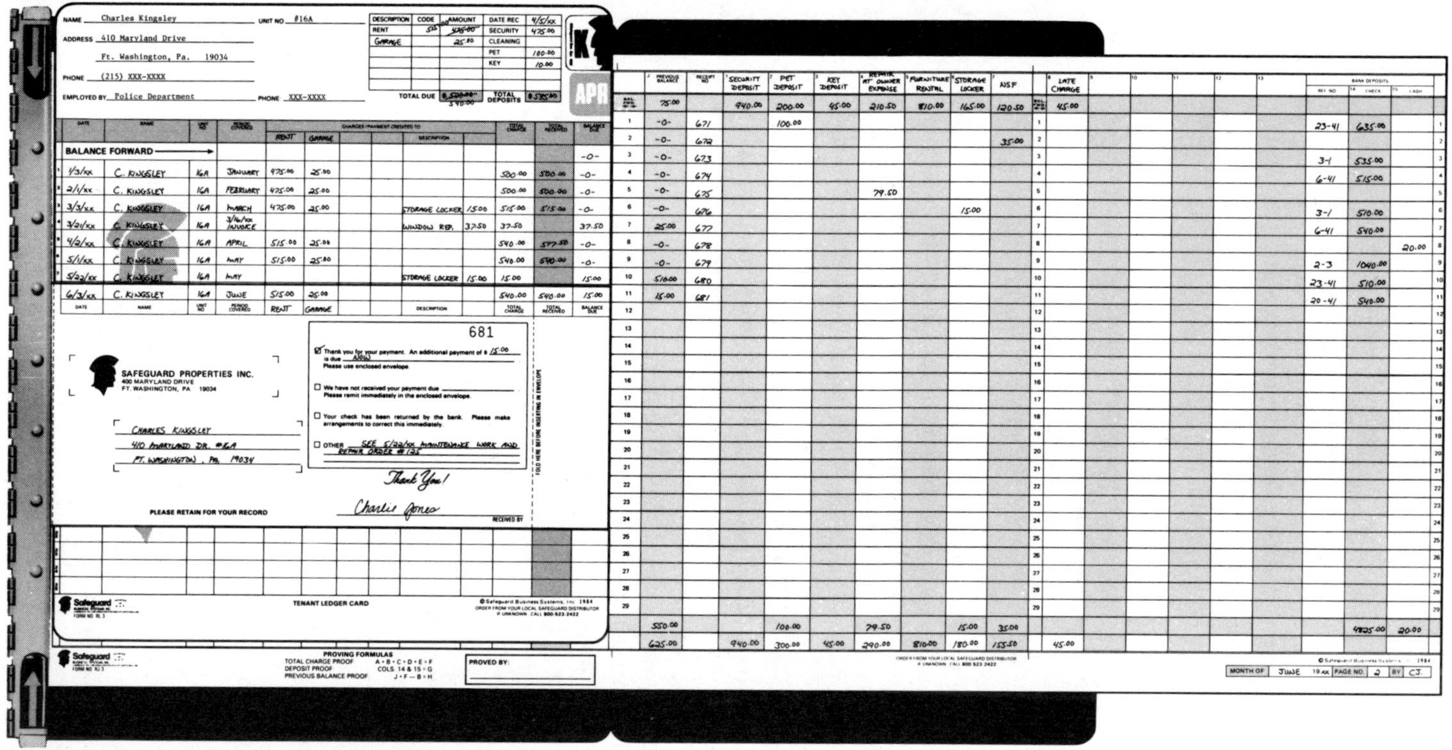

Figure 10-3 Safeguard Rent Receipts System.

Computer Systems

Computer systems are becoming more and more popular today. The standard system usually provides a multipart receipt; the top copy goes to the resident, the second copy to the manager, and the third copy to the data processing department for input to the computer. The reports that formerly were generated manually are now prepared by the computer.

A few caveats are in order if you are considering purchasing a computer. GIGO: Garbage in, garbage out. Computers are very stupid; they only process information infinitely faster than we can. But do not buy a computer expecting it to do all your thinking for you, because it can't. If you don't understand the information going into it, you won't understand what comes out of it.

Also remember that initially computers do not save you time, and they create more paperwork than you can imagine. Much of the paperwork used in property management is more useful in hard copy rather than buried on a computer disk which may only be accessible to one or two people in the office who have learned how to operate the computer.

If you make the decision to purchase a computer, shop for the software package first. Most people buy the hardware first and then are limited to the software packages available to that particular model. The hardware is not much more than a little black box that runs the program. Also, personally check five or six references for customer satisfaction before committing to any computer purchase.

Finally, it is important that you understand your manual system and that you stay on it for at least the first 90 days that you are setting up your new computer system. However, it is not unusual for it to take up to 6 months to a year to work the "bugs" out of the system, in which case you will be very glad that you maintained the manual system in the interim. It is not an uncommon story to hear of a management company going back to the old pegboard system after a year of frustration and aggravation with its new computer system.

Ledger Cards

An individual ledger card is maintained for each resident as well as each source of income (e.g., laundry, vending, pay phone, recreation room), which provides you with a chronological record of all financial transactions with that resident or entity.

The ledger card should have a column for the receipt number of each entry for your audit trail. If you have a question about any entry on the ledger card, it will be cross-referenced to the original entry in the receipt book by the receipt number.

The ledger cards, which are filed alphabetically, provide a cross-reference to your resident files, which are filed by unit number. If you only have an address, you can find the resident's name by looking in the files. If you only have a name, you can find the unit number by referring to the ledger cards.

TICKLER FILES

A tickler file is an index box with index separators for January through December and 1 through 31. Write the item you want to remember and place it behind the date that you wish to recall it. Include items such as the following:

1. *Lease expiration dates.* File these 45 to 60 days prior to the lease expiration date in order to renegotiate or terminate the lease with adequate notice.
2. *Month-to-month tenancies.* File these 45 to 60 days prior to the annual anniversary date of move-in. It is preferable to raise rents once a year so that the rent increases are modest, predictable, and reasonable. It is also recommended that you keep your rent increases staggered so that you are not on the receiving end of an organized rent strike, which can happen when rents are raised across the board at one time.
3. *Warranty expiration dates on equipment.*
4. *Insurance policy expiration dates.*
5. *Service contract expiration dates.*

FIELD AUDITS

Finally, part of the area supervisor's job is to spot-check periodically the on-site files and records to make sure that company policies are being followed. The first indication that there is a problem comes when reports are consistently late or completed improperly. Bookkeeping reports that are not crossfooted and balanced also indicate that the resident manager does not understand what is required of him or her. Field audits, however, may reveal other serious problems that indicate a need for immediate remedial action or additional staff training.

The office should always be neat and organized. Papers and files should be in their proper place, not scattered on desk tops and piled on filing cabinets. When spot-checking resident files, the applications should be adequately documented on the back. The original lease and move-in inspection report should be in the file, dated and signed by all adult occupants. Signatures should be in blue ink on the original, not black ink, so the original can be easily distinguished from photocopies. After reviewing a file, you should note the front of the outside file jacket with your initials and the date of review. Approximately 4 to 8 percent of the files should be checked each month as part of your routine property inspection.

Ledger cards should be checked periodically. If a one-write system is used, all collection entries should be in carbon, never posted directly to the ledger in ink. An adding machine tape on the month-end balances should reconcile with the accounts receivable report. The pattern of collections (i.e., timing and amount) on individual income sources should be reviewed for consistency. The petty cash receipts and cash on hand should always equal the petty cash fund amount.

Do not make the mistake of allowing the resident manager to develop the mind set that the on-site records are his or her personal property. No matter how smoothly the on-site operation appears on the surface, it is the rule, rather than the exception, to find inadequate maintenance of files and records when a manager leaves a property; you may even find yourself in the middle of defending a lawsuit. Maintaining proper records is part of your legal fiduciary responsibility to your client; it reduces many of your management headaches and increases the efficiency and effectiveness of your management operations.

CHAPTER 11

Maintenance for maximum profits

James H. Koch
Aquarian Advertising Associates, Inc.
New York, New York

Good maintenance of your property, with an eye on future profits, requires a program of *doing a little all the time* so that no system of your building deteriorates before it has completed its normal useful life. If real estate owners treated buildings as well as most people treat their cars—with periodic checkups and replacement of parts—buildings would last longer and cost less to maintain.

PERSONAL BUILDING INSPECTION

Regular building inspection should spearhead an owner's maintenance program. Unless you are a major real estate owner with a trustworthy manager working for you, *inspect your buildings yourself* and, in addition, do it *with professional help from time to time.* Whether your buildings are residential or commercial, next door or a thousand miles away, let your own eyes and common sense size up the condition of your property. You probably remember the ancient fable about the elephant which various handicapped people saw in different ways. There are few things more subject to a *variety of perceptions* than real property. A frustrated tenant may consider it "in decline," and a landlord may see it as a brilliant investment. It may be throwing off sizable operating profits because maintenance is neglected. There will come a day, of course, when neglect will cause considerable expenses or a reduction in the asking price when the building goes up for sale.

COMPETITION FOR QUALITY PROPERTIES

The current real estate market in the United States is highly competitive; new buildings compete with old; the consumer has the money, the credit, and the intelligence to shop around, either to buy a personal residence or to invest in income property. Professional advice is available to the buyer as well as to you, the seller. In the long run, therefore, you will deceive no one with a building that is not well-maintained. The prices offered will take into account the lack of repair—you can count on that.

You can anticipate and prevent trouble by beginning your program with a professional analysis of the property's condition. Continue with periodic inspections of your own, and, after a time, a repeat visit by the inspector, particularly if something seems to be going wrong—symptoms such as greater and greater bills for energy, leaking, unusual cracks developing, stains forming in the plaster, water seepage, and other creeping disasters.

SYSTEMATIC MAINTENANCE

The checklist for maintenance on pages 252–254 has stood the test of time; one like it is used by professional inspectors in all parts of the United States. Note that it specifies the possible points of disrepair and how often to inspect them. Figure 11-1 shows many of these checkpoints, with their names and position in the integrated operating system of a house.

On the checklist below, P stands for periodically, S for spring, F for fall, and A for annually.

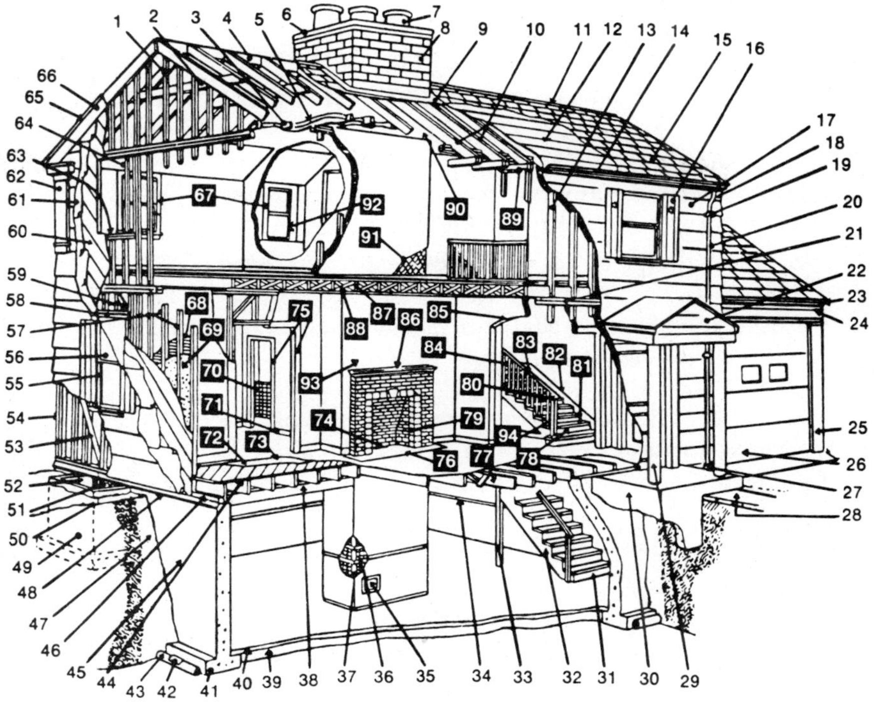

Figure 11-1 A building's key places of wear and tear.

1. Gable stud
2. Collar beam
3. Ceiling joist
4. Ridge board
5. Insulation
6. Chimney cap
7. Chimney flues
8. Chimney
9. Chimney flashing
10. Rafters
11. Ridge
12. Roof boards
13. Stud
14. Eave gutter
15. Roofing
16. Blind or shutter
17. Bevel siding
18. Downspout gooseneck
19. Downspout strap
20. Downspout leader
21. Double plate
22. Entrance canopy
23. Garage cornice
24. Fascia
25. Door jamb
26. Garage door
27. Downspout shoe
28. Sidewalk
29. Entrance post
30. Entrance platform
31. Stair riser
32. Stair stringer
33. Girder post
34. Chair rail
35. Cleanout door
36. Furring strips
37. Corner stud
38. Girder
39. Gravel fill
40. Concrete floor
41. Foundation footing
42. Paper strip
43. Drain tile
44. Diagonal subfloor
45. Foundation wall
46. Sill plate
47. Backfill
48. Termite shield
49. Window well wall
50. Grade line
51. Basement sash
52. Window well
53. Corner brace
54. Corner stud
55. Window frame
56. Window light
57. Wall studs
58. Header
59. Window cripple
60. Wall sheathing
61. Building paper
62. Pilaster
63. Rough header
64. Window stud
65. Cornice moulding
66. Fascia board
67. Window casing
68. Lath
69. Insulation
70. Wainscoting
71. Baseboard
72. Building paper
73. Finish floor
74. Ash dump
75. Door trim-casing
76. Fireplace hearth
77. Floor joists
78. Stair riser
79. Fire brick
80. Newel cap
81. Stair tread
82. Finish stringer
83. Stair rail
84. Balusters
85. Plaster arch
86. Mantel
87. Floor joists
88. Bridging
89. Lookout
90. Attic space
91. Metal lath
92. Window sash
93. Chimney breast
94. Newel

CHECKLIST FOR SYSTEMATIC MAINTENANCE

1. **Foundation and masonry:** basement, exterior walls: to prevent seepage and condensation problems

a. Check basement for dampness and leakage after wet weather.	P
b. Check foundation walls, steps, retaining walls, walks, patios, driveways, and garage floors for cracks, heaving, crumbling.	S
c. Check chimneys, deteriorated chimney caps, loose and missing mortar.	S, F
d. Maintain grading sloped away from foundations walls.	A

2. **Roofs and gutters:** to prevent roof leaks, condensation, seepage, and decay problems

a. Check for damaged, loose, or missing shingles, blisters.	S, F
b. Check for leaking, misaligned or damaged gutters, downspouts (leaders), hangers (straps), gutter guards, and strainers.	S, F
c. Clean gutters, leaders, strainers, window wells, drains. Be sure downspouts direct water away from foundations.	P
d. Cut back tree limbs growing on or over roof.	F
e. Check antenna supports for sturdiness and possible source of leakage.	S, F
f. Check flashings around roof stacks, vents, skylights, and chimneys as sources of leakage.	S, F
g. Check vents, louvers and chimneys for bird nests, squirrels, and insects.	S, F
h. Check fascias and soffits for paint flaking, leakage, and decay.	S

3. **Exterior walls:** to prevent paint failure, decay, and moisture penetration problems

a. Check painted surface for paint flaking or paint failure.	P
b. Check siding, shingles, and trim for damage, looseness, warping, and decay.	P
c. Check exterior masonry walls for cracks, looseness, missing or broken mortar.	P
d. Cut back and trim shrubbery against sidewalls.	S, F

4. **Doors and windows:** to prevent air and weather penetration problems

a. Check caulking for decay around doors, windows, corner boards, and joints, and recaulk as needed.	F
b. Check glazing putty around windows.	F
c. Check weatherstripping.	F

5. **Electrical:** for safe electrical performance

a. Learn location of electrical panel box for breakers or fuses. Never overfuse.	P
b. Trip circuit breakers every 6 months and ground fault interruptors (GFI) monthly.	P
c. Mark and label each circuit.	P
d. Check condition of lamp cords, extension cords, and plugs. Replace at first sign of wear and damage.	P
e. Check exposed wiring and cable for wear or damage.	A
f. If fuses blow or breakers trip frequently, have a licensed electrician determine the cause.	P
g. If you experience a slight tingling shock from handling or touching any appliance, disconnect the appliance and have it repaired. If lights flicker or dim, or if appliances go on and off unnecessarily, call a licensed electrician.	P

6. **Plumbing:** for preventive maintenance

a. Check faucets, hose bibbs, and valves for leakage.	P
b. Drain exterior water lines, hose bibbs, sprinklers, and pool equipment.	F
c. Check for leaks at sink and house traps and at sewer cleanouts.	P
d. Draw off sediment in water heaters monthly or per manufacturer's instructions.	P
e. Have septic tank cleaned every 2 years.	P

7. **Heating and cooling:** for comfort, efficiency, energy conservation, and safety

a. Change or clean furnace filters, air conditioner filters, and electronic filters as needed.	P
b. Clean and service humidifier.	P, A
c. Have oil burning equipment serviced.	A
d. Clean around heating and cooling equipment, removing leaves, dust, and overgrown shrubbery debris. *Be sure power is off!*	P

8. **Interior:** general house maintenance

   a. Check bathroom tile joints, tub grouting, and caulking. Be sure all tile joints in bathrooms are kept well sealed with tile grout to prevent damage to walls, floors, and ceilings below. — P

   b. To prevent freezing, keep garage doors closed in winter, and wrap exposed water lines and drains with insulation. — P

   c. Close crawl vents in winter and open in summer. — S, F

   d. Check underside of roof for water stains, leaks, dampness, and condensation, particularly in attics and around chimneys. — A

   e. Keep attic louvers and vents open all year round. Check louver screening. — A

9. **Know the location of**

   a. The main shut-off valve

   b. The main electrical disconnect switch or breaker

   c. The main emergency shut-off switch for the heating system

YOUR BUILDING, SYSTEM BY SYSTEM

Within the framework of a regular maintenance scheme, consider your building system by system, from top to bottom, in your own periodic inspections. Presumably, you checked out these systems carefully when you bought the building. If you didn't, do it right away. Remember, benign neglect may work in politics, but it doesn't work in operating a property for profit.

The Roof

Shingles. If the shingles are wooden, have they begun to rot and let water through? If they are composition, such as asphalt, have they remained intact? If they are metal or slate, have some fallen off? Do some shingles need replacing? Does the entire roof need replacing? Most roofs in harsh climates last only about 20 years.

Flashing and valleys. These are usually of copper or similar durable metal and serve as a conduit for roof water at angles in the roof or where dormers nestle into the main slope of the roof. If they have been damaged, punctured, or torn, they might let water leak through. The flashing around a chimney is particularly vulnerable to corrosion and deterioration. Check, too, the mounting of a TV antenna to see whether it has damaged the flashing or shingles into which it is fastened.

Flat roofs. Does the roof feel squishy underfoot? Are there bubbles or separation of roofing felt or paper? After rain, are there large puddles which take a long time to evaporate and threaten to leak through?

Gutters. Inspect gutters to be sure they are draining properly, are not filled with silt and decayed leaves, and do not leak. Depending on your climate, you may want to have deicing cables looped along the eaves; if installed, they will require periodic testing. Downspouts sometimes clog. Sometimes they need a length of heating cable to stay functional during alternating winter freezes and thaws.

Attics and Ceilings

Check for water stains in wood or plaster. They are a simple and natural warning that the roof system may be leaking and require attention. If your attic has no natural light, you sometimes can find leaks in the roof by entering the attic (and putting a cardboard temporarily over the ventilation louvers) and looking for spots of daylight showing through cracks or joints. Check carefully around the chimneys and under valleys and gutters if you have a gabled roof with dormers.

Note whether there are wasp nests in your attic or evidence of squirrels or mice nesting there. Wasps can be deterred with vespicides; they usually come in through cracks in the eaves or through ventilation louvers that have no screens. Mice and squirrels sometimes get in through these same gaps and can cause endless harassment to you or your tenants. Once they get into the attic, they have access to walls, make nests, raise families, and multiply at your considerable expense. They can raise havoc with your insulation system. They may even gnaw old-style electrical wires and cause a short circuit, and possibly a fire.

With contemporary construction techniques, water vapor sometimes becomes a problem because it cannot escape. As it gets into the attic, it may condense and cause water stains even though there are no leaks in the roof. That problem is usually solved by strategically placed vents that let moisture escape (some heat, too), but to compensate there is insulation in walls and ceilings to prevent heat escape from below. Because moist, warm heat rises, the problems accumulate in the attic of a steamy building; it is particularly important to have proper ventilation if there are dishwashers, laundry equipment, a greenhouse, or a solarium with many plants in the building.

Walls and Windows

In older buildings, it is often easy to tell what insulation went into the attic ceilings because the joists are exposed. It is hard to know what went into lower, secondary ceilings and into walls. Years of opening walls to rewire, place strategic electrical outlets, and install TV aerials, additional telephones, and the like may have seriously impaired the insulation system and caused a great deal of heat loss. That is why, in older buildings, you may want to look into possible renewal of the insulation system with blown-in material.

Again, if very much moisture is generated in rooms such as kitchens, and there is no vapor seal in the wall, the moisture may condense within the walls and cause the outside finish of paint to peel. Conversely, if your walls are masonry and there are cracks or faulty pointing (the mortar between the bricks or blocks), you may have water coming in, particularly if a wall is exposed to the driving rain or prevailing winds. Such a condition may require repointing of the mortar and waterproofing of the building blocks or bricks with a silicon solution.

Windows and storm windows require painting and occasional reputtying to be sure cold winds do not literally blow through cracks and crevices. The new aluminum double- and single-pane window systems with storm and screen inserts are a boon to home owners with aging backs or who lack the patience to deal with stuck window sashes and meticulous painting of mullions. If you have colonial windows with mullions, you might consider the aluminum inserts for screens and storm windows only. Get the inserts finished in white and preserve your colonial style with no need to paint.

Floors

Aside from maintaining the finish of floors, replacing tiles, and occasionally scraping to eliminate stains or warping, you may encounter sagging floors, which put everything at a tilt. These floors may require substantial rebuilding, such as positioning a steel beam or Lally column on a new concrete base. In the country, such sagging may be caused by dry rot or termite attack on the support system of your building. If you see a widening of floor cracks, you should call in a contractor or engineer right away. Poorly built foundations or erosion of natural support may cause a whole section of your building to sheer away from the rest. Timely correction of the fault can prevent an extensive and costly catastrophe. Sudden changes in floor position usually signal a shift in the foundation, an uneven settling of your building.

If by chance your building has cement floors that have been covered by flooring or asphalt tile, check carefully to be sure there is no moisture accumulating in the flooring material. The cement will not let spills or leaks run off properly. If the moisture accumulates or surface moisture is allowed to seep through to the cement, you will soon have warping of your expensive flooring. Parquet floors on cement are especially vulnerable to this subtle and costly deterioration. Vinyl tile will also loosen.

If termites get into your house and floor joists, or other floorboards fall prey to their jaws, you might some day have an expensive collapse that could not only damage a large portion of the building but also expose you to negligence suits by tenants. Be sure you inspect regularly for termites if your structure is partly wood and is located in the middle or lower tier of states, where termites survive the winter. Unless you are extremely knowledgeable about termites and have fought them successfully in the past, it's better to have a professional exterminator look at your suspected visitors and see what can be done. Then, perhaps, you can learn how to continue the treatment.

Stairways and Halls

If these are not well lighted or have loose treads, you are asking for trouble. Living with such unsafe conditions may bring serious and expensive accidents, such as a child or senior citizen falling down a stairway and breaking a limb. In some old buildings, the stairways are steeper and the treads less wide than in modern buildings. Strangers in the building, not used to the difference, may slip. It may be negligent of you not to post or otherwise emphasize the danger. Be sure you have a secure railing so that the young and the old can help themselves up and down unfamiliar territory.

Basement

In the basement of the building you may encounter any number of failing systems. The lowest toilet or sink is the one in which backups will occur first. Sometimes, if the building is hooked up to a sewer, there will be a trap or cleaning outlet *outside* the house. This is the place to enter the line to free it of roots or other obstructions.

Sniff the air of the basement and check if anything seems to be leaking, such as heating oil, sewage, or possibly gas, if you use that for fuel.

Check to see that floor drains in the basement floor have not overflowed—you will see stains on the cement or other flooring. They are the low point of your interior drainage system and give a clue to a possible obstruction in the system. Sometimes they have been installed improperly and have no gas trap—an elbow filled with water that prevents methane gas from the sewage system from backing up into a house. Such a backup can happen with septic systems as well. The best septic or sewer systems are situated below the level of the house so that backed-up liquids have a chance to announce their presence through traps outside the building. Without such traps, they could back up into the basement.

Foundation walls, often around windows, may show cracks caused by excessive or uneven settlement. You may also find evidence (mud tunnels) of termites or growing fungi, which would suggest rotted floor joists.

Examine the lower part of basement walls and all the floors for waterlines from past floods. If you were not there for the actual flood, try to find out what caused it so that you can prevent a recurrence.

Check wooden support pillars and makeshift reinforcing to be sure they can continue to give reliable support.

Heating System

If your home is heated by oil, be sure that the storage tank does not leak and that pipelines into the house do not cause smelly and dangerous puddles of oil on the basement floor. Many oil suppliers offer a low-cost checkout service to be sure that all valves and controls are in good working condition. The checkout should include recommendations for dealing with soot in the chimney, if applicable. At the beginning of the heating season, a check of all heating ducts and radiators should be made to be sure that heat reaches throughout the house.

If you have hot-air ducts through which a fan blows air, be sure that the fan is in good working order and that the vents in each room are not obstructed.

If you have heat pumps, air conditioning, or varieties of solar heating that use liquid to transfer heat, be sure all pipes are sound and not dripping—either because of leaks or because of condensation of moisture. Be sure to insulate all pipes that carry cold water, for they will show condensation on warm, muggy days. If there is enough condensation, water can begin dripping and cause damage wherever it collects.

Examine the water heater to be sure it is functioning efficiently and has sufficient capacity for the family or families inhabiting the building.

Exterior Walls

If the exteriors are painted wood, they will need painting about once every 5 years, with perhaps a touch-up of the side most exposed to the weather in between. Excessive peeling or flaking usually indicates a moisture problem; see if you can track it to inadequate ventilation of an interior room or perhaps a leak in the water system within the walls. A good paint job will not peel or crack on a sound wall; rather it will turn dull and "dust" off gradually.

Most buildings present too many problems for the amateur painter:

scaffolding, brushing and scraping, repairing windows, recaulking around metal fixtures, and handling shutters. Choose the best paint available on the advice of a professional. Observe how a professional goes about painting, and perhaps the next time you can save money by doing part of it yourself. Painting has become popular summer work, and college students and teachers often form painting crews. They are often good painters, and it is a way to help them through school. But they are *not* professionals, and *you* should learn some of the tricks of the trade first so that you can give adequate supervision to such a crew. Kids have the strength for the job and often the neatness, but they don't always know the method for putting paint on so that it will last for 5 years or more. Be sure you have liability insurance to cover painters and other workers.

If your house or garden walls are brick, building blocks, or tailored stone, you may have a problem with the mortar—particularly in an old installation. The mortar may have to be repointed, that is, partly scraped out and replaced. A mason can do that for you; it is also easy, these days, if you want to do these chores yourself, to get prepared mixtures of mortar to which you add water. If the bricks need a complete stripping and you will have to put up scaffolding, it's better to call a mason or painter.

GETTING RELIABLE REPAIR PEOPLE

When something goes wrong, you can always run to the Yellow Pages of your local telephone directory and call someone. But this is not the way to get the best maintenance service and make the most profit on your building.

Ask among your neighbors which electrician, plumber, and heating contractor they think are the best in your area. Ask several people for names, but be aware of relatives recommending relatives. Yet do not be put off just because someone is the cousin of a neighbor; the person recommended may be the best in the line. Just get another recommendation or two that support the quality of the work.

After you have obtained a few names, get estimates. Have the person come to size up your problem and give you an estimate of how much labor, how many parts, and how much material will be required. Get two or three such estimates, and give the job to the company that seems the most competent and reasonable in price. Get the contract terms in writing and explore the question of guarantees and ongoing maintenance. Get those details in writing, too.

This may seem a lot of fuss for minor repairs, but the screening will stand you in good stead later when you may need a backup for a repair person who may be on vacation, retired, or just too busy. Good repair workers, in the country as well as the city, seem in as much demand today as brilliant surgeons. They know their worth, and sometimes their competence "goes to their head." That is why it is a good idea to try a person out on a small repair job. You may find someone who, during a slack season, can help you remodel or construct an additional room, an outbuilding, or whatever you may decide will increase the usefulness and value of the property.

While maintenance service primarily helps the buyer or owner of a building by eliminating sudden discoveries of malfunction, obsolescence, illegal improvements, and needed repairs, it also protects the seller from embarrassment because of defects not previously noticed, which can become the basis for a lawsuit. It limits the liability of the seller by providing an outside professional who can vouch for the condition of the building as presented.

Methods of inspection and the format of the inspector's report may vary, but every inspection by a member of the American Society of Home Inspectors (ASHI, located at 1629 K Street NW, Washington, D.C., 202-842-3096) must include all the following systems: central heating, air conditioning, interior plumbing, electricity, roofing, insulation, ventilation, walls, ceilings, floors, windows, doors, and foundations.

USING BUILDING INSPECTION TO CONSERVE ENERGY

While the building inspector is on your premises, ask him or her to suggest energy conservation measures. Inspectors now receive training in the application of new heating and cooling systems and can give you practical tips about what will pay off and what will not.

Most owners of buildings are not yet aware how simple procedures and modifications of existing buildings can cut energy bills drastically. In percentage of improvement, these simple changes often run circles around expensive installations that generate solar heating and electricity. With the cost of heating oil already high and the cost of electricity rising, the operating costs of the average building have risen at a frightening rate during the past few years. Whether the present oil situation is a temporary famine or glut situation does not make that much difference. The overall impact on cost is here to stay on the upside. Thus it is worthwhile to make at least the modest repairs and alterations that can cut about 30 percent from your heating bills.

Insulation
Improper insulation is the most common cause of inefficient heating. This defect is most easily remedied by working with the local building supply store, which probably has sold insulating materials to owners of any number of building like yours. You don't need special skills or tools, just patience for laying the insulation everywhere it is required and at the proper thickness. It belongs anywhere there is space between heated and unheated areas, such as exterior walls, attic floors, and basement ceilings. You can make one of the most significant improvements by adding 4 inches of insulating material to the 2 or 3 inches already placed in most attics. Because hot air rises, your heat goes to the attic and through the ventilator to the great outdoors; with the right amount of additional insulation (varying with geographical region) properly placed, you can reduce your fuel bills substantially.

Weather Stripping
Probably the most noticeable change in physical comfort derives from weather-stripping windows and doors that did not have such protection. Although insulation will cut fuel consumption to a greater degree, weather stripping (including storm windows or installation of double-glazed panes properly weather-stripped) will give you creature comfort that you can sense and enjoy right away. If you previously did not have *any* weather stripping, you will sense a dramatic difference in drafts and sustained warmth; if you had *some* weather stripping or weather stripping that has lost its effectiveness because of changes in flooring, settling of the house, or careless painters, renewing the defective material will produce a noticeable effect. It is a good idea to review *all* the weather stripping in your building and replace it where necessary. This can be done inexpensively and easily. In most cases, you can do it yourself, even if you are not especially handy.

With metal windows and doors, sprung jams may cause unsuspected leaks. The new metal-framed screen–storm-window systems and door systems often need delicate adjustment when installed because the openings are not entirely square. If these adjustments are not made and the variances not sealed, the effect of multiple panes of glass is counteracted by leaking around the edges. Windows not in active winter use should be locked, with the sliding parts drawn up tight against one another. This is particularly true of old-fashioned wooden-sash windows, which do not have modern weather-stripping features built into the runners.

When sealing in storm-window frames, there is a need to leave weep holes where moisture condensing between the two sets of windows can escape. Thus you eliminate the threat of rotting window sills.

Caulking

You can use caulking compound as a flexible filler between two different materials, such as metal, plastic, or wood, which might react differently to changes in the weather. You cannot expect caulking to last forever; that means periodic inspections and replacement when necessary, another possible do-it-yourself task. Different caulking compounds have been created for different situations, and it is important to know how to apply specific materials. Otherwise the compound may not stick to both of two different surfaces, and no real seal will take place. Your local hardware dealer can advise you about this. The right compound, applied the right way, will ensure longer lasting protection against weather leakage through cracks. Caulking is a process complementary to weather stripping and fitting of storm windows and door frames.

Necessary Ventilation

If you are a thorough weather stripper and insulator and your building has a vapor seal intact, undisturbed by electrical or plumbing alterations, you may approach a condition in which your building no longer breathes. In a residence, this can be remedied by opening a door or window, usually at night, as a precaution against stuffy air while sleeping. You will then have to judge whether the occupants' personal habits—their comings and goings—allow enough air into and out of the house to provide a good supply of oxygen and an escape of carbon dioxide and moisture.

The average leaky house changes its entire air supply once within about 2 hours. With modern sealing and energy conservation techniques, the air-supply change could be cut down to once every 10 hours. And you will notice the lack of fresh air and accumulation of moisture (from cooking and human breathing) by condensation on the inside of the windows, odors, and a general feeling of lack of air and increasing dampness. This situation can be overcome by running your air conditioners on the ventilation or exhaust setting. In commercial buildings, for example, a mechanical ventilation system can change the air, heat it, dry it, and deliver a fresh supply to the desired area. The private residence can accomplish the same thing through machines or through natural use of open windows and doors. You will have to experiment to get the right combination for your building.

LANDSCAPING AND GROUNDS

Growing trees, shrubs, flowers, and lawns, and installing improvements such as pools, sculptures, driveways, and shorelines add greatly to the pleasant appearance of buildings but only slightly to profitable operation. All require maintenance, for an unkempt appearance can quickly discourage tenants. Let these environmental extras deteriorate over many years, and you will have to make costly replacements.

Most owners want to keep up the appearance of a building as a matter of personal and community pride. You may be upgrading the property to produce greater income or simply holding it as an investment with the hope of selling it later at a profit. Beyond profitable repair, your level of maintenance is a matter of conscience—what sort of citizen you want to be.

THE PRINCIPLE OF CONTINUING MAINTENANCE

You will learn quickly from owning a property of its continuing challenge of repair and replacement. You can keep your cost lower if you use your building and equipment in a conservative way. Each checkpoint of a house has its characteristic wear and tear, but you can minimize these by formulating rules of use.

You can *use* or *abuse* your land and buildings. But the greater profits usually come to those who *use* their property with common sense and a commitment to conservation. Reading the maintenance manual of your car—or any other appliance—will give you an idea of how a profitable maintenance program can work on your real properties.

An inspector of key systems will, first of all, get you acquainted with the property and its buildings, including strengths and weaknesses. You may discover old repairs, badly made, that ought to be done over in more durable fashion or using another technique (makeshift roof repairs and patches are an example) to prevent a more serious breakdown at a later date.

If you have not had your property inspected by an engineer or architect as part of the buying process, go around the premises with such an expert early in your ownership. Ask him or her to suggest what maintenance routine would give longer life to the various systems of your building. Take notes and make a schedule of the suggested repairs and their timing. Put the notes on a piece of cardboard or have them typed on paper and inserted into a glassine folder in a looseleaf binder. Keep them in a drawer in your office, kitchen, or workroom. In the same drawer you can collect advertisements from stores for various materials and suggestions for good maintenance, just as you might collect recipes and cookbooks. On a similar sheet or cardboard, keep the names and addresses of principal repair and service people. When something goes wrong, you simply reach for this listing and telephone the appropriate person. It is worthwhile to jot down what the person charged for various jobs. It will give you an idea of what system on your property—electrical, plumbing, or heating—is cutting the most into your profits. It may give you a sense of timing and proportion concerning when an appliance or system requires replacement. Suit the sophistication of your record keeping to the size and complexity of your real estate investment. Check your local stationery store for preprinted forms and notebooks, or design your own using a typewriter and print a supply with a copying machine.

WARRANTIES AND SERVICE CONTRACTS

If your property is a home or apartment building, you undoubtedly have bought equipment and applicances for it with guarantees of performance of one kind or another. Keep these forms in one place; they can save you money on repairs required before the lapse of the guarantee. In fact, a prudent owner should make a point of inspecting any new machinery a reasonable time before the warranty runs out. The manufacturer owes you a usable machine or tool, not a temperamental lemon that causes more expense than it is worth. If you are an investor in property that you do not live in, you will still want to keep track of these guarantees. If you have a property manager, insist that he or she keep them on file.

Sometimes various appliances such as dishwashers, electronic door openers, and the like come with optional service contracts. Well-known brand-name manufacturers and major merchandisers offer these contracts, which are sometimes worthwhile. But you will have to test them to see if they actually save you money. Try one or two of the most attractive service offers on an appliance or two and see whether you get your money's worth over a year or two based on your level of use and maintenance. If you are satisfied, extend the contract.

LEASING EQUIPMENT

If you have income-producing property and your accountant has set up a tax schedule of operating expenses, you may find it advantageous to lease rather than buy some appliances, such as heavy-duty maintenance equipment or a personal computer to keep track of your program and its costs. There is often the possibility of a big savings through a leasing contract that requires the lessor to keep the machine running satisfactorily. When leased equipment konks out, you simply call the lessor, who will fix it, usually at no charge (if that is what is spelled out in the leasing contract—and be sure it is!).

Aside from the service you get on equipment that is leased, you can write off lease payments as expenses as they occur. You do not depreciate such equipment over many years; you deduct the cost as an operating expense right away. This may be particularly attractive to owners of property who do not intend to hold on to it for any length of time.

Unlike land and buildings, most of this equipment declines in value, like a family car. The decline in market value roughly parallels the depreciation. On the other hand, land with buildings (and lately mobile homes) increases in market value, although for tax purposes you still can claim depreciation on it if it generates income. Thus with implements and machinery costing so much, you may find it to your advantage to lease rather than buy. They will not be worth more in the future than now, and the tax and service advantages of leasing are considerable if you have short-term plans.

Talk over with your accountant whether leasing can possibly improve your profits as well as your ability to maintain your building. Talk with him or her, too, about tax credits for maintenance and replacement projects, such as energy conservation.

THE BUILDING INSPECTOR AS PART OF YOUR MAINTENANCE PROGRAM

There is a new professional on the real estate scene. He or she is usually an architect or engineer who wears an extra hat; this person will give you a written report on the condition of the structure and systems of a building you want to buy, improve, or simply maintain well.

Before these professional inspectors became widely recognized, their role was anticipated by architects, engineers, or perhaps plumbers, carpenters, or contractors who evaluated present conditions as they prepared to repair or improve them. There was a definite danger, however, in hiring these moonlighting contractors as inspectors. Their opinions were not unbiased because they had something to earn from the recommended repair or improvement. Also, although well able to evaluate their particular specialty, they were often not competent in peripheral trades. The plumber could evaluate the plumbing system, and the electrician, the electrical system—but neither could give a comprehensive and competent judgment on the whole structure. During recent years these shortcomings have been remedied by the emerging professional inspector, who takes training and accumulates experience in giving a written opinion on the condition of a whole building and all its systems, including its economical use of energy.

CHAPTER 12

Insurance

Roger E. Lipman
R. E. Lipman Insurance Brokers, Inc.
San Rafael, California

As a property manager, you're faced with many day-to-day decisions which affect the assets of others. One of those decisions involves the purchase and administration of insurance. A familiarity with insurance terminology and basic contracts will assist you in becoming a better and more knowledgeable manager.

This section of the handbook is more general than others because most insurance terms are nonspecific. Most terms will apply equally to a shopping center, apartment house, or manufacturing plant. The items covered here are those at the core of any insurance contract. There are more coverages and insurance contracts available, but the goal of this section of the handbook is to provide a working familiarity rather than an exhaustive compendium. For "fine" details, you should work with your broker using the language and information you have acquired.

WHY HAVE INSURANCE?

Every time we sit down and write an insurance premium check to our broker or agent we may wonder why this is necessary. Is there a way to avoid spending these hard-earned dollars for something so intangible?

If you have never had a major loss or needed the coverage afforded by an insurance contract, paying premiums may seem hard to justify. To understand the need for insurance, look at the situation in which one would *not* need insurance. For persons with no assets, no future income, and no sense of responsibility for their actions (now or in the future), clearly insurance is totally unnecessary.

An understanding of the two main areas of insurance, *indemnity* and *liability*, is important for the protection of assets. *Indemnity* is the function of making you "whole" after a loss. An example would be a fire in an insured facility, for which an insurance company pays to make the repairs and reimburses lost income: The company indemnifies you. *Liability* is the responsibility imposed on you for your actions by a third party (someone not named as an insured on your contract). The typical lawsuit states that you were negligent and caused bodily injury or property damage.

A person in business has a responsibility to others beyond the immediate sphere of that business:

The *public* expects that you have insurance as the financial means to pay for your negligence or to restore your business services to the community.

Employees expect you to provide the statutory coverages of workers' compensation and employee benefits and to protect them from lawsuits in which they might be named as defendants because they work for you.

Clients (tenants) expect that you will have the necessary coverages to repair the facility so that they can get on with their lives or business (insurance may be contractually required in your lease).

The *government*, in most areas, requires that evidence of insurance be provided prior to commencing construction. The requirement for workers' compensation is mandatory, and in most states so is automobile insurance. Also, insurance may be necessary to obtain government-secured loans (e.g., Small Business Association).

Owners (stockholders, partners, limited partners) expect as a basic fiduciary responsibility of the management that their assets will be protected against the possibility of physical destruction or court-imposed liability.

Lenders or *mortgagees* have a material interest in the guarantee of their loans. As loss payees, they require the insurance contract to provide coverages in the correct amount as well as in a form which minimizes their financial risk.

WHAT IS INSURANCE?

The format of insurance has changed since its beginnings in antiquity. (Some may say the contracts have changed little since then.) Traders having commodities transported across the inland seas were at risk of the ship carrying their goods being lost in a storm or plundered by raiders. Accordingly, some of the shippers (farmers) of the region formed cooperatives, agreeing that if one shipper's goods were lost all the others would give that shipper a portion of their production to make up for the loss. Thus each shipper's assets were protected against loss from the perils of the sea. The members of the cooperative enjoyed the improved security and knew that they would only pay a portion of their crop to share in the benefits of the program.

Today, in lieu of sharing of a portion of production, all transactions are based on the dollar. We hire an administrator to secure the ideal contract (the broker) and an intermediary to handle the contract (the insurance company). For each of these services, a fee is paid, which is included in the premium. Ideally, the amount of premium collected would be exactly equal to the amount of losses to be paid. However, the factor of time and uncertainty of the amount of payment to be made (consider a court-awarded judgment) create a situation of unpredictable total financial risk. The insurance company takes this risk as its business. Therefore, it collects the premiums from many persons or companies in advance, invests the money, and expects that the total claim payments will occur sufficiently in the future that they will have made a profit on the use of the funds.

THE INSURANCE COMPANY

There are two sides of an insurance company: the *underwriting* and the *investment* departments. You typically deal with the underwriting department when you contract for insurance coverages.

Generally, of every dollar that the underwriting department collects, 65 cents will be paid out in losses; the balance includes the broker's commission, insurance company operating expenses, and profit. However, this is an ideal underwriting proportion and rarely attained. Insurance companies have a significant cash flow. In a strong economy the investment department requires a higher than average cash flow to generate a higher return.

Companies therefore are willing to allow their underwriting department to operate at a loss to generate the high cash flow. The high cash flow is created by the lowering of premiums, which brings in many more policyholders and, in the aggregate, more cash. Thus the theoretical underwriting formula gets distorted: The ideal of 65 cents paid to losses becomes 90 cents or, in some cases, over a dollar.

Under these circumstances, the underwriting department may lose more than it collects! However, if the investment department is generating enough profit on its investments, the insurance company can afford these losses. This practice will last only as long as the investment markets are profitable. When the investment market goes flat or turns downward, pressure is placed on the underwriting department to make profits sufficient to make up for all the investment losses.

The process underwriters use to begin their profit cycle requires cutting internal operating expenses—selecting only those insurance customers who have the lowest probability of losses and raising premiums to a level which will ensure a profit.

This premium up-and-down cycle normally runs 5 to 8 years. The wise insurance purchaser is aware of these cycles and anticipates when to shop for price or for insurance availability and insurance company stability. Although there are other factors which affect the price of insurance, this cycle is the primary cause of changes in pricing and availability.

THE INSURANCE DELIVERY SYSTEM

There are more than 1800 insurance companies in the United States. Some use the services of agents or brokers (we use these terms interchangeably), whereas others have their own sales employees. These companies offer a full range of services consistent with their underwriting goals. While the underwriting goals of each company may vary, companies are consistent in their quest for profitability. A company which has its own sales employees is called a *direct writer.* These are companies such as Allstate, State Farm, and Farmers. Most other insurance companies use the services of brokers and agents.

The insurance industry, like most others, has wholesale providers as well as retailers. You normally deal with the retail broker. It is worth knowing that the broker with whom you transact your insurance may be purchasing through a standard insurance company or a *surplus lines broker* (wholesaler). Surplus lines brokers provide the normal retail broker with a much larger spectrum of insurance companies. The normal retail broker has only five to ten insurance companies with whom there is a continual flow of business. Thus the surplus lines broker is a source of special insurance for the substandard or unusual needs of a client.

Insurance companies are rated by their quality of management, underwriting judgment, and financial stability (size). This evaluation is called the Best's rating. Best's is an insurance trade publication which is the standard of the industry for evaluation of insurance services. Each year Best's publishes a guidebook on all insurance companies. The insurance company ratings range from A+ to C for quality of management and underwriting quality (A+ indicating the highest rating), and from I to XV for financial size (XV indicating the companies with the greatest assets). There are many good companies in the B+ to A+ range. As a consumer you should ask the rating of your insurance company *before* you complete your insurance purchase.

EVALUATING YOUR INSURANCE NEEDS

A first look at the needs for insurance seems a simple matter, but a full evaluation yields an overwhelming array of alternatives. There are four basic actions in the insuring process.

Avoidance. A business does nothing which will expose its assets to any potential loss. This means that the business takes no action, and as such ceases to exist as a functioning business. Avoidance could be used, however, when an action would not affect a material portion of the business; for example, not installing a diving board at a swimming pool significantly reduces the possibility of a lawsuit.

Self-insurance. A business may assume the entire burden of protection of its assets without the benefit of insurance or it may use very high deductibles to self-insure partially. The worst situation occurs when a business, through an error in its insurance program, is unknowingly self-insured. Such an error can have disastrous consequences.

Transfer. When a business is involved with other businesses, the dominant company may require the subordinate company to provide its insurance. This situation exists in most leases: The "hold harmless" clause effectively transfers a portion of the insurance burden to the lessee. Thus the lessee is providing some (if not all) of the coverage for the lessor. Having an entity named as an "additional insured" is another means of transfer. (The insurance contract must be clear regarding what coverage is offered through or to the additional insured versus the named insured.) It is important that if transfer is involved, it be effective and enforceable. A poorly executed transfer can lead to full or partial self-insurance.

Insurance. The purchase of an insurance contract is the typical means to provide protection of the assets of the business.

COVERAGE

Deciding what to cover and how much coverage is required can consume many hours. Preparing an organized plan is a more efficient means than randomly picking and choosing what exposures to cover. The basic process starts with reviewing the organization's overall objectives and evaluating the specific operations and how each contributes to the goals of the business. You can determine priorities of physical assets and liability exposures according to which are critical to business survival and which are relatively unimportant. A full listing will provide a clear picture of the business value of each of these exposures (see Figure 12-1). Finally, you can assign the dollar values which would be required to replace or optimally protect the business operations.

In valuing physical assets, you should incorporate appraisals, purchase documentation, and current market replacement values into the listing. The dollar limit of exposure to liability is rather difficult to determine. Questions arise such as: What are the typical court judgments currently being made? What is unique to the business operation which could make judgments greater than normal? What level of protection is enough? Is a liability limit of $500,000 too low or is $10,000,000 too high? What is an affordable insurance purchase? These are decisions which you, your management, and your broker must make.

HOW PREMIUMS ARE DETERMINED

Insurance ratings (how the premium is computed) are based on "units of exposure." For real and personal property, this is the value, expressed in dollar terms. The rates are determined by the insurance company, which has developed its own rates or uses a central insurance rating organization: the Insurance Service Office (ISO). Thus the rate multiplied by the value equals the premium. Your broker can provide you with the ISO fire rate if your property is specifically rated. Liability exposure is based on payroll, sales, area, or units of production. Classifications of liability exposure units are grouped by analogy. Some businesses are not specifically designated. In housing and most real estate insurance, there is a fairly clear division of classes. Again, the rates are company generated or based on the ISO standard.

COVERAGE REVIEW

1. General areas of policy to review

Named insured:

Additional named insured(s):

Address of property:

Mailing address:

Subsidiaries—name(s):

Subsidiaries—address(es):

Loss payee(s):

Number of units:

Square footage (if known):

Policy—date:

Policy—premium:

Policy—signature:

Insurance company—*Best's* rating (if unsure of company):

30-day notice of cancellation:

2. Property

Building(s)—insured to current value:

Building(s)—coinsurance:

Multiple buildings—blanket coverage:

Building(s)—replacement cost endorsement:

Building(s)—stipulated amount or agreed amount of endorsement

Contents—insured to current value:

Contents—coinsurance:

Rents—insured to current value:

Rents—coinsurance:

Deductible(s)—building(s):

Deductible(s)—contents:

Deductible(s)—rents:

Coverage—"all risk": provided ________

3. Special endorsements (if necessary)	Included
Glass:	________
Earthquake:	________
Flood:	________
Increased cost of reconstruction:	________
Demolition:	________
Boiler and machinery:	________ limits: Deductible:
Difference in conditions:	________
Extra expense:	________

Figure 12-1 Coverage review.

4. General liability

Limit as requested: $500,000 CSL ________
$1,000,000 CSL ________ Other ________

Medical payments:
Limits: per person ________ per occurrence ________

Coverage—comprehensive general liability form:

Broad form endorsement—attached:

Attached or special endorsements:

General liability coverages

Premises and operations:
Products and completed operations:
Elevator (if any):
Independent contractors:
Owners' and contractors' protective (if any):
Personal injury:
Liquor liability—host:
Employers' nonowned auto:
Hired auto:
Blanket contractual:
Property damage—broad form:
Cross liability (partnerships):

Management agent—named as additional insured:

5. Auto coverage not necessary: ________

Limits—bodily injury: $________
property damage: $________
CSL: $________
uninsured motorists: $________

Medical payments: $________

Physical damage—deductibles:
collision: $________
comprehensive: $________

Loss payee(s)—current:

Endorsements:

Driver of other cars:

Employers' nonowned auto:

Hired auto:

Scheduled vehicles—current:

Check and/or correct:

Schedule of authorized drivers

Check and/or correct: Name(s) ________ Address(es) ________
Driver's license # ________

Figure 12-1 (*Continued*)

Check and/or update: M.V.R. ________
Date of last report: ________

6. Fidelity

Employee dishonesty limits: $________

Form—commercial blanket bond: ________

other: ________ type: ________

7. Special items of review unique to this policy

____

____

____

____

____

Figure 12-1 (*Continued*)

SELECTING A BROKER OR AGENT

The process of selecting the person or organization to represent you to the insurance companies is an important element in your insurance program. Choosing a friend or brother-in-law may not be in the best interest of the owners or others who depend on the insurance contract. Brokers vary widely in their basic competence to handle business accounts. Some brokers are specialists in personal lines of coverage, such as personal auto, home owners, or boat insurance. Selecting a broker who has a good reputation for handling your type of business will provide you with the highest probability of getting an adequate insurance contract. The broker should represent a cross-section of insurance companies. These companies should be stable and capable of writing the correct insurance contract. The service you pay for in the contract should be provided willingly and with precision. There is a commission in most insurance contracts unless you make a fee arrangement in advance with your broker. This fee is the revenue which the broker collects for services provided.

Brokers are your employees with regard to their duty to you. The fees your premium provides pay the salaries of brokers and their staff. They should earn their pay!

Your broker should provide you with a written outline or proposal of your insurance program. It should detail what is covered, what is not covered, an outline of the terms of the coverages, and what the payment terms are. Additionally, your broker should clearly define the advantages of various deductible amounts for both property and liability coverages and explain the financial advantages of including a higher than average deductible.

The broker should present more than one insurance carrier's proposal for your review. From this you can see what various insurance companies are offering and note the whole range of premiums. By taking this action you can make sure that the broker has reviewed more than one insurance company. If for any reason the company you select cancels or withdraws, your choice of an alternative insurance company may be an easier task. There may be situations in which there is no really competitive alternative insurance carrier or the next carrier's bid is far higher in premium. An "only" bidder can mean that the insurance market is restrictive in coverage availability. A very low bid could mean that the bidder has made an error in the computation of the premium. Remember, if an insurance company makes an error in its premium, it normally expects to be able to adjust the premium to its satisfaction at any time or cancel coverage.

Insurance contracts are somewhat unique in the standard of fairness by which they operate. If you cancel coverage mid-term, they will assess a "short-rate" penalty, approximately 10 percent of the earned or annual premium. However, if they cancel they are required to give only 10 days' notice. (Having a 30-day notice of cancellation clause in all insurance contracts is important because it allows time to secure alternative coverage. The 30-day notice clause is given by most carriers without much resistance.) Note that for nonpayment of premium the notice is only 5 days! If the insurance company cancels, it will settle on a *pro rata,* or "actual premium used" basis.

When presented to you, a proposal of insurance should have all the alternative coverages and programs you discussed with your broker when the original data were gathered. Select the plan which meets the goals of your organization as you originally defined them.

INSURANCE TERMINOLOGY

Each profession is filled with its own terminology. The field of insurance is no exception. You should be familiar with some basic insurance terms.

Two words often misused are *coverage* and *peril. Coverage* refers to what the insurance will do or how it will respond to an event. The phrase "you're covered" means that the insurance carrier recognizes that your contract is valid and will handle the claim.

A *peril* is the event which may occur. Examples are a fire or a lawsuit for alleged negligence. The typical property perils addressed in an insurance contract are fire, smoke, hail, lightning, damage from vehicle or aircraft collision with the property, windstorm, riot, civil commotion, vandalism, and malicious mischief. These are called the *named perils.* To these you may add events such as sprinkler leakage, earthquake, and flood. When the policy is written with the named perils, only those events which are specifically named are covered. An *all risk* policy states that the property is covered for all events of physical damage except those detailed in the exclusions. The exclusions itemize many things which may need to be covered. Earthquake, flood, and boilers and machinery are among the most important exclusions.

It is true in most contracts that "the large print giveth, and the fine print taketh away." The insurance industry has attempted to provide "easy-to-read" contracts, the majority for personal lines of insurance. The legal requirements of the commercial contract make the provision of "easy to read" not easy to meet. You usually have to rely on professional interpretation from your broker or attorney.

When discussing liability perils, the contract gets a bit clearer (just a little bit). The perils here are claims or lawsuits which allege that your negligence has caused bodily injury or property damage to a third party. The perils of personal injury (e.g., libel, slander, defamation of character, false arrest, wrongful eviction) should normally be included. The liability contract has exclusions which are important to consider. An intentional act is normally excluded. An example would be an eviction initiated by you under the standard legal procedure that because of some error in process gives the person evicted a cause to sue. Since the act of eviction was intentional, the wrongful eviction may be excluded from coverage.

No-fault insurance is available in some states, usually applying to automobile insurance. No-fault is an insuring technique which facilitates more expedient claim settlement and tries to avoid costly litigation. Operating in a state with no-fault insurance requires that you verify with your broker that your insurance program is adequate for that state's requirements (as well as those of all the other states in which you operate).

It is impossible to define the boundaries of liability-related litigation. Because the liability perils are many, a clear and effective liability insurance program is essential. Property and liability perils may be discussed at length; you and your broker should develop a plan for all the events that may happen.

TYPES OF COVERAGE

Coverage relates directly to what needs to be insured. If the inventory of items on your list is incomplete, you may suffer a loss in areas in which you are "self-insured." The following is a brief summary of the basic items which need to be considered.

Real Property

Buildings and other structures which are permanently attached to the land make up *real property.* The coverage for most perils does not include site improvements, foundations, or subterranean improvements. Basically the "ground up" is what is covered. Earthquake and flood policies normally cover foundations.

Personal Property

Personal property includes the contents of the buildings, or those items which are removable (e.g., stock, inventory, furniture, fixtures, equipment). For insurance purposes, personal property does not include vehicles, goods in transit, or goods held for others; these are covered under other portions of the insurance contract.

Earnings

The purpose of being in business is to earn a profit. If your means of earning the revenue is damaged or destroyed, you may not have the continuation of cash flow to stay in business even if the facilities are rebuilt. (Reconstruction may take 6 months to 2 years or more.) This cash flow is insurable. Titled *loss of earnings, rental income, gross earnings,* or *business interruption,* these insurance contracts provide a means to protect cash flow. The data required to arrive at a proper limit are exacting, but the result of the effort is a very high level of financial security.

Boilers and Machinery

The term *boilers and machinery* refers to coverage for the equipment on which your business runs, such as the air conditioning, heating, air pressure sources, and electrical distribution panels. Small buildings with no steam boilers are usually not in need of this coverage. When there is a critical element of safety or necessity, boiler and machinery coverage provides for the cost of repair and replacement of the equipment and the consequential loss of earnings which may result from an outage.

If a shopping center's main power transformer which feeds power to all the tenants fails, who is responsible for the loss of percentage rents to the owners? If an office building's main chiller system fails, who has to pay for the repairs and the rental of a temporary unit? Boiler and machinery coverage provides this security by covering the object, loss of earnings, expediting expenses for critical parts, and inspections.

Electronic Data Processing Equipment

Computers, software, and related equipment are used in all aspects of business, and insurance is available to cover the special needs of users of this equipment. The policies are titled *EDP floater* and cover a broad range of perils which are not included in the standard personal property coverge, such as electronic interference and consequential water damage. The systems engineer should review the available forms and select the coverage which best meets your needs.

Valuable Papers

The documentation of most business is difficult but not impossible to replicate. The problem is that the time and expense may be so great that the company may not be able to survive the wait for information. Valuable papers coverage provides funds to pay for the creation of new records—not just the paper on which they are written. Think of how many person-days it would take to replicate every important paper in your office if they were all destroyed. Again, the key documents in the organization need to be identified. Also, an investment in fireproof file cabinets is normally well worth the expense.

Accounts Receivable

Which of your accounts would not pay in the event they knew your records were destroyed? Coverage here provides payment when the records are not complete due to a loss. A duplicate set of records, frequently updated, is a valuable asset. The coverage limit is based on the normal outstanding receivables and the annual average.

Extra Expense

Extra expense coverage provides funds to operate temporarily through another facility or operation. It pays for the emergency setup of phones, rental of a short-term storage facility, and so on. Consider the immediate and temporary needs of your business in the event a facility becomes unusable.

In Transit

If your operations have goods and equipment being transported on your own or common carriers, coverage is needed to protect that cargo in the event of a loss. The standard property coverage does not extend to items in transport. If your maintenance staff moves high-value items frequently or you purchase goods "FOB factory," it may be worthwhile to consider goods-in-transit coverage.

There are other property-related coverages, and your broker will work with you to determine if they are necessary and/or cost efficient.

GENERAL LIABILITY

Liability, as discussed earlier, includes various coverages which are deemed essential to your protection. The basic general liability contract covers the events which may occur on your premises. Using that policy as the foundation, many coverages are added which are essential to the operation of a property-oriented operation. First, the policy should be a comprehensive general liability policy. This form provides an expanded group of coverages which "broaden" the contract. Items which should be included are as follows:

Employees as Additional Insureds
This coverage includes your employees under your policy so that they do not have to provide their own defense; also, they will not be induced to become hostile witnesses to protect their own interest.

Independent Contractors (Incidental)
When you have small jobs accomplished on your premises by independent contractors, this coverage extends your policy over that of the independent contractor in the event you are named in a suit as a result of their actions. This coverage is no substitute for owner contractors protective coverage, which is for your protection over major contracts. Securing certificates of insurance from subcontractors is a very important step to limit your liability.

Blanket Contractual
This part of the policy covers the contracts which you encounter in the normal course of business. The *hold harmless* is the typical contract in which you assume the liability for another person. Blanket contractual protection extends your coverage over the contract you have made.

Personal Injury
Personal injury coverage pertains to libel, slander, defamation of character, false arrest, and wrongful eviction. The insurance contract should be written so that it deletes the employee exclusion. This action provides coverage, normally excluded, for actions brought against you by your present or former employees. Most insurance contracts do *not* cover discrimination, which is interpreted by most companies to be an intentional act and therefore excluded.

Product Liability
This aspect of the policy covers any products you may sell or deliver to a third party. In housing there are few products sold other than products

available from vending machines and provided at parties held in your recreation rooms, which are sources of potential claims. If there are commercial occupancies in your building, you may be involved in a products suit because you "knew" that the product being sold was unsafe.

Host Liquor Liability

This coverage protects you from suits which arise out of your serving liquor or allowing it to be served to others. No coverage will be provided if you sell liquor or serve it to minors. You cannot be in the business of serving liquor. This coverage is important if you have a liquor sales establishment in your building. You should be named as an additional insured on that establishment's liquor liability policy to protect the allegation that you are "in the business" whether true or not.

Broad Form Property Damage

You need this coverage if you and your employees work on or in another person's property. Although basic liability coverage applies to the area where the work is performed, it does not cover beyond that area. Broad form property damage coverage would be needed if a maintenance person working in a bathroom for some reason damaged property in the bedroom.

Incidental Malpractice

When someone provides medical care, even in an emergency situation, there may be a claim for medical malpractice. While most states have "good samaritan" laws regulating liability, this coverage provides legal defense and will pay the judgment. If you operate a medical clinic, full medical malpractice coverage should be purchased.

Other Liability Coverages

Employee nonowned automobile. This coverage provides excess insurance over the automobile insurance of your employees who drive as part of your business. Your employees also should have their own automobile insurance. If one of them is involved in an accident when conducting your business, the other injured party will most likely sue your firm in addition to the employee. The plaintiff's attorney wants to ensure that there will be sufficient funds to pay the client's claim. The "deep pocket" theory of recovery has been sustained many times. This coverage is of nominal cost and is mandatory if you have any employees who drive as part of your business.

Hired automobile. If your firm rents or hires automobiles, this coverage extends your liability limits for these vehicles. Note that physical damage (collision and comprehensive) to rented vehicles is not covered. If you rent frequently, you may find it advantageous to enter into an insurance arrangement with the rental company. This can limit your liability and most likely save you money in rental charges due to the avoidance of the insurance charges normally included.

Occurrence versus claims-made liability contract. See the newly passed industry rules on page 291, effective January 1986.

Automobile Liability

This coverage is required to protect your firm against claims which result from accidents involving company-owned automobiles. If you have trucks hauling any goods interstate, there is a federal minimum insurance coverage defined under the Transportation Act of 1983. Automobile liability, like product liability or medical malpractice, results in some of the largest judgments awarded.

One extension of coverage which is imperative and usually affects the principals of the firm is called *drive other auto* (DOA) coverage. The business automobile policy is very different from the personal auto policy in that coverage is *not* extended to the drivers of the automobile when driving non-business-owned automobiles. The business automobile policy covers business vehicles only. If a person has no personal automobile insurance and usually drives a business-owned vehicle, she or he will have no insurance when driving a nonbusiness vehicle. If the insurance on the other vehicle is inadequate or it is uninsured, the individual will be subject to an uninsured loss. This coverage is added by scheduling on the policy the specific drivers to be covered. If they are not listed on the policy, they will have no coverage.

Professional Liability

This coverage is important to consider; it protects you from financial errors and omissions which result from your failure to act or your acting improperly. You normally will be sued by owners who feel you have financially wronged them. Examples are failure to increase rents and inciting a rent strike by failure to maintain property. While this coverage is moderately expensive, has high deductibles, and is limited, the benefit of the legal defense alone is worth the premium.

Cross-Liability (Severability of Interests)

This endorsement creates a severability of interest in the named insureds. If there is more than one named insured, each has the right to sue the other, and the policy will provide coverage to each as though they were individuals (but not to exceed the policy limit of liability). This is a standard inclusion in condominium policies. The owners have the right to sue the association even though they are named in the policy as insureds.

Fire Legal Liability

A standard exclusion in a general liability policy is that goods or items in the named insureds care, custody, and control are not covered in the liability contract. The portion of the building you lease as an office is in your control and therefore not included if you are deemed negligent in damaging it. Your contents are covered by your personal property coverage, but the building is not. If you negligently cause a fire in your office and destroy the unit of the building you rent and the neighbor's unit, your liability policy covers the neighbor's property and the rest of the building which is not in your control. However, the building owner's insurance company would repair the building and sue you for all the damage. If you did not have fire legal liability coverage you would have *no* coverage. A means to avoid this problem is to secure a mutual waiver of subrogation in your lease. A way of avoiding insurance, this waiver states that you agree not to sue the landlord and she or he agrees not to sue you.

Directors' and Officers' Liability

This coverage is to indemnify the directors of a firm or organization from lawsuits which allege that they have failed to perform their duty in the best interest of those they represent. This is protection from owners' suits in condominiums or stockholders' suits in corporations. The coverage is very precisely defined and has broad exclusions (e.g., failure to purchase adequate insurance, theft). It is a necessary coverage if there are outside directors, who usually will not serve without protection.

Umbrella Liability

An *umbrella policy* is an additional level of insurance which protects above the limits of the general liability policy. Usually the general liability policy has limits of $500,000 (or more) combined single limit (CSL) of liability for bodily injury and property damage. When a much higher limit is needed, the umbrella policy is used: It is less expensive and the high limits are usually beyond the primary company's insurance capacity. Umbrella policies may be written up to $100 million or more.

Umbrella policies contain various clauses which define how they pay a claim. Some state they will "pay on behalf of . . . ," which means that the insurance company will pay the claim from its account. If the policy states "will indemnify . . . ," however, this means that the insured may have to pay and seek reimbursement from the insurer. Not many firms have a spare 10 million to pay while waiting for the insurance company to reimburse. Another important clause is the agreement to defend. Do the defense costs come out of the limit of liability or is there no defense coverage? You might assume that the primary carrier has the obligation to defend and that the umbrella carrier will pay the claim when it's settled. Unfortunately, it's not quite that easy. The primary carrier may present its check for its total limit of liability to the court and not attempt to defend because it doesn't feel it can win the case. Thus you are left with the cost of defense on behalf of the umbrella carrier.

Beyond liability, other areas of insurance relevant to business include crime, fidelity, workers' compensation, and employee benefits.

CRIME AND FIDELITY

There are several major types of crime and fidelity policies: *employee dishonesty, money and securities* (inside and outside the premises), *depositors' forgery,* and *counterfeit currency.*

Employee dishonesty is the prime concern for property management operations. There are three types of employee dishonesty contracts: *Named position* contracts are written according to the title of the job (e.g., controller, bookkeeper), *named individual* contracts cover specific persons, and *commercial blanket* policies, the most frequently used, cover any and all employees acting alone or in collusion.

A major problem with bonds is determining what the limit should be: Federal government–controlled properties require at least 2 months gross potential. Some condominiums require a limit equal to the total liquid assets of the association. You should select a limit which will protect you and your owners' solvency. A clear definition in your management contract as to who is the actual employer—the owner or the management agent—is important to the bond. If the agent insures his or her employees and the site employees are determined to be employees of the owner, there most likely will be no coverage. Conversely, if the site employees are the agent's employees and the project purchases the bond for the owner, there also will be no coverage. Make sure you know who is the named insured, because the bond only pays for losses to that person.

If an employee steals from a tenant, there will be no coverage.

An important addition to the employee dishonesty coverage is an espousal endorsement. If a manager and spouse live on-site, the bond by itself will cover only the employee. If the spouse of the employee steals, there would be no coverage. The espousal endorsement extends the coverage to the spouse of the manager.

A money and securities policy (inside and outside) provides coverage for cash and securities on-site or in transit off-site. Most properties require that there be no cash on site and that rents be paid only by check or money order. This rule avoids the many problems which result from the temptations of cash to employees, burglars, or armed robbers. If there is cash on-site, the coverage limit should be written to cover the maximum amount which could be taken in a loss. Frequent bank deposits minimize the amount of cash on premises.

Counterfeit currency coverage protects against losses resulting from the acceptance of counterfeit money and money orders.

Depositors' forgery protection covers the loss caused by the alteration of any check, draft, or promissory note drawn on or upon your account. The settlement date with your bank may expire prior to your discovery of the loss. It is always recommended that the person who writes the checks for an account not be the one who reconciles that account.

WORKERS' COMPENSATION

Workers' compensation is statutory insurance to provide first-dollar medical care and loss of income benefits to workers injured on the job. The history of workers' compensation goes back to the earlier part of this century when workers had almost no rights. Although they could sue the employer for negligence, the employer, who had much more power, could counter with the "assumption of risk" defense. ("You knew the job was dangerous.") In order to avoid this frequent litigation, workers' compensation laws were enacted, which removed the employees' right to sue and the employers' defense. The resulting system led to the present no-fault coverage protecting all employees.

Workers' compensation rates are determined by separate classifications. The rates reflect the expected losses and expenses for each class of labor. Most states have a central rating organization which annually computes and establishes rates. There are various discount techniques available. Most insurance companies pay dividends (after the policy expires) to the insureds. Based on individual loss experience (the lower the losses, the greater the dividend), premiums over $2500 qualify for most dividend programs. Each insurance company has its own dividend schedule, so comparison shopping is worthwhile.

Some insurance companies and brokers make a lot of promises and provide little performance. Check the history of the insurer first. There is more to workers' compensation than dividends. A dividend is determined by the amount of workers' compensation losses you experience. Monitoring your losses is important. An insurance company creates loss reserves when it expects the loss to be much greater than the amount they have already paid. They will reserve the claim for an amount they feel will be sufficient to pay the claimant in the future. Even though the insurance company has not paid out all the money, it computes a reserve as a loss. Reserves and actual payments result in the lowering of your potential dividend. Follow up on all losses to verify the reserves which have been established. If you feel a reserve is improper, make your broker or representative resolve the issue on your behalf.

Workers' compensation is provided by either state funds (organizations run by the state), insurance companies, or both. In some states, only the state fund is available. If you operate in many states, you will need to purchase a policy in those states that have their own funds, as your policy may not provide coverage in "state fund" states.

Not carrying workers' compensation exposes you to almost unlimited liability. Having "independent contractors" as your site managers may result in their alleging, if injured, that you are their employer. If you have no workers' compensation insurance for this site, you could be "on line" for your total assets.

EMPLOYEE BENEFITS

Employee benefits are an important element of your insurance program. Group health, life, and long-term disability insurance provide your employees with a level of security. This security allows them to work without fear of the disastrous economic consequences to them and their families of a major illness or death. The purchase of such benefits can be distributed among all properties and therefore not necessarily be an excessive economic overhead burden. A good plan of employee benefits tends to reduce turnover and therefore reduce training and other costs associated with new employees.

CONTRACT TERMINOLOGY REGARDING COVERAGE

Following are brief explanations of insurance contract terms regarding coverage that you may encounter when working with your broker.

Declarations

The first page or pages of the policy state the named insured, items covered, locations covered, policy number, effective date, expiration date, insurance company name, and premium, and list the various forms attached by their reference number. These are called the *declarations.*

Endorsements

Amendments or changes to a policy, *endorsements* are part of almost every policy. When they are added after the policy has been issued, they may create an additional premium or credit.

Audits

All workers' compensation and most general liability policies have *audit* requirements. This means that if the rating basis used by the underwriter at the inception of the policy differs from the actual units of exposure at the end of the policy term, there will be an additional premium or a return of premium.

CONTRACT TERMINOLOGY REGARDING PROPERTY

Blanket

All locations in one policy are written with an aggregate limit. Thus any variation in value among the locations will not be considered by the insurance company as material. For example, if you insured five buildings and the value of one was not exactly the correct amount, you would not suffer a coinsurance penalty because it was undervalued if the total limits of all property are adequate.

Replacement Cost

Most policies are written on an actual cash value basis (ACV). This is defined as *replacement value less depreciation.* Since insurance depreciation is different from book depreciation, you will clearly benefit from a replacement cost basis of loss settlement. Basically, replacement cost is "new for old."

Coinsurance

Without any doubt, this is the most confusing area of property insurance. *Coinsurance* is a contractual agreement between you (the insured) and the insurance company. What it states is that you agree that the value you have assigned to the property is 80, 90, or 100 percent of its actual value. The value must be declared as either replacement cost or a depreciated value (ACV). Coinsurance clauses assure the insurance company that they are securing full premium for the total exposure. By the threat of coinsurance, the insurance company will have the capacity to penalize you if you have not insured your property to value. The formula is as follows:

$$\frac{\text{The limit you had}}{\text{The limit you should have had}} \times \text{your loss} = \text{payment}$$

An example:

Building value $100,000 at 100 percent coinsurance
Insured value = $100,000
Loss = $26,000

Settlement (\$100,000/\$100,000) × \$26,000 = \$26,000
Payment = \$26,000; coinsurance penalty = \$0

Another example:

Building value \$100,000 at 100 percent coinsurance
Insured value = \$75,000
Loss = \$26,000

Settlement (\$75,000/\$100,000) × \$26,000 =
.75 × \$26,000 = \$19,500
Payment = \$19,500; coinsurance penalty = \$6500

If you are "insured to value," coinsurance plays no part in your loss settlement; you will receive 100 percent of your loss less deductibles up to the policy limit.

Agreed Amount (Stipulated Amount)
This is an amendment to the property insurance contract which waives the coinsurance provisions. To secure this agreement, the property has to have a recent appraisal or meet the insurance company's valuation requirements.

Deductibles
Insurance underwriters will give rate credits for large deductibles. Deductibles have traditionally been at the \$100 level. (Think in terms of present value; a \$100 deductible was adequate in 1940.) A nominal deductible today is \$250 or \$500. Determining how much premium you will save by using a higher deductible is worthwhile. If you save only \$200 by increasing your deductible to \$1000 from \$250, it may not be worth the change. Have your broker provide quotations using various deductible amounts.

IMPORTANT EXCLUSIONS AND COVERAGES

If your property is in a redevelopment area or other area where the city is trying to force updating of structures, you may find that the zoning regulations require demolition of a building which is over 50 percent destroyed. An insurance company will only pay for the actual damage to a structure. Thus if the building was 60 percent destroyed and the city says "tear the remainder down," the insurance company is going to pay the 60 percent and you pay the balance. If you know you are going to be faced with this problem, you should add *demolition coverage* to your property insurance. The dollar limit is determined by the damage percentage in the ordinance.

INCREASED COST OF RECONSTRUCTION

In most cities the zoning is updated to keep up with technology, which creates a problem for the building owner. The insurance company will pay to put the building back the way it was before the loss. However, the city may not allow it to be rebuilt unless it meets current codes. This cost differential will not be paid by the insurance company unless you have an endorsement which limits the effect of the "operation of building law." Again, this limit is set by you, usually with the help of a contractor to estimate betterment costs.

Always read the exclusions portion of your policy. You may negotiate with an insurance carrier to purchase back an exclusion.

CLAIMS

In the event of a claim you should be aware of your responsibilities. Your insurance contract spells out the procedures which are necessary to secure your claim. As with any contract, set everything in writing to prevent the possibility of a claim denial due to an error. Property losses are usually clear-cut and quantifiable. When there is a property loss, notify the carrier or your broker by phone and follow up with a statement in writing as soon as possible. Be prepared to substantiate all values. Having appraisals, income statements, and full duplicate records assists in rapid settlement. In the event of a large loss, public adjusters will solicit you to "negotiate" your claim (for a percentage of the settlement). Check with your broker and/or attorney prior to signing any public adjuster's contract.

If there is a loss of any type, have a responsible employee complete an "incident report" (see Figure 12-2). An incident report is the who, what, when, where, and how information which documents your files for any claim. Because the claimant sometimes has 2 years to file the claim, you may not have any people or witnesses to aid in your defense. You may not have sufficient information to help the insurance company defend your claim. Once a claim is in process, keep track of the action through your broker. Knowing how much the claim has been settled for and when will provide better data for future insurance negotiations. Underwriters determine rate credits and debits based on your losses.

When closing a property claim, you will be asked to sign a "proof of

INCIDENT REPORT

DEVELOPMENT: ______________________________

DATE AND TIME OF OCCURRENCE: ______________________________

LOCATION OF OCCURRENCE: ______________________________

PROPERTY DAMAGE/INJURIES (DETAIL WHO, WHAT, WHEN, AND HOW):

____

____

____

____

ROBBERY/BURGLARY (DETAIL WHAT TAKEN, VALUES, ATTACH LIST):

____

____

____

____

VANDALISM (DETAIL EXTENT, WHAT CAUSED DAMAGE):

____

____

____

____

COMMENTS/POLICE REMARKS (GET OFFICER'S NAME, BADGE #):

____

____

POLICE REPORT #: ________ (COPY ATTACHED, IF POSSIBLE)

WITNESSES,—NAMES AND ADDRESSES:

____

____

PROJECT ADMINISTRATOR'S SIGNATURE: ______________________________

Figure 12-2 Incident report.

loss." Make sure that this document reflects the full and accurate settlement. Having one person in your organization tracking all losses will assist in proper control of claims.

CONCLUSION

Managing insurance can be a confusing and frustrating experience. Knowing some of the terminology and what the contracts mean will provide greater ease in running the total business operation. The foregoing is a sketch of a very complex picture. The need for a qualified insurance professional to work with you is clearly important. Asking "good" questions will avoid overspending on premiums or failing to purchase adequate coverage. Think of your insurance person as you do your legal counsel and accountant: a professional whom you can rely on and can expect to provide you with clear and precise information.

Occurrence versus Claims-Made Liability Contract

In order to limit its long-term liability, the insurance industry has revised its contract for general liability from an occurrence basis to a claims-made basis, effective January 1986, as mentioned on page 282. An occurrence is the event which triggers coverage, i.e., the accident or incident.

Occurrence policy. When a claim is presented to an insurance carrier, the policy in effect at the time of the occurrence, no matter how far in the past, provides coverage.

Claims-made policy. For a claims-made policy to respond, the occurrence *and* the claim must be presented to the carrier in the current policy period. This limitation reduces the insurance company's long-term exposure. Every claim is in the present.

As a result of the reduction in the carrier exposure, the premiums for a claims-made policy are substantially lower. With the claims-made policy the insured has the opportunity to extend the policy (for a fee, of course) backward for "prior acts" coverage or forward for an "extended discovery period" to minimize the uncertainty of a claim not being covered.

You must work closely with your broker to verify that your needs are met by this new contract and that the cost savings are fully considered prior to accepting the contract.

CHAPTER 13

Property taxes and assessments[1]

Dennis S. Tosh
University of Mississippi
University, Mississippi

In most parts of the country, the largest single source of revenue for local governments is the property tax. City and county governments use the taxes collected through property assessments to provide governmental services to the general public such as fire and police protection; construction and maintenance of public schools; and upkeep of streets, libraries, and parks. In short, were it not for the money generated through property taxes, local governments would be severely if not completely limited in the services they could provide.

As a property manager, it is imperative that you have a clear understanding of how your local government taxes the property you are managing. This is important because the taxes your property owes can be a significant percentage of the total income you collect in rent, perhaps as high as 10 or 15 percent. Clearly, any operating expense of this magnitude warrants your complete understanding. In addition, you may discover that the properties you are managing are carrying

[1]Neither the contributor nor the editor is involved in offering tax, legal, accounting, or other professional services. State and local tax laws vary enormously between jurisdictions and may have a significant impact on the contributor's comments. In addition, federal (and other) laws are constantly being changed and reinterpreted. If expert advice is desired, you should go to a competent practitioner.

more than their fair share of taxes compared to similar properties. As a property manager, you have a duty to your investors and owners to manage their property correctly, and this function includes saving them from paying more than their fair share in property taxes. If you do not understand how your property is assessed and how the appeals process works, it will be difficult, if not impossible, to know if the property you are managing is being treated fairly in terms of its tax burden.

Finally, unpaid property taxes give the taxing jurisdiction the legal right to lay claim against your property through the recording of a lien in the public land records. If after a prescribed period of time the taxes have still not been paid, the taxing authority can and will take the necessary steps to sell your property at a public sale. While you may reclaim your property by payment of the taxes due plus the interest penalty, the end result of such unpaid taxes can be the loss of your property. As a property manager you certainly would not want this to happen. Thus the need exists for you to understand property taxes fully, including how the amount due is calculated and what steps you can take to ensure that you are not paying more than your fair share.

DETERMINATION OF PROPERTY TAXES

Property taxes are referred to as *ad valorem* taxes, a Latin term meaning "according to value." For real estate, this means the tax due is based on the *assessed valuation* of the property. Each parcel of real estate is taxed based on a proportion or percentage of value; thus the higher the property value, the greater the tax. Historically, the theory of taxing property held that property owners of more valuable real estate were the wealthier people, who were therefore more financially able to pay the tax. What evolved was an *ad valorem* tax as we have today rather than a specific property tax per acre or a unit tax such as the current tax on a gallon of gasoline or a package of cigarettes.

In order to determine how much tax is due on a particular parcel of real estate, the following steps are necessary:

1. Determination of local budget expenditures
2. Appraisal (assessment) of all property
3. Assignment of taxes due to each property

Determination of Local Budget Expenditures

The determination of the local budget expenditure is a function of both the quality and quantity of services the local government wishes to provide, such as schools, road maintenance, and fire and police protection. The cost of each of these services is estimated to derive the amount of money needed for the local government to function. From this figure, revenue sources other than property taxes are subtracted. These additional sources include such things as federal revenue, local sales tax, income tax, and various licensing fees. The difference between what is needed to operate the local government and what will be available from these other revenue sources is the amount that must be generated through property taxes.

Appraisal

The second step in property tax determination is an appraisal or assessment of all property within the taxing jurisdiction. This is a time-consuming process that for the most part is never-ending. As land is developed new parcels are added to the tax rolls, and this improved land must be reassessed. In addition, inflation and higher demand both cause market values to increase, which in turn calls for property reassessments. Thus the assessment or reassessment of property continues.

A local, either city or county, tax assessor's office has been established in most jurisdictions. One of the primary functions of this office is to determine the assessed value of all real property within its taxing jurisdiction. In some areas of the country this job is contracted to private companies, while in a few states property assessment is handled at the state level. At whatever level this occurs, the manner in which property is assessed is central to the determination of taxes due.

Market value approach. Assessment procedures vary from jurisdiction to jurisdiction, but the process normally used in founded on one or more of the traditional approaches to value. In many jurisdictions the assessed value of a specific property is based on that property's *market value,* that is, the price at which a willing buyer and willing seller will agree, and at which neither is under any undue pressure and both are negotiating at arms' length with complete knowledge of the market. This approach is particularly suited for residential property, for which there is sufficient market activity to establish market value. For income-producing property or special-purpose property, however, there may not be enough market activity to establish a true market value. The primary justification for using this approach is that the market is the true determinant of value and a property's worth in the marketplace is a true and accurate indicator of its value; thus property taxes due on the property should be based on market value.

Cost approach. A second approach used in estimating value for tax purposes is based on the *cost approach,* which is a method of estimating value based on the economic principle of substitution. This approach is based on the assumption that the value of a building cannot be greater than the cost purchasing a similar site and constructing a building of equal utility. The cost approach is particularly well suited for unique or special-purpose property and is the means by which assessment values are derived in many jurisdictions.

The starting point for this method is an estimate of *reproduction cost new,* that is, the total cost in today's dollars to build a similar structure. Since it is often impossible or impractical to estimate the cost of reproducing an exact replica, many tax assessors start by estimating *replacement cost new,* which is the cost of producing a structure of similar utility using modern materials and building techniques. Since the assessor is attempting to derive current value of the building, *accrued depreciation* must be subtracted from the reproduction or replacement cost to derive an estimate of value. Accrued depreciation is considered to be any diminishment of utility or value from the replacement cost new and can take one of three forms: (1) physical deterioration, (2) functional obsolescence, and (3) economic (locational) obsolescence.

Physical deterioration allows for the actual wear and tear of the building. Since the replacement cost new has, by definition, no allowance for actual wear and tear, an adjustment (subtraction) must be made, without which an overestimate of the building's value would result. *Functional obsolescence* allows for conditions *within* the structure which make the building outdated compared with a new building. For example, inadequate loading facilities in a warehouse subtract from the value of the warehouse; an adjustment for this condition would be necessary to reflect actual value based on the cost approach. Finally, *economic or locational obsolescence* considers factors outside the property such as desirability of the neighborhood, surrounding land uses, or public services.

While all three types of accrued depreciation are difficult to measure, each must be estimated and subtracted from the replacement cost new to estimate the present value of the building. These factors are particularly important to the property manager since the assessed value assigned to a particular property is the basis on which the amount of taxes to be paid is calculated. The property manager should make certain that adequate subtractions have been made to cover all of the accrued depreciation. It should be noted that the cost of improvements is based on the cost in the marketplace, not the cost to an individual builder. This means that costs include materials, labor, indirect costs, and a reasonable builder's profit. Once the total accrued depreciation has been subtracted from replacement cost new, the difference is an estimate of the building's value. To this figure the value of the land is added to give a total property value based on the cost approach.

Income approach. The third and final approach used in estimating assessed value is the *income approach,* which is based on the assumption that a property's value is equal to the *present worth of future rights to income*. To state this assumption another way, the value of income-producing real estate is a function of the income generated by that property. If the income increases, the value of the property increases. As the income of property decreases, there is, in turn, a decrease in the value of that property.

To use this approach, the tax assessor must first estimate the *net operating income* (NOI) of the property. Net operating income is calculated by subtracting total estimated expenses from the rental income collected. After that, an appropriate *capitalization rate* is selected. A capitalization rate, or *cap rate,* is simply a rate used to convert an income stream (NOI) into a lump-sum dollar value. The third and last step in this approach is to apply the capitalization formula (value = income/capitalization rate) to the information derived from the first two steps. When this is done, an estimate of value based on income can be derived. By examining the formula, value = income/capitalization rate, one can see that the value estimate is determined and thus affected by two things: (1) net operating income and (2) capitalization rate. By changing either or both, the value estimate also changes. Since the tax assessor is responsible for estimating net operating income as well as choosing an appropriate capitalization rate, the estimate of value is entirely dependent on information gathered and analyzed by the tax assessor.

Although these three appraisal approaches are all available, not every property is appraised using all three methods. In fact, tax assessors normally use only one of the three methods, and the specific one chosen is normally a function of the type of property being assessed. In assessing residential real estate, tax assessors usually go with the market approach since in most communities there is enough market activity to generate sufficient market information for the assessor. For income-producing property such as apartments, office buildings, and warehouses, the appraisal approach taken is not as straightforward. First of all, there may be little or no market information with regard to the selling price of similar properties (assuming they exist), so the assessor is forced to turn to one of the other two generally accepted appraisal methods.

In the majority of taxing jurisdictions, tax assessors turn to the cost approach and use it as the basis on which to estimate assessed values. For property managers and owners, this may mean a higher than expected assessed value since the cost approach often sets the upper limit on value. If one or both of the other two approaches are not available, the property manager should be ready to show why the cost approach is too high and thus not appropriate for assessment purposes.

In some jurisdictions, the appraised value and assessed value are the same amount. For instance, a warehouse is appraised for $200,000 and if assessed at *full market value* would be assessed at $200,000. In most taxing jurisdictions, however, property is not assessed at full market value but at a fraction thereof, for example, 40 percent. For the warehouse, then, the assessed value for tax purposes would only be $80,000 ($200,000 × 0.40 = $80,000).

Furthermore, not all classifications of property are assessed uniformly. In one state, for instance, commercial property is assessed at 60 percent of value, industrial property at 40 percent, residential property at 30 percent, and agricultural land at 20 percent. What is important to the property manager in all of this is not so much the percentage used, but rather if in fact two properties of equal classification are assessed at the same rate. Consider two apartment complexes with appraised values of $500,000 for one and $1 million for the other. If each has been properly assessed, and if in fact the second is worth twice the first, then taxes on the $1 million property will be double what they are on the $500,000 project, regardless of what percentage of appraised value is used.

Assignment of Taxes

The final step in the determination of property taxes is the assignment of taxes due to each property. Before this can be done, however, the taxing jurisdiction must determine exactly how much property is available to be taxed. This is necessary since certain types of property located within every taxing jurisdiction are exempt from taxation. Examples include public land, streets, governmental buildings, schools, and churches. Once these properties are identified, the remaining property must absorb the full burden of the taxes to be generated. To illustrate this step, assume that the total assessed value of all the property in a jurisdiction is $90 million. If the revenue that must be raised through property taxes is $1,800,000, then by dividing ($1,800,000/$90,000,000 = 0.02) it is concluded the jurisdiction must collect 2 cents (2 percent) for every dollar of assessed value. This 2 cents, or 2 percent, can be stated in one of three ways: (1) dollars per hundred, (2) dollars per thousand, or (3) millage rate. If the assessment rate is stated in terms of *dollars per hundred,* as is done in many jurisdictions, the warehouse assessed for $80,000 would have a tax bill stated as $2 per hundred, or $1600 ($80,000/$100 = $800; $800 × $2 = $1600). Based on a rate of *dollars per thousand,* the 2 percent rate would be stated as $20 per thousand and the tax due would be the same, $1600 ($80,000/$1000 = $80; $80 × $20 = $1600). Finally, as a *mill rate* the tax rate is stated in terms of mills per dollar. Since 1 mill equals one-tenth of a cent, the 2-cents-per-dollar tax rate would be stated as 20 mills ($8000 × 0.020 = $1600).

APPEAL PROCESS

Once the tax bill on property has been received, the owner of record has a certain period of time in which to challenge or appeal the assessed value. This statutory period normally runs between 15 days and 6 months. Property managers or owners who file a protest within this period of time are given the opportunity to present facts and reasons why the assessment is incorrect. The standard procedure followed in the majority of jurisdictions involves either meeting with the tax assessor or appearing before a local appeals board or board of equalization. The job of the board is to listen to your complaint and decide if your property has been incorrectly assessed. If you are still dissatisfied, many taxing jurisdictions provide a tax court which periodically reviews cases not settled by the appeals board or board of equalization.

Property managers should certainly make use of the appeals mechanism if they feel the property they are managing is overburdened in terms of the amount of assessment placed on it. To do anything less is to fail to represent the best interest of the property's owner.

There are numerous means by which you can check the fairness of the assessed value of your property. While some of the market data necessary may not be readily available, you should be able to collect sufficient information to check the fairness of your assessment. The following assessment ratios can be used to assist in your analysis:

1. Total assessed value as percentage of market value:

$$\textit{Example: } \frac{\$800{,}000 \text{ (assessed value)}}{\$2{,}000{,}000 \text{ (market value)}} = 40\%$$

It is easy to compare your property with similar properties, since assessed values of all property are public information. While you may not be able to calculate the exact market value of similar properties, there more than likely is enough market activity in your city to give you a good indication of market values. If your $2 million property is assessed at 40 percent and similar properties are assessed at 30 percent, your tax bill is a full one-third more! Such a fact would be cause for an appeal.

Once you have determined how your property compares with similar properties, the next step is the splitting or breaking up of the total assessed value into land assessment and building assessment. This step simply serves as another check on the fairness of your taxes. In many jurisdictions, land values are crudely assessed; that is, all land in a given area may be assessed at so much per acre or a set amount per square foot with little if any regard for actual differences in market value. And while good comparison properties may be difficult to find, the same analysis for comparing either land or building assessments can be used as is done in comparing total property values.

2. Total property taxes as percentage of market value:

$$\textit{Example: } \frac{\$2500 \text{ (property taxes)}}{\$100{,}000 \text{ (market value)}} = 2.5\%$$

This percentage varies from jurisdiction to jurisdiction and from property to property: however, if all the property within your jurisdiction is assessed uniformly, theoretically the percentage should be the same for all property. On investigation, you may find that your property's percentage is higher than others, and if so, your property is carrying more than its fair share of the load.

Generally over time the ratio of property taxes to market value will decrease for all property due to the periodic and, in some instances, constant increases in market values during periods when property taxes are not being raised. Then suddenly—POW—reassessment, and the result is a significant increase in this percentage!

3. Ratio of property taxes to gross income:

$$\textit{Example: } \frac{\$2500 \text{ (property taxes)}}{\$37{,}500 \text{ (gross income)}} = 7.5\%$$

This ratio, or percentage, is a good indicator of your property's tax burden since it states rather plainly what you are actually paying in property taxes as a percentage of what you are collecting in rent.

While it will be very easy to calculate this for your own property, you may have a tough time acquiring figures for your competition. However, at worst you can probably estimate gross income for comparable properties and thus conclude whether or not you are paying more than your fair share.

4. While the ratio of property taxes to gross income is an excellent overall ratio, you may want to break it into specifics:

Property tax per unit:

$$\frac{\$2500 \text{ (property taxes)}}{17 \text{ (number of units)}} = \$147.06$$

Property tax per room:

$$\frac{\$2500 \text{ (property taxes)}}{68 \text{ (number of rooms)}} = \$35.76$$

Property tax per square foot:

$$\frac{\$2500 \text{ (property taxes)}}{7000 \text{ (total square footage)}} = \$.36$$

All these calculations can be done for either gross or net space and should be easy to calculate. Again, exact calculations for comparable properties may be difficult to acquire, but approximate figures will at least give you the opportunity to compare your property with other property in your jurisdiction.

UNPAID PROPERTY TAXES

Property taxes are billed and normally due within a stated period of time. Unpaid property taxes become *specific liens* on your property and as such are superior to private liens such as an unpaid mortgage. Unpaid taxes beyond a certain grace period allowed by a jurisdiction can result in the selling of the property at *public auction* to satisfy the tax lien. As a propety manager, you need to know when taxes are due, what the late payment penalty is, and what happens if your taxes are not paid.

SPECIAL ASSESSMENTS

From time to time, jurisdictions may levy a special assessment on property you are managing. This may be done for the purpose of paying for the cost of a public improvement such as a sewer or sidewalk. Unlike *ad valorem* property taxes, special assessments do not occur annually nor are they based on the assessed value of the property.

For example, you may be managing a building located on an unpaved street. The city decides to pave the street and agrees that it will absorb one-third of the total cost. Each property owner's share is determined by front footage rather than current market value or assessed value of the property. Generally, such a special assessment does not have to be paid in the year the improvement is made; rather, the total is divided by a certain number of years, for example 10, and one-tenth of the special assessment is due each year along with the normal property tax. Special assessments should be included in estimating total property taxes due.

A FINAL WORD

As has been stated on numerous occasions, only two things are certain—death and taxes. If in fact this is true and if property taxes fall within the category of taxes, you as a property manager are going to pay property taxes. That much is certain. What is not certain is the amount you will pay, and even though you do not set either the tax rate or the assessed value on your property, you certainly should take the steps necessary to assure yourself and your owners and investors that you are not paying more than your fair share. To do anything less is to fall short of your professional duty as a property manager.

CHAPTER 14

Dealing with government agencies

Gerald E. Kimmer
Realty Management Services, Inc.
Minneapolis, Minnesota

"Red tape" includes the rules, regulations, guidelines, forms, policies, directives, procedures, and format under which an organization functions. To say that a company, group, or government body imposes red tape is to acknowledge that all organizations operate under a set of rules and procedures. To the organization, they are the necessary procedures under which they function. Although we are all guilty of generating red tape to a degree, government bodies find most of the sarcastic use of the term *red tape* directed at them. Although all of us will agree that a certain amount of organizational procedure is necessary, when it reaches a saturation level, we invoke the "red-tape curse."

All housing enterprises have regulations that have been imposed by some government body. These start at the township or city level, where there are codes and zoning requirements to be met. From there, as one might expect, they get more complicated. The process of getting government approval at any level uses many of the same techniques to achieve positive results. Following are some of the general government bodies and agencies the property manager might encounter in attempting to obtain approval of a proposal:

1. Townships and cities
2. City and county housing and redevelopment authorities (HRA)
3. State financing agencies
4. Area, regional, and central housing and urban development agencies (HUD)

In this chapter we cover the management agent's trek through government red tape. We look at the government agency, the owner of the property that is monitored by the government agency, and the role of the manager in this process. The manager plays the role of intermediary between the residents-tenants and the owner on the one hand and between the agency and the owner on the other.

A main point to remember is that the manager works for the owner. Although a government agency may be required to give approval of the appointment of a manager, the management contract is between the manager and the owner of the property.

PROPERTY MANAGER AS INTERMEDIARY

As an intermediary between the owner and the government agency, it is the manager's responsibility to promote the owner's goals and objectives through the agency's procedural process, or red tape. We will discuss the process of carrying out the owner's objectives as they relate to government rules and regulations, thereby reaching the goals set by the owner. This action will require, in many cases, overcoming the red-tape logjam. In general, the logjam slows, and sometimes stops, progress through the agency.

Since time is usually of the essence, a thorough understanding of the entire process, including all the communications among owner, manager, and agency, is important. There are three main areas that must be understood to travel these paths successfully: (1) Know the agency that you are dealing with—its goals and objectives and its relationships with owners and managers; (2) know your owner's goals and objectives, as well as his or her relationships with managers; (3) know the manager's role in all of the preceding relationships.

KNOW THE AGENCY

In order to move something successfully through a government agency, you must know how the agency works. Agencies are made up of people;

therefore, you must know the people and the rules they work under to understand the ebb and flow of the agency's procedures.

The first step in understanding the procedure of the agency is getting to know the people at the agency. Establish personal relationships with these people, and begin to understand their work. Get to know the people you will be dealing with, especially the person directly in charge of your project. Find out if that person is single or married, learn his or her likes or dislikes, and be interested in his family and how he spends his free time; the opening conversation when contacting this person needn't be a statement of the problem at hand but something like, "How was your vacation?" The idea is to get the person on your side, sell him the idea, and make it difficult for him to turn down the objective because it would be like turning you down personally.

Each person has limitations, some set by the job—"I have to ask my supervisor"—and some set by the individual—"I don't think that's a good idea." Once you understand the limitations, you know whom you must sell.

Understand Your Contact Person

If your contact person does not think your objective is a good idea, you must try to change that person's mind. To do this, you must first know your contact person's objection to your proposal. The objection could be purely personal, or the proposal could run counter to an agency regulation. In either case, try to win your contact person to your point of view. If you cannot get your contact person to change his or her position, see if you can at least get her to pass your proposal on. See if you can get her to ask her supervisor so that the process may continue.

On the other hand, if you have done a good job in presenting your position and have in effect sold your contact person, your contact may be the one who sells your position to her supervisor. Once your proposal goes to the supervisor, make sure that your contact has all the information necessary. Provide the tools and in some cases even the argument, if it is a good one, so that your contact can take your entire case or position to the supervisor.

If the Decision Goes Against You

You must know your case and your position better than anyone. If the decision should come back against you, find out why. Was it due to established guidelines, policies or procedures, rules and regulations, or a directive? If the obstacle was a guideline, remember that guidelines may be changed. Assume it can be, and look for ways around the guideline. Give the person who invoked the guideline a way around his logjam. If the guideline cannot be circumvented, find out who established it, and see if a meeting can be set up with that person. Try to keep going until you can work through to whoever has a solution to the situation. This procedure can be used whenever you encounter policies, procedures, or directives you don't agree with.

Working with Rules and Regulations

Changing rules and regulations is more difficult than changing guidelines and sometimes is impossible. You must determine whether your objective is worth the time and effort necessary to attempt such a change. The most you might be able to accomplish is to get someone to bend the rules and regulations or ignore them. That situation creates its own unique problems.

Start at the Bottom

The preceding ideas and procedures make up a plan or direction to use to achieve the owner's objectives. Start at the bottom, or the beginning of the "tape," work with individuals at the bottom, get those persons on your side, and move up the tape. Know each person's position along the way and how the paperwork travels. Know the forms necessary to proceed from one end of the tape to the other. Be meticulous in filling out the forms. Do them completely. If there is a question on the forms or procedures to use, ask your contact person. Get that person involved. Try to make your position his position, so that the two of you are working toward the same goal. Know and understand what happens to the forms, where they go, what is done with them, and who gets them next.

Sometimes, due to the nature of the objective you are trying to reach, you must start at an upper level of the agency bureaucracy. Here again, find out what the person involved needs to work on your objective and achieve the results you are looking for. Provide as many details as possible so that you have a total package for that person to evaluate. In addition, find out who the person's assistant is and do as much of the preparation work as possible with the assistant. Try not to take up much of the upper-level person's time. While working with the assistant, if problems arise find out what he needs, and work through the details with a lower-level person. Get to the bottom of the paperwork pile. Start back up with forms filled out properly and your goals in mind. On your way back up the red tape, work through the people that you will be dealing with and again sell them your ideas. Get to the position where they are helping you through the paperwork and up the red-tape chain. Keep in mind that a "paper bureaucracy" responds to correct paperwork. Inspect your forms, clarify your position, and make sure that each point is presented clearly so that your proposal may continue on its way to a positive conclusion.

Who Has the Power?

Many times you are not sure where you should start on the red-tape path. One approach is to start where you have the best contact or where you feel the best and work your way up until you reach a solution.

Another approach is to find out who has the power. Do these persons delegate power or keep it for themselves? Find out how far down the power goes, that is, what decisions are made at what level. Start at the lowest decision level and aim for the highest power level to get your proposal accepted. Carry your proposal yourself each step along the way, unless you can get your contact person in favor of your proposal and willing to carry it for you. Try to get decisions on all of the situations that come up. Work through each objection at the lowest level possible.

At the lower levels, you encounter the fewest obstacles and objections, involve the least number of people, and thus encounter the least red tape. At the lower levels, you should make your objectives seem ordinary and simple. Once you get up to the higher decision levels, the involvement in rules and regulations, guidelines, and directives creates more obstacles and red tape. In addition, when more people get involved your objectives seem to take on more significance, and it becomes much more complicated to obtain your objectives. Complications are things that stir up red tape, which we all want to avoid. Keep things simple, use the simplest form, see the fewest people possible, and get approvals at the lowest level possible.

Determine How High You Must Go

If you can get your objectives into the "routine" category, your red-tape path is cut. Before starting, try to determine to what level you will likely have to go to get approval; however, always try to achieve approval at the lowest possible level. You are more likely to obtain this approval if you do your homework. Prepare forms properly, work through your lowest level contacts, and get them in favor of your objectives. Head for the ultimate decision maker.

Successful cutting of red tape involves getting through the approval process expending as little time and energy as possible. However, do not let the red tape hold you back; follow the tape until it can be cut. Make sure that you do not cut your personal relationships when you cut the tape, as they are the key to red-tape cutting.

To say that you cut the red tape is to be unaware of the fact that only the creator of the tape can cut it. It follows that the red-tape cutter is also a red-tape generator.

Forms that are not completed properly can be sent back for reworking, buried on desks, or sent to the wrong person for approval. These are delays we don't need and red tape we can avoid. Know the track of paperwork, know the forms, and fill them out completely. Know the people who get the information, what they need, when they need it, and, if possible, why. Find out what these people do with the paperwork provided, and show interest in their work. You may learn something that will allow you to suggest changes and speed things up; more important, let the person you are working with know she has an interesting and important job.

Step-by-Step Procedure

Where does the report go next? Who needs it and why? Where does it end up? Ask questions, and, more important, get the answers. Know the system from beginning to end. Understand the system better than those in the system do! Help people get the paperwork off their desk by knowing how it is filled out and where it goes, and helping them get it there. Be prepared so that delays are as short as possible; keep the flow moving and your issue going. If your proposal stops for a logjam of red tape, you are stopped and may possibly invoke the "red-tape curse." Get your proposal to the decision maker as quickly as possible.

Help each approval person along the way so that your proposal keeps moving. Make sure that you are doing everything that has to be done along the way so the decision maker can look at the issues in your proposal quickly. She should be able to read the presentation and see that everyone below her has approved your proposal. You have done a major portion of the decision-making work. You just may have given the decision maker a proposal tied up in a package that can be rubber-stamped, thus allowing you to reach your objective.

Set Up Your Own Schedule

The procedure outlined may take you much longer than you anticipated. In the beginning set up a schedule, including people to see, places to go, and things to be done, along with time schedules indicating when each item must be completed. If you are on a very tight time schedule, you will need to complete all items more quickly. However, try not to short-circuit the process. When you do that, you may be taking advantage of a contact person. Even though your proposal may get through this time, it may not the next time. When you come back with a new problem, as you know you must when dealing with a government agency, you may find yourself without a contact person and jammed up in red tape. If you must "use" someone for your proposal, make sure the issue is worth the use. If you have no other avenues open to you and you feel the expenditure of a contact person is justified, go ahead. Make sure, however, that you very carefully assess the situation, since it usually is best to keep your contacts open. Match the procedure you will use to go up the tape with the goals you are trying to achieve. If you follow through as outlined, you will have the best chance of reaching your objectives.

When you reach your objective, it is time to work back down the red-tape chain. Share your pleasure and results with all persons down the line. Thank them. Let them all know that they helped and that you appreciate all they did for you. One word of caution: Don't try to buy them. Your thanks and happiness will be payment enough. They will be happy and pleased that they helped. If you feel you must do something special, make it simple: a thank-you card, or a phone call. However, saying thank you in person is the best. The person not only hears the pleasure in your voice, he or she can see it on your face. Remember to let all these people know the role they played and how important that role was to the success of the objective. Remember, keep your contacts and relationships open.

After all is said and done, your issue may be rejected. Still, thank all those involved for their help. Keep your communication paths open, because as sure as problems are a part of management, red tape is a part of problem solving, and you know you will be back. If your issue is rejected, it is time to go back to the owner.

KNOW THE OWNER

All the processes you went through with the agency were the result of a goal or objective of the owner. As managers we work to achieve the goals and objectives of owners. Now you need to come back to the owner and say, "Here is how far the issue got and here's what happened. What would you like now?" Try again? Use new approaches or change the issue slightly and try again? Think up entirely new positions? Drop the issue?

By knowing owners and working with them, we can obtain the results they require. How do we get to know owners and where do we start? Spend time with them. Learn their wants, needs, and desires as they relate to the project you are working on. Learn all constraints under which they must function with regard to government agencies. Look at regulatory agents, partnership agreements, and any other binding obligations to learn owners' positions. As a manager, you will be trying to achieve owners' goals and objectives, and you must know and understand the rules that govern all relationships.

The Regulatory Agreement

The owner in most cases operates under a regulatory agreement with the agency, consisting of all the agreed-on obligations between the two.

The agreement establishes the rules and regulations that govern the agency's reaction to your problems. One of the first questions asked on setting a goal or an objective should be: Is it in violation of the regulatory agreement? If the goal is not referred to directly in the regulatory agreement, it may fall into a gray area. In such cases an interpretive position can be taken and a course of action started. The agent acting on the owner's behalf can proceed, as previously described, up the red-tape line. Prior to proceeding, however, there must be a thorough understanding of the regulatory agreement and all other relevant agreements.

Learn the Owner's Goals and Objectives

When getting to know the owner, spend time with him or her and ask questions. Make the owner's goals and objectives with regard to the project your goals and objectives. If you have problems with any of the goals and objectives of the owner, they should be discussed at the beginning. We all know how difficult it is to sell an idea that we don't believe in or we think is not the way to go. If a true difference of opinion exists, and it cannot be resolved, the best solution may be a split, allowing the owner to hire a different management agent. That would be an extreme solution, since the owner's goals and objectives are usually in the best interest of the project, and the agent is also looking out for the best interest of the project. Once the goals and objectives are established and you know the rules that govern the situation, you know the path that must be followed through the agency and you can proceed.

A good time to find out the goals and objectives of the owner is at budget time. Establish a budget, discuss it with the owner, and see that the budget meets his or her goals and objectives. Since the budget is usually for 1 year, this may also be a good time to look at some far-reaching goals and objectives of the owner—maybe a 5-year plan of extras. See if there are any special projects that might need to be accomplished, and always be looking to see if that special project will need agency approval. If so, a determination can be made as to the priority of the objective. In addition, a determination can be made as to the difficulty in getting the specific proposal through the agency. Try also to predetermine how far each item should be pushed and to evaluate the price that might be required to reach the objective. Each time something is pushed through the red-tape chain, it has a cost associated with it—and I don't mean money. Be sure that each item on the special project list is evaluated, and remember that the meeting at budget time is an opportune time to assess the time and cost associated with achieving desired results.

Make sure you set aside a specific amount of time for the owner. The owner's goals and objectives must be thoroughly understood by the agent for the best results. Another good time to meet with the owner is at the monthly review of the operating report, or possibly, a quarterly review of progress. At the least, a semiannual meeting should be held: Evaluation is essential to see that the owner's goals and objectives have not changed. As managing agents, we record and track the operation of the project on a daily basis and report monthly. We are constantly working toward the goals and objectives established at budget time. Keep in mind that changes do come up, and they should be addressed whenever they come up. These can be investigated at the regular meeting with the owner, and corrections and corrective procedures can be taken to ensure that, once again, you are working toward the most current goals and objectives of the owner.

As I have mentioned previously, the agent must stay between the owner and the agency. The agent must take the owner's goals and objectives, decide on a course of action with the owner, carry out the goals and objectives, and work them through the agency. Although the agent is the intermediary, there may be a time when only the owner's interaction with the agency can resolve the situation. At that point the owner should come in, present his or her position, and take part in the follow-up discussion on the subject. Once that step has been concluded, the owner should leave the agent to finish up the details. The meeting should be kept small and short. Also, try not to allow an antagonistic situation to develop between the owner and the agency. The contractual relationship between the agency and owner is normally for a long period of time; therefore, that relationship must be maintained.

KNOW AND UNDERSTAND THE MANAGER'S ROLE

The final ingredient in dealing with government agencies is understanding the role of the managerial agent. The manager must know and understand the relationship between a manager and an owner and that between a manager and an agency. As mentioned previously, the manager has a contract with the owner. In most cases the government agency has a third-party approval and is not directly or contractually associated with the manager. In most management agreements, however, there is wording that governs to a degree the manager-agency relationship. As the manager, you must fully understand this relationship. Know the dollar limits that require agency approval, what type of approval is needed, and who gives the approval. As you can see, all of these processes are interrelated. As noted in the segment on agencies, you must know who the agency contact person is, who the approval person is, and what or who is on the red-tape chain. All procedural processes and people must be known so that progress can be made and owners' goals and objectives achieved.

Since the manager has a direct contractual relationship with the owner, the process must start with these two principals. The owner's goals and objectives must be set and understood by the agent, and a schedule for achieving the goals and objectives must be established. The manager must also anticipate possible conflict areas in which the goals and objectives of the owner might be in conflict with the position of the agency.

Be prepared, do your homework, know the procedures, forms, and people to see. When a time schedule of achievement has been established, contact the owner to ensure that he or she is informed of the scheduled plans and that they are consistent with the current established goals and objectives. If changes must be made before getting started, reestablish a schedule and plan of action so that the owner's goals and objectives are correctly presented to the agency.

IN CASE OF A CONFLICT

If a conflict is anticipated, use the process outlined at the beginning of this chapter. Start at the lowest level person, use personal relationships, get your contact person informed of the issue, and strive for a positive solution. To ensure that this process is working effectively, try to find out the agency's probable position beforehand and prepare your case. Do your homework, know your position so well that you can anticipate where the problem areas will be.

Know the agency's position as well as your own; however, do not argue the agency's position for them. They will be more than adequate at presenting their own position. As a manager, you must sell the owner's position to the agency, and to do this you must make the owner's goals and objectives your goals and objectives. They are goals and objectives that were selected as positive improvements for the project; therefore, the agency must be made to see that a positive situation for the project is in its best interest. All parties involved are trying to achieve the best results for the project.

Difficulties usually arise regarding which direction to take to achieve the desired results. If the disagreement is on which approach to use, the approach can usually be modified to achieve the desired results. If the conflict is with the ultimate goal, the process of getting approval becomes much more difficult. However, if you have gone through all of the steps outlined, a positive conclusion with the agency is much more likely.

The results demonstrate that you have worked with the government agency—through the established red tape—to a positive conclusion. The relationships that have been established are intact, and the goals and objectives of the owner have been achieved. Since the owner's goals and objectives are in the best interest of the project, the conclusion can be a positive one for all involved. Afterward, you can begin to prepare for the next presentation to the agency.

PART 5

Rent control and discrimination

CHAPTER 15

Antidiscrimination

Louis B. Hansotte
Hansotte, Nostrand & Lange
San Diego, California

BACKGROUND

There may be no issue related to the law of property management that is more emotional and therefore more controversial than the *legal* restrictions and requirements associated with racial and other forms of discrimination. And there may be none in which the pitfalls involved in failing to understand and apply the many related laws, regulations, and cases can be more disastrous.

Regardless of the property manager's personal feelings in the matter, whether sympathetic with or adverse to the underlying problems and concerns of society and the legislatures in enacting antidiscrimination laws, it is important for the manager to know:

1. What the law is
2. What it prohibits as well as what it requires
3. How it is enforced
4. What guidelines must be followed to avoid the potentially serious consequences of commission or omission associated with these issues

It is these areas of concern, not the sociopolitical aspects of discrimination, that are the focus of this chapter.

It might be interesting to note that discrimination per se is not illegal. Each specific type of discrimination must be made illegal by law, regulation, or judicial decision. There are many examples of conduct in the business world that are clearly discriminatory yet neither illegal nor judicially punishable because the particular form of discrimination is not prohibited by statute or case law.

Under the general precepts of the law, one's conduct is presumed to be legal unless it can be shown to be otherwise. To prevail in an antidiscrimination action, therefore, it is necessary to do more than merely allege or even prove discrimination. It must be shown that the specific kind of discrimination is illegal and that the person alleging the discriminatory conduct is one who is entitled to protection under the umbrella of the antidiscrimination laws.

In one New York case, for example, a prospective tenant filed a discrimination complaint stating that the landlord refused to rent to her because she was an opera singer and was told that her daily rehearsals might be offensive to other tenants in the building. In upholding the landlord's right to refuse the rental, the court stated that since there was no statute or case law protecting opera singers from discrimination, no law was broken. Another court came to the same conclusion when a landlady refused to rent to a bald man; the woman claimed that bald men tend to throw wild parties. Note, however, that neither of these cases alleged discrimination based on sex or race.

The first two important considerations in discrimination cases, therefore, are to determine what discriminatory act is alleged and whether that particular form of discrimination is prohibited by law.

FEDERAL LAWS

There were few prohibitions against discrimination at common law; most are creatures of statute and of the case law which has developed pursuant to those statutes in fairly recent years.

The five federal laws, cases, and regulations which provide the important bases for most discrimination cases are as follows:

1. *The Civil Rights Act of 1866,* 42 U.S.C. 1981–1983, which holds that "all citizens of the US shall have the same right, in every state and territory, as is enjoyed by white citizens thereof to inherit, purchase, *lease,* sell, hold and convey real property" (emphasis added)
2. *The Civil Rights Act of 1968,* also known as the Fair Housing Law of 1968, 42 U.S.C. 3601–3619, as amended by the Housing and Com-

munity Development Act of 1974, and particularly Titles VIII and IX thereof, which makes it illegal to discriminate against all persons and requires them to be treated equally, with no difference in terms, conditions, and without denial of equal opportunities

3. *Shelley v. Kraemer,* 334 U.S. 1 (1948), which held that deeded land restrictions prohibiting the ownership or occupancy of real property by persons other than those of the Caucasian race could not be enforced by court order
4. *Jones v. Mayer,* 392 U.S. 409 (1968), which reaffirmed the Civil Rights Act of 1866 and interpreted it to outlaw racial discrimination in all forms of housing
5. *Executive Order no. 11063,* which directs all federal agencies to take any action necessary to prevent discrimination in housing and related facilities owned or operated by the federal government or provided with federal financial assistance, as well as in residential lending practices

In *Jones v. Mayer,* an important civil rights case related to housing, Mr. and Mrs. Joseph Lee Jones, responding to a newspaper advertisement, went to a newly developed subdivision in St. Louis County, Missouri, known as Paddock Woods, to consider the purchase of a lot and home. The subdivision was owned by two corporations, both of which were under the control of Alfred H. Mayer, who was also a licensed real estate broker. The Joneses applied to purchase a home but were refused on the grounds that Mr. Jones was black, and it was the seller's policy not to sell houses or lots to blacks.

The *Jones* case was dismissed by the Federal District Court for failure to state a *cause of action* (failing to allege any actionable wrongdoing), and the dismissal was affirmed at the appellate court level because it held that Section 1982 of the Civil Rights Act of 1866 applied only to state actions and did not reach private refusals to sell.

In reversing the decision, Justice Stewart, speaking for the U.S. Supreme Court, ruled that Section 1982 bars *all* racial discrimination, private as well as public, in the sale *or rental* of property, and that the statute thus construed was a valid exercise of the power of Congress to enforce the Thirteenth Amendment to the U.S. Constitution.

STATE LAWS

In addition to the federal laws and cases outlined, the laws of each state must be considered in determining whether a discriminatory act has been committed, particularly if a real estate licensee is involved.

California, for example, has a number of statutes and regulations that address the issue of discrimination, including the following:

1. *Sections 51 to 54 of the California Civil Code,* popularly known as the "Unruh Civil Rights Act." This act bans discrimination in "all business establishments of every kind whatsoever," and business establishments include housing units for sale or rent. Potential damages include payment of $250 for *each* member of the homeseeker's household, compensatory and punitive damages, and attorneys' fees.
2. *Sections 125.6 and 10177 of the Business and Professions Code,* which subject licensees to disciplinary action for engaging in specified discriminatory conduct. Section 10177(1) allows the real estate commissioner to suspend or revoke the license of any licensee who "solicited or induced the . . . lease . . . of residential property on the ground, wholly or in part, of loss of value, increase in crime, or decline in the quality of the schools, due to the present or prospective entry into the neighborhood of a person or persons of another race, color, religion, ancestry or national origin."
3. *Regulations of the real estate commissioner,* found in the Administrative Code, including Sections 2780 through 2782, which implement the foregoing sections of the Business and Professions Code.
4. *Sections 35700 through 35745 of the California Health and Safety Code,* popularly known as the "Rumford Fair Housing Act." This act applies to all publicly assisted housing units and to most multiple dwelling units whether or not publicly assisted. The act bans even an oral inquiry about the race or other related characteristics of the proposed homeseeker. Violations of the act may be reported to the state Fair Employment Practices Commission (FEPC), which, on a finding of discriminatory conduct, has authority to order that the unit be rented to the complainant, or that a like accommodation be made available to the complainant, or a payment be made of up to $1000 in damages if a satisfactory unit cannot be made available to the complainant.
5. *Sections 35800 through 35833 of the California Health and Safety Code,* which embody the Housing Financial Discrimination Act prohibiting discrimination in lending practices.

ILLEGAL ACTS

Each of the following acts is expressly made illegal by the 1968 federal law if based on or related to race, color, religion, sex, or national origin or if they are expressed or implied attempts to exclude or adversely affect *protected* classes of persons:

1. Refusing to rent, deal, or negotiate with any person
2. Steering a person toward or away from a particular neighborhood or area
3. Making an otherwise available dwelling unavailable for showing or renting
4. Discriminating in the terms, conditions, or privileges of the rental agreement
5. Refusing to accept a bona fide offer to rent on otherwise acceptable terms or conditions
6. Carrying out an owner's instructions to make a dwelling unavailable to a prospective tenant or to avoid its rental to that tenant
7. Delaying, hindering, avoiding, obstructing, or discouraging the rental of a dwelling
8. Performing any act, making any notation, asking any question, or making or circulating any written or oral statement that expresses or reasonably implies a limitation, preference, or discrimination based on the status of the protected person
9. Discrimination in advertising by limiting rentals to persons of a certain race, color, religion, sex, or national origin
10. Denying that housing is available for inspection or rental when in fact it is
11. "Blockbusting," or persuading owners to sell or rent housing by telling them that minority groups are moving into the neighborhood
12. Denying to anyone the use of or participation in any real estate service, such as multiple listing services, realty board services, or other facilities related to the rental of housing

Most of the foregoing discriminatory acts are prohibited by the 1866 Civil Rights Act as interpreted by the decision in *Jones v. Mayer,* and many are prohibited by state laws, which in some cases are more restrictive than their federal counterparts.

Even though discrimination may result, the following acts are *not* covered by the Fair Housing Law of 1968:

1. The rental of rooms or units in owner-occupied multiple dwellings for two to four families, provided discriminatory *advertising* is not used
2. Limiting the rental of dwellings owned by a religious organization to

members of that organization, provided membership in *that religion* is not restricted regarding race, color, or national origin

3. Limiting to its own members the rental or occupancy of lodgings owned by a private club or operated for other than commercial purposes
4. The rental of single-family homes, provided:
   a. No discriminatory advertising is used
   b. No real estate broker is employed in the transaction
   c. The home is owned by a private individual
   d. The individual owner does not own more than three such single-family residences
5. Rental of multifamily dwellings containing four or fewer units, provide the owner lives in one of the units

Caution: Even if the 1968 federal Fair Housing Law does not prohibit the foregoing acts, *that does not mean that they are not prohibited by other state or federal laws(s).*

FAIR HOUSING POSTER

Under Department of Housing and Urban Development (HUD) regulations effective in 1972, a fair housing poster similar to that shown in Figure 15-1 is required to be posted or displayed by real estate brokers, mortgage lenders, and others subject to Sections 804–806 of the Fair Housing Act of 1968. Posters "shall be prominently displayed so as to be readily apparent to all persons seeking housing accommodations or financial assistance or brokerage services in connection therewith."

The complete wording of the regulations may be found in the *Federal Register* of January 5, 1972, and February 16, 1972. Failure to display the poster will create a prima facie, or "first glance," presumption that the firm or broker is engaging in discriminatory conduct.

PROVING A DISCRIMINATION CASE

In rental cases, proof of discriminatory conduct requires the court to make a determination or finding of *each* of the following elements concerning the complainant:

1. He or she is a member of a protected minority group.
2. He or she applied for and was qualified to rent the property.

EQUAL HOUSING
OPPORTUNITY

We Do Business in Accordance With the Federal Fair Housing Law

(Title VIII of the Civil Rights Act of 1968, as Amended by the Housing and Community Development Act of 1974)

IT IS ILLEGAL TO DISCRIMINATE AGAINST ANY PERSON BECAUSE OF RACE, COLOR, RELIGION, SEX, OR NATIONAL ORIGIN

- In the sale or rental of housing or residential lots
- In advertising the sale or rental of housing
- In the financing of housing
- In the provision of real estate brokerage services

Blockbusting is also illegal

An aggrieved person may file a complaint of a housing discrimination act with the:

U.S. DEPARTMENT OF HOUSING AND URBAN DEVELOPMENT

Assistant Regional Administrator for Fair Housing and Equal Opportunity
450 Golden Gate Ave. P.O. Box 36003
San Francisco, CA 94102

Figure 15-1 Fair housing poster.

3. He or she was rejected.
4. The housing or rental opportunity remained available to others thereafter.

As simplistic as these criteria may seem, the two most difficult and important aspects of discrimination cases are determining (1) whether the alleged victim of discriminatory conduct belongs to the class of persons intended to be protected from discrimination and (2) whether the particular conduct alleged has resulted in a form of discrimination which is prohibited by law.

In order to make these determinations, one must be able to:

1. Identify the complainant as a member of a protected class
2. Recognize discriminatory conduct

The examples in the following section illustrate the process used to identify a member of a protected minority class.

TYPES OF DISCRIMINATION

When the term *discrimination* is used, most of us think primarily in terms of some form of racial discrimination (race, color, national origin). In fact, the trend in the law is to bring far more classes of protected persons under the umbrella of antidiscrimination statutes.

Some, if not all, of the antidiscrimination laws now include prohibitions against discriminating against any person by reason of:

1. Race
2. Color
3. Religion
4. National origin
5. Sex
6. Marital status
7. Age
8. Physical handicap
9. Ancestry
10. Medical condition
11. Employment based on sexual orientation

IDENTIFYING A PROTECTED PERSON

Assume you are a property manager faced with each of the situations in the chart that follows. If you refuse to rent an available apartment to any of the persons described, *you have violated the law!*

An important step in the determination of discriminatory conduct is to be able to identify a member of a "protected," or minority, class. Table 15-1 illustrates the process of qualifying a person as a member of a protected (minority) class.

DISCRIMINATORY CONDUCT

Actionable discriminatory conduct may be classified as class A (direct) or class B (indirect).

Class A conduct is usually intentional, obvious, and relatively easy to identify. "We don't want this neighborhood to turn into a 'little Puerto Rico' " doesn't leave too much to the imagination.

In *Brown v. Loudon Golf Club,* 573 F. Supp. 399, a black golfer, the guest of a member of the club, was asked to leave the course because of his race. He brought suit in federal court alleging both violations of antidiscrimination statutes and the intentional infliction of emotional distress. The court stated that he would have a valid cause of action on *both* counts, if the club does not qualify under the private club exemption. Instances of this type of conduct are serious and offensive, and not difficult for the property manager to identify since they are so obvious.

Class B, or indirect conduct, is much more difficult to identify, and indeed is frequently not intended to be offensive or illegal.

It is extremely important to understand that one's conduct may be discriminatory and illegal even though all parties are being treated alike, and no discrimination is intended, if the results of that conduct are discriminatory!

The elements of class B discrimination are as follows:

1. Conduct or actions which *tend* to exclude or otherwise harm members of a (protected) minority group
2. Conduct or actions which *either*
   - *a.* Have no valid business purpose, or
   - *b.* Have a valid business purpose but could be accomplished in some other way without having an exclusionary or harmful impact on minority groups

There are many actual and potential examples of this type of discriminatory conduct. Examine the following practices to see why they are (or

TABLE 15-1 Examples of Protected Classes

Subject	*Type of protected class*	*Basis of discrimination*
Susan is a 30-year-old single woman	Females; unmarried persons	Sex; marital status
Aaron is Jewish	Jewish persons	Religion
Laslo is Czech and blind in one eye	Czech persons; handicapped persons	National origin; handicap
Sarah is divorced and has three minor children	Females; unmarried persons; children	Sex; marital status; children
Sean is Catholic	Catholics	Religion
James is black	Blacks	Race
Rajah is from India, is Hindu, and attends a local college	Indians; Hindus	National origin; religion
Nuyen is a Vietnamese refugee and a Buddhist	Vietnamese; Buddhists	National origin; religion
Maria is a Mexican national on a legal visa and a Catholic	Females; Mexicans; Catholics	Sex; national origin; religion
Arthur is black and his wife, Velma, is white	Blacks	Race; marital status
Frank and Zelda are unmarried but want to rent an apartment and live together	Unmarried persons	Marital status
George is white, single, age 22	Males; unmarried persons	Sex; marital status
Sam and Henry are white and over 21, are leaders of a gay activist group, and want to rent an apartment together	Males; unmarried persons	Sex; marital status

may be) discriminatory, and note how such conduct could be unintentionally or inadvertently engaged in by property managers with no actual intent to discriminate:

1. Imposing a requirement that prospective applicants for an available apartment unit must have two references from present tenants in the building, when the overwhelming majority of current residents are white
2. Limiting rentals to specified professionals (e.g., doctors, lawyers) in a community in which minority groups do not have reasonable representation in the designated professions

3. Allowing military personnel to apply for rental units but requiring that they be of a stipulated rank or grade (e.g., senior officers), when minority members are not reasonably represented in those ranks or grades.
4. Holding out rentals to retired members of a previously all white trade union, company, group, or association
5. Limiting rentals to retired persons earning specified minimum incomes which would not normally be available to minority groups

To help identify discriminatory conduct, review the cases which follow. It should be possible for you to determine whether each is a prohibited act, and what type of discrimination is depicted:

1. Property manager urges Henry, a white prospective tenant, not to rent in a particular apartment complex because the neighborhood is predominantly black and the tenant's family would not be safe there.

This is discrimination in treatment based on race. Violations include delaying, avoiding, channeling, and steering.

2. Carla, an Italian woman, applies for an apartment in a complex you manage in a predominantly Irish neighborhood, and you tell her there is no vacancy. Earlier the same day you had told Erin, an Irish woman, that although there was no apartment presently available, you would be happy to place her name on a waiting list for the next available apartment.

You have discriminated on the basis of national origin by allowing differing terms or conditions.

3. A manufacturing plant in your city has recently begun hiring a large number of assembly line workers, most of whom are of Hispanic background. The owner of the apartment complex you manage near the plant informs you that he has adopted a new policy and instructs you to restrict future rentals to employees of the plant who are at the foreman level of management or higher.

This is discrimination on the basis of national origin. Violations include refusing or failing to show or rent and making the dwelling unavailable.

4. Lawrence, who is white, married, and of legal age, has been discouraged from renting an apartment in a building owned by a church with a predominantly black membership. The apartment is operated as a profit-making enterprise. Lawrence is not a member of that church. The property manager has been instructed to give preference in renting the units to members of the church that owns the building.

Larry has been discriminated against because of religion and race.

The manager has violated the law by carrying out instructions to discriminate; delaying, avoiding, discouraging, channeling, or steering; and expressing or implying preferences in renting.

5. Vlad, a Polish man, was told that apartments in a complex in which he wanted to live were being rented only to doctors, dentists, attorneys, accountants, or similar professionals. Although there is a considerable Polish-American population in the community, less than 1 percent are in the professional categories specified by the rental agent. Vlad is employed as a lathe operator and moonlights as a mechanic's helper. His income is more than sufficient to allow him to meet the rental payments.

There is discrimination on the basis of national origin. Violations include refusing or failing to rent or show and delaying, avoiding, and making a dwelling unavailable.

6. When Miyako, a Japanese man, went to rent an apartment near a new factory, he was told that apartments in the building were to be rented only to employees of the factory. Miyako is a chef at a local sushi bar.

This constitutes discrimination on the basis of national origin. Violations include refusing or failing to rent or show, carrying out instructions to discriminate, and making a dwelling unavailable.

7. A broker in a real estate firm obtained exclusive leasing rights to a new apartment complex. The apartments are designed to appeal to young, single adults. The broker feels that it will be easier to rent all of the apartments if he rents the first half of the units only to females. He refuses to rent a unit to an otherwise qualified single adult male.

The broker has discriminated on the basis of sex. He has refused or failed to rent or show and made a dwelling unavailable.

8. Richard and Martha, who are white, are tenants in an apartment complex. They applied at the office to reserve the use of the main common-area party room and were asked if they planned to invite any black persons to the party as guests. When they informed the manager that a few blacks might be attending the party, they were told that they would have to use the smaller reception room at the rear of the complex, even though the main party room was available that evening. The manager defended her actions on the basis of complaints from other tenants in the past.

The manager has discriminated on the basis of race by imposing differing terms, conditions, privileges, or services.

9. Howard, a black man, recently won a fair housing suit against the apartment complex in which he now resides, based on their refusal to rent to him because of his race. They were compelled to rent to him by the court action. He has been informed by the property manager that neither he nor his guests will be permitted to use the shower, locker rooms, sauna, or hot tub, because other tenants have said they will move if he is allowed the use of these facilities.

The refusal constitutes discrimination on the basis of race. The manager has imposed differing terms, conditions, privileges, or services.

10. The property manager of a residence for the elderly, operated under the supervision of the Department of Housing and Urban Development, has had complaints from tenants about having to share their shuttle bus with three elderly American Indian women. The manager felt the complaints were unjustified, but resolved the problem by setting up a timetable which allowed for separate use of the bus by the Indian women.

This is discrimination based on race. The manager has imposed differing terms, conditions, privileges, and services and has encouraged discrimination.

TESTERS

As we have already seen, in order to obtain a conviction for violation under any of the civil rights acts, it is generally necessary for the prosecution to prove each of the following elements:

1. That a specific property was available to rent at the time a member of a protected minority made application for it
2. That the person was refused the rental
3. That the refusal was based on a prohibited form of discrimination
4. That, thereafter, the premises remained available for rental purposes to others

It is relatively difficult for an applicant who has been denied the right to rent available premises to establish conclusively and singlehandedly all of the elements necessary for a successful prosecution under the law. Rarely will the owner or agent admit that the basis for the refusal involved an intentional violation of the law. To achieve success in the prosecution of these cases, it is common to use teams consisting of members and nonmembers of the protected minority operating in association with each other, unknown to the owner or agent. These teams are called *testers*.

The usual procedure in using testers is to verify the existence of a rental unit by having the nonminority team make inquiries concerning availability, rent, and other terms on which the property may be rented or leased. A team of minority members visits the same premises shortly after the availability and terms of the rental have been established. If the unit is claimed to be unavailable, or available on different, more restrictive terms, a second team of nonminority applicants returns to the unit and makes application for it.

If this second team is successful in renting the unit on the terms and conditions presented to the first nonminority team, a prima facie (presumptive) case of discrimination has been made, and a conviction can probably be obtained in court by the testimony of the three teams of testers.

The use of testers has been questioned on both legal and ethical grounds. However, the legality of their use has been decided by the U.S. Supreme Court. In *Bush v. Kaim,* 297 F. Supp. 151, decided by a federal district court in 1969 in an action brought under the 1866 act, the court commented that "such tactics [the use of testers] are, indeed, not to be favored. Nevertheless, had the plaintiffs not utilized such tactics to acquire possession of the premises, they would have found themselves without a remedy once the home had become occupied by another tenant who was without knowledge of the prior discrimination."

In the 1982 case of *Havens Realty v. Coleman,* 105 S.Ct. 1114, the Supreme Court allowed a tester (as well as the fair housing group which employed the tester) to bring suit against the owner of a Virginia apartment complex for giving false information concerning the availability of an apartment in the complex. The decision was based on an interpretation of the Fair Housing Act of 1968, which provides that it is a violation of the act to falsely represent that an apartment is unavailable if the underlying purpose is to avoid renting it to a member of a protected minority.

In this case, a black prospective tenant was informed on several separate occasions that there were no apartments for rent in the complex, while white testers making inquiry during the same time period were told that apartments were available.

Whether or not the use of testers is justifiable ethically is not for consideration here. The importance of the foregoing cases is in demonstrating that their use is legal, and that pending other means of establishing and proving a case of discrimination, such use will presumably be continued.

THE PENALTIES

Violations of civil rights laws, even unintentional violations, can be severely punished. In addition to the enforcement facilities of both state and federal fair practices and housing departments, the victims may and frequently do use the judicial system to obtain significant financial judgments.

In *Parker v. Shonfeld,* 409 Fed. Supp. 876, an appeals court upheld a jury verdict of $30,000 for a discriminatory refusal to rent based on race. An additional $6443 was awarded for attorneys' fees and costs.

In *Wharton v. Knefel,* 562 F. 2d 550, another case involving refusal to rent based on race, and one, incidentally, in which the court did not allow the testimony of testers to be used, a total of $8500 was awarded, most of which went for attorneys' fees for both the trial and appeal.

SUMMARY AND ADVICE

Legally actionable discrimination is a creature of statute; if the alleged discriminatory conduct is not expressly or by implication prohibited by statute, it is not in violation of the law.

To determine whether or not specific conduct is prohibited by law, first, of course, it is necessary to review the statutes and cases. Following that, one must determine if the alleged victim is a member of a protected (minority) class and, if so, whether the conduct itself was discriminatory.

Remember that it is *not* necessary to show a specific intent to discriminate for the law to have been violated. If the *result* is discriminatory, the intent is irrelevant.

Discrimination may occur even though there are other, valid grounds for refusing to rent, such as bad credit. It is important to use credit reports and other screening devices uniformly for *all* prospective tenants, not just those who may appear to be poor credit risks.

The use of testers to determine the existence of violations, and to prove them in court, has been judicially approved. Do not be surprised if prospective tenants turn out to be testing for violations of the law, rather than true candidates for rental vacancies.

Maintain adequate records to establish the nonexistence of apartment units, if rentals are refused, and be prepared to prove the reasons for turning down prospective applicants if there are available vacancies.

The property manager's main concerns about discriminatory conduct lie in the advertising, showing, and rental of properties; in ensuring equal availability for use of the facilities by all tenants and guests; and in supervising his or her employees to be certain that they are not involved in discriminatory conduct for which they are personally liable and for which the property manager and owner may be also. A good way to accomplish this is to schedule formal training sessions with employees, in which the manager reviews and discusses the situations covered in this handbook and others as they present themselves in practice.

In short:

1. Be aware of the law and of the means of enforcing it.
2. Be consistent in management practices.
3. Be prepared to meet and carry the burden of proof of nondiscrimination if a complaint is filed, and do not rely on the usual presumption of innocence as a valid defense to such a charge.

CHAPTER 16

Rent control and regulation

David L. Ganz
Ganz, Hollinger & Towe
New York, New York

Rent control is prevalent throughout the United States, although found most commonly in large metropolitan cities. It is a political hot potato, because tenants (large numbers of whom are voters) demand its continuation, and landlords (many of whom are campaign contributors) demand its extinction.

BACKGROUND

Rent control, price stabilization, and *regulation* sound like words of a wartime era. Such laws constitute an abridgment of the historical right of contract, but they also represent the legislative determination, which came out of social necessity, that the price landlords are able to charge for rental of their space should somehow be regulated under the auspices of a legislative body or municipal administrative agency.

Price controls on rent have the effect of government intervention into the free market, and their origins are in a shortage of housing or commercial renting stock. Supply and demand principles of traditional economics govern housing as any other commodity. If there are

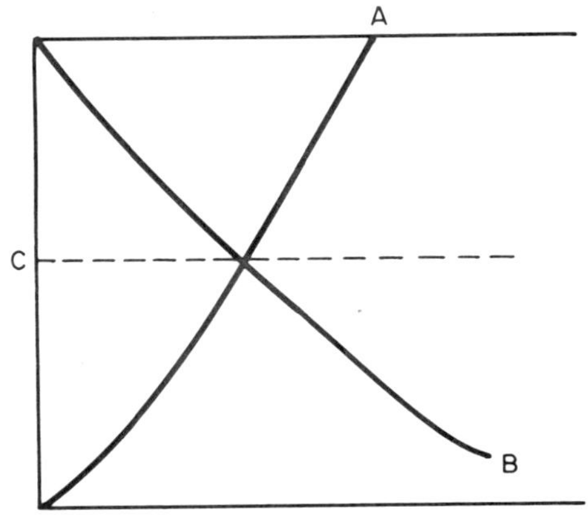

Figure 16-1 Simple supply-and-demand pricing for housing. A = number of units of housing or commercial rental stock. Few units in a free market where they are desirable means prices will be high. B = price. As the number of units in the marketplace increases, prices fall. C = level above which rent control supposedly assists housing and commercial space.

too few houses or apartments for the number of people seeking them, the prices tend to rise. This is the supposed evil that rent control or regulation seeks to correct. Rarely, however, does rent control seek to deal with the other side of the economic spectrum: an overabundance of housing or commercial space, which normally causes prices to fall, as Figure 16-1 indicates so clearly.

COMMERCIAL RENT CONTROL

Rent control frequently is thought of as an issue for residential tenancies only—an erroneous view. In fact in the 1980s, increasingly, there has been pressure placed on legislatures to create equivalent rights for commercial tenancies, principally for small businesses.

In large cities such as New York, one of the problems as viewed by the legislature is that small ma and pa businesses, some service-oriented stores (such as dry cleaning establishments, grocery stores, fruit and vegetable stands, and the once-ubiquitous 5- and 10-cent store), as well as small, light manufacturing businesses, are no longer being offered renewals of their leases at rental rates that are commercially reasonable for the tenant or with terms that used to be referred to as long-term leases.

At one time, it was not uncommon for a 5- and 10-cent store or a hardware store to have a 30-year lease (usually a series of 5-year leases with renewal options at increased rental rates). In the 1960s and 1970s, however, inflation became so rampant that these older leases no longer seemed to offer the landlord (or, more commonly, the landlord's successor by purchase) a reasonable rate of return on investment.

An Example of Commercial Rent Control

In 1958 a landlord rents a space at $1000 per month for a restaurant, and the lease is written as a standard 10-year lease (common among restaurants then) with a series of three 5-year options (rent rising to $2500 per month in the twenty-fifth year); such a lease was commercially reasonable at the time and offered the landlord a good return together with the security of knowing that the tenant would be there for a quarter of a century. In the succeeding years, however, property values increase, the landlord sells the premises (subject to the lease), and it is subsequently resold for a still higher sum. Meanwhile, the desirability of the space occupied by the restaurant increases to the point at which it is worth $7800 a month—but is still locked in at the old rental rate.

Pragmatically, this leaves the landlord in a bad way, and makes any prospective buyer of the premises prior to the expiration of the lease speculating as to future rental—although returns could be substantial on expiration.

Potential for Exploitation

The tenant in this situation also can be exploitative; with restaurant space at a premium, this space—available at well below market price—is a salable commodity. In fact, as long as there is a sublease clause (or a corporation whose stock can be transferred), the restaurant can be transferred and the landlord left without profit.

When the lease is up, the landlord is in a position to triple the rent (or possibly, increase it even more, depending on the view of the market at that time), leaving the restaurant proprietor with a choice: renew at a substantially higher rental or decline and either close or move to another location. The higher rental may not make sense, because the clientele of the establishment know precisely what the prices are; if the prices were to rise enough to cover a trebling of the rent, they could become double what they were.

The problem is identical for service industries, such as a shoe repair shop. Old leases calling for $500 a month rent were met by applying toward them $5 from each of 100 customers' average charges. If the rent goes to $2000, the same 100 customers must now have $20 of their average charge apply toward rent. That the average sale is less than this price means the shoemaker must move instead of renew.

Choices must always be made by landlords and tenants. But what commercial rent control attempts to do is reestablish the bargaining power by giving tenants a longer time in the premises and providing for certain renewal rights.

In some cities, such as New York, it is difficult today to obtain a lease from any landlord for more than 3 years. The pragmatic problem presented for small businesses is that capital improvements on the premises rarely can be depreciated over this amount of time. (The better solution to this, of course, is to amend the tax law, rather than limit the landlord's rights.)

The issue of rent control is a live one that will continue, through most of the 1980s, to cause problems that must be addressed and invite solutions that will allow landlords to make a reasonable return on their investments which *they*, not the government, determine.

RESIDENTIAL RENT CONTROL

Housing Shortage

In a number of cities throughout the country, there remains a shortage of middle-class rental housing, including apartments, single-family homes, and multiple-family homes. There is also a shortage of reasonably priced commercial space. Both situations have initiated legislative solutions, which have been in no short supply.

Some observers have suggested that rent control is the reason for the shortage in housing stock, for it is now more profitable for a landlord to convert rental stock into salable property (either as single-family residences, condominiums, or cooperative stock corporations) than it is to rent it. The rates for commercial space are so high in some cities (and additional space so unlikely to appear) that moderate leases are simply not being renewed on their expiration. As leases expire, convenience and service-oriented stores and other commerical ventures with long-term leases are pushed on, in the name of progress, and profits.

Restricting Rental Alternatives

The shortage of rental housing is so acute and the development of condominium and cooperative apartments proceeding at such explosive rates that there is some consideration being given at local and state levels to regulating the number of cooperatives and condominiums that may be placed in the marketplace. Typically this is done by governing the terms and conditions of eviction plans for existing residences or through altering the requirements for a prospectus to pass the muster of a state attorney general as part of standard "blue sky" securities regulation.

Regulation of commercial space, particularly for smaller users, is also spoken of as a distinct possibility. Its avowed purpose would be to maintain existing small businesses in the central city and to prevent a vast wasteland from being created. Detractors suggest it will destroy smaller landlords, whose income may be a simple building, or "taxpayer."

From a landlord's standpoint, maintaining rental stock is clearly less desirable in a rent-controlled city than is an outright sale. In offering an apartment for sale, even under the most stringent of securities laws, a landlord need only amend the prospectus to change the price of the unit being offered. If mortgage money is plentiful or the interest rates change, the seller can easily adjust the price.

Stabilization

Such adjustments can't be made under rent control, or under rent stabilization—the hydra that combines the problems of rent control with the knowledge that landlords would sell off their entire stock if prohibited in any form from raising prices. Stabilization, as practiced in many cities, allows the landlord to obtain a "going price" but stabilizes subsequent increases, usually providing for what some legislative committees term a "reasonable" rate of return on investment.

Rate of Return

Rate of return on investment, of course, is what being a real estate landlord is all about. To be sure, ownership of real estate offers tax advantages in the form of depreciation, interest expenses on mortgages, and even extensive property tax deductions and tax credits. But the bottom line is whether an owner will get a reasonable rate of return on the underlying investment. In some cases, rent control—coupled with spiraling costs of wages, utilities, and other services—has caused the return to dip from single-digit numbers into the negative.

Spread of Rent Control

At a time when government borrowing on treasury bills is yielding 9 percent or more on a regular basis and interest rates have gone as high as 21 percent, it is unreasonable to expect landlords to maintain housing stocks for minimal rates of return that are less than these amounts.

Some decry the inability to contract freely in the marketplace. Some believe, as well, that were rent control invented today, it would be invalidated as an unconstitutional infringement on the power to contract.

However, rent control and regulation are so deeply ingrained in the American system that their outright elimination, or even a declaration of their illegality, would be nothing short of startling on the part of a court, or political suicide on the part of a legislature.

Surveys of the laws of the 50 states disclose that rent control statutes or regulations exist, to varying degrees, in about 30 percent of the country. Recent court cases concerning rent control have been reported in about fifteen different jurisdictions.

HISTORY OF RENT CONTROL

Modern rent control probably originated during World War I, when an inability to provide housing in the District of Columbia brought about legislation in October 1919. Although a subsequent Supreme Court decision found that rent control was not justified if all that remained of the underlying war conditions was a mere increase in the cost of living, a valuable precedent was set. During World War II, federal regulations of rentals in housing accommodations were instituted, and two-family homes became a staple of American city and metropolitan-area life.

Following the war and the demise of federal legislation, local municipalities and state governments acted swiftly to continue the trend.

New York State Rent Control

New York State's rent control law is typical of the period. Entitled "an act in relation to the regulation, control and stabilization of rents and rental agreements and to proceedings to the recovery of possession of certain commercial space in cities having a population of more than one million, and to actions, proceedings and related matters involving unjust, unreasonable and oppressive rents or agreements for rent with regard to premises used or occupied for commercial purposes, and declaring a public emergency," the law by its terms was designed to apply solely to the city of New York—the only municipality in the state with more than 1 million people.

Clearly the premise of the legislation was the police power that governments are granted to protect their very existence. The New York law, typical of many, noted this indirectly by declaring itself "to be a measure designed to protect and promote the public health, safety and general welfare, to aid essential civilian activities, and to prevent inflation, and is made necessary by an existing public emergency."

Interestingly the "emergency" legislation was reenacted on an annual basis and in substantially the same form until, in 1963, the legislature enacted Section 8538 of the Unconsolidated Laws, apprising the world that "the emergency herein described is hereby declared to continue until December 31, 1963." Of course, New York's trial and tribulation with rent control did not end in 1963; the law has since been reenacted with modifications in the form of rent stabilization, with a confusing patchwork designed to trap the unwary—unfortunately, but inevitably, a synonym for landlord. The original rent control law explains succinctly the underlying theory of rent control for both housing and commercial space. The original law of 1945, duplicated in many other jurisdictions, originally set a rent ceiling at 15 percent above the rent charged on March 1, 1943, but allowed for a judicial determination of "reasonable rent" under tightly defined circumstances.

New York originally controlled commercial and residential space. The underlying rationale for commercial controls is stated in the following declaration:

> Unjust, unreasonable and oppressive leases and agreements for the payment of rent for commercial space in certain cities having been and being now exacted by landlords from tenants under stress of prevailing conditions accelerated by war, whereby a breakdown has taken place in the normal process of bargaining and freedom of contract has become an illusory concept, and whereby have come into existence conditions threatening to obstruct the production and distribution of essential civilian commodities, and to cause inflation, . . .

None of these conditions sounds especially awful to those of us who have suffered through the inflationary spiral of the 1970's. However, the declaration continues:

> And all of the foregoing situations and conditions being a threat to essential civilian activities, and to public safety, health and general welfare of the people of the State of New York, it is hereby declared that a public emergency exists without promise of relief so long as conditions brought about by war continue, and that action by the legislature is imperative and will not permit of delay. It is hereby found by the legislature that for the duration of such emergency, the establishment of maximum rent for commercial space at level of 15% above rents charged on March 1, 1943 . . . will curb the evils arising from such emergency and will accomplish the purposes hereby sought to be achieved.

Not content with just regulating commercial space, a comparable prohibition was created with respect to residential tenancies.

Rent Control Across the Country

Similar legislation has been put forth in major American counties and cities. Sometimes the rationale behind the legislation was the government itself. As Earl Warren recounts in his autobiography, *The Memoirs of Earl Warren* (1977), the city of Los Angeles condemned substantial amounts of land of the purpose of obtaining a watershed. The former owners became, in essence, tenants, and while all other landlords were prohibited under rent control regulations from raising rents, Los

Angeles tried to raise the rents of some tenants by as much as 50 percent. Warren relates that he signed a bill into law binding the city of Los Angeles to the same rent control prohibitions as any other landlord.

Los Angeles County still has rent controls, as do some municipalities in Connecticut, Florida, Hawaii, Illinois, Maryland, Massachusetts, Missouri, New Jersey, New York, Ohio, Pennsylvania, Wisconsin, the District of Columbia, and the American territories of Puerto Rico and the Virgin Islands. Other state and local entities also allow for residential or commercial rent control and regulation or are considering it. The concept, however, is plainly not one that is limited to the United States.

Foreign Rent Control

In Canada, the province of Quebec has the *Régie du Logement,* created in 1979, which has jurisdiction over the leasing of dwellings and allows for a fixing of new rents. In Italy, the ordinary rules of the civil code relative to rents have long been abrogated by special legislation which both froze rents and extended the terms of leasehold by legislative fiat. The Fair Rental Act of 1978, law number 392 (enacted July 27, 1978, and still in effect) does not permit a residential lease to be offered for a term of less than 4 years or a commercial lease to be offered for less than 6 years. The amount of rental is also fixed at an amount equal to not more than 3.85 percent of the current value of the premises as determined on parameters which include its size, location, age, and condition. Even agricultural leases are covered under a separate law (number 203, enacted May 5, 1982), which says a 15-year minimum lease must be offered with separate criteria. (The Italian rules are apparently predicated on a leasehold having a certain life of no more than 25 years with the rate of return fixed accordingly.)

France also has laws relative to commercial and residential leases. Commercial leases, for example, must be given to tenants for a period of 9 years as of right; a tenant may terminate at the end of 3 years, and should a landlord find a way to remove a tenant, the tenant has what is called a *droit au bail* or *propriété commerciale,* which must be compensated for. Rent ceilings are imposed on residential premises based on floor space, the amount of sun, air, and other such amenities, as well as the national index for revisions.

Socialist societies are not immune to rent control either. The Soviet Civil Code, Article 304, allows for the rental of dwelling unit space, provided rent does not exceed fixed limits.

What these facts show, of course, is that rent control is pervasive in society. The real questions are what the landlord can do about it and how the landlord can *use* rent control to help increase profit.

HOW TO DEAL WITH RENT CONTROL

There are a number of ways in which rent control can be mastered, and there are actions that every landlord (and landlord's agent) ought to consider carefully when dealing with rent-controlled property, whether residential or commercial. Consider this checklist describing how a landlord can increase profits with rent control:

- Choose your investment properties carefully, noting which are covered by rent control or stabilization and which are not.
- Use any rent control system to its maximum extent. Apply for any increase that you are entitled to, no matter how small.
- If permissible, make your tenants responsible for their own utilities; install separate electrical metering and (if feasible) electrical climate controls in each apartment.
- Explore converting a rent-controlled or rent-stabilized building into a condominium or cooperative. Converting creates profits and can eliminate some controls.
- Always keep on hand current copies of rent control regulations and learn them.
- Watch for changes in owners or residents of apartments or commercial buildings; if the change allows termination of controls, pounce on it.
- Know where your residential tenants *really* live. Some jurisdictions allow rent control only for genuine residents. An application form designed to ferret out this information may be suggested.
- Look for violations of the tenancy that can rid you of a rent-controlled tenant.
- Foreclosure by a prior mortgagee can sometimes rid a building of tenants.
- Familiarize yourself with the landlord-tenant judicial process.
- Use your leases (even on new construction, or in areas which do not have rent control) to defeat rent controls.
- Have increases for any lease built in, have the tenant waive a right to rent control in the future, put in cost-of-living riders or a specific percentage, or both (whichever is high).

There is a good cause to examine portions of the preceding checklist at greater length, since it can be of immeasurable assistance in learning to live with rent control; use it to your maximum advantage as a landlord or agent. Above all, *choose your investment properties carefully*.

Know the Law in Your Area

It is axiomatic that ignorance of the law is no excuse, but it is equally true that a little knowledge is sometimes very dangerous. For example, an assumption that because rent control is in effect in your jurisdiction it applies to every residence or business can be a costly mistake. So, too, can failing to apply for all rental increases that you are entitled to if the premises are subject to control. Anyone who tries to operate in a rent-controlled or rent-stabilized jurisdiction can attest that the law is a morass seemingly designed to trap the unwary. The unwary person, more often than not, is the landlord.

If you understand what the law is in your particular jurisdiction, you are one step up. If, for example, rent control or rent stabilization is not in effect in one- and two-family dwellings, you may reconsider the acquisition of property containing three or more families. If private residential homes are exempt, this also may translate into a positive advantage. The key is to consider these factors along with rates of return as relevant in making an investment decision.

Good property management depends on knowledge of existing rent control and rent stabilization laws. Frequently, compliance with those laws is essential if a tenant is to be evicted. In some jurisdictions, noncompliance with stabilization or control laws is an affirmative defense of a tenant against whom eviction is sought—even for nonpayment. One way around the emergency stabilization and control laws is for the owner to take the rental housing out of the marketplace entirely or convert it for his or her own use. There are restrictions to this approach, and inevitably it can be challenged as being insincere, but it nonetheless can be quite workable.

Such conversion works particularly well in a multiple-family dwelling, in which a close relative or growing child may be offered an apartment. Usually, eviction proceedings are necessary before a rent-stabilized or rent-controlled tenant can be removed, but in almost every case the tenant is ultimately compelled to leave. The key in almost every case is that the landlord keep the apartment off the market for a period of at least 2 years, and sometimes more. If a landlord acts in bad faith, the removed tenant has legal remedies ranging from fraud to whatever the rent control or stabilization laws provide for.

Understand Rent Control Economics

It is intriguing to undertake a simple economic analysis. In New York City, for example, where luxury apartments can rent for $2000 a month or more (even a mere two-bedroom unit of 1000 square feet or so), the identical apartment, if rent-controlled, could rent for $200 a month. If the unit is stabilized, meaning that the original rent-controlled tenant has left, and the apartment is put back on the market at its fair rental price (determined by the landlord) and subsequently stabilized in terms of increase, the monthly cost would depend on when all this took place. If it occurred 10 years ago or more, the odds are strong that the apartment rented in the $500-a-month range.

The economics of this are as follows. If the apartment is rented at $600 a month, it yields the landlord $7200 a year. Over a 2-year period of withdrawal from the marketplace, the apartment would have brought $14,400 of income. Yet in the third year, an additional $7200 of income would have been received for a total of $21,600. At $2000 a month, that entire sum is recaptured, to a profit, in the third year. (During that time, of course, the family member using the apartment could pay rental to defray the costs partially.)

Typical limitations will not allow a landlord to do this at the expense of a rent-controlled tenant if there is other space available in the building. Therefore, it becomes a process that, if not painstakingly slow, must be undertaken with extreme caution and care, and almost always after consulting with local counsel.

To the extent that your jurisdiction allows a rent-controlled apartment that is abandoned (usually when the tenant dies) to be placed on the rental market at "fair market" value and continues to subject it to stabilization, there are several additional remedies that property managers may take.

The first remedy relates to the lease term. If this is not regulated by statute, you should consider trying for a term which, under the law, will allow for maximum increases. When appropriate, clauses should be inserted in the lease to provide that the tenant pay for a portion of any real estate or other tax increase that may be imposed on the building. An additional clause to have the tenants pay for their own utilities, or a portion of the total utilities in the building, is also appropriate. Consider, too, a clause requiring the tenant to pay a proportional share of any increase in a union contract for workers in the building.

Riders of this sort are quite common in commerical leases. They are less common in residential leases, but if bargained for they can usually be obtained and upheld. Eventually, the entire building will fall under leases such as this, and the landlord will be reasonably well protected and able to maintain the equity of an investment in real property.

It is also useful to remember that while commercial rent control is generally no longer in effect, it is conceivable for it to be legislated or imposed in a constructive way, via taxation. It can (and should) be protected against in a rider to a commercial lease allowing for increases and for "reimbursements" and other landlord rights. Any tax designed to take a portion of a landlord's profits over and above a certain level can be guarded against by requiring commercial tenants to pay all additional costs.

Use the System

Equally important in any system of rent control and stabilization is using the system to its maximum extent. This means that if you are allowed under local ordinance to apply for an annual rental increase, you should do so. If you are entitled to a fuel surcharge, you should add it. No matter how small the increase may appear or how complicated the paperwork actually is, every increment gives a higher yield on your overall profit.

In some cases, the added charges may be sufficient to encourage tenants to move elsewhere. Typically this causes a rent-controlled building to become stabilized, or even entirely free of controls.

In almost every jurisdiction, a landlord is deemed to be presumptively entitled to a fair and equitable rate of return. While the details vary by statute, in some instances landlords may apply for automatic rent increases following a resale. Local ordinances should be consulted before undertaking such a program. Also, landlords are entitled to additional reimbursements from tenants for fuel surcharges, modifications to the energy system, and similar upgrading items.

Handling Utilities

If permissible, a landlord in a rent-controlled or stabilized facility should try to have the tenants pay for their own heat and electricity rather than bear the charges in each apartment. Sometimes, electrical units can be separately installed, with the tenant having the responsibility for payment. This arrangement is particularly useful as the costs of heating tend to rise. Although in some areas there are outright prohibitions against requiring the tenant to pay, if it is legal, it is a worthwhile investment that can increase the landlord's stake in the building many times over.

Conversion

Conversion of a rent-controlled or rent-stabilized building into a cooperative apartment or condominium is sometimes a viable option. There are two types of plans to convert a building: an eviction plan and a noneviction plan. The easiest, by far, is the noneviction plan.

If a noneviction plan is chosen and the tenant does not desire to leave, the landlord (or new owner) keeps the existing tenant under the old rent-controlled or rent-stabilized rate. The person purchasing the apartment (which may be the entire building) or any other private individual is entitled to depreciate the apartment at its full acquisition cost yet receive in return the modest rent-controlled or stabilized rental.

In this case, the purchaser puts himself in the landlord's current position. He can wait out the rent-controlled tenant or not, as he chooses. In some cases this option can make good economic sense, given depreciation. Consider the following as an example: An apartment costs $120,000 with $20,000 down and a $100,000 mortgage. Assume the mortgage is at 14 percent, meaning annual interest in the amount of $14,000. Also assume that the rent-stabilized price is $500 per month, or $6000 per year.

From the $120,000 price, depreciated over a 15-year period, there is an $8000-per-year tax deduction. On a typical 20-year mortgage, the monthly payment would be about $1200. The tenant would be contributing $500 a month toward the mortgage and maintenance (which, typically, would be 50 percent deductible but over and above other costs). There is a small net operating loss after taxes that accrues to the owner, but if the value of the apartment increases, the deal may be a viable one. And if the tenant leaves and the apartment goes back on the open market, then truly the value is recaptured.

Keeping Up to Date

Perhaps one of the most important things any property manager can do is to maintain current copies of the regulations and rules that apply to rent control and rent stabilization in the municipality in which the premises are located. Keeping up to date may not be easy, for in some jurisdictions obtaining a copy of the local rules—especially current ones—is impossible. Although it is frequently said that it is a citizen's obligation to know the law, it is quite rare indeed that every citizen has equal access to the pertinent statutes.

Simply by examining the statutes, in particular any changes that have been made, a manager of real property can pick up on a minor change that can be used to the benefit of his charges. For example, there might be a minor change affecting the residency requirements for stabilized or controlled property, which can be capitalized on quickly by an astute manager. An owner who keeps up with the various changes that take place may suddenly ascertain entitlement to a minor increase in price or a means by which another benefit can be derived, such as through some improvement.

One of the easiest ways to inquire about current regulations is to write, telephone, or visit the local control board; typically, the board has a current set of regulations available for tenants to look at. You, the manager, or landlord, can also avail yourself of this service. You should do it frequently, for the rules do sometimes change. Be aware, however, that most government-related publications have a particular slant, usually tenant-oriented. You can't necessarily take what is said at face value, but such publications provide a valuable starting point.

Know Your Tenants

One way to ensure effective property management is to watch for telltale signs of a change in occupancy of an apartment. In a number of jurisdictions, rent control and stabilization are available only to a named tenant. Frequently, particularly when one spouse leaves the other, it is difficult for the remaining person to carry the apartment rent alone. Taking a roommate, whether of the same or opposite sex (inevitably not permitted by a lease) is sometimes the solution the tenant arrives at. The most likely signs of this include a new name on a mailbox, additional rent checks, or even an entirely new rent check.

In cities where rent control and stabilization have brought tremendous competition for those apartments, subtenancies are not infrequent, the most telltale sign of which is a check with a name that does not match the rent bill. Since a doorman or building superintendent is often the first to know about changes of arrangement, every rental agent or manager should cultivate these persons more seriously than the tenants do. When a sublease is prohibited or the addition of a roommate is grounds for termination, scrupulous attention should be paid to the pertinent statute. If a notice to cure must first be served, it should be in accordance with the statute. The landlord or agent can then proceed to try to obtain what is rightfully hers. It is useful to recall that a number of housing courts—sometimes called landlord-tenant courts and usually handling both residential and commercial relationships—have stringent rules and regulations that must be followed to the letter. Whereas other courts may routinely allow pleadings to be amended to conform to proof, some tenant-oriented courts will not permit it, requiring a landlord to begin anew. Check the rules, plan accordingly, and make the system work for you.

Subletting

Just as a change of ownership in a residential tenancy can have an impact on the establishment or continuation of rent control, a similar change may have an impact on control in commercial space. Although more often there is a right to sublet commercial space, if there is not, you can use such changes to your benefit.

One confounding problem is related to the situation of a corporate lessee and a change of corporate stock ownership. Sometimes such a change is a method of sale, but other times it is subterfuge. In either event there may be a right to claim that if the principals are no longer the same, the tenancy isn't, either.

A curative provision that possibly can be placed into a *future* lease is to prohibit subleasing for any reason whatsoever without the landlord's consent (and provide that this consent *may* be unreasonably withheld), and secondarily to provide that if the stock in any corporation is transferred from the existing owners (you can require a tenant to supply a current listing), the lease likewise is deemed terminated. You should always place a contingency backup in the lease to apply in the event a sublet takes place and you find out about it later; such a provision will allow you to recapture the profits.

In a number of jurisdictions, a "prime residency" test is employed. The purpose of this is to make sure that a person who has a rent-controlled apartment is not using it as a pied-à-terre for the purposes of ripping off the landlord and other potential apartment dwellers. In New York City, for example, one proof of residency now being used is whether or not the tenant filed New York City income tax in the preceding year. (Nonresidents of the city of New York are not required to file such taxes unless they work in the city.) Given the fact that tax rates differ dramatically between residents and nonresidents, a number of individuals who used rent-controlled or rent-stabilized apartments as alternative residences several days a week and filed taxes from a country home found themselves in for a rude awakening.

There are other ways to check on residency: by finding out the location of a person's driver's license (almost always available quite readily from the Department of Motor Vehicles of any state on application), by checking voters' registration cards, and by checking many of the other accoutrements that people use to define where their true "home" is. If this sounds messy, it really isn't; several well-placed letters can bring forth most of this information. More important, this information may be beneficial, ultimately, in either renegotiating with the tenant for a higher rental rate or for taking over the apartment by the landlord in its entirety. That of course remains the goal in almost every rent control or stabilization situation—allowing a landlord to recapture the apartment and subsequently put it back on the market at its fair market value.

Landlords can often obtain the necessary information from tenants themselves. The easiest way is to do so initially when the tenant makes an application to rent the space. The application (as long as it is not unreasonable) usually can ask for everything from a copy of the driver's license and a listing of all bank accounts to a variety of other information that no one would ordinarily give to anyone else.

For tenants residing in a controlled unit for a considerable period of time, there may be statutory limitations. But if possible, it can be immeasurably useful if the information that ultimately defeats the tenant is provided by the tenant.

Violations

Watching for violations of tenancy is another way that a stabilized or controlled apartment can ultimately be reverted to the landlord. An example would be making sure tenants pay their rent on time, and if they don't promptly sending letters remonstrating against the failure. Other breaches of the lease, whether major or minor, can be called to tenants' attention together with a demand that they be cured. When a tenant interferes with the comfort and safety of others or allows the premises to be used for an occupancy which will subject the landlord to civil or criminal penalties, these are often grounds as well for removal of the tenant.

Another common ground for refusal to renew a lease that is controlled or stabilized is the tenant's failure to allow the landlord in the apartment to make repairs. Repairs can be many things: They can be beneficial to the building, beneficial to the landlord, and, incidentally, beneficial to the tenant. The general rule in the United States seems to be that the landlord is entitled to the preservation of his or her property, and a tenant who denies that right oftentimes can be removed.

Foreclosure

Foreclosure of a real estate mortgage is another possible way for rent control to be ended. If the mortgage predates the tenant, virtually every real estate lease contains a clause in which the tenant agrees to subvert his rights to those of the mortgagee. What this means, as a matter of substance, is that if a prior mortgage is foreclosed, the tenant whose interests come subsequent to that mortgagee, if properly served with judicial process, can be cut off. In a number of buildings, of course, mortgages have long since expired; in others, however, imaginative and creative financing in the form of extension or consolidation as well as modification allows for substantial mortgages to exist which could be foreclosed in a manner that would fully protect the mortgagee and mortgagor but not the tenant.

Such a procedure requires a sophisticated knowledge of foreclosure law in each jurisdiction, as well as principles of equity and the manner in which a foreclosure takes place. There may be instances in which some tenants are deemed desirable, and (in most cases) these tenants do not have to be served with process. Their tenancies thus continue as before; they are exempt from the foreclosure proceeding and continue living in the building. The undesirables, however, can usually be removed by way of a summary proceeding.

Understanding the Judicial Process

Familiarization with the entire judicial process is strongly recommended for those who have to live with rent control and rent stabilization on a day-to-day basis. There is nothing to be afraid of in the courts, although their procedures are time-consuming and often expensive. A landlord who goes to the landlord-tenant court often wonders why they don't call it the protenant court; nevertheless, in certain narrow instances a landlord can obtain justice.

The knowledgeable landlord who is not afraid to use the legal system ultimately will have tenants who are more cooperative: As word spreads that a landlord is not afraid to go to court on an issue, tenants may be far more responsive to the landlord's demands than before. After all, it takes the tenant time to go into court and defend a lawsuit (even if without a lawyer); the tenant is placed in the position of having to take time off from work or other activities.

This is not to recommend that you be litigious; rather, if you have a legitimate beef that you think can be best resolved by the legal process, you should not allow yourself to be intimidated.

New Construction

A final word is due regarding jurisdictions which impose stabilization in new construction; this advice is equally applicable to jurisdictions which allow the landlord to put out a new lease at one time or another. The new lease should reflect the landlord's desires and goals; it should have tax escalations, fuel increases, wage and porter increases, and other such items, including provision for taxes that may be imposed in the future. The landlord should anticipate the possibility of a rental freeze by providing in the lease that should a freeze be imposed, if the freeze is lifted, any monies not paid by virtue of it may be retroactively collected. The lease may also provide (if the landlord thinks this appropriate) that any claim or controversy arising out of the lease shall be settled exclusively by arbitration, as opposed to using the court system. Use of the court system may be effectively precluded in this way. Leases may also provide that the arbitrators be required to award legal fees to the prevailing party—thus tending to inhibit tenants from frivolous arbitration. Use of the American Arbitration Association is a possibility, although the landlord should realize that the association charges a substantial filing fee in commercial matters.

The foregoing are some of the areas that ought to be seriously explored by anyone who is commercially using property in a jurisdiction which has rent control or stabilization or may have it in the future. The suggestions provide ways to survive rent control and rent stabilization as landlords have done for hundreds of years.

The most important thing for landlords to remember about rent control and stabilization is that these are tenants' (and voters') laws. Instead of saying that the law is unfair and unworkable, you can find a way to make the law work to your benefit.

PART 6

The future of property management

CHAPTER 17

Computers in property management

E. William Hahn, Ph.D.
Marlene M. Hahn, Esq.
Hahn Computer Systems, Inc.
McLean, Virginia

Property management is an area of the real estate business that adapts readily to the benefits of a computer. The management activity may involve only a small number of rental units (e.g., 50 individual residences) or a large number of rental units, including apartments, condominiums, shopping centers, warehouses, and other commercial and industrial properties. Automating the management activity through the use of a computer can enhance the administration of any department, large or small.

What are the benefits of an automated system? First of all, such a system allows a tremendous *time savings*. For example, a manager operating a department that handles 100 individual residences spends a great deal of time writing checks to lenders, owners, and outside vendors as well as reporting to the individual owners periodically on the status of their properties. Not only does this work require a great deal of time to complete, it is also quite tedious. By its very nature, however, it adapts perfectly to being programmed into the automated-system.

Believe it or not, a properly programmed system can frequently cut work time down by 60 to 75 percent. This means that money can be saved in not paying someone to do time-consuming paperwork manually. The property manager can use time ordinarily spent in supervising (or performing) these time-consuming activities to generate new business and bring in more revenue to the company.

Any budget or accounting activity takes hours of time without a computer. Anyone who has done such activities manually knows the frustration involved in the detailed accounting activities. However, an automated system will assist property managers in preparing *timely and accurate* accounting reports on properties. The accounting may range from a simple income-expense report for the owner of a single-family property to detailed financial reporting for owners of apartment complexes, commercial or industrial buildings, and shopping centers. Furthermore, an in-house computer system allows management instant access to the budget and financial figures necessary to keep control over both the income and expenses involved in operating the property.

An automated system provides a *uniform and formalized* system of accounting and reporting. It helps management keep control over the quality of financial accounting and gives the client a standardized set of records that the client can rely on. This is particularly important when dealing with the management of condominium and homeowner associations. Boards of directors that contain volunteer members with little or no management expertise often select a management company based on its strength in providing concise and comprehensive computerized financial reports.

Use of an automated system can allow the management company to *increase business without substantially increasing expenses.* Because a computer can perform in minutes tasks that might take hours to do manually, property managers can use existing staff members' time to go out and seek new business. Furthermore, if the company provides good management service along with timely and accurate reports, it can build a reputation that has clients seeking its services.

Many management companies are able to obtain new clients by showing samples of the types of financial statements they provide and by making the clients aware that all the necessary management tasks will be performed quickly and efficiently. Management companies concerned about providing a personalized service may find that the use of an automated system allows them to expand their client base without sacrificing the personalized service which has gained them their reputation.

Finally, but most important, an automated system can help the property management firm keep *better in-house records.* By automating the accounting and financial record-keeping functions, the firm can quickly determine the status of clients' accounts. Furthermore, the system can automatically generate reports and keep accountings as required by the various regulatory bodies. Some examples include preparation of year-end 1099 statements to the IRS, tracking and reporting tenant security deposits, assessing interest to security deposits if required by the jurisdiction, and preparation of statements required by the Department of Housing and Urban Development (HUD) for qualified apartment buildings.

After all is said and done, however, service to people is still the basis of property management. Property managers must be able to deal effectively with owners and tenants alike. A computer can help in both areas. While it cannot replace the people-to-people communication that only an expert manager can provide, it can produce reports that help managers communicate more effectively (and accurately) and retain control over the many details involved in leasing and management activities.

Some of these activities are discussed in more detail later in this chapter. However, examples of useful management reports include tenant lists, vacancy lists, lease-termination reports, delinquency reports, and current balance reports (sample report figure).

SELECTING AN AUTOMATED SYSTEM

Note our use of the term *automated system* instead of *computer*. This term is used for a specific reason. Many people mistakenly believe that computer equipment, or hardware, is the key to automating an office. They have been led to believe, mainly through advertising media and hardware vendors, that all that is necessary is to buy the computer and plug it in. Somehow, magically, it will think for them.

These are the people who go out and buy a computer thinking that they can shop around later for a program. They all too frequently believe that any program will work on any computer, or that a program can easily be adapted to their particular computer. These people are generally very disappointed. They may even decide that their first venture into automation has been too expensive. At this point, many just give up and continue to use their manual systems—a step back into the Dark Ages.

An experienced professional manager knows that the process of automating a property management office takes a great deal of planning along with the right software—the programs that communicate with the computer, or instruct it in performing its functions. To automate an office properly, one must follow some basic guidelines. The guidelines may not alleviate all the problems that arise, but they can provide some basic insurance against making any big (and expensive) mistakes.

The following sections discuss the major considerations in automating the property management office. These factors should be considered whether the automated system consists of a small business system (a microcomputer and printer) or a larger system with multiuser and networking capability.

Requirements Analysis—Where's the Pain?

Make no mistake: The process of changing procedures and long-standing habits is time-consuming and requires a great deal of commitment. Therefore, in determining whether or not to automate the property management office, a major consideration is *pain.* If everyone is satisfied with the present system, it would be foolish to change anything. However, if expansion and efficiency are important factors, the advantages of automation become apparent. The following steps should be taken in the initial evaluating process—the *requirements analysis.*

Gather information. All key personnel in the office will have to cooperate in this planning stage. Find out what they are thinking. What do they expect to get and to give in the process? There should be a number of meetings and planning sessions to focus on answering such questions as:

What do we need in a system?

What would we like in a system?

Who is going to use it?

Where are we going to locate it?

What procedures do we want to change?

What procedures do we need to change?

Who will be responsible for coordination efforts?

Do we need a consultant?

Let's discuss each of these questions in depth.

What do we need in a system? Answering this question is perhaps the most difficult task of the requirements analysis. It means that all key staff members must review in depth the various facets of their responsibilities (including those functions performed by personnel they supervise). Time must be spent itemizing in detail not only the functions that the system must perform, but also the basic types of reports required, along with the information each must contain. It may even be advisable to select desirable formats for some reports that are particularly useful. Oversights and unnecessary haste at this stage of the analysis will undoubtedly prove costly, in terms of both expense and loss of efficiency and productivity during the transition from a manual to an automated system.

What would we like in a system? Not only must the requirements analysis plan for today, it should also plan for a practical amount of growth. This stage of the analysis also has its pitfalls. Sometimes people get so wrapped up in their "wants" that they forget to be practical. They find that the system they want is too costly, and they forego a more modest system that fulfills many of their needs and allows for some growth.

At the opposite end of the spectrum are people who spend unlimited amounts of money to purchase a system that they can never realistically expect to use to its full capacity. While it is wise to plan for some growth, it is generally foolish to purchase an automated system that provides capacity far in excess of the business growth reasonably anticipated in the company's projections.

Who is going to use the system? In order to control the accuracy of input and limit the accessibility to confidential information, the analysis should include consideration of the following questions:

What are the security needs of the system?

Which staff members should have access to the system?

What limitations should be put on accessibility of information? (Should all staff members who use the system be allowed to access *all* information?)

Who has the authority to input information?

Is it desirable to hire a person from outside to teach the use of the system rather than selecting in-house personnel for this responsibility?

This phase is most important because it involves delegation of responsibility. If everyone were responsible, then no one could accept full responsibility. Hence the automated system may never be used to its best advantage.

Where will the system be located? This question is most important with a large system with many components and a number of terminals. For example, if a management firm is responsible for many apartment complexes, it may be desirable to have a terminal at each location or at designated major locations.

Even with a small management department that is part of a residential firm, however, there is some planning required. It may be desirable to locate the microcomputer away from the general flow of traffic so fewer people have access to it. If the system is to be shared with another department (e.g., accounting), both location and time scheduling are necessary so that both groups can have adequate time allocated to benefit fully from the system.

What procedures do we want to change? Every professional property management team is constantly monitoring its procedures and systems to determine better ways of serving clients and performing the necessary duties. The requirements analysis stage is a good opportunity to spend time as a group selecting procedures most in need of change. This analysis time can result in time and money savings as well as assist in streamlining the overall operation of the property management group.

What procedures do we need to change? The transition to an automated system will most likely result in some necessary changes in operations of the management group. This stage of the analysis focuses attention on the types of changes which must occur, ranging from something as simple as the format of reports to a complete reorganization of the management department staff responsibilities.

This is the time for the staff members to do some group "soul searching" to determine which of the changes they are willing to make and which they are not willing to make. (To some extent, this may depend on staffing and budget considerations.)

Who will be responsible for coordination efforts? The process of automating involves many people and activities. Not only must staff time be spent in performing the requirements analysis, but the information must be put into a logical order to begin the systems evaluation, that is, the evaluation of the software and hardware that best suits the purpose of the property management group.

Other aspects of this coordination effort include gathering information from vendors, arranging demonstrations, ordering software and hardware, arranging any program modifications or customization, scheduling delivery of the system, and handling training and integration into the office. Depending on the size of the system, coordination could be a full-time effort. In some instances, this will be the responsibility of the consultant, which leads to the final consideration of the requirements analysis.

Do we need a consultant? Whether or not a consultant is involved, the property management staff must take an active role in the requirements analysis. Without this valuable staff input, the best consultant in the world cannot perform his or her job effectively.

Before selecting a consultant, determine what is expected. Unless a highly qualified person has already been recommended, several potential applicants should be interviewed. At a minimum, discuss in detail the following:

- The credentials of the consultant, including experience with automated system integration, real estate property management, and the type of hardware and software systems under consideration. Ask for references.
- The type of agreement with the consultant—for example, hourly contract or fixed fee. Determine if the consultant is required to perform to any degree prior to payment of consulting fees.
- What responsibilities the consultant will undertake. If the recommended solution fails, who pays the additional cost to find the solution?
- The amount of time the consultant will devote to this project.
- The time schedule allotted for completion of the work.

SOFTWARE—SEARCHING FOR BURIED TREASURE

If the initial effort in the requirements analysis has been completed in sufficient detail, it is now time to begin the search for software. At this point there are several alternatives to consider:

- Buy a software package off the shelf.
- Buy a package and have it customized.
- Have a programmer develop a package to conform to the specifications obtained from the requirements analysis.

Each of these options has some benefits and some problems. Let us examine each in some detail.

Buy a Software Package off the Shelf

At first glance, this seems by far the easiest and cheapest method of obtaining software. There are at least 100 different products on the market today that are purported to be "property management" programs. The real trick is to determine what these products do, not an easy task since the buyer seldom has the opportunity to see a program work. Consequently, words that mean one thing to a property manager may have an entirely different meaning in the product description. Generally, if you open a package that was sealed in plastic, you have purchased the software.

Most of the sales personnel in the computer and software stores know little or nothing about the individual programs or about the property manager's needs. Therefore, all they can do is suggest that the package is wonderful, and that it will do "everything" any property manager needs. Most of these programs leave a lot to be desired. Some of them do not even work properly, and there is seldom anyone to call on for help in the event of a problem.

Buy a Package and Have It Customized

This certainly is better than the previous option, particularly since there is an identified professional involved. If the vendor is available to customize the program, most likely the vendor is available also to offer assistance in the event the customer needs help. There are pitfalls, however.

Frequently the costs of modifications and customization are very high. The reason for this is that in any detailed software system, there are many parameters to consider in making changes. Therefore, a change in one portion of the program requires corresponding changes in other parts of the program. If all these changes are not made, parts of the program will operate improperly or not at all. This situation results in "bugs," dreaded by software developers and users alike. If the vendor is willing to work with the customer, and the customer is willing to pay the necessary cost, the chances are good that some packaged programs can be modified to satisfy the requirements of the property manager.

Have a Programmer Develop the Program

This is by far the most expensive and probably the most hazardous course to pursue in obtaining a real estate management software. In order to develop software that is easy to use and free of most bugs, a substantial amount of time and effort is needed. In addition, the developer ought to have some idea of the operations performed in a property management office. Otherwise, software can be developed that appears to meet the specifications given the programmer but fails to meet the practical uses in the business.

There is nothing worse than having a really wonderful product that is too difficult to use or even understand to be practical. If the property management department decides to have a special program developed, the criteria to follow should be the subject of another study. In this chapter, we limit discussion of the software evaluation process to software obtained "off the shelf" and used as is or with some amount of customization.

Evaluating Software

How does the software evaluation process occur? First, all the information obtained from the requirements analysis must be sorted and coordinated in some logical order. After this is completed, a search for available software can begin.

Remember that the success of the automation process in the management group is highly dependent on the quality of the software. The chances are good that there are no real bargains in the management software marketplace. While price alone is no indication of quality, there is a high risk that a program that is substantially less expensive than that of the competition will work poorly or not at all.

The following are suggested guidelines to follow in the evaluation process:

1. Determine the functions that the software must perform.
2. Search for several software packages that are available for property management.
3. From this information begin to evaluate the individual packages to determine which most completely fills the requirements.
4. Evaluate the capabilities of each of the packages.
5. Determine if the cost of the program, along with necessary training, customization, and ongoing maintenance, meets the budget allocated.

Determine the Functions That the Software Must Perform

If the requirements analysis has been completed and the information sorted and compiled, there should be a list of specifications including "needs" and "wants." This part of the evaluation should be relatively simple to complete; however, be sure that the list includes sufficient information, including the following:

1. Timing of various activities—entering and storing invoices weekly; check writing on the first and fifteenth of the month
2. Total number of properties to be stored and in what categories—individual residences, number and size of apartment buildings or complexes
3. Types and amounts of data to be stored in each category
4. Types and information necessary on reports

Search for Software Packages for Property Management

There are two general types of software on the market today: the general packages used by homes or businesses that are non-industry-specific and the *vertical* market software, which is industry-specific. A vertical package is usually more expensive than a general package, because it has been written for a smaller base of users. Another characteristic of the vertical market is that it may take a lot of searching to find the best available products. The programs are not always available off the shelf in a store, nor are they often advertised in computer magazines.

The best way to find vertical packages is to check the trade magazines, seek referrals from associates who are using automated systems, and review software guides, of which there are several available for the real estate industry. Another possibility is to check with the local board of Realtors,® who may have a library of information on software programs or a computer specialist on the staff.

Begin to evaluate individual packages. Clearly, this initial evaluation will be subjective in many respects; however, the information-gathering process may have brought in twenty or more responses. At this point, it is time to review the initial literature, including looking at the advertising material. If the system obviously does not meet most of the needs specifications (or if it tells little or nothing at all), it can be discarded. After going through in detail all the literature of systems that have some applicability to the specifications, it may be necessary to set up a checklist to note the capabilities of each package. From this initial evaluation, select the five or fewer packages that meet the specifications. (Note: Since there is substantial variation among residential, apartment, condominium, and commercial management functions, it would be impossible to find any one package to meet all specifications. The selection and evaluation process would require going through the same procedures for each individual package.)

Evaluate the capabilities of each package. There are two ways to go about evaluating capabilities of packages. The first way is to arrange an appointment with the software vendor to see the software package demonstrated. The second, which is usually done when there is a great distance involved, is to order a demonstration program disk and manual. For many reasons, the first option is far more desirable. In a face-to-face meeting, the customer has an opportunity to ask questions about the package, learn the feasibility and cost of any modifications or customization, and determine to some extent the vendor's knowledge and understanding of the property management business.

The very least that is necessary to judge a software program fairly is a thorough review of the demonstration program disk and manual. Whether the vendor demonstrates the software package for you or you view the demonstration disk and review the documentation yourself, there are several aspects that deserve attention. These most important and often overlooked factors include the following:

- The ease of program operation, including loading the program, backup procedures, and actually using the software
- The clarity and conciseness of any menu or screen displays
- The procedures for correcting mistakes and whether the program prompts for errors
- The quality and format of the reports

You cannot ask too many questions. If there is any caution that you should heed when searching for software, it is: *Do not assume anything!* Generally, if something is not advertised, it does not exist. Even if it does exist, it may not work as expected. For example, a program may be advertised as having an automatic check-writing capability. In some programs this means that you press a button, and all checks in a category (e.g., first mortgage checks) are written. In other programs it may mean that all of the information must be entered each time the checks are written.

Another concern is for the capacity of the system. There are software packages that may operate quite satisfactorily for a small number of properties. As more property information is entered, however, the processing time increases, causing the operation of the entire system to slow down. Some packages are limited to the processing of a given number of properties.

Either type of capacity limitation is acceptable as long as the system meets the user's reasonable expectations. However, it is quite easy to assume that a program that operates well with 50 properties will operate equally well with 500. It is a great disappointment to find that the processing time has increased beyond the frustration tolerance of the person using the system and beyond its practical value as a time-saving device.

A final consideration at this point is to determine if the program seems to follow a logical pattern. There are some functions that logically flow together. For example, if you are inputting property record information and make a mistake, it makes sense to be able to stay within that general area of the program to correct the error.

Once you have looked at the functional operation of the software, it is time to review the manual. Much of the documentation for programs is poorly written. This occurs for a number of reasons, the most important of which is that frequently the total program package is put together by a group of people. Therefore, the program designer is not necessarily involved in the actual programming, the programmer may know nothing about the practical use of the software in the property management office, and the technical writer may be lacking some understanding in either area.

The user's manual, your most available source of immediate assistance, thus may have some important voids, or it may be entirely incomprehensible. If after reading it carefully you can understand it and reasonably follow it, the chances are good that it will be of value. If you cannot understand it or follow it at this point, the chances are that you will have no better success using it when you have a real problem that needs solving.

Once you have chosen the one to three programs that seem most desirable, it is time to do some more in-depth evaluation. Obtain from the vendors the following information for review:

1. Reference list of users
2. Sample licensing agreement
3. Sample maintenance and support agreement, if available
4. Background information on the company
5. Information on vendor support, training, and other services, along with cost estimates for each
6. Availability and cost of enhancements
7. List of hardware with which software is compatible
8. Specification of any other software necessary to operate program

Determine If Cost Meets the Budget Allocated

When your group finishes its initial requirements analysis, undoubtedly there will be some budget allocated. At this point, when it is time to enter the final selection process, the budget becomes a prime consideration. The following items have to be considered in the overall acquisition:

Original cost of hardware

Original cost of software

Cost of modifications

Cost of new furniture (if necessary)

Cost of remodeling or refinishing space for system (if necessary)

Cost of supplies

Cost of training

Cost of ongoing hardware and software support and maintenance

Some of these costs are self-evident. Clearly the acquisition cost can be relatively low. However, some companies go to the expense of investing in custom designing a space in the office for their data processing department. In many cases this is an investment that pays off, but it is an individual decision.

What many people do not realize is that to get the most from their investment in the automated system, they must invest in training and ongoing maintenance for their software as well as their hardware.

While few people would purchase a new car or even a new typewriter without expecting ongoing maintenance costs, many believe that there is little need for ongoing maintenance and enhancement for computer software. Although most people are willing to accept the fact that the hardware may need "fixing," few realize that the software also needs periodic updating or that there may be bugs that have to be eliminated. It is necessary to plan for this ongoing maintenance and support.

You must plan, too, for training of new personnel when necessary. It is far less expensive to invest in training than to have an entire system fail because an inexperienced person made some serious mistakes. More likely than not, any expenses incurred in support, maintenance, and training will be well worth the money spent.

HARDWARE—IT'S DOWNHILL FROM HERE

The discussion up to now has concentrated on the software aspects of the system. There are several reasons for this sequence. First, the hardware options are many and varied. Because they require a technical background for full understanding, the real estate professional may get frustrated. Consequently, he or she may postpone the decision to automate.

However, a more substantial reason to discuss the software first is the dependence of the hardware options on the selected software package. In short, most software is developed to run specifically on a given hardware configuration. If the hardware does not match, the software selection simply will not work. In fact, the requirements study and the software evaluation activity in general leave the question of hardware options moot.

Since the hardware decisions are dictated and outlined for you by the previous studies, it makes sense to give them a lower priority initially in the selection process. However, you must be aware of some basic hardware fundamentals as you undertake the software vendor evaluation.

All computer hardware systems can be broken down into three basic subsystems (see Figure 17-1):

The central processing unit (CPU)—primary memory, arithmetic operation, and control unit

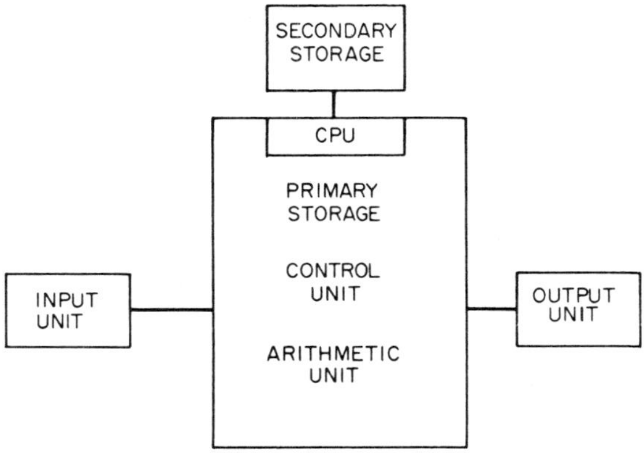

Figure 17-1 The three basic subsystems of all computer hardware systems.

The secondary memory

The input-output system

For the real estate professional investigating computer systems, the important feature of the CPU is its primary memory, or capacity. There is no need to be concerned initially about the arithmetic operation or the control unit, because they deal with the internal speed of processing and are generally comparable with similarly priced computer systems. However, since the capacity of the primary memory is measured in thousands of characters of storage, the user generally has options with respect to the amount of storage required to perform the necessary functions. For example, a typical microcomputer may have a primary memory capacity of 128,000 characters (known as *bytes*) of information. The user must determine if the primary memory is sufficient to handle the requirements of the selected software.

The secondary memory is also measured in thousands of characters of memory. In microcomputers the secondary memory is composed of the disk storage—either the *hard disk,* with approximately 10 to 20 million characters, or the *floppy disks,* with approximately 300,000 to 600,000 characters each. Again, the storage requirements are dictated by both the software and the amount of data processed.

For example, if a company with 150 individual units buys a program that requires 1000 characters of storage per unit, then a floppy disk system will not only meet its current needs (150,000 characters) but allow for growth potential as well. Notice that the total memory capacity needed can exceed the primary memory (as given in the example above of 128,000 bytes) because the secondary storage shares the burden by switching the data back and forth between it and the primary memory.

RECEIVABLES ACTIVITIES

PERIODIC REPORTS
2. Display/Print Tenant Status Report.
This report presents the accounting information for each unit within the apartment complex.

TENANT REPORT STATUS
4/14/83

PROPERTY NO. 1 ROBERT JACKSON
1123 DRAGON DRIVE

Starting Balance: $0.00

DATE	TRANSACTION	AMOUNT	TOTAL
3/25/83	PARKING	$ 12.50	$ 12.50
4/1/83	RENT	$475.00	$487.50
4/14/83	POOL DUES	$ 25.45	$512.95
4/14/83	PMT RENT	-$475.00	$ 37.95
4/14/83	PMT POOL DUES	-$ 25.45	$ 12.50
4/14/83	PMT PARKING	-$ 12.50	$ 0.00

PERIODIC REPORTS
3. Display/Print Current Balances.
This selection allows you to obtain the current ending balances of all the units.

CURRENT BALANCE REPORT
3/18/83

ACCT NO. 1	101	DEAN SMITH	$ 182.00
ACCT NO. 2	102	JAMES ROBINSON	$ 898.00
ACCT NO. 3	103	ART TEACHER	$1,185.40
ACCT NO. 4	104	JOE REPORT	$1,217.90
.			.
.			.
.			.
ACCT NO. 20	120	JASON DENNY	$ 525.00
ACCT NO. 21	121	JACK QUINCY	$ 525.00
		******TOTAL	$4,978.80

Figure 17-2 Samples of reports from a computer system.

YOUR COMPANY NAME
7777 LUCKY AVENUE
MCLEAN, VA
22101

DELINQUENCY REPORT
10/21/81

TENANT NAME	UNIT NO.	ASSESSMENT	AMOUNT
DEAN SMITH	101		
	# 1	BILLED RENT	$100.00
	TOTAL AMOUNT DELINQUENT		$100.00
DEAN SMITH	101		
	# 1	BILLED RENT	$200.00
	TOTAL AMOUNT DELINQUENT		$200.00
VACANT			
		BILLED RENT	$120.00
		ASSESSMENT 2	$ 20.00
	TOTAL AMOUNT DELINQUENT		$140.00
JOE REPORT	104		
	# 4	BILLED RENT	$120.00
		ASSESSMENT 2	$ 20.00
		ASSESSMENT 3	$ 59.00
	TOTAL AMOUNT DELINQUENT		$199.00
VACANT	105		
	# 5	BILLED RENT	$120.00
		ASSESSMENT 2	$ 20.00
	TOTAL AMOUNT DELINQUENT		$140.00
BILL DATE	106		
	# 6	BILLED RENT	$300.00
		ASSESSMENT 2	$ 15.00
		LATE FEE	$ 20.00
		ASSESSMENT 3	$ 35.00
	TOTAL AMOUNT DELINQUENT		$370.00

Figure 17-2 *(Continued)*

BILLING REPORTS

3. Aging Delinquent. This report presents a listing of all delinquent accounts with the respective aging of these delinquencies.

AGING OF DELINQUENT ACCOUNTS

OWNER NAME	PROPERTY	CURRENT	30 DAYS	60 DAYS	90 DAYS
ROBERT JACKSON	123 WEST	0.00	0.00	0.00	0.00
			TOTAL =	0.00	
JACK & JILL MASON	124 WEST	665.45	0.00	0.00	0.00
			TOTAL =	665.45	
BILL WEAVER	125 WEST	49.35	0.00	0.00	0.00
			TOTAL =	49.35	

BILLING REPORTS

9. Print Late Notices/Labels. This selection allows you to prepare late notices/ mailing labels to all delinquent tenants.

ACCT NO: 3 DATE: 4/14/83
UNIT NO: 125 EAST BALANCE DUE: $49.35
APARTMENT: HOLLYWOOD TOWERS

Your fee for this month has not been received. If you have mailed it, please disregard this notice. If not, please forward immediately using the payment card previously received.

--- A LATE FEE IS ADDED ON FEES RECEIVED AFTER THE 15 TH ---

BILL WEAVER
125 DRAGON DRIVE
FALLS CHURCH, VA
22090

Figure 17-2 *(Continued)*

The third subsystem in the computer hardware configuration is the input-output system, which gives the user the capability to communicate with the system. There are many options available, such as keyboard, modem, cathode-ray tube (CRT) screen, printer, plotter, and mouse. Again, the selection of input-output equipment is generally dictated by the software selected. For example, if the software is written for a single-user computer, it is not feasible to plan to use it on a central computer with several terminals—barring a miracle, it just won't work!

All this information about hardware may seem confusing—and it is. The best solution may be to follow the vendor recommendations, confining shopping to price comparisons. Another option is to have a computer professional put together a *turnkey system,* which is a complete package including all hardware and software along with training or other services if necessary.

WHY CAN'T ONE PROGRAM DO IT ALL?

All competent real estate professionals know that there is a world of difference between residential and commercial brokerage activities. Of course this difference extends into the area of management as well. Therefore, a program that adequately meets the needs of a residential property manager who is responsible for 300 individually owned units cannot meet more than a few basic needs of an apartment manager, and almost none of the needs of a commercial manager (see Figure 17-2).

In the course of the overall selection, therefore, the company must plan for the automation of each of the specific areas of management activity performed. The selection process then can be geared to the requirements of each specialty group.

CHAPTER 18

Tomorrow's industry

Bowen Ballard
Ballard Realty Companies
Montgomery, Alabama

The field of property management has undergone significant changes during the early 1980s, owing to transitions in the marketplace and innovative programs. When the dust settles, however, property management will continue to be basically the same industry it always has been, that is, one person looking after another person's property. When Adam told his sons to go out and look after the fields, property management began; since that time, the work has been done by slaves, serfs, overseers, and now, computers. The first landowner had more land than could possibly be handled by one person, and the need for help was obvious. Now the land is so specialized, management has got to be specialized to keep up. Either we have taken a simple idea and made it complex, or our industry has become so complex that simplicity has become a lost art. Whatever the case, the mechanics surrounding successful property management are constantly undergoing change.

ASSET MANAGEMENT

One of the most obvious changes in our industry has been reflected in the change in our name. As *property managers*, the parameters were somewhat set: You were given certain improved property, for a certain period of time, for a certain commission. You were the central source of knowledge for the property, and any decisions made concerning this property were based on data supplied by you. Our parameters have increased because of the logical progression of expertise to the point that the term that best describes our industry—a term coined by the industry—is *asset management.*

Property management is more than taking care of a building or an apartment; those property managers who don't realize this will not be around in 5 years. As the name implies, asset management concerns any type of real property from raw land to income property. This means that asset managers have to broaden their base of knowledge to meet new demands.

The Old Days Are Gone

Gone are the days when the clerical help made sure the tenants made their monthly payments and possibly coordinated repairs on or inquiries about the property. Gone are the days when a 2-year management contract satisfied both the owner and the manager. Now we must address multiyear projections, multiuse possibilities, and multiowner possessions.

The selection and training of personnel have also changed considerably. The right person for the management of certain real property assets must possess a good bit more sophistication in the areas of law, economics, financial responsibilities, and marketing techniques and tools, not to mention architecture, landscaping, and one of the most important areas, maintenance.

The Importance of Public Relations

An area which touches all the other areas mentioned is public relations. With the advent of the impersonal computer, everybody is privy to everybody's information. However, the personal element is still necessary for final decisions, and the asset manager of today and tomorrow must employ a global attitude in dealing with owners and investors. The economic factors that affect a piece of property on the West Coast certainly are not the same as those affecting an apartment complex in New Jersey. Asset managers of yesteryear did not have to worry about such factors since they generally managed properties in a limited locale. To do the job properly today, asset managers must know about rules, regulations, and laws of other counties and states and the interaction of the federal system with them.

Asset managers of residential property have to be aware of such factors as the local housing market, the demand for various lots and apartments, and whether the area is ready for condominiums. In commercial asset property, each lease or sale of the units may be subject to negotiation. Some may have a set price, while others are based on the income of the commercial tenant, or buyer, or both. In the area of finance, the asset manager must really shine, for it is here that big decisions are made, primarily regarding ownership. The income, expenses, improvements, and salaries all have to figure into the "magic formula" that makes the "numbers work" with an ever-changing economy. This area has become crucial: Previously, increases or anticipated increases in goods and services were gradual. Now such increases can be overnight nightmares. The asset manager has to realize that with our present system, there is very little chance for a reduction in prices but an almost certain chance of an increase. The most obvious problem this scenario presents is lack of parity with rent.

Marketing

The marketing that asset managers use to present their property for lease or sale no longer can be accomplished by the person handling the account in the classified section of the local newspaper. The marketing of property takes place on a fierce battleground. People today are not looking for a simple "two bedrooms and one and a half bath." They want ambience, both in their residence and at work. The asset manager has to be able to translate a feeling, a setting, or a mood into something the property can project, and know the props necessary to accomplish this, such as building materials and landscaping elements. Whether the asset manager is in on the creation of the project or has to maintain it ex post facto, his or her knowledge of architecture, landscaping, and maintenance has to be more than fair to middling.

The availability of new tools of marketing pertaining to asset management has increased, and the classified section in the local newspaper is not the last stop anymore. Radio, television, video cassettes, promotion, and other means of communication now give the asset manager unlimited possibilities for the right presentation.

PLAYER PROFILE

Before looking at the people involved, it is helpful to say a few words about past participants and their evolution into the present-day professionals. In the past, persons who did well in business and had some capital to invest would turn to stocks or real estate as a sound investment. With real estate appreciating at a rapid rate, a small amount invested almost always guaranteed a good return. During the early 1980s, however, real estate changed for all time. Money was not to be had, and if it was found the rates were impossible to work with. The days in which a person could pick up a run-down piece of property for practically nothing, fix it up, and sell it for a profit are gone. Real estate is still appreciating and is still a good investment, but the means of investing in real estate have changed.

Creative Financing

Creative financing has provided a variable market from which to choose the appropriate vehicle to invest in real property, and investors also come in many shapes and sizes. It is by no means an innovative idea; however, it once represented a small segment of real property investment and is fast becoming the norm.

Stocks

Stocks are the other area of heavy investing; real property and stocks are converging in the form of multiple owners of real property, which has had a major impact on asset management. When times are bad and foreclosures are frequent, individual owners or small-group owners are bought out or taken over by groups such as insurance companies and mutual funds—the people with deep pockets. This trend creates the problem of distance: The property generally is located on the other side of the country, away from the owner, and local management is the best way of seeing that the property operates properly. The distance gives local asset managers greater opportunities and responsibilities, since their expertise in a particular locale must be conveyed to the faraway owner, who relates to asset management better in his or her part of the country.

Owners

Although there probably always will be individual owners and developers, a greater percentage of asset property owners now are groups of investors in either joint-venture partnerships, corporations, or syndications. The common ground, generally, is that these entities are looking for one thing, primarily, in the asset property: a return on their investment. It is true that tax shelters play an important part in investment packages, but the term has become an ugly word, with its connotation of finding a way to make sure Uncle Sam does not walk off with most of the earnings. A little public relations work is needed to change this negative image and focus on the fact that asset management deals with investments and that one aspect of these investments is the tax shelter.

Buyers

Because of the trend described, potential buyers are becoming, more and more, institutional buyers, since corporations have the necessary funds to purchase a project outright, thus eliminating the problem of fluctuating mortgage rates. Another type of buyer who has had a major impact on asset management is the foreign investor. If ownership can be maintained from 2000 miles away, it can also be handled from a continent away. Again, this situation increases the need for local asset managers or companies with the expertise to set up a local management system.

What these new players have done for asset management is force the evolution of a high level of sophistication and professionalism in the asset management industry. This process has been painful for some, but only when there is resistance to the inevitable changes brought about by national and global situations.

THE WORKING MECHANISM

New participants in the management of the age-old product—land—have brought asset management into a new era, with changes that are complex but extremely gratifying. How are these new elements going to interact to fulfill our original task of looking after someone else's property? One of the most significant factors in this interaction is the computer.

The Computer Revolution

The computer has revolutionized our entire society—and asset management as a part of it—with the technologies of word processing, electronic spreadsheets, electronic mail, and time management programs. Quick projections and analyses are available at the touch of a button, and because of the many fluctuations in our industry, future planning has become extremely flexible. With competition becoming fierce, asset managers, with the help of computers, can look for better ways of getting the most for the property owners at the least cost. Although this sounds like something out of Economics 101, it is the goal you must shoot for, and the computer is ready to assist you.

Although it may seem that the time-worn principles of yesterday should apply today and tomorrow, that is not the case. With the radical changes and fluctuations in financing of income properties, it has become necessary to address management of income properties from a different perspective.

Asset Manager as Communicator

Asset management is probably the only segment of real estate which is at the forefront of the changeover to the computerized information-conscious society. Deductive reasoning would support this statement, since asset management is basically communication of information with investors and tenants. Understanding the interaction between the goals of each group is the job of the asset manager. If asset managers are going to be flexible, they have to have a broad range of knowledge and must get away from the victim-villain concept of the landlord-tenant relationship. Long-range planning with cost accounting analyses and the ability to make flexible adjustments when fluctuations from external influences occur will give successful asset managers the edge on their competitors. Since we are broadening the areas of expertise of asset managers, we might as well add a few more hats to wear. With the many connections of this mega-network asset managers can make just being in the industry, there is plenty of opportunity to compete for the management of a particular asset. Of course, the competition will be there; however, if new business leads seem to dry up, asset managers need to hook up with developers and create their own products. To what extent participation is involved will be determined by the size and scope of the asset manager's operation.

Goals of the Manager

The ideal direction for asset management is toward translation of the asset manager's broad data base into input for the development of future business. This process almost has a life of its own. We note the appearance of a cyclic pattern since the industry started with the entrepreneurial businessperson who wanted to invest those hard-earned dollars into sound real estate. The owner/developer participates in this cycle, but in a consulting role rather than an ownership one.

Asset managers are compensated with a development fee, along with the management fee, and if the situation warrants, maybe a piece of the deal in the form of a joint venture or syndication. The asset manager gives the project the feel for the property that is easily lost with absentee landlords who go through either public or private funds to obtain property, have little knowledge for input or control, and probably never see the property. Some of the larger groups controlling properties have asset-management teams, but in either case local knowledge of the property will have to be mastered. If the local or regional managers are out-of-house, they will be under the gun to prove that they can consistently get better return for the investors than in-house managers. This competition keeps the industry healthy and continually aware of new trends and innovations.

Public Scrutiny

Owners are now under the scrutiny of the law in many instances to provide disclosure and maintain financial obligations that have been set out in public or private offerings in the case of syndications or partnership agreements in joint ventures. Failure to meet these obligations could result in disciplinary action, making the bottom line subordinate to prescribed dictates. This situation is a lot different from the ma and pa operations that have owned income property in the past, which would receive a statement once a year and not even look at that unless the property was losing money.

Strict legal guidelines require that the asset management team make weekly, monthly, and annual reports and summary reports, along with 5-year plans and 10-year plans, all according to the way the project was structured. People do not view the real estate industry as speculative in the same way they view stock, oil, movies, and so on. The average person on the street feels that real estate can do no wrong. Such people might think real estate is somewhat risky but nowhere near as risky as movies, oil, or other investments with similar write-offs. If you strike an oil well, fine, everybody's happy; if you lose one, fine, you lost that one. In real estate, however, if you have an apartment project or housing project that goes down the tubes, that's a big deal and people don't understand how it happened. Generally it's not a matter of luck or public opinion that you have to deal with, as in the movies, when no one knows whether the public will like the movie or not. In real estate, there are statistics and studies available to help make things happen right. In other words, there is little room to make a mistake, and most of the risks have to be eliminated or at least provided for before a project is started.

Restrictions

In dealing with the state and federal security laws monitoring these projects, you may have conflicts between laws in states where the investors live and those where the property is located. A lot of this bureaucratic red tape will be alleviated as multiple ownership in the form of syndications becomes more commonplace and favorable legislation is passed. These types of restrictions are good for the investor, but create nightmares for the developer who is trying to make the numbers work. The situation has forced creative financing to blossom, with packages and deals never heard of before. This in turn affects what happens to properties, and the relationships and roles of asset managers can change quickly.

If performance is down and not in accordance with the structured plan going into the project, the roles of the developer and/or asset manager could be changed by substituting another manager. In the past, it was possible to get a loan payable in 25 or 30 years or longer on a project, with little fluctuation in the way the project was managed. Now, short-fuse loans and participation loans place people in positions in which they have to buy, sell, or make changes quickly, which certainly affects the project.

The Spreading Ownership Base

The new flexibility and volatility in ownership have attracted more people to the real estate industry as an investment. It certainly is more appealing to know the property is owned or backed by a national company, and the ease of purchasing a piece of these properties through security exchanges and brokerage houses opens the market to a new group of investors. People now can put up a small amount of money and become an owner, whereas before it took a great deal of personal wealth, a complex understanding of financial and tax structures, and the ability to take risks. Those elements are now addressed by the seller, and we have government agencies to make sure that the investments are structured properly. Small investors can limit their investment, risks, and exposure. Millions of people can now invest, as stock firms market real estate almost like any other commodity.

The marketing of real estate on a nationwide level, whether income producing or residential, gives asset managers a juggling act to perform regarding who owns the property, who they are going to be working for, and who they are going to be putting in the property—along with what marketing processes they see evolving that will affect each of these groups. We have discussed possible owners and some of the various combinations of groups who may hire the asset manager. It is now time to look at the customer who will inhabit the residence, apartment building, or office space.

DEALING WITH THE TENANT

What is happening with regard to consumerism, how does this affect the tenant and/or owner, and what is the ultimate effect on the asset manager? One of the most obvious changes has been in the size of families. People are content now with one or two children. Less space is necessary to accommodate these mini-families and consequently less time to maintain the residence. Having less to maintain is the most significant factor in the popularity of patio homes, zero lot lines, town houses, condominiums, and cooperatives. It is hard to believe that the public will pay the same price for patio garden homes with practically no yard as they will for single-family dwellings with a good-sized lot, but that is the case, and density does not seem to bother the prospective owner and/or tenant either.

Even though we have become somewhat impersonal, with our computers and numbers, we still have the need to have other people around. It appears we have become somewhat introspective, have taken notice of detail, and realize that we do not need big cars, big houses, and big families. However, we still have the need for group identification, and the asset manager along with the other key players in a development must create and maintain a mood or a feeling—the ambience which personalizes and separates one area from another.

How do you create ambience? Experience counts heavily, but it is only adequate for dealing with changes or shifts in an area's moods or needs created by surrounding factors of which we have very little control. The best way to know what is going to happen before it happens is to undertake the feasibility study.

The Feasibility Study

You, the asset manager, should realize the value of this most important tool in formulating your game plan for making a project work. It is essential for new asset developments, ongoing projects, and distressed projects. A feasibility study involves the assimilation, compilation, and distribution of essential information. This might sound like the work for a super sleuth, but it isn't. It is the gathering of data about a specific area and interpreting that information.

You need to know where the trends are and in what direction they are heading, what factors in the economy affect these movements, and how much control you are able to exercise to meet the related problems that will arise. Much of this information can be obtained from your local chamber of commerce, city planning and zoning department, or street and transportation systems, to name a few sources. If your staff does not allow for this type of data gathering, you can turn to market study firms and consultants who can do the work for a set fee which will vary according to the amount of information you need. The use of an outside consultant gives you a more objective view of the proposed project, since the consultant usually does not have a formed opinion about the property and is open to formulate an opinion as the data are received.

With a market study, asset managers can create their environment by picking and choosing the necessary elements such as design, tenant mix, amenities, and building materials. This market, or feasibility, study is not a one-time shot. It is advisable to update the study every 6 months or at least annually, given the rapid changes we are continually undergoing.

So much of the risk is eliminated by these studies that the asset manager who accepts them as tools of the trade will be ahead of the game. You have to be able to zoom in on your target area; although market study information can become voluminous, the computer makes it possible to keep abreast at the touch of a button.

Applicability of the collected information to proposed developments is relatively new for seasoned property managers who are fast learning they are asset managers of mini-villages consisting of single-family homes, zero lot lines, clusters, garden homes, condominiums, and cooperatives. This creates a big change from the old tenant-landlord relationship, but the necessary implements to meet these new management challenges have evolved with the change and are ready to make the job as sophisticated as the mind can fathom.

Mobility

Another factor influencing the trends affecting property management is that the mobility of today is a lot different from that of yesterday. People are becoming more mobile and less mobile at the same time. They are more mobile in that through the use of computers and other communication devices such as visual telephones, intercity meetings are now possible without leaving the office or home. We have telecommunicating on important business matters involving two or three cities, and we have grocery store inventory appearing on our television screen giving the homemaker a comparison of two or three stores at the touch of a finger. Communication without moving is the result. This information should have an impact on the decision to locate close to the grocery store or to work.

Role of the Property Manager

With the aforementioned changes in lifestyle and family structure, it becomes apparent that the seasoned property manager is in a good position to benefit. Apartments and apartment living have been around for a while, but as mentioned earlier, rents are not in parity with the ever-increasing costs of maintaining apartment complexes. Individual ownership in the form of condominiums, cooperatives, town houses, and garden homes is the natural result, but there still needs to be some type of overseeing or management, and we are back in the ballgame better equipped than ever to do just that. The asset manager will have to be there to see how the roof on the clubhouse is doing, how the shrubs look at the entrance, and if the residents are frowning or smiling—barometer readings that let the investor know that his or her 10-year development plan is working and evolving from stage to stage. Is it time to convert the apartments into condominiums? Do we need more office space in the office park? These demands and changes have put a strain on attempts to zone the property properly from the outset. If you ask an asset manager where the apartments, office park, and garden homes should be located, according to his or her expertise and the results of the feasibility or market study made for that project, the answer will still be no more than a guess. Once a project has begun, the extenuating circumstances over which you have no control begin to arise and you try not to be locked in location to the point that the project may not survive.

The planned unit development. In the planned unit development (PUD), a mixture of land uses, such as housing, shopping, and industry, are zoned at one time on a large tract of land. This innovative type of zoning has become popular as it gives the investor/developer and asset manager the flexibility necessary to make whatever changes need to be made to ensure that the project continues to work. You can eliminate most of the development risks with careful research and evaluations, but what do you do when a new highway cuts right through the property and your proposed apartment complex? This happens all the time. With the PUD you have some idea of what will be next door.

The PUD is not a new concept, but I believe it is the best trend for providing for a large development to be approved in stages, but which can start off with a proposed mixture of land uses. Again, the asset manager is the best judge regarding the direction a development is taking based on the needs of the residents, and careful consideration from his or her perspective will count heavily.

Home Relocation

Another trend I feel will influence the asset management industry is the movement of the population and the people who work and live in the environments we create and maintain. People today are less likely to consider their present location the only alternative. When things got bad in the past, families would wait out the situation and stay close to home; now, with the many similarities in business, whether it is marketing cars, potatoes, or clothing, crossovers from one business to another are made more frequently. If the new job means moving south or to the West Coast, the move is made.

How does this mobility affect the plan of the asset manager? Suppose a new plant opens close to your apartment complex or development. With it will come several employees from the home office. These people are changing from one way of life to another, and they will be bringing many changes with them. The asset manager will have to accommodate them and at the same time keep the existing tenants or residents happy. There are no pat solutions for these situations, but a computer or an absentee landlord will find it hard to make these decisions—only the local asset manager has the experience and ability to make them.

Office Management

The asset manager will find that an effective program for commercial and office space is very similar to a residential program. People are wanting style and mood in their places of work. You are constantly hearing today about the psychological aspects of work, what can be done to encourage motivation, and what is the most effective surrounding for the best work output. The trend toward considering aesthetics and comfort in an office, turning it into a place you'd want to spend a lot of time, is being supported by creating attractive environments.

The asset manager of an office building or complex needs to be a kind of matchmaker, putting compatible businesses together to project the image the office building or center has been set up to create. Amenities such as a place to get something to eat and a fitness center in the building or close by make the office more inviting.

Office identification activities such as charity promotions, softball teams, and public service programs should be encouraged or organized by the asset manager. It is important to support the human element of group identification, since business has become somewhat impersonal, with the machinery and robotized mechanisms that do so much of the work for us. As stated previously, families have shrunk in size, but the social needs of families haven't changed; one of the best means of supporting those needs is bringing people with common goals, interests, work habits, and incomes together in some type of joint effort. What better place to do this than at work?

Another way of getting business tenants involved with their cotenants is through promotion of personal hobbies such as photography or arts and crafts with exhibits held in the lobby area of the building. More and more businesses are getting involved with the arts, and you would be surprised how many hidden artists or craftspeople are sitting staidly behind desks. Putting together exhibits is also a good way to generate traffic if you have vacancies.

The Planned Retirement Community

An area of asset management that is becoming more prominent and will become even more so is the planned retirement community. The children of the post–World War II baby boom are coming of age, and the right kind of living facilities to accommodate the senior baby boomers are already on the drawing boards and being built. The planned retirement communities vary in design and amenities much like any apartment complex, but with age and the progression of age kept in mind. Whether the retirement community consists of rented space or separate ownerships, the asset manager is again in great demand. In the past and still in the present, it is quite evident that nursing homes provide an alternative to retirees who leave the work force. The only problem is that the majority of retired persons do not want to throw in the towel; they have earned the right to enjoy their golden years in style. The market certainly is there and is steadily growing.

A planned retirement community is created primarily with *safety* in mind. The prospective tenants want the peace of mind that comes from knowing they are in a safe place with regard to both security and hazards that may cause accidents. The rest of the planning or maintenance of the retirement community will vary with the age range targeted and amenity package offered. Convenient medical facilities are another factor to be considered, along with proximity to shopping or at least transportation to and from retail and grocery areas. Of course, minimal maintenance for the occupant will be an important element, which means the asset manager will have a greater amount of maintenance to contend with. The asset manager might propose management plans to local churches since many of them have foundations that could provide financing for a planned retirement community.

The College Crowd

College students are also making changes which will set the trend for years to come. If you have a college-aged child, you can reasonably assume that he or she will be studying for at least 4 years. One of the headaches associated with the beginning of each term is the search for a place for your child to live. Although a good percentage of students live in college-run dormitories and sorority and fraternity houses, a good percentage also live off-campus. Condominiums are a good solution to the problem of student housing and another great investment for the real estate investor.

The asset manager will set the leasing program up according to the school semesters. Student housing offices will gladly furnish the names of prospective tenants, and the parents who invest in the units will be glad to know that something is appreciating while their child is at the university. Another possibility for student housing condominiums is the conversion of older, outdated school buildings on campus. The asset manager needs to investigate such possibilities and draft proposals for private investors and for the school itself. Even though the school is the owner, it will take someone like an ambitious asset manager to present a detailed management proposal to convert a building that otherwise would most likely be torn down.

Conversions

Schools and other institutions and commercial businesses are looking to the condo conversion. The high cost of money, decreasing availability of land, and constant problems of construction will continue to plague those who want to make a project work. Consequently, more developers will be investigating building rehabilitation as an alternative.

Asset managers and investors are catching on to the Madison Avenue approach of face-lifting, new-naming, and overall remarketing programs which revamp, revitalize, and rejuvenate property. The feasibility or market study will tell you what market is out there and what the people want; all you have to do is give it to them. If you remove some of the risk involved in guessing what the market is, you may find that a property can easily be turned around. The really hard part is finding a building to work with. With the population increasing, it makes sense that everything built will be used at some point. When you visit a metropolitan city, you quickly can find a great income-producing property across the street from what appears to be an abandoned building. If the market can hold up one property, it will certainly take care of another. The market is there, and it is up to you to find it and rehabilitate the property to meet it.

If you are an asset manager who is always wringing your hands about the availability of properties to manage or the fact that someone else has all the good properties, you need to open your eyes and look at the rundown property you passed on the way to work this morning, and use your imagination and the expertise you have acquired over the years to make something new happen out of the old.

The climate is right for rehabilitation or conversion; the nation is supporting a general "recycling" effort. If nothing else, it seems like a great way to clean up undesirable properties that usually have a wealth of building materials in them.

The government is also doing its share in renovation by providing financial programs that can make a project move quickly. Patience is a good lesson to learn with these government programs, however; when asset managers, developers, or investors look toward this way of producing the product, they must be prepared to be on target. Generally local governing bodies, such as planning commissions, zoning boards, and historical associations, will go the extra mile to help you with a project. One test these properties have stood is the test of time, and if they have withstood a little age they more than likely, with the proper planning, can serve the investor again and again.

Not only are individual buildings being considered for conversions or rehabilitation, but complexes such as shopping centers and industrial parks are being given a face-lift. With the right planning, a small shopping center can become a mini-village, or a factory shutdown-casualty in the form of an industrial park can become the latest shopping center. The asset manager must realize that property management does not have to be bland and boring. Given just a small amount of creativity, an eyesore can become beautiful; the asset manager has the product, and the investor usually has a great investment in an attractive financial package with the special charm of age.

THE SELLING OF THE ASSET MANAGER

The changes in our industry are numerous, but none of them are as great as the changes in the people who identify themselves with the industry. Property management is only the early stage of asset management. We are specialists and professionals dealing with the soundest, most lucrative commodity our system has to offer. You do yourself and your industry an injustice by thinking otherwise. We deal with the most important aspects of individuals' lives—their home and their work. There is no room for compromise, and we owe it to the tenants, owners, investors, and others to give them what they expect. Therefore, we have to equip ourselves with the proper training, experience, and continued education to get the job done.

Our curriculum is much broader than it used to be. The management of land from raw acreage to high-rise complexes requires a vast amount of knowledge, and young persons who want to be successful in the business must look long and hard at what kind of commitment they are willing to make. As in other professions, much of this business is learned through experience. What you learn from textbooks will always be different from what you encounter in the real world—of that you can be sure. However, there is an overall schematic way of looking at property through an asset manager's eyes which can apply across the board. This view of course takes practice, experience, and constant revision. A warehouse no longer looks like a warehouse: You see the shape, the size, the building materials, and the potential. With practice, you will be able to gauge the time frame necessary to accomplish what is sought.

The numbers in this industry have swelled, and the competition is tough and will get even tougher as the rewards and compensation increase. You will have to polish your own skills, whichever form of management job you choose to take. With an increase in managers, new forms of the management job have evolved to provide more options.

As stated in the early part of this chapter, in the past clerical employees saw that the rent was paid, placed an advertisement in the classified section of the newspaper, and called the plumber when the faucet started leaking. Now the asset manager can contract out his or her services much like an accountant or attorney; she can join a real estate company that specializes in management or join a bank, insurance company, mutual fund group, stock brokerage firm, or syndication firm. The possibilities are endless, because all businesses must have an office and everyone must have a place to live. Although this sounds basic, it is necessary to look at what our job really is: helping the work force take care of its properties.

Selling the Owner

Once you are convinced of the importance of the asset manager's contribution, how do you convince the landowner that you are the one to do the job? The most obvious way would be to offer a better deal. If you are in a large company that manages several properties, volume usually will take care of the discounted management fee very much like a large department store, which depends on volume rather than price. Another way of securing management contracts is proposing renovation projects for existing buildings, as mentioned earlier. Even buildings being used at their highest market value can be improved or enhanced, and owners welcome the chance to increase the return on their investment. A third way of getting business is to connect with a developer or builder who needs your expertise to crystallize an idea and translate it into a project. As mentioned before, this is the ideal way since it allows you input from the beginning.

CONCLUSIONS

The framework for maintaining properties has changed quite a bit and will continue to do so. Nothing has been lost, and our perimeter has widened. The changes have been for the good, and the trends look even better. Real estate as a whole has gone through quite a few upheavals recently, but growing pains usually make us uncomfortable for a short time only.

Like so many other industries in our nation, the transition from the old to the new is sometimes painful and hard to understand but is inevitable. Through the increased availability of information in our society, we now are aware of the slightest changes in factors that affect the developing, buying, and selling of real estate. These trends, as most of you well know, can occur almost overnight. In order to function properly and to do well, therefore, we must keep our ear to the ground and be ready to shift gears when the moment warrants. Now we have to be financial experts, promotional directors, marketing specialists, and civic-minded men and women who are aware of what is going on everywhere in our society and understand why a situation on the other side of the world will reverberate to us.

We are rapidly approaching a time when the "global village" concept will become a reality, and only those who are willing to make the transition will survive and profit by it. Flexibility is the key word, and the ability to adjust quickly to any changes in the industry will be the deciding factor to success.

INDEX

INDEX

ABOUT THE EDITOR IN CHIEF

Robert Irwin has been a successful California real estate broker, investor, and property manager for more than twenty years. Having been a consultant to lenders, investors, and landlords, he has helped steer hundreds of properties onto stable and profitable courses. His publications include *The McGraw-Hill Real Estate Handbook*, *Computerizing Your Real Estate Office*, *Time-share Properties*, *The New Mortgage Game*, and *How to Buy and Sell Real Estate for Financial Security*, all published by McGraw-Hill.